A MEMOIR

The
SMART MONEY

How the World's Best
Sports Bettors Beat the Bookies
Out of Millions

MICHAEL KONIK

SIMON & SCHUSTER

NEW YORK   LONDON   TORONTO   SYDNEY

SIMON & SCHUSTER
Rockefeller Center
1230 Avenue of the Americas
New York, NY 10020

SIMON & SCHUSTER and colophon are registered trademarks
of Simon & Schuster, Inc.

Designed by Joseph Rutt

For information regarding special discounts for bulk purchases,
please contact Simon & Schuster Special Sales at 1-800-456-6798
or business@simonandschuster.com

Manufactured in the United States of America

10   9   8   7   6   5   4   3   2   1

Library of Congress Cataloging-in-Publication Data is available.

ISBN-13: 978-0-7432-7714-3
ISBN-10:   0-7432-7714-7

For my lucky Charm,
who bet on me when I wasn't the smart money.

AUTHOR'S NOTE

Some of what's described in this book is either a matter of public record or commonly known to members of the gambling cognoscenti. Much of it, however, is not.

Members of the Brain Trust continue to operate around the world. So as not to compromise their ongoing success, I've changed names, identifying details, and some chronologies.

CONTENTS

Contents

GLOSSARY

Added games: Nontelevised, lightly bet contests of interest only to home-town fans, degenerate gambling addicts, and sophisticated sports bettors prowling for weak lines.

Baccarat: One of the simplest table games in a casino, akin to calling heads or tails on a coin flip. Players wager on which of two hands, Player and Bank, will make a point total closest to 9. The dealer distributes cards according to pre-established rules, and there is no further decision making for bettors. Although casinos distribute pencils and note cards for tracking "trends," there's no betting system or money-management scheme that can beat this faux glamorous game.

Circled games: Sporting contests for which the casino has lowered the betting limit, usually to half of the standard maximum, sometimes even less. Games get "circled"—literally, a circle is drawn around them on the toteboard—when a key player's status is in question or some other crucial piece of information remains uncertain.

Kelly Criterion: A mathematical formula that expresses a gambler's optimal bet size. Crudely put, the criterion says that an aggressive gambler should wager a percentage of his bankroll equal to the percentage advantage he enjoys over the game. For example, when a blackjack card-counter determines that he has a 1 percent advantage over the dealer, he ought to wager 1 percent of his total bankroll. To avoid increased risk of ruin, most professional gamblers apply half Kelly or quarter Kelly to their wagering decisions.

Key game: The nationally televised, heavily bet sporting contest that draws betting action from every stratum of gambler, from casual to professional. For example, *Monday Night Football.*

Line: Also known as "the point spread." The line expresses the power differential between two teams. A professional football team that is 2 points better than the opponent is considered a small favorite to win. A team that is 17 points better is considered a prohibitive favorite. To encourage equal betting action on both the stronger and the weaker team, the line-makers allow bettors to add or subtract the point spread from a team's final score. For example, if the Bears are a 7-point favorite over the Bengals, Chicago's bettors must subtract 7 points from their team's final score or add 7 points to Cincinnati's final score. Thus, if Chicago triumphs by a final score of 24–21, they lose ($24 - 7 = 17$) or *fail to cover the line,* and people who bet on Cincinnati win their wager ($21 + 7 = 28$), thanks to the extra points.

RFB: Casino host parlance for "room, food, beverage." Players who earn RFB status enjoy the full range of complimentaries, or comps, the casino has to offer, including shows, limousines, room service, and entrance to VIP events like boxing matches and invitation-only casino parties. Achieving RFB status requires betting different amounts at different casinos, but most top-drawer Strip properties like to see $250 a hand or more from their RFB suckers.

Send-out: The original point spread suggested by linemaking services in Las Vegas and the Caribbean, which bookmakers use to determine their opening numbers. The send-out for the following week's football usually occurs late Sunday afternoon, shortly after the conclusion of the day's games; it's literally sent out via computer and fax to subscribers. By the time the line is published in *USA Today* the following morning, it's been heavily bet by early action shoppers in Las Vegas and offshore.

Smart money: The well-informed betting syndicates that wager enormous sums on sporting contests. The smart money's "smartness" is derived from having sophisticated information on injuries, weather, and psychological factors, as well as powerful computers that can process millions of bits of data—game statistics chief among them—and produce a more accurate point-spread line than the bookmakers. Thus the bookies fear and despise the smart money.

Squares: The average, unsophisticated gambler whose decision making is based on hunches, media manipulation, or spurious systems that cannot overcome the bookmaker's inherent mathematical advantage. Thus the bookies love and cherish the squares.

Totals: Also known as "over-unders." Bettors wager on the *total* number of points scored in a game, gambling on whether the final score will be over or under the bookmaker's posted number. For example, in the 2005 Super Bowl, the official total for New England and Philadelphia was 47. The teams scored 45 points between them (24–21). Gamblers who bet on the under won. Those who bet over lost. One more field goal and the results would have been reversed.

Vig: Short for "vigorish." The vig, or "juice," is the tax gamblers must pay the bookie every time they wager. When two fellows make a gentleman's bet between themselves, each man puts up an equal amount, say my $10 against your $10. Bookies typically require their customers to bet $11 to win $10. The losers pay the winners and the bookmaker keeps the vig. At 11–10 odds, the industry standard, bookies enjoy a 4.54 percent advantage over their customers, which means bettors must select more than 52 percent winners to break even.

Whale: A huge bettor. A whale is generally a casino's or bookmaker's best customer, the high-rolling, money-means-nothing-to-me bon vivant who craves action and attention more than long-term profits. The criteria vary from casino to casino, but whales generally have $1 million lines of credit or more.

Wiseguy: Someone who bets with or for the smart money. Wiseguys generally get the best point spreads and wager on the most profitable teams. Since these sophisticated gamblers seldom make bad bets and seldom play hunches, wiseguys win in the long run. Bookies intensely dislike wiseguys.

PREFACE

Gambling is America's second-favorite indoor pastime. Casinos, home poker games, bingo halls, state lotteries—wherever Lady Luck can be courted, we're eager to stake our money on the turn of a card or the bounce of a ball.

Particularly the bounce of a ball.

Betting on sports is an American obsession. If you yourself don't participate in an office pool, or have a local bookmaker, or maintain an offshore Internet account, you probably know someone who does. Betting on football and baseball, hockey and basketball—even NASCAR auto racing and PGA Tour golf—makes the most banal athletic competition exciting. It imbues the ordinary with drama. It gives viewers a personal stake in the outcome of the contest, no matter how inconsequential the final score might be in the course of world events.

Since almost all sports betting in America occurs in the shadows, hidden from the scrutiny of actuaries, putting a definitive number on the size of the sports betting industry is impossible. But most reliable estimates, based on data from the highly regulated Las Vegas sportsbooks, extrapolate stunning figures that would be the envy of anyone in the entertainment business. Most experts estimate that the bookmakers who take the bets gross billions of dollars a year.

The reason the bookies win so much money is that, in the long run, almost nobody can beat "the line." Also known as "the point spread," the line expresses the imbalance between two unevenly matched teams, thereby reducing every contest to the mathematical equivalent of a coin flip. For example, if the Los Angeles Lakers played against the Hollywood High School basketball team, no one but the mentally ill would bet on the high school squad. But if gamblers who wanted to wager on the mighty Lakers had to give the adolescents an 83-point head start— well, even fans of Kobe Bryant would have to think twice. In the real world, when the Lakers play the Chicago Bulls, the Lakers are usually forced to give the weaker team an 11- to 12-point handicap. About half the time the Lakers win by more than 11, and half the time they don't.

Every NFL football game, every NCAA basketball game, every NHL hockey match has appended to it a point spread—indeed, many newspapers, including *USA Today,* publish the daily lines. Though the TV announcers aren't supposed to make reference to the point spread (which the NCAA likes to pretend doesn't exist), sly innuendo—"With one minute to go, Duke is up by twenty-two, but there's still some business to be decided!"—suggests that the television networks understand that gambling on sports keeps viewers fixated on otherwise meaningless contests.

Except for the illegal drug trade, sports betting is probably America's biggest, most lucrative unregulated business.

The bookies count on the line to be accurate—or at least accurate enough that half the people in America will like the favorite and the other half will go for the underdog. Traditionally, bookmakers act as brokers, a human clearinghouse for their customers' compulsions. The standard bet requires gamblers to lay $11 to win $10. If you bet $10 with a bookie you don't win $10; you win $9.10. In the classical bookie business model, winners are paid with the losers' money and the house keeps the "juice," or "vig." Ideally, when the Patriots play the Panthers, Joe Bookmaker's clients collectively bet $550,000 to win $500,000 on New England and $550,000 to win $500,000 on Carolina. Unless the game ends in a point-spread tie, or "push"—for example, the line is 3 and the final score is 20–17, a 3-point differential—Joe Bookmaker collects $550,000 from the losers, pays $500,000 to the winners, and keeps $50,000 for his trouble.

It's a very nice business—particularly because the combination of an accurate line (a point spread that accurately expresses the disparity between two teams) and the 11–10 juice is almost impossible to overcome. Common wisdom says that over the course of a long football season the average American man—or his girlfriend, dartboard, or pet monkey—will pick approximately 50 percent winners. Thanks to the juice, the only one who profits in this scenario is Joe Bookmaker. In fact, sports bettors must pick 52.4 percent winners just to break even.

The line is generated by highly paid consultants in Las Vegas and the Caribbean who weigh the relative strengths of the teams and, more important, the public's perception of those strengths. Because of regional prejudices—people in Chicago, for example, think more highly of the Cubs than do people in New York—the line can vary slightly from shop to shop. Furthermore, on games where the bettors are disproportionately betting on one team, bookies will incrementally adjust the line to make the underbet side more attractive. Thanks to the general brilliance and accuracy of the point spreads, gamblers who can consistently beat Joe Bookmaker are as rare as honest politicians.

But it can be done.

The bookies fear (and despise) a tiny coterie of professional bettors known as "wiseguys," or "the sharps." Fewer than 0.0001 percent of gamblers, the proverbial "one in a million," are able to consistently pick point-spread winners. But there are betting syndicates privy to the most up-to-date information on injuries, weather, game plans, and, most important, *the real power of the teams involved.* These wiseguys are often able to derive a more precise, more accurate, more *valuable* point-spread line than the oddsmakers. Essentially, they create their own theoretical line on the same slate of games offered by the bookmakers. Then they compare their numbers against the bookies'. When the sharp players spot a discrepancy between their line and the one the bookies are offering, they bet.

A lot.

Hundreds of thousands of dollars. Sometimes as much as $1 million on a single game.

The avalanche of money that cascades down upon the bookmakers is what moves the line. When you see that the Jets have gone from a 3-point favorite to a 4-point favorite, it's often because the smart money (and the hordes of followers who try to track their bets) likes the boys from the Meadowlands.

The members of the MIT blackjack team made famous in *Bringing Down the House* are small-timers compared with the biggest sports bettors.

In some ways, the gulf between the big betting syndicates and recreational gamblers is as wide as that between Wall Street's institutional investors and an unemployed speculator sitting in his underwear at home dabbling at day trading. But the professional bettors have something in common with the millions of people who gamble on the weekends: They desperately want their team to win, to cover the point spread. The big difference is that instead of sweating a hundred-dollar wager, the smart money sweats millions every weekend.

Gamblers whisper about a legendary—some think apocryphal—syndicate known as the Brain Trust, a sobriquet earned because its members seem to understand more about sports betting than anyone else. Though they operate in secret, the Brains are the most influential force in the world of sports betting. They're to gambling markets what Warren Buffett is to the New York Stock Exchange. Everyone involved in sports gambling wants to know what the Brains are doing—which matchups they favor, which teams they're investing in on any given weekend. Everyone who bets on sports—from the degenerate action junkie to the half-sharp sports fiend who watches ESPN sixteen hours a day, from small-time professionals to big-time bookies—they all try to figure out how the Brains do what they do. And, especially, what they'll do next.

I'm one of the few people in the world who can tell you. Because for several years I was one of them.

THE SMART MONEY

INTRODUCTION

November 2000

The Western Tanager calls Central America home, but during its annual migration observant bird-watchers can spot this little beauty in the most unlikely locations—even in the densely populated hills rising above the industrial cacophony of Sunset Boulevard, in Hollywood, California. You don't have to be an expert ornithologist to notice the Tanager. It's canary yellow, with a brilliant red head that looks like the logo on the helmet of the Phoenix Cardinals. It has a black back, like the home jerseys of the Jacksonville Jaguars. And one white and one yellow wing bar, a design that no NFL team has yet co-opted. When it's not breeding, it lacks the glowing cap, and the bird books say that in this state it's common to mistake the Tanager for a male American Goldfinch or a female Bullock's Oriole—which is what I must have done, I tell myself. It's nearly Thanksgiving; any Tanagers that once nested here in the palms of Los Angeles must be currently enjoying the tropical sun down in Costa Rica, where, along with dozens of species of tree frogs, butterflies, and serpents, many of the world's biggest bookmakers permanently reside.

Still, the flash of yellow and orange outside my living room window catches my eye, and that's not easy to do when football is on the television. The antics of the brightly colored gladiators, heavily muscled warriors outfitted as gaudily as macaws, seem to matter to me more than to the average sports fan. Actually, at this point in my life I no longer care about the interstitial running around and tackling, the passing and catching, the playing of the game. I'm concerned only with the little box in the corner of the screen, the one that shows the score.

I brush aside a pile of papers on the coffee table, a stack of spreadsheets with numbers on them that I barely understand, and I grab my binoculars. I use them to spot the green parrots (pants of the Miami Dolphins) and Western Scrub Jays (Minnesota Vikings), and the dozens of hummingbirds and finches that flit around the gardens of my house. I'm not really a "birder." I don't maintain a life list or spend my vacations in Louisiana swamps searching for rare species of woodpecker. But I do enjoy looking at the winged creatures around the neighborhood. Observing their grace and beauty gives me a sense of peacefulness, a calm, that most of my waking hours sorely lack. When I pick up my field glasses, I'm momentarily transported to a tranquil sanctuary, where some of Hollywood's biggest movie stars aren't calling me to scream about their "investments." Where no one cares about the supercomputer I've got stashed in a Massachusetts apartment. Where it doesn't matter what legendary gambler is on my speed-dial.

If an uninitiated visitor wandered into my living room, he would observe what seems to be domestic normality: the dog asleep underneath the piano, the TV flickering in the corner, the late-afternoon sunlight streaming through the large picture window, the man in his thirties attired in a sweatshirt with cold pizza stains on the sleeve. Few would guess that this modest Hollywood bungalow is the home of a serious professional gambler. I'm the owner of the house and *I* can't believe it. Just three years earlier I was an earnest middle-class American, a writer searching for a good story.

I found it.

It was hidden between the lines, enmeshed among the Las Vegas point spreads and betting odds, like a sparrow camouflaged in bougainvillea vines, almost invisible until you look more closely, with a telescopic visual aid or an expert teacher.

The New York Giants and their 4-point lead over the Washington Redskins can wait; I'm determined to positively identify the wayward

Tanager I think I've seen streaking past my window. I raise the binoculars to my eyes and scan the trees across the street. It's all an emerald blur. I focus. The individual branches come into view, but no birds. Wait, there's something! Oh, just a dove. No sign of the lurid yellows and oranges that signal toxicity to predators but look so fine to our human eye.

I put down the glasses and scan the street with naked eye, hoping for a burst of color, some frantic movement. Everything is static. I see houses built on granite bedrock, noble firs unruffled by wind, parked cars. Nothing animated.

Then a glint of light twinkles from across the way. I bring the lenses back to my eyes and look for something moving. Slowly, like the establishing shot in an epic western, I pan from the left side of my quiet residential street to the right. Stalks of bamboo. A cypress tree. Pink impatiens. The pavement on my neighbor's driveway. A white picket fence. A Buick.

A Buick with a balding man slouched low behind the steering wheel. Looking straight at my front window. Through binoculars.

I pull the magnifiers from my eyes to see the big picture from a normal perspective, because, surely, the pressure of the past year has started to get to me and I must be seeing strange and troubling things.

Before I can get another peek at the Buick's occupant, the car roars away, its tires screeching like a flock of parakeets.

I run out my front door, down the steps, and out to the sidewalk. I look up the street. Nothing. He's gone.

None of the neighbors seems to be around, and if any are, they're staying inside their home with the shades drawn, safe from spying interlopers. I feel alone, as though I'm the only living person in a ghost town, with only my dog and a tangle of increasingly frightening thoughts to keep me company. My impulse is to lock myself inside the house and phone my mentor and protector. But before I make the call, I entertain an even more disturbing notion: perhaps he's the one having me watched.

I trudge back to the living room. The Giants have widened their lead to 7 points. My famous colleague Captain Beefcake, who ought to be worrying about the box office numbers of his new thriller and not the score of a meaningless NFL game, has left what is probably an irate message on my voicemail. And the birds, the ones I've seen and the ones I suppose I'm only imagining, have left the feeders and returned to their nests. The only creature to watch, it seems, is me.

I close the curtains and double-bolt the door. Then I squeeze into a corner of the couch, cover myself with a wool blanket, and wait to see if Washington can make a late score.

One

A PROPOSITION

June 1997

Rick "Big Daddy" Matthews and I are playing golf at the Sherwood Country Club, not far from his summer home near Santa Barbara, California. Founded by David Murdock, the gentleman who owns Dole and much of the island of Lanai, the club is a rarefied playground where some of the most privileged people in America dig up the sod. The clubhouse is the size of a respectable basketball arena, albeit one outfitted with leather furniture and a staff of full-time shoe-shiners. Tiger Woods has his annual postseason invitational here. This Sherwood isn't the kind of place where ordinary Robin Hoods might enjoy a game of golf. Initiation fees are reportedly more than $250,000, an impost that ensures that the first tee remains accessible to the celebrity membership, which allegedly includes Jack Nicholson, Kenny G., and Janet Jackson— although discretion prevents the club from commenting on such delicate matters.

Rick Matthews moves comfortably in these elite circles. A millionaire many times over, he's built a four-state empire of "casual gourmet" restaurants, where patrons pay premium prices for a fine dining experience uncomplicated by menus written in French. He has all the trappings of extraordinary financial success: a private jet, a fleet of luxury cars, and a stable of mansions (some of them with actual stables). Big Daddy gives generously to charities, to institutions of higher learning—which cour-teously rename academic buildings in his honor—and to politicians who are sympathetic to his concerns. The man is a vital member of society.

And he got where he is by taking a gamble.

Actually, thousands of them.

The restaurants, the mansions, the ear of the senator—the whole tow-ering monument to the American dream is built on a foundation of bet making. Not wagering on the stock market or an obscure foreign cur-rency, but the kind of gambling most citizens of the United States can vaguely understand from firsthand experience. Big Daddy Matthews made his fortune betting on sports.

The man has always had a penchant for games of chance. For taking a risk, even a foolish one. Before becoming the kingpin of American sports betting, he won and lost millions of dollars on roulette, blackjack, and other negative-expectation casino games. At one time Rick Matthews, son of a church deacon father and a schoolteacher mother, was one of the most valued customers in Las Vegas, a certified sucker with a drink-ing problem who was prone to blow $1 million or more per visit. The Golden Nugget, in downtown Las Vegas, kept a suite on permanent hold for Matthews and would dispatch the casino's airplane whenever Mr. Rick got the itch to do a little gambling. He had a profitable fast-food chain called the Fryer back home in the deep-South Arkansas-Mississippi-Alabama region, where customers unafraid of the ravages of bad cholesterol could get all manner of oil-drenched comestibles, in-cluding battered Snickers bars. Whenever the betting bug bit, Rick would siphon off money from his own company, leaving it on the brink of bankruptcy. Fortified with greasy cash, Rick Matthews would lose every penny of his quarterly earnings during his forays to Sin City. But as long as the lard kept bubbling he could count on a steady stream of money to donate. It wasn't that he didn't *want* to win—he tried every spurious bet-ting system and useless angle he could find. Matthews just didn't know *how* to beat the house.

And then, after years of fruitless exploration, the lifelong action junkie finally discovered the key to the casino vaults. Rick Matthews figured out which football teams to bet on. The rumor going around Las Vegas was that Matthews had some sort of supercomputer tended to by a coterie of experts known as the Brains.

It wasn't precisely a license to print money. But when you win three and lose two over and over, day after day, season after season, your fortune starts to stack skyward, like a pyramid in the desert. Unlike many sick gamblers, whose compulsions prohibit them from holding on to their winnings, Rick Matthews conquered his alcoholism, invested wisely, avoided leaks (bad decisions that inexorably erode a gambler's bankroll), and continued to raise his bets while he was ahead. Which is a smart play when you're on a twenty-three-year winning streak.

His name isn't well known, but Rick's prowess at prognosticating football games is famous. Even the hacks at my golf club in Los Angeles, who participate in a weekly pool, know that there are supposedly a few guys who can beat the point spreads consistently. My golf buddies have never met any of these wizards and couldn't tell you what they look like. But the boys like to repeat the rumor that there's a genius in Las Vegas who's built his multimillion-dollar restaurant empire with capital earned from his sports betting exploits.

To the gambling cognoscenti, Rick Matthews is no rumor. He's credited as the emperor of an operation that inspires fear in bookies and jealousy in aspiring professional punters. He's the Michael Jordan of the wagering business, a man to whom the cliché "living legend" may be applied without embarrassment. One man moves the Vegas line. One man influences the way millions of people bet on sports. One man is a celebrity in a milieu otherwise devoid of stars.

Knowing I was eager to meet the legend for an interview I hoped to publish in a national magazine, a friend of a friend, another member of the secretive fraternity of professional gamblers, introduced me to Rick Matthews. Before I shook Rick's hand and proposed that he allow me to include his tale in a book I was researching, my friend warned me about Rick Matthews. "The guy is totally charming. A real sweetheart. But don't let the southern gentleman deal fool you. When it comes to getting the best of it, the guy's a stone-cold killer. You've heard of ice water in the veins? Rick Matthews has liquid nitrogen."

On the sixth tee, I watch Matthews hit a towering drive, an elegant parabola that rockets out to the right and slowly curls back to the left, coming to rest three hundred yards in the distance, bisecting the fairway. It's the kind of golf shot I hit regularly—in my fantasies. I'm envious of Rick's prowess, but not surprised. Before Big Daddy Matthews hit upon the secret to beating sports, he earned the bulk of his gambling winnings on the golf course. Rick, in fact, is one of the greatest golf hustlers of all time. Major champions like Lee Trevino and Fuzzy Zoeller have played with him, and they don't look forward to wagering against him again anytime soon. Rick's the rare bird who can shoot just about any score he needs to. When he was a bit younger, the talk around Sherwood Country Club was that Rick ought to take a crack at the Champions Tour when he turned fifty. But then everyone came to his senses and realized Big Daddy Matthews could earn a lot more money at golf staying at home playing against oil barons and telecom CEOs.

Now nearing sixty, Rick can still shoot in the seventies. And since there's almost no amount of money he won't play for, it's impossible to make him nervous. When you're dealing with a fellow who regularly wagers a million dollars on a football game, detecting a racing heartbeat during a friendly golf match is awfully difficult. So I've got no chance of winning today. Not a prayer.

Even against me, a nine-handicap with a piddling bankroll, the old hustler is loath to give away even the slightest edge. To make a fair match, I know I should be getting at least three shots a side. Rick insists on only giving me two—"and that's too generous!" he complains.

We're playing for twenty dollars.

I wonder: Does Big Daddy love to win? Or is he pathologically afraid of losing?

I've been eagerly anticipating my day on the greens with the legendary bettor. Since our introduction six months ago, we've spent several cordial and productive evenings together in Las Vegas. I've crafted excerpts from our chats into a story about sports betting, hoping to publish it in one of the slick periodicals during the heart of football season. It's a good article, even if some of the choicest anecdotes were delivered off the record. Big Daddy has a habit of starting a fascinating story and then stopping in mid-sentence, smiling sheepishly, and declaring, "Naw, I don't think we should talk about that." But I can tell he likes me. Although I'm not officially part of his world—I don't win and lose the average American's yearly salary in one feverish night of action—I'm fluent with the vocabulary of people who look at life as a series of risk-versus-reward decisions. Most regular folks outside the surreal subculture of professional gambling see the high-rolling inhabitants of this parallel universe, where a "dime" means $1,000, as maladjusted freaks who could use a healthy dose of psychological counseling. The regular folks may be right. But there's also something seductive and oddly respectable about men who are willing to back their convictions with a large portion of their net worth.

Ever since age five, when my great-grandma taught me how to play gin rummy, I've enjoyed card and board games: Scrabble, Stratego, Mastermind, Monopoly, hearts, poker—the excitement of an athletic contest and the intellectual challenge of problem solving have always appealed to me, a nerd with a competitive streak. But growing up with a healthy respect for money—my family never seemed to have quite enough of it—I viewed gambling with the cultivated skepticism of a striver inculcated in the twin virtues of Work and Study. Casino games fascinated me, since they were *games* after all. But losing hundreds of dollars at roulette and craps and slot machines, "recreational pursuits" that seemed as rigged as a carnival barker's ring toss, was anathema to my stolid constitution. Part of me wanted to be a big winner. I wanted to take the risk. I wanted to overcome the odds with my wits and my guile. But I didn't have the heart for it. Perhaps that's why I was attracted to the rare fellows who did.

When I meet Rick Matthews in the summer of 1997, I'm thirty-two, moderately successful by the standards of "normal" American life but an inconsequential piker compared with the people I profile in the world of professional gambling. As a freelance writer, I contribute articles to a wide array of magazines, including several men's publications that like to publish stories about wagering and Las Vegas, about big scores and big characters who heroically do what all of us working stiffs haven't the heart for, men and women who play by a set of rules different from the ones we good citizens assiduously follow on our road to the pension and retirement home. These journalist assignments require monthly jaunts to Nevada, which remind me how much I like games, *winning* at games, and also how blasé and predictable my middle-class life is, how devoid of risk and its fraternal twin, reward. My biggest gamble involves appearing on a televised game show (and losing). My average blackjack bet is ten dollars. The poker tables I sit at produce wins and losses in the hundreds, not hundreds of thousands. I'm tickled when a casino pit boss offers me a comp dinner at the coffee shop (drinks not included). I pay the mortgage, I save for the future, I buy clothes and cars and concert tickets—and it all amounts to a rather ordinary variation on the theme of American triumph: You work hard, you endure the countless indignities of the unprivileged plebian, and then you go quietly.

The excitement in my life revolves around Vivian, my girlfriend of a year, a woman who is decidedly, willfully not average, not the usual middle-class gal obsessed with marriage and children. Vivian is what moralists would call a "bad girl," a libertine who refuses to subscribe to the code of feminine conduct prescribed by church and state. She's a pagan, a voracious reader of philosophy and science, and an omnisexual hedonist. To Vivian, Las Vegas is an adult playground, where every day is Mardi Gras and even the nicest people can be corrupted by temptations of the flesh. In Los Angeles, where we live together, Viv is an executive at a hotel company, a competent and presentable corporate achiever in a proper pantsuit. But when I've got a story assignment in the desert she likes to let down her hair (literally) and sate her carnal appetites. We gamble and flirt and go to underground adult sex clubs to play, and I feel at those fantastic, extravagant moments that I'm not just another anonymous young man hoping to find his way in the world. I'm *doing* something extraordinary.

When I began pursuing Big Daddy for my book project, I wasn't conscious of wanting to work for him. If anything, I was simply keen to be let in on the secrets, to be given a glimpse of the recipe for his particular brand of special sauce. To see how one of the real rebels staked his claim to a grand slice of the American dream. Now, on Sherwood's eighth green, I tell Rick Matthews, "I respect your accomplishments. And I reckon a young man like me could learn an awful lot from someone as sharp as you."

Searching for ulterior motives, Big Daddy stares at me intently, as though I were a poker player he's assessing for signs of weakness. Then he grins and says, "Well, that might work."

A few holes later, riding up Sherwood's closely manicured eleventh fairway, Rick Matthews nonchalantly asks me, "Hey, pards, how'dya like to make a little money this football season?"

Would my dog like a rare porterhouse for lunch? Like most American men, I bet a recreational pittance on the NFL games, and, like most American men, I win a bunch of games and I lose a bunch of games. I'm sharp enough to pick winners approximately half the time, but the juice, the bookies' 11–10 vigorish, eats me up in the long run. I'm lucky if I break even.

I tell Rick, "Sure, I'd like to hear how I could make some money betting on football. But could we talk about it later, after the round? I need to concentrate. I'm playing for twenty bucks after all."

"Sure we can," Big Daddy agrees, chuckling softly.

We golf. He goes about his business with chilly precision and I don't, so the outcome of our match is never in doubt. No matter how much I try to concentrate on tee shots and birdie putts, for most of the time I mull over whatever proposition might be awaiting me after the round.

When we're back in the clubhouse, Rick spells out the plan: We're going to be "partners," which means I'll bet his money as instructed. I'll be part of his team of bettors, a squadron of associates who help him wager the enormous amounts of money he invests on every game. I'm not to play hunches. I'm not to divulge his picks to anyone. I'm not to reveal the source of "my" handicapping skill. And I'm supposed to wager all that I can.

Because of his reputation and the low limits the casinos impose upon him, Big Daddy Matthews can't bet his own money in most places, and he certainly can't bet enough to make it worth his while. He needs people like me to help him "get down," to get his huge bankroll in play. In return for this valuable service, I'll be entitled to 10 percent of the net profits. If we lose ("which ain't gonna happen"), he absorbs the hit; if we win, I get paid a potentially substantial fee. I pay taxes on my share, he pays on his, and everyone gets rich. "Plus, one day when we're all through you can write a helluva book."

I'm going to contribute a small minority interest in the bankroll, which will mean I'm betting my own money as well, but the casinos may look upon this distinction as rhetorical hairsplitting. I ask Rick why he just doesn't get one of the usual suspects, a salaried sportsbook runner, a human mule, to do the deed. He tells me that it would look better if a hotshot Hollywood type—or at least a guy who can play the part—flew into Vegas each weekend, looking like hundreds of other high-rolling suckers. Plus, Rick explains, I'm comfortable in the casino environment; I know the vernacular, and I can convincingly imitate the habits of a hopeless loser.

And most important, he says, he's got a strong instinct that he can trust me.

Big Daddy Matthews has just invited me to join his team, the organization that those in the know call the Brain Trust.

I nod soberly and tell him I'll think about it.

But I already know I'm in.

The next week I have supper with my friend Spanish Jack, one of the best seven-card-stud players in the world. Over margaritas at a downtown Los Angeles Mexican restaurant, I tell Spanish Jack about my opportunity to work with Big Daddy. Jack says that Rick Matthews has a reputation throughout the gambling world as a snake, a rat, a back-stabber, and every other lowdown epithet you could imagine. "He's the most successful gambler of all time. He's probably won fifty to a hundred million. But you don't want to be his partner. He just can't stand not getting the best of every transaction. I'm sure he's great to work for. He pays, and pays well. But you don't want to have to trust him."

I've heard similar innuendos before from other professional gambler acquaintances, but I don't want to believe them.

I'm still deliberating two weeks later when a men's magazine assigns me to write a story about Las Vegas. It's a good excuse to interview Eric

"Jox" Brijox, the man who creates the Las Vegas line, the guy whose job it is to make it difficult for people like Big Daddy to make a living. We're sitting in Jox's office, a brightly lit workspace decorated with sports memorabilia, in a corporate park not far from the Vegas airport.

Jox, a former statistician with a major aerospace concern, has a pasty complexion and thick eyeglasses befitting a fellow who spends most of his waking hours in front of a computer monitor analyzing batting averages and rebounds per game. The Las Vegas casinos—and dozens of others around the world—pay Jox a monthly fee to help them set their opening point-spread numbers, which Rick Matthews and friends subsequently comb for weaknesses to exploit. Jox doesn't like Big Daddy. He says Matthews is a compulsive liar and a scoundrel in general, a guy who refuses to follow the casinos' rules on betting limits. I can see the distaste on Jox's pale, boyish face when he talks about his chief nemesis.

Without revealing that I'm pondering joining the Brains, I tell Jox that I'll probably take a shot at beating football this season. I tell him I've come into a substantial amount of money and that my neighbor, a computer whiz, has a program that can pick something like 60 percent winners (52.4 percent is break-even). Does Jox have any thoughts?

He tells me he's skeptical and says that if I ended up the season losing only a little he would consider it a huge success.

I glance over Jox's shoulder at the framed photo of Secretariat winning the Triple Crown at Belmont. I say I'm confident of my system. "I'm planning on betting a lot. Might as well put my money where my mouth is, right? Any reason I shouldn't?"

"Because you're probably going to lose!" Jox predicts, chortling. "I make a pretty good line, you know."

I think about how Jox sets that line, how hundreds and thousands of sports statistics are fed into a computer on an hourly basis, stats that are analyzed by a program created and fine-tuned by Jox and his crew of geniuses. For the average sports gambler, Jox's line is tough. "The best," I reply reverentially. But I'm thinking, *It's not infallible.*

Outside Jox's window, another plane lands at McCarran Airport, depositing hundreds of fresh suckers in the desert. Their cumulative wisdom about gambling wouldn't come close to equaling what Eric Brijox knows about risk and reward. Yet even he, I realize, can't stop syndicates like the Brain Trust from beating the Las Vegas sportsbooks. There's a reason they're called the Brains: They simply seem to know more than anyone else does. To most casual players, the point spreads are as solid as the commemorative baseball bat, signed by Reggie Jackson, hanging on the wall behind Brijox's head. To Rick Matthews, they're as fragile as a crystal champagne flute.

"Here's my plan," I explain. "Either I'm as good as I think, or I'm going to go down in flames. So I'm going to bet as much as I can afford." We talk about the Kelly Criterion, a formula for determining the optimal percentage of one's bankroll to wager on each game, and other mathematical arcana beloved of serious gamblers and math wonks—but really I just want to put the proposition in front of Jox. I know if I end up betting big sums, some sportsbook manager is going to call Jox the Linemaker and ask, Who the hell is this precocious kid? If Jox tells them I'm just some punk writer, things might look suspicious; if he says I'm a gambling author with the dumb luck to have a big bankroll and a funny idea in his head that he can beat football—well, then they'll probably be happy to take my action.

Jox asks how much I want to bet. I tell him I don't know—$20,000 to start, $30,000, maybe even $40,000, depending on how good my system is. Jox laughs. "That's going to be tough to bet that much. There's only one guy who knows how to get that much down. You want that kind of action, you better get in tight with a guy like Rick Matthews."

I swallow hard and try to keep a straight face.

SEASON ONE

Autumn 1997–Spring 1998

Two

HIGH ROLLER

When my girlfriend Vivian and I arrive at McCarran International Airport at 8:30 on a Friday evening in September 1997, I ring Big Daddy's cell phone, as instructed. He tells me he's glad I've arrived and asks me to call him back after I've checked into Caesars Palace, one of the first super-luxe themed casinos on the Las Vegas Strip and one of the few older properties to keep up with the increasingly hip and modern Vegas. The excesses of the Roman Empire are celebrated at this world-famous resort, where every man, no matter how plain his title back home, can be an emperor. Lurid blue lights illuminate the front of the hotel, whose building-sized marquee and ornamental fountains have appeared in dozens of movies and television shows as visual shorthand for Vegas grandiosity.

It's the second week of the college football season. Since our fateful golf date, Big Daddy and I have had one terse conversation during which I agreed to his generous terms. I was fully briefed on my responsibilities. Then, using my real name over a series of increasingly credible phone calls, sweet-talked the casino management into believing I'm a whale, a big-betting sucker worthy of the finest amenities—despite the fact that the biggest wager I previously placed at a Las Vegas sportsbook was $220 to win $200 on a football game.

Now the real fun begins.

Every employee at Caesars wears a uniform that is supposed to suggest ancient Rome, however tenuously. Even the parking valets, who take our rental car and summon a bellman for our luggage, are dressed up as some sort of characters, though I'm not sure as what exactly. (Well-kept slaves?) So many incandescent lights glow near the front entrance, a horseshoe of glass doors on top of a wedding cake of stairs, that the air is measurably warmer near the doors than on the expansive stone driveway. At the front desk, a great slab of white marble, the nice lady checking my reservation tells me that thanks to my management-approved status, I could have availed myself of the Invited Guest Lounge, where patrons hand over their credit cards and driver's licenses while attendants bearing canapés speak in hushed tones and fetch cool drinks.

I call Rick Matthews from our room—a "superior" model, with a Jacuzzi, a circular bed, and a mirror on the ceiling. It's not the *Rain Man* suite, but the abundance of gold-plated faucets and marble flooring suggests that the casino wants the room's occupants to feel like patricians of Caesar's empire or, at the very least, facsimiles of Tom Cruise. The bathroom amenities are arranged on platforms held up by miniature Doric columns, and the pay-movie channels, I discover, don't require payment. They're all activated.

Viv and I have been together for more than a year. We've been to Vegas a dozen times before. We've never stayed in a place like this.

Big Daddy tells me to meet him out front in thirty minutes. "I'll be driving a black four-door Mercedes," he says in his lazy drawl.

Half an hour later, after escorting Viv to her bubble bath, I'm waiting alone under the porte cochere, watching the limousines and taxis disgorging passengers. Rick pulls up and waves when he spots me in my white Shadow Creek golf cap. Only the loftiest of high rollers get invited to play at this ultra-exclusive North Las Vegas private course, where people like Michael Jordan and Phil Mickelson keep lockers. Journalist credentials allowed me to sneak through the filter that's supposed to keep out people whose net worth is below $10 million. (And I bought a hat to commemorate the occasion.) Now, I'm thinking, the Shadow Creek me-

mento will broadcast to the world—particularly the management at Caesars Palace—that I'm a terribly desirable casino customer. After all, I've played at Shadow Creek.

On the passenger seat of Rick's car is a legal document that acknowledges my participation in the Brain Trust betting syndicate and a list of the games I'm supposed to play. It's a plain white sheet of paper, with black type, frank and unadorned. Big Daddy says, "Howya doin', pards? They treatin' you all right?" as I climb inside.

Before I can answer, he says, "Let's make a visit and go get you some money."

We drive downtown to the Union Plaza. As we pass successive casinos along the Strip—Mirage, Treasure Island, Frontier, Riviera—their lights winking like flirtatious girls, Rick eviscerates the city of Las Vegas. "I'm so disappointed by what's happened to this town," he admits, shaking his head. "They all smile at the suckers, pretending that everyone has got a decent shot at winning. But, Mike, you're gonna find out: If you show any speed whatsoever they'll bar you in a second. Bunch of frauds, these people are," he mutters.

I look over the list of the Brain Trust's picks. A few are popular televised national matchups, such as Wisconsin vs. Illinois. But most are obscure regional games, which, I fear, will set off alarm bells with the bookies. Akron vs. Toledo, Western Carolina vs. Ball State, Ivy League contests. Even I know only wiseguys play these games.

Rick parks outside the Plaza and leaves me in the car. I read and sign the legal document, which basically says I'm holding a lot of the Brain Trust's money. Then I rewrite the shopping list of football games in my own messy scrawl.

He returns a few minutes later with a leather bag containing $400,000 in bundled hundred-dollar bills. I hold the satchel between my legs. It feels as though there's a bowling ball inside. I'd have to write one major story a month for close to eight years to accumulate what's in the bag.

Back at the Palace's front entrance, Rick and I transfer the money into two shoe bags—golf shoe bags. FootJoys. "Go win some bets!" Big Daddy says.

"Yes, sir," I reply and bolt into the casino.

Realizing I've forgotten my Shadow Creek hat, I dash back to the curb. He's still there, watching me.

I go directly to the sportsbook, a cavernous room with a forty-foot-high ceiling and wide-screen television monitors blanketing the space like animated wallpaper. The back wall behind the service counter, where patrons make bets, and which looks like the hotel's front desk, is entirely dedicated to a digital toteboard listing the current betting odds on hundreds of contests. The backdrop of ESPN's *SportsCenter* set is modeled on such a toteboard. Dina, the night supervisor, greets me. Gino Miceli, the vice president of sports and horse racing (and Dina's boss), a former Brooklyn pizzeria owner turned casino executive, told her I'd be coming and to take good care of me. I phoned Gino earlier in the week and he didn't seem too interested in my fanciful story of hitting it big in Hollywood and wanting to scratch my action itch. He just wanted to know when I was coming and how he and his staff could make my visit to Caesars special. "Let me win!" I barked.

I plunk the shoe bags on the counter. "I'd like to open a betting account," I tell Dina as she eyes the mountain of money. "And oh, by the way, could you scare up a couple of buffet tickets?"

A portly woman with round cheeks, Dina titters obsequiously at my joke. Her entire face jiggles when she laughs. I'd previously seen a couple of small-time bookies, outlaws who operated out of basement poker rooms and sports bars. Dina's not what I pictured a professional casino bookmaker would look like.

The sportsbook air is filled with the low hum of televised highlight shows and the pungent aroma of cigarettes and perspiration, the by-product of excessive adrenaline and anxiety. Dozens of sports fans congregate beneath the broadcast screens and toteboard, silently wishing and praying and willing their team to win tomorrow's game so that they too can win. There's a sense of desperation already, and none of the contests have even started.

For the next hour we fill out paperwork and count the money. Though two clerks work on the stacks of bills, counting them into $10,000 packets, it takes thirty minutes, and I quickly exhaust my supply of small talk, leaving me and Dina in uncomfortable silence. I'm given tickets to a VIP table, in the middle of all the screens, a prime location to root and holler and play out private dramas in public. While the employees count and package, I make some noise about being a big poker player down at the Horseshoe. But no one seems to care where the money came from, only that it's probably going to end up staying with Caesars Palace.

Dina asks me if I want to bet tonight. I say yes, and as a courtesy she gives me an updated list of the current lines so I don't have to wait for my games to appear on the toteboard, like stocks flickering past on a ticker. To my dismay, *none* of the games are posted at the point-spread numbers Big Daddy has ordered. It's only a half point or so that they're off, but the rule is clear: Wrong number, no bet. I tell Dina I'm going to get something to eat and come back later, after I've had a chance to "analyze" the lines.

With $400,000 at my disposal, I walk away from a wall of bets and return to the hotel room. Viv tells me Rick phoned and expressly asked for me *not* to call this evening. Saturdays are fourteen-hour workdays, so he goes to bed early the night before. I tell her my dilemma, that he gave me ten plays and none of them are bettable. She wrinkles her nose and says I should probably wait until morning.

We order room service and dine on our circular bed.

Big Daddy calls at 7:30 a.m. This is Vegas. On a Saturday morning. After a Friday night in Sin City, I didn't think anyone ever rose before 10:00 a.m.

I tell him I refrained from betting, and he says I did the right thing. Then he gives me five or six plays and tells me to get downstairs and fire away. After I do I'm supposed to call him with confirmation from my room or a pay phone out of sight of the sportsbook management.

"And by the way, Mike," he says, "before you go back out there we gotta get you a nickname, a code name, just in case anyone from the hotel is trying to listen. We don't want them to know I'm talking with you."

"All right," I say, feeling for a moment like a clandestine operative behind enemy lines.

"You got one?"

My boyhood pals used to call me Koney—but that doesn't seem secretive (or cool) enough. Neither does Viv's favorite sobriquet, "honeybuns." While I'm thinking, Big Daddy proposes "Shakespeare." He says, "You know, the writer."

I remember how my grade school basketball coach, an ex-military man with a crewcut and a copy of *Playboy* stashed in his desk, never called any of us by our names, only our jersey numbers. "Hey, 44!" he would shout at me. "More passing, less shooting! Play some defense, 44!"

"How about 44?" I ask.

"Just the number? 44? Well, okay." Big Daddy seems to have expected more from a writer, something clever, like "Shakespeare."

"Yes. Call me 44."

"Well, okay, Mr. 44. Go on and make those bets."

I throw on some jeans and hurry to the casino.

The Caesars Palace line manager, Stevie "the Pencil" Masters—he's known for always scribbling something while he balances the action—is already there, getting ready for a big day of college football. Stevie, only thirty-two but already going gray around the temples, is painfully thin and bouncily hyperactive, as though he were jacked up on a potent mixture of coffee and point spreads. Rumor is that he was an adolescent math genius who got kicked out of a prestigious East Coast boarding school for booking bets on the intramural lacrosse games. Then he got expelled from Princeton University for booking bets on college basketball. Eventually he landed in Las Vegas, where no one begrudges him his penchant for accepting sports wagers.

Clutching *The Gold Sheet*, a weekly tout pamphlet filled with "best bets of the week" recommendations that ought to brand me as a half-sharp clod who thinks he knows something, I introduce myself to Pencil Stevie. Although the Code of Vegas decrees that the enormous amount of money I have on deposit is supposed to earn me some instant deference, I can feel him giving me the once-over, gauging, trying to get a read. His boss, Gino the Suit, has briefed him (warned him?) about me, but the Pencil seems to be the kind of guy who likes to make his own judgments. He asks me if I want to make some plays.

"I wanna bet fifty-five thousand dollars to win fifty thousand on the

Southern Cal game," I announce. It's a big televised battle against Tennessee. Everyone is watching it—and betting on it.

Without a hint of regret, Stevie says, "I can only let you bet twenty-seven thousand five to win twenty-five thousand. I'm really heavy on that game." He means all the money is coming in on USC.

I shrug and say, "That's fine. My buddy Tommy—you know, the sportsbook manager over at the Gold Coast—he told me everyone likes USC. That's the only reason I'm betting it."

"You know Tommy?" Stevie the Pencil asks.

"Oh, yeah. Long time."

"Good man," Stevie says.

"The best." I nod emphatically and move on to the next game, Florida, for another $55,000, against a nonconference punching bag—which the Pencil again lets me bet for $27,500.

And the Miami of Ohio game, another $27,500.

And Kansas State.

"These are all added games, buddy," he says.

I play dumb. "What do you mean? They're all football games that have been on the schedule for weeks," I say, although I know what he's getting at. "Added games" are typically untelevised contests of regional interest. The average gambler wants action only on the games he's sweating, the ones he's suffering through live. Only wiseguys play untelevised games.

Already I'm feeling the heat, and I've been playing only two minutes.

As soon as I return to the room and report my bets, as well as Stevie's comment about the added games, Big Daddy sends me back down to bet a few more. They're all "board" games, but Stevie still mutters something about me betting a lot of the hot sides, the teams that everyone else (including the wiseguys) is taking. I tell him I don't know what he's talking about. I just want to gamble.

When Rick sends me back down again an hour later to bet the *other* side of the Florida game—the line has moved from –41 to –44, meaning now Florida has to win by 45 in order for bettors to cash a ticket—the Pencil gets furious.

"You're not betting both sides of the game!"

I say I'm just trying to hit a middle, what's the big deal? If Florida wins by 42 or 43, I win *both* bets. If they win by 41 or 44, I win one bet and tie the other. And every other result costs me only the juice on one bet. For example, if I bet $27,500 on Florida –41 and $27,500 on the underdog, Podunk State, +44 points, I'll probably win one bet (and collect $25,000) and lose one bet (forfeiting $27,500), for a net loss of $2,500. But those magical times when the final score falls in the middle of my point-spread numbers, I win $50,000 for the $2,500 I'm risking. I'm getting 20–1 on my gamble. (The odds are effectively even better than that, because when the final score falls directly on one of my point-spread numbers, 41 or 44. I win one bet and tie the other, thereby saving the $2,500 juice.)

Pencil Stevie tells me he smells a rat; that he's got half a mind to shut down my account; that he gets a bad gut instinct; that he's heard rumors about the big syndicates bringing in bettors disguised as tourists; that I seem to be playing some awfully hot games.

Casinos are private businesses that reserve the right to refuse service to people they don't like: namely, anyone who has a realistic shot at beating them. With a built-in house advantage, why should they cut into the profits produced by legions of losers? Expert blackjack players and sometimes even professional video poker players face the prospect of being barred from the casinos, even though all they're doing is using their minds. But I've never heard of anyone getting barred for betting on sports. Instead, the casinos prefer to do what Stevie the Pencil is doing: refuse individual wagers or severely limit their size.

I tell the Pencil I don't know what he's talking about. Syndicates? Is that some sort of Mafia insinuation?

Outwardly I act aggrieved. But I'm shaken. The first day of the first week of what the Brain Trust hoped would be a long, profitable season, and I'm already lit up with Vegas neon.

When I tell Big Daddy of my steamy status, he laughs, promising that our next few plays will definitely change the Pencil's opinion of me. "Nobody in the world is betting a dime on these games. You gotta look like the biggest sucker in the world."

I mumble, "You want me to make bad bets?"

"Come on, now, son," Big Daddy chuckles. "There ain't no downside to these games. You know me better than that. I ain't gonna give these sumbitches a nickel."

I go back to the book. The Pencil is mildly conciliatory. He says he's going to be straight with me: There's a lot of talk going around about the big syndicates like the Brains sending in a team of previously unidentified bettors. I, of course, feign ignorance. Although I've never once in my life assembled power ratings or crunched team statistics through a computer, I tell the Pencil that I consider myself one of the best handicappers he'll ever meet, and that I expect to win.

"I appreciate your confidence, but look at it my way," he says. "I can't risk getting hurt by a big gambler who knows what he's doing. And by the way, I'm going to call Tommy, our buddy at the Gold Coast, to check up on you, if that's all right."

"Sure," I say, nonchalantly, making a mental note to have Big Daddy talk to Tommy (a man I've never met) before the Pencil does.

Then I give Stevie a bunch of ice-cold plays: Rutgers getting 39½ from Texas; BYU getting 8½ from Washington; Stanford giving 29 to San Jose State. He seems a little more relaxed. But I know I'm being watched like a recidivist felon.

"If those plays don't cool him off, nothing will," Rick Matthews tells me when I call to report the bets. I tell Big Daddy about the Tommy incident, and he says he'll take care of it—but that in the future I should let him know if I'm using anybody as a reference. "We need to cover our tracks, 44."

For the rest of the afternoon I join Viv in the spa, where we get massages and mud wraps. We're treating our weekend at Caesars Palace like a holiday—me from the constant chase of freelance writing and she from her marketing responsibilities. We pretend we're strangers. We pretend we're movie stars. We pretend we're an old married couple. Mostly we act like two kids in love.

Although bettors typically float in and out of the sportsbook to check on scores and changing point spreads, I'm glad to stay away. It's a relief to be out of the casino, away from the flame of inquisition and mistrust.

Big Daddy Rick and I talk once more—he beeps me as my massage is concluding—to review our positions. He continues his rant about what a disappointing con game Las Vegas is, and says we're done for the day. "But keep your beeper on, 44, in case something comes up."

I'm hoping nothing does.

After a gluttonous dinner at Nero's, the steakhouse, I stroll to the sportsbook with Viv to check the scores. Knowing my worried gaze and pleading voice wouldn't affect the outcome of the contests, only my blood pressure, I've refused to watch any of the games. Now we'll find out how the beefy scholar-athletes from around the country performed on our behalf.

I scan the giant, wall-sized toteboard, ticking off the wins and losses in my head. USC: winner. Florida: winner. BYU: loser. Sixteen games in all.

I look at Vivian with wide, astonished eyes. She smiles back at me. We've finished the day 10–6, up about $91,000.

In one pampered day I just earned $9,000.

The boss man calls at 7:30 a.m. on Sunday morning with two "total" plays and instructions to bet them for $20,000 to $25,000. Totals are known as "over-unders": gamblers bet on the total number of points scored by both teams. Will it be higher or lower than the number posted by the bookmakers?

The Pencil is already up and working, scribbling furiously, with his chin propped on his fist. But he barely acknowledges me when I pop into the book. "Morning!" I say cheerfully, striding up to the long counter, separated from the seating area by low partitions, like a savings bank. He nods silently and scowls.

The cavernous room, soon to be filled with gamblers screaming at the jumbo screens, is almost deserted. One disheveled fellow sitting at a cocktail table is bent over a stack of papers, with his forehead in his hand, like Kant working out the meaning of life. Another guy, balding and pot-bellied, stands beneath the toteboard with his hands stuck in his pockets, his head tilted upward, and his mouth hanging open, as though he were admiring Michelangelo's handiwork on the ceiling of the Sistine Chapel.

I make my bets for $20,000, and the clerks take them without discussion. Then I hang around the window for a few minutes, as if I'm studying other bets. I ask a few stupid questions and stroll away. But before I do, I sincerely thank Pencil Stevie for not letting me bet the other side of the Florida game—he saved me $27,500. I get a dirty look.

Back in the room the phone rings. Rick asks me how they took the action.

"It was cool," I tell him.

"Don't remind Stevie about the Florida game, 44. It will only piss him off," Big Daddy says offhandedly.

I wonder if Big Daddy is having me watched, making sure I'm not placing any renegade bets or giving up his picks to other bettors. From that point on, I take special notice of the faces I seem to see repeatedly in the Caesars Palace sportsbook. I suspect one middle-aged redheaded woman, but I can't confirm my suspicions. It's like being in the middle of a movie spy thriller, with everybody—including the guys on my team—watching my every move. Suddenly I don't want to step into that place again.

But Rick gives me another Brain Trust play—an icy play, he assures me—and I go back down. It's the Tennessee Titans +6 against the Miami Dolphins. I bet $55,000 to win $50,000 and Stevie takes the action without blinking. That's the way I like it.

During the morning NFL games I have brunch with Viv and try not to fixate on the heat or lack thereof my bets are generating. I tell her I'm thinking of bringing in an associate, someone to run from the room to the book so I don't draw attention to myself. I assume casino surveillance is watching to see if I go to a pay phone immediately after I wager. Then again, Big Daddy probably wouldn't appreciate the potential security leak, so I shelve the idea.

When we check the scores, I discover we're handily winning our two morning games. In the midst of high fives, Big Daddy calls again with our after-lunch special. "You gotta have something to sweat in the afternoon, right, pards?"

I bet the Jacksonville Jaguars –4½ against the New York Giants for another $55,000. Again, the nice folks at Caesars take the bet without hesitation, as though I were wagering ten bucks. Then I depart for an afternoon round of golf at the Desert Inn, courtesy of the casino. When

I say good-bye to the Pencil, I ask him if I'll be seeing him again next weekend.

"You still want to come?" he asks.

"If you'll still have me," I say. "Oh, and by the way, could you arrange tickets to the De La Hoya fight?" I ask brusquely, remembering that I'm a high roller and entitled to such perks.

He says he'll see what he can do. Call him tomorrow.

With no work scheduled for the evening, Viv and I have a splendid (comped) meal at the elegant Chinese restaurant and go to a show at the Stratosphere, where she gets hypnotized and levitated. When we get back, around midnight, I do a final check of the scores, and I feel as though I'm floating myself: We've won everything.

For the weekend, the Brain Trust has gone 14–6 and taken $231,500 of the casino's money.

I could get used to this.

But I suspect Caesars Palace never will.

Back in Los Angeles, I talk to Stevie the Pencil on the telephone. He's very cordial, almost apologetic. Seems his bosses weren't too happy about my performance. Seems they want to impose new, lower limits on me: $30,000 for pros, $15,000 for college. Normally, when someone makes a large wager, the bookmaker moves the line to attract money on the other side. The Pencil assures me that if I bet and they *don't* move the line, I'm welcome to bet them again at the full limit.

I tell Stevie, Be honest: We wouldn't be having this chat if I didn't do so well, right?

He says not necessarily. A lot of my plays were similar to the bets of the suspected computer teams.

I play the Iggy and ask him to explain. He does, telling me how a syndicate like the Brain Trust works. "These big groups, they use a computer to get their number. The Poker Players, Blair and Ferdy, the IBMs, Ricky's Brain Trust—all these different syndicates, they figure out their lines with a computer. Then they bet a pile of money all around the world. They use guys like you to help them get down."

"Fascinating," I say.

Perhaps excessive bravado, I reckon, will make me look like the kind of idiot Caesars wants to keep as a customer. I tell the Pencil that I'm good. Damn good. A super sharp handicapper—and I'll put my winner-picking abilities up against anybody.

The Pencil patiently says, with all due respect, there's no such thing as a sharp handicapper who plays twenty games on a weekend.

Which is just what I want him to say. "So how come you're lowering my limits then?" I ask, logically. "Because you're scared of how good I am, right?"

He tells me if it were he, personally, he would take any amount from anybody. It's the bean counters who make the rules. And so forth.

"Fine," I say. "But you watch." I promise I'm going to be the best handicapper Caesars Palace has ever seen.

I can almost hear him sneering over the phone line.

Big Daddy and I review the latest developments. He calls the casinos a bunch of dummies and decries their hypocrisy. "We'll just have to set you up at two places at once," he says. Maybe, he suggests, I could get set up with the Hilton, or some other joint that purports to cater to big shots like me. In the meantime, we're stuck with one shopping outlet. That week, I busy myself with my usual routine of pitching story ideas to magazine editors and working absentmindedly on the ones they commission. All I can think about is flying across the Mojave to the parallel universe Rick Matthews is allowing me to inhabit.

Finally, Vivian and I return to Caesars Palace on the Friday afternoon before the big De La Hoya vs. Camacho fight. There's a sexual charge in the air, an undercurrent of power and money. Pretty hoochie girls everywhere, their gambler boyfriends and sugar daddies not far away. Guys in track suits; guys with fight credentials hanging from their necks; guys who look like *players*. It feels good to walk through the casino knowing I've got $631,500 sitting in an account with my name on it. Even if I'm not really the kind of player the casino thinks I am. Or wishes I were.

Our room, booked through VIP Services, is comped, per the Suit and the Pencil. It is, as requested, in the Olympic Tower, nearest the sports-book. And though it's not quite as "superior" as last week's, it does have an even bigger mirror over the bed.

I don't read any sinister motives into our mild downgrade. On a fight weekend, I'm glad to have any sort of comped room in Las Vegas. And even gladder to have two $600 tickets to the fight, courtesy of my gener-ous hosts. What a town. I even get to see Oscar and his entourage down in the casino.

I call Big Daddy, who tells me he's got a special cell phone for me all set up. He'll call me back at around 6:15, when he can talk more.

He doesn't ring until 9:30, when Viv and I are in the middle of a glori-ous French meal at the Palace Court. The maître d' brings me a portable phone, saying I don't need to push any buttons, it's all ready to go. How Big Daddy knew to reach me at this particular restaurant, one of nine at Caesars, I can only guess. "Hey, pards, you gonna be ready to go anytime soon?"

I tell Big Daddy it will be around thirty minutes. He says this might be our only opportunity to bet a whole bunch of games. I tell him I can sneak out for a few minutes, if necessary. He asks me if I'm there with a whole bunch of people. No, only my girlfriend Vivian, I tell him. I can go if he needs me to. "That's all right," he says, being gentlemanly. "Just call me as soon as you're leaving, 44."

As the waiter places our chocolate soufflé on the table, I ring Big Daddy back. He gives me eleven Brain Trust plays—one of which is the big Michigan television game; four of which are added games; and two of which, he warns me, are superhot.

Viv and I walk to the sportsbook, wineglasses in hand. I'm in a suit and tie. She looks smashing, an expensive plaything, pouring out of her little white dress. If I'm the sucker high roller from Hollywood, she's the high-priced escort on my arm. And I'm enjoying the masquerade.

The moment we come in view of the counter, Viv discreetly whispers to me, "We've definitely been recognized. Three people behind the counter started talking to each other and looking our way, like they've been expecting us."

I'm all smiles and handshakes—a fun-loving party boy who, with the help of the wine, doesn't have to fake it too hard. Everyone—the clerks; Dina, the night supervisor; Little Mikey Brown, the night manager (and former heavyweight prizefighter)—is genuinely nice. Like they're real pleased to see me. I ask Dina for an updated odds sheet and a statement of my balance. When she brings out the sportsbook's list of accounts, I make a big deal of having Viv turn away, so she doesn't see how much (shopping) money is available. As I verify my number—$631,500—I sneak a glance down the sheet and note that about twenty individuals have accounts open, and the total balance of these accounts is approximately $1,100,000. I've got more than half the money on account in the casino sportsbook. No wonder they're hawking me.

Every play Big Daddy has requested is available except one total bet, and Dina takes my action without pause, making sure only that I haven't exceeded the new, lower limits the Pencil has prescribed. I ham it up a bit, telling her such and such is my play of the week—even though I don't have the faintest idea who the coaches are, let alone the starting quarterbacks. Viv tells me I look like a good-time Charlie who thinks he knows something the whole world doesn't. In other words, a real idiot.

After betting, we hang around for ten minutes, watching highlights of De La Hoya's past fights on the video screens. Vivian has a huge crush on Oscar the Golden Boy. I admit to her that I have a huge crush on the fantasy world I've entered, where pleasure and power and risk and reward all intersect.

Cheered by the casino's warm reception, Viv and I stumble off to our room, where we giggle at our ceiling mirror.

I wake up at 7:00 a.m. and realize I missed a bet. The total play that I thought wasn't listed—Miami of Florida—was there all the time. I had been looking at Miami of Ohio. (Ah, red wine.) Slightly panicked, I dash down to the book.

Pencil Stevie and all his day-crew boys are there. I say hello and shake some hands and get a mildly cordial reception. The number is still what Big Daddy ordered, so I don't have to tell him about my mistake. I bet it and linger a little longer, as if I'm thinking about some other plays. I ask a few inane questions—"Hey, you think that LSU number might go to ten?"—and chat about the big fight. I say to Stevie, "Is anybody actually betting on Hector Camacho?" He tells me yeah, because he's only making a hundred-dollar spread, cheap for a boxing line. I tell him that's pretty good. He says, "Not for me it isn't!" I laugh, genuinely pleased that the Pencil is joking around with me. Maybe he's getting comfortable. For crissakes, I just gave him eleven plays before the first snap. He's got to love me. Conventional wisdom says that the more games you play, the more money you're going to lose in the long run. The more results the bookie can churn through his mill, the more profit he's able to grind out.

Seconds after I return to the room, Big Daddy Rick calls for a report. He chuckles bitterly when I reiterate the limits they're allowing. "All right, pards. I'll get back to you."

He does only once, another total play. It's a light, low-pressure afternoon. I get a massage; Viv gets a full day of spa treatments. Every so often I pop into the book to check my results. With eight of our twelve plays complete, we're 4–4, but up about $18,000, a decent if unspectacular result. We leave for the pugilistic festivities with $80,000 in wagers undecided.

The De La Hoya fight, like all big Vegas fights, buzzes with the kind of manic hum generated by celebrity, money, and hundreds of beautiful women in clinging, low-cut dresses. Viv and I enter the arena through a VIP entrance, where camera-toting autograph hounds have staked out spots to ambush the famous athletes and movie stars who pass this way. Our seats afford a terrific view and all the complimentary cocktails and salty snacks we desire. Oscar takes care of business. Big Daddy never pages me for emergency Brain Trust action. And we have a fine and raucous time.

Upon our return to Caesars, I discover the Brains have gone 2–2 in the night games, but the two we've lost were slightly bigger bets than the winners. For the day we're up a piddling $1,600. I console myself: At least now the Pencil and his cronies will probably be more comfortable with my play.

We cap off the evening at a private party for Oscar at the execrable

Planet Hollywood, where, to Vivian's delight, we meet a couple of naughty girls. One of them, a slender brunette with pouty lips and a pierced tongue, seems to be a good candidate to join us in our room, but turns out to be a flirtatious bust. Instead, Viv ends up buying us a hooker—on my credit card.

I'm officially a Vegas high roller.

Three

BUILT IN

After only one week of proving my usefulness, Big Daddy desperately wants me to get built in at the Las Vegas Hilton, where the self-proclaimed "Superbookie," Moe Farakis, one of the tightest managers in the business, runs the show. Rick Matthews has heretofore been unsuccessful in cracking the Farakis defenses. Like one of those talented truffle-hunting pigs in Italy, Moe sniffs out Big Daddy's Brain Trust associates and tosses them from the Hilton sportsbook like unwanted trash—along with countless other profitable customers.

To reinvent myself as the new Hilton boy, Rick implies, will require an astonishingly convincing (and brazen) act. But I figure if I can crack Caesars Palace, where whales from around the world frolic, I can surely swim into the Hilton sea. So I call up a casino host and drop some names and tell him what a big shot I am and how I want to be "taken care of" and all the usual megalomaniac blather. The host puts me in touch with Nick Cerruto, the sportsbook supervisor, who tells me the Hilton would *love* to accommodate me and my special needs—but that Super Moe will have to make the final call. And he's on vacation.

"That's fine," I say, curtly. "But just so we don't waste each other's time, let me explain the kind of player I am."

Per Big Daddy's coaching, I tell Nick I want to bet ten to twenty games a weekend (true sucker action) at anywhere from $30,000 to $50,000 a pop, sometimes higher. Nick Cerruto says that for this kind of patronage *everything* will be taken care of—full RFB (casino parlance for room, food, beverage), fight tickets, you name it. I can almost hear him salivating. But his boss, Nick reminds me, has to make the final call.

A couple of days later, Super Moe calls me from a speakerphone, with Deputy Nick at his side. Moe asks me to reiterate the action I expect to play. After my extravagant spiel, in which I insinuate that I care more about deluxe freebies and obsequious toadying than betting lines, the Superbookie says he thinks they'll be able to accommodate a player of my "magnitude." For $75,000 a day in betting action, he can take care of my room. More will get me meals and other amenities. I tell him I won't have any problem living up to those numbers. Hell, I might bet that in two games.

"I think we'll be able to make you extremely happy," Super Moe assures his pigeon.

"That's nice," I grunt, very much enjoying being a demanding prick.

The boss man answers on the first ring.

"So, what's the story, morning glory?" Big Daddy asks excitedly.

"I'm in."

"Well, how 'bout that? Mr. 44 at the Hilton!"

We talk about the logistics—money transfers, getting the plays, how to handle tough questions (act ignorant is Big Daddy's advice)—and I ask him some tough questions of my own. The first experimental foray at Caesars, I know, can't possibly be business as usual. No one goes 14–6 week after week. "You're right about that, 44," Big Daddy admits. "I'm good, but I ain't *that* good. If all goes as planned," Big Daddy continues, "you stand to make seventy-five to a hundred thousand in a few months. I expect a three percent return on investment, minimum. Based on how much action we can get down, you can figure your share. The longer you stay alive, the more dough you can expect to make."

I start daydreaming about down payments on a country home in Great Britain, and my heart quickens. It's all too fantastic. "And the downside?"

"None," Big Daddy says. His lawyer has drawn up another document for me to sign, which will protect us both by making us bona fide business partners, albeit with drastically disproportionate shares of the company. "It's all upside, 44. I'll talk to you later in the week, pardsy. Over and out." Then he hangs up.

Three days later, the day before I'm scheduled to fly to Vegas, a Thursday, Big Daddy calls to say Farakis, that no good so-and-so, has taken down half the games. Just took them off the board. No longer accepting bets. I'm made to understand that Mr. Farakis is a genuine dogshit. And worse. Big Daddy says it looks like we're only wasting our time at the Hilton. He sighs hotly. "I guess we'll have to confine our plays to Caesars for now."

Like the degenerate loser I'm attempting to portray, I rationalize that Caesars' complimentaries are half the reason for taking on such a high-pressure assignment. And there's relatively less scrutiny from the management. Unlike the Hilton, Caesars, which is accustomed to hosting the highest of rollers from around the globe, is used to seeing monster $50,000 bettors in its sportsbook. That's why the Pencil doesn't have the ball-busting rep that Super Moe does.

So I call up and cancel my Hilton reservation. Deputy Nick asks if there's a problem. "Yeah," I say impatiently, "there is." To subtly reinforce Big Daddy's message, I tell Nicky I'm going to play at Caesars, where they have more games to bet on, where they don't take half the games off the board late in the week. While Nicky stammers an explanation, I say good-bye and hang up.

Then I reconfirm my Palace dates. Everything's all set.

Allowing myself to fantasize, I tell Vivian that I'd be happy—all right, thrilled—if I could clear $2,000 to $4,000 a weekend. And it's not beyond the mathematical pale. So long as I'm not found out.

Reasonably intelligent people play slot machines and roulette wheels because of sporadic positive reinforcement. They know intuitively that these games aren't fair contests, that the casinos are able to offer visitors prime rib and lobster tails at the money-losing price of $7.95 because the shortfall is subsidized by gambling winnings, but otherwise clearheaded individuals soldier on anyway. Gamblers remember the one time when they lined up three sevens, or when their birthday number came in. They console themselves with fond memories of the past—or, if that's not too sunny, a bright future. They tell themselves things will be better tomorrow or later in the evening. Maybe even on the next spin.

It's my second weekend as a Vegas playboy, and, it seems, the magic has already vanished. The Brain Trust is merely breaking even. And I catch myself reciting the litany of affirmations that bettors rely upon during the darkest hours: "It will get better. Remember last week. Big Daddy promises."

We win the Syracuse game; we lose the Penn State. We win Michigan State and Northwestern back-to-back; we blow the profits on Iowa and Baylor. As the great critic Pauline Kael was apt to say about movies she disliked, we can't get any rhythm going. Bored and increasingly superstitious, I watch bits of the games on television. Spoiled by early success, I catch myself on this gloomy Saturday muttering curses at the steroid-enhanced hoodlums dropping passes and missing tackles, for no reason other than to rob me and my cronies of our richly deserved winnings. Bastards!

Walking to the sportsbook through the hordes of narcotized zombies planted at blackjack games and video consoles, I catch a glimpse of my face in the reflective surface of a keno machine. I have the grim look of a slot junkie.

I crack a smile and resolve to order a really nice bottle of Bordeaux at dinner.

On Sunday, Big Daddy calls at 9:00 a.m. with the NFL orders, three solid plays and two provisional ones, which I'm instructed to bet if the line moves in our favor. It doesn't. So our weekend hinges on two games: the New York Giants –2½ against Baltimore and the San Diego–Oakland game going over 36½ points. Win, and it's another profitable weekend; lose, and it's a free room and all the Château Haut-Brion you can guzzle.

The Giants, winning and covering the spread with a few minutes to go, give it away on a late turnover. Our weekend is now certain to be a loser, no matter what happens in the late San Diego game. I'm grouchy.

To make matters worse, when I check the incidental charges on my in-room video, I discover that the Pencil didn't take care of Vivian's over-priced salon and spa charges, as promised. The nearly $500 in beauty treatments on my bill wouldn't rankle me nearly as much if I were winning, say, $40,000, instead of losing as much. I go downstairs and tell the Pencil I'm taking down my money—all $589,000 of it. The truth is, I have to go on a writing assignment out of the country for a couple of weeks (for a *Traveler* story about Scandinavia), and Big Daddy tells me dispassionately that he doesn't want a messy situation if, you know, somehow something happened to me or the airplane I'm flying on. Better to cash out and start fresh if and when I return.

But I don't tell Pencil Stevie any of this; I let him think I'm pissy because Caesars didn't pay for my girl's pedicure. After about half an hour of paperwork, a clerk escorts me to the main cashier's cage, where another clerk tells me it's going to be a while. I take the opportunity to chat up Dick Rollins, a smooth casino host, seeing if he'll check me out of my room at the VIP desk, knowing that if any of the unwanted charges show up, I might be able to convince him of the cleverness of comping them. He looks over my player profile on one of those slant-top monitors built into reception desks. Sure enough, after perusing my particulars he's eager to help. Remembering that "I" have more than a half-million dollars on deposit at Caesars Palace, and that "I" have just lost more than $40,000 in two days of sports betting, I—the real me—have a right to be truculent.

Dick Rollins makes some feverish calls while I tell him, You know what, don't bother, it's just the point. As he pulls his strings, I finally retrieve my cash, big bricks of hundreds that weigh about twenty pounds. I put them in a plastic Caesars Palace laundry bag. I poke my head into the office to say good-bye to Rollins the Host, who wonders out loud if maybe I wouldn't like a cashier's check instead. He hands me his card and reminds me to call if there's *anything* he can do for me.

I just shrug and walk out.

Viv meets me at the valet. She sits in the passenger seat of our rental car, a purple Dodge that, it occurs to me, does not befit a player of my stature. Next time, I remind myself, I need to request a limousine. I gently place the laundry bag of money on her lap—"Jesus!" she exclaims;

"holy shit, that's a lot of money!"—and drive to a gas station about a mile from the hotel, on the way to the airport. The whole way I'm thinking how comical it would be if I were to crash and hundreds of thousands of hundred-dollar bills were scattered across Flamingo Road. Upon further consideration, I decide it probably wouldn't be very funny at all. We arrive at the prearranged meeting spot without incident. Big Daddy is waiting in the parking lot with an associate, Sergeant Clark, sitting beside him in the big Mercedes. I don't dare ask about the Sarge. Anything to do with the Brain Trust network, it's been made clear, is none of my business.

I introduce Viv to Rick, who, in his most courtly, southern-gentleman fashion, says what a pleasure it is to meet her. She says likewise, and I hand the laundry bag to him through his rolled-down window.

"How much is this?" he asks.

I tell him, "Five hundred and eighty-nine thousand. I left a hundred on deposit to keep the account open."

Big Daddy nods. "All right, then, 44. I'll see you in a couple of weeks."

I tell him I'll call when I return from my travels. As I turn to go, Big Daddy says, "Hope your trip's okay, pards." Then he rolls up his window and drives away.

Viv and I drive onward to the airport. I'm thinking that maybe I should have asked for an advance on my winnings. "Maybe I should have had Rick count the money. You know, to verify my trustworthiness. Maybe *I'm* too trustworthy."

She tells me to stop worrying. "These gamblers just do things differently than normal people. And, by the way, you didn't tell me: Big Daddy is really cute!"

I tell her I hope she still thinks so when this adventure is all over.

For the next two weeks, while I'm traveling in Europe for my real job, I notice myself watching the sports scores on CNN, wondering which teams "we" bet, and if "we" are winning. In my absence the guys at Caesars, I assume, are checking up on me, talking about my wins and losses, attempting to discern a pattern that will answer definitively: Who is this guy? And, more important: Do we really want his action? I imagine two scenarios upon my return. Either they'll take me back warmly—and even consider raising my limits to the first-week levels, as befits a sucker who somehow got very lucky but now shows signs of coming back to Earth. Or they'll say, "We've done a little investigating. Don't ever step foot in here again."

I want to be welcomed back, brought into the casino's comforting fold, where the danger of being found out, of losing, of *winning* heightens the senses and sharpens the mind. Eating alone at a restaurant in Copenhagen, I scan the menu. The dishes. The prices. Numbers. Little numbers.

Real life seems hopelessly banal compared with the sporting life. A modest life of quiet desperation seems, well, so *quiet* compared with the operatic anxiety of having your fortune teetering on the precipice of a field-goal kicker's toe. During the days leading up to my return to Vegas action, I find myself distracted, daydreaming, unable to concentrate fully on my work. Writing a story about resort hotels in Denmark seems dull and annoying every time I consider what I'll be doing over the weekend. For the first time in my life I feel what it's like to be a nine-to-fiver. You function for five days a week, but you *live* on the weekend.

Finally, it's time to be reborn. Vivian and I go to Vegas on a Friday evening flight from Los Angeles, one of those peculiar airborne symposia where everyone seems to have a hot gambling tip, a scheme, a system. The guy sitting next to me volunteers a few "sure thing" college football games to bet on. I thank him for his generosity and wink at Viv.

When we land I call Big Daddy from an airport pay phone. He directs me to ring him again as soon as I've checked into Caesars Palace. He says, "I'll have a guy bring some money over as soon as we know your room number."

The hotel does not have me listed as a VIP. Only my room is comped—I'm R, not RFB. This disturbs me, but I figure I'll get it rectified when I see the Pencil in the morning.

I call Big Daddy from the room, a spacious suite with his-and-hers showers. He says Sarge Clark, the guy we met a couple of weeks ago, will come by in the next thirty minutes with $200,000. For what seems like the twentieth time, Big Daddy asks about the betting limits I've been given. I go over the new, lower terms—$15,000 and $30,000 for college and pro, respectively—and he mutters, "That's no good. This is hardly worth my time, or yours." Nonetheless, he gives me four plays—all televised regular games—to make when the money arrives.

Room service and the Sergeant knock on the door almost simultaneously. While the waiter sets up the table for our late-night supper, Sarge sits in a corner chair, with a large black satchel on his lap. As soon as the Palace employee departs, Sarge opens the satchel and pulls out a handgun and a folded paper bag, which he opens wide for me to inspect. "It's all bundled," he says.

Eyeing his weapon—I've never seen one before, except in movies—I pull out the bricks of hundreds, counting in $10,000 units. "Two hundred thousand," I say. Viv pretends to watch television.

Sarge calls Big Daddy and reports the delivery. Then I get on the phone to confirm. "It's all here, Daddy. Nice and neat."

"All right, pardsy," Big Daddy drawls. "I'll talk to you in the morning."

Vivian and I eat our dinner with the money sitting portentously on the bed, like a mute guest, impossible to ignore. Occasionally we look at it and laugh.

"This is frickin' weird," Viv says, grabbing a brick and tossing it from hand to hand like a tennis ball.

"Surreal," I mumble, looking out the window at the other hotel-casinos lining Las Vegas Boulevard. How many other rooms on the Strip this night, I wonder, have $200,000 in cash sitting on a mattress?

When I go downstairs to deposit the money, Dina waves to me. She's clearly been waiting for my arrival. When I approach the counter she says, "I've been on the lookout for you. Everything all right?" I unceremoniously plunk my brown paper bag on the counter. Slipping back into my high-roller persona, I tell her, No, in fact, I did not appreciate the incident at check-in, which, I tell her, made me feel like a nickel slot player. "Was this your way of telling me you're not really happy to have me betting in your casino?"

She apologizes and says she's sure Stevie the Pencil will take care of everything in the morning. Do I want her to call him?

"Of course not," I say, petulantly. "I don't want to be a jerk about it."

Dina reveals that she's been instructed to call him when I arrive, anyway. Seems the Pencil wants to know how much money I brought and which games I'm betting.

Utterly unsure what any of this means, I shrug. "Whatever," I say.

After they count my bricks and I make a few bets, I give Dina and one of the clerks some souvenir currency from my trip abroad and join Viv in bed, where I stare at the ceiling, wondering if I'm living or dying.

Big Daddy calls at his customary 7:30 a.m. All he wants is confirmation of last night's plays, and he says he may release me after 11:00 a.m. "We're not gonna do much today," he drawls. Caesars has posted close to fifty games on the toteboard today, college-football Saturday. Did the linemakers come up with sharp point spreads this week? Is the Brain Trust computer broken? Has the boss man detected too much heat emanating from his supernumerary at Caesars Palace? Has Big Daddy lost his golden touch? But I don't ask for an explanation.

Eleven comes and goes, and Big Daddy never calls. When I reach him, he confirms that we're through for the day. He suggests that I spend the afternoon meeting other sportsbook managers around town, seeing if I can't establish some new relationships. "The limits they've got you at now, at Caesars, they're not gonna work. See what you can do."

At the Hilton, where curmudgeonly Moe Farakis holds court, Vivian and I are greeted warmly. Nicky Cerruto, who remembers me from my inquiry a few weeks earlier, is clearly eager to have my business. Over the phone, I pictured a young Al Pacino. The person I'm looking at is more like an old Tobey Maguire, with big puppy eyes, neatly combed brown hair, and cheeks a grandmother would love to pinch. We agree on limits: $50,000 for NFL and $25,000 for college, with $10,000 on added games. And on "key" games, television matchups, and so forth, they'll often let me bet double. And if I want to bet more, just ask. And as far as taking care of me and my spa-loving girlfriend, if I bet what I say I'm going to bet, everything—*everything*—will be courtesy of the house.

If I'd like to start playing with them tomorrow, on Sunday, they'd love to have me, Nicky says. I tell him I'll think about it—I've got to run this by Big Daddy—but in the meantime, I say, sign me up for next weekend. Deputy Nick seems genuinely pleased to have another big fish on his hook. And I'm pleased that we seem to be back in the big leagues, where the swings (the volatility of results) could make me relatively wealthy. It's a lot easier to win $250,000 in a weekend when you're betting $25,000 and $50,000 than when you're betting $10,000 and $30,000.

When our taxicab returns us to Caesars Palace, I call Big Daddy with the news. He quickly decides to move our operation to the Hilton next weekend. But he counsels me not to burn any bridges at Caesars, to be polite and stress that I would like to keep doing business with them if they change their limit policy.

Meanwhile, ironically, we've lost the first three of our four games. The Pencil, I'm sure, is cursing the lower limits he's been forced to impose on me. Perhaps he's thinking I'm not such a wiseguy after all.

When I go downstairs to check on my final bet of the day, Pencil Stevie is there, and he's not in a good mood. I ask him if, in fact, I'm RFB in his casino, and he answers me shortly, "Yeah, you are." I tell him what happened at check-in, and he says the casino just won't take care of sportsbook customers, that he's going above and beyond for me. He tells me to eat in any restaurant I want, take my girlfriend, it'll be taken care of. And then he says, "Look, Mike, if you don't like the way we're taking care of you, you don't have to play here."

I don't get confrontational. I just nod and say, "Okay."

But the Pencil continues his rant, like a brokenhearted lover who knows he's losing his paramour. "I'm sure Nicky will take very good care of you over at the Hilton."

Apparently these sportsbook people talk to one another.

I check the scoreboard. We're resoundingly winning the last game, Washington University laying the points, so Viv and I can go off to dinner—a comped dinner—losing "only" $25,300 for the day.

Groggy from too much champagne and Sauternes the night before, I go downstairs early on Sunday morning and bet two NFL games, a morning and an afternoon matchup, at $33,000 each. One of them is the Battle of the Bays, Green vs. Tampa, a nationally televised, superhyped conference showdown. (The Brains like the favorite, the Packers.) I expect the Caesars management will let me bet more on this game, since everybody in the joint is wagering on it. No, an apologetic clerk informs me; Pencil Stevie isn't in at the moment, and he's the only one who can authorize a bigger limit. But he'll be here in half an hour, if I'd like to wait.

"I need my action now!" I exclaim, perhaps a bit too maniacally.

I bet at the usual limit and return to the room. Big Daddy is, predictably, bitter. "Biggest day of the week and the boss isn't in the shop. I'll tell you what . . ." He sighs and directs me to play another game, San Francisco −5½.

When I arrive at the sportsbook, the number we're looking for has already changed by a half point. Per my instructions, I'm required to back off. When I call to report the news, Big Daddy seems perplexed, a bit peeved. "Somebody's pickin' off our numbers, bettin' 'em before we can. Guess we gotta move faster," he says.

An hour later, almost three hours before the start of the late games, Big Daddy sends me down to bet Arizona in another afternoon tilt. The Pencil is unusually jovial. "Mr. Konik," he says cheerfully, "you're all taken care of, all RFB."

I nod and say thanks.

"Take your girl to dinner tonight, it's all set up."

I can never figure out what makes the guys on the other side of the counter happy or sad, but the Pencil is back in his "let's be pals" mode. In the casino business, everybody loves a loser.

And lose we do. Both the Packers and the Cardinals give up late leads to let the underdogs get in under the spread. For the weekend we go 2–5 and drop another $62,000. When I talk to Big Daddy late in the day, he sounds subdued, mildly frustrated, as any shell-shocked gambler might. "What happened with the Packers?" he asks. "Weren't they leading twenty-one to three at the half? And Arizona? How did they ever let Minnesota get the ball?" I hear in his voice a trace of human fallibility, as if he were just another fan, not the greatest sports bettor on Earth. I want to comfort him. But I also want him to be strong.

I trust Big Daddy to make me a winner.

Sarge comes by several hours later to take home what's left of the money. Viv and I go to Palace Court, the French restaurant, and mistakenly order a $450 bottle of '88 Cos d'Estournel. (We meant to select the '89, at a mere $250.) When we check out of our suite, we discover that our $800 dinner for two indeed has been "taken care of."

God bless Las Vegas.

The following week, back in Los Angeles, Vivian returns to her windowless office at the hotel. I return to pounding out a thousand words a day and halfheartedly chasing down editors who might grace me with the opportunity to earn for an entire article what I make on one Brain Trust football bet. Eager for Friday to come, I talk to Deputy Nick Cerruto, who confirms my room reservation, betting limits, and RFB status. He's also dispatching a limo for me at the airport.

His pitch is this: "If you bet what you say you're going to bet, we'll have no problem taking care of everything. When you check in, the account will be open and subject to billing. But as soon as we see your play, we'll adjust everything to RFB. No problem."

Vivian makes appointments for massages and wraps and whatever else she has done in the spa, gleefully skipping around our house like a child who's just learned she'll be spending the weekend at the carnival. I'm hopeful that all will go smoothly. But the outcome, like almost everything else Brains-related, is ultimately in the hands of Big Daddy Rick. When I talk to him midweek, he's upbeat, pleased that we'll be able to bet some serious money. But he also warns me that Moe Farakis will be watching me like a hawk hunting rodents. "He'll have a camera on you, looking to see if you've got a beeper or a cell phone," Big Daddy warns me. "Make your bets and leave. Don't hang around the casino floor." We agree to communicate on a cell phone and only in the room. Big Daddy also promises to have documents for me to sign, and that the money—more than $400,000—will be ready for delivery shortly after I check in.

Before we hang up, he asks me how I left things with the Pencil. I tell him that ol' Stevie was happy to raise my limits—as long as I wanted to bet Sunday night on the next weekend's games. I expect Big Daddy to scoff at such a notion. Instead, he tells me, "You tell Stevie, if he wants to let you go first, you'd be happy to play with him. Truth is, couple of local guys, guys named Jimmy and Billy, get to bet the games first." He explains that some of the boys behind the Caesars counter allow a few neighborhood gamblers to bet into the point-spread lines before the Brains and the other syndicates can, before the numbers get pounded into shape by professional handicappers. "You tell Stevie if he wants to let you bet before the local hotshots, before you go back to Los Angeles, you'd be happy to oblige," Rick advises. "Hell, he wants to do that I'll light him up like a Christmas tree!"

We both laugh heartily. It's the first time I've heard that sound from Big Daddy since the start of football season.

The Hilton limousine is very nice. The suite with a putting green outside the glass door is very nice. Room service is very nice.

I must remember that this is all a façade. The niceness could disappear the moment I start betting—and winning.

The Sarge arrives shortly after I check in, bearing $300,000. He hands me a mobile phone that works on a digital radio signal, supposedly impossible to intercept. After I count the bricks of hundreds he says, "You're in business, kid." Sarge tucks his pistol into the waistband of his pants. "I think we got one play for tonight. Get in touch with Rick and he'll give it to you."

I call Big Daddy on the new device. He counsels me once again on security—I can't be too careful in this joint—and, after some consideration, agrees with me that it might look funny to make only one bet tonight. Better to wait until the morning, when he says he might find something else for us to play. I feel the impulse to suggest certain games, as if I've garnered several decades' worth of experience in a mere month. But I know better. I know my place.

Still, I make a record of the games *I* would play if the handicapping were up to me. Just in case I possess a previously unmanifested natural talent for picking point-spread winners.

After concluding business with Big Daddy, I go downstairs to the cage to deposit the money. Unlike Caesars, the Hilton compels me to buy $5,000 denomination chips. Which means I've got to walk around the casino with $300,000 in negotiable instruments in my pocket. For the first time on the job, I have an urge to do a little renegade gambling on the side. Nothing major, maybe a few thousand on the craps table, maybe $5,000 on blackjack. And if I lose, there's always more where it came from. I've got to win eventually, right?

I stop myself before the dangerous nonsense gets out of hand. I'm feeling blue. Vivian and I have had a bad fight and are on the brink of breaking up. Despite the allure of the Hilton spa she's remained in Los Angeles, stewing over real and imagined slights suffered at the hands of her increasingly gambling-obsessed boyfriend. Seeing so many sexy women in the casino has given me a big-wad complex, an urge to show off my huge bankroll. Win a few thousand. Rent a hot whore. Live it up.

I'm starting to understand why casinos can be so addictive to lonely middle-aged men all across America.

Psychological motivation aside, the odds of putting a few easy hundred (or thousand) in my pocket are enormously favorable. When you've got tens of thousands to play with, winning a few hundred is almost a statistical cinch. I briefly consider returning to the casino and grinding out a quick profit, but decide to stay in my room and read. No gambling, no girls. No trouble.

I call Vivian before turning out the lights, but she doesn't answer. Dreaming fitfully of touchdown passes and fumbled kickoffs, I rise early and wait for my usual Saturday morning call. When it comes, shortly before eight, Big Daddy has five plays for me, including the highly anticipated Ohio State–Penn State game, an NFL game for the following day, and two more games on television. "They're gonna love you, baby," he says cheerfully. The Penn State game is a key game, so I can bet double my usual limit. One of the others, Stanford-Arizona, is supposedly a circled game—limited betting because of an injury question or a vulnerable line. Nonetheless, when I go down to play, the supervisor on duty takes all my bets (including the Arizona game) without blinking and treats me with utter graciousness.

If there's heat on me, I don't feel it.

The security of my new radio cell phone makes me feel even more at ease. Already I've bet close to $200,000 and haven't had any reason to sweat.

Big Daddy calls back twenty minutes later with another play, Navy +1 vs. Air Force. "The game starts at nine, 44, so get down there quick." I have twenty minutes.

When I bet, Nicky Cerruto, dressed in a blue suit and red tie, looking like a lad on break from boarding school, walks over to shake my hand. He's as nice as could be, inquiring if I want to go eat anywhere, if I'd like a pass to the SuperBook's exclusive Hall of Fame Room to watch the games in privacy, if there's anything he can do. I request lunch and dinner reservations and tell him I'll probably go to the health spa later, too. "No problem," he says, smiling, revealing gapped front teeth. "I'll call it all in and it'll be taken care of." Before I go, Deputy Nick asks me if I made any more plays since my original five. I told him I just bet Navy. "You gotta like their running game," I remark, as if I know what I'm talking about. He nods and says good luck.

"He's got to love that play," Big Daddy tells me when I call with confirmation. "Good sucker play." Then he says he'll get back to me sometime later. Which means that I'm supposed to wait in my room, out of view of the security cameras, unsure when I'll be needed again. The waiting was easier when Viv was here with me to pass the time. With only $80,000 left to gamble with, I'm hoping Big Daddy will have a few more games for me soon and release me for the day. When he calls later and finds I've slipped out to the coffee shop for brunch, I get a mild scolding. "Now, 44, you aren't on vacation. You need to be available." I apologize, make two more bets, and return to my gold-trimmed cell.

My relationship with the Hilton seems to be going smoothly. We lose the first two games on last-minute misfortunes, but given the casino's abhorrence of winning players, the tough beats may be good for me in the long run. Deputy Nick confides that he needed the losing Navy squad, too. "We were rooting for the same side." This is wonderful, the surest way to stay ice cold: bet what the casino wants you to bet. I hope we'll have more games like this.

Big Daddy calls to see how much money I have left to wager. I tell him $25,000. "Well, we need twenty-seven five to bet the LSU game. Hey, pards, I'm a little short, you think you could loan me twenty-five hundred?" Before I can respond, Rick breaks into a hearty laugh. "I'm a little short!" he repeats, guffawing. "We need this Ohio State game to end so we can have something to play with."

Ohio State leads by a touchdown and is getting 7 points on the spread. Problem is, the game might not end before the 4:00 p.m. kickoff of the LSU-Florida tilt.

I suggest that I should go down to the casino and watch the end of the game. If it concludes in time, I'll bet the LSU game and the Nebraska game, another play the Brain Trust favors. If it doesn't, I'll just bet whatever I have left on whichever game Big Daddy prefers.

"Yeah, good idea, pards," Rick responds. "Go on down there."

As I sweat the closing moments of the key Ohio State game, Nick tells me that he needs the same side as me. (Good.) The game is close, with the lead going back and forth. But for the entire second half, Ohio State stays within the 7-point spread. I'm watching the game clock and the real-time clock; it's going to be close. For a moment, I'm rooting hard for two different propositions—for the Ohio State side *and* the game to end—applauding every small Ohio State triumph and cursing the miscues. I'm an authentic, money-crazed sports junkie.

With a few minutes left in the game, it becomes clear that the end will not come before 4:00 p.m., so I'll have to bet what I can on the Nebraska and LSU games. But at least I know I'll be collecting a juicy $50,000 win fifteen minutes later. Since Deputy Nick will let me bet only $10,000 on the Nebraska game—Nebraska is favored by 41 points, and that kind of spread normally kills the betting action—I decide to split what I have left on the two games. At 3:59, I bet $11,000 apiece and hope the boss will approve.

I figure he'll be in a good mood as soon as Ohio State hangs on to its point-spread victory. But then, with a minute left and Penn State trying to pick up a first down to seal a 4-point win, the big Nittany Lion running back barrels through the line and rumbles toward the end zone. Miraculously, Ohio State defenders take him down at the three-yard line. With thirty-nine seconds left, there's time for two more plays. If Joe Paterno decides to ram in another score, they'll cover the point spread and I'll be screwed.

The Hilton SuperBook is in a state of delirium. Half the crowd in the book is yelling at the fifteen-foot big screen: "Go for it! Cover the spread! Go!" The other half is screaming, "Stop! Stop!" I'm holding my breath.

The Penn State quarterback gets under center, snaps the ball . . . and takes a knee.

Yes!

For me, it's a $105,000 kneel-down.

I hurry back upstairs and call Big Daddy with my bet confirmations. Fortunately, he's pleased with my decision to split the money on two games. "Just too bad Ohio State didn't end a few minutes sooner."

"What a game," I say, reminding him that we squeaked out a big win.

"Tell you what, that big old back almost made it in."

"Yeah, my heart stopped there for a moment," I admit.

"Me, too. He goes in I'm one sick puppy, I guarantee you."

"Gotta love that kneel-down."

"Yes, sir. I was glad to see him take a knee," Big Daddy says light-heartedly.

"Excellent decision by Mr. Paterno. He's quite a gentleman."

Big Daddy chuckles and tells me I'm done for the day. "We'll talk in the morning, pards. You go enjoy yourself tonight."

"You, too, Big Daddy." I attach my phone to the charger, and I wonder. I wonder if Big Daddy goes out to party on a Saturday night after pulling off a big college football win. Does he dance? Does he chase women? Does he buy new Porsches? Or is it just another work night, a brief interregnum before Sunday's NFL battles? I hope he invites me to join him one of these weekends, after the work is done. I hope he lets me behind the veil of secrecy. For now, our worlds intertwine only when the Brain Trust needs to bet a pile of money.

On this night I join my friends Craig and Pamela Fullbright, managers of the poker and slot tournament operations at the Golden Nugget. Craig has been a trusted source for many of my best gambling stories and is a thoroughly honorable guy in general. He and many of his cronies in

the gambling world have included me in their hermetic fraternity precisely because I've proved that I can keep a secret. I know, in turn, that I
can tell Craig and Pam some of what I've been up to without its becoming public knowledge. Over dinner at Hugo's, an elegant restaurant in
the basement of the downtrodden Four Queens casino, on Fremont
Street, I hint at my association with the Brains. The Fullbrights are fascinated but concerned. "You can't be too paranoid, Michael," Craig counsels. "People talk. They investigate." He nods significantly. "Be careful."

For the image I'm trying to cultivate—"Poker Mike," action junkie—
Craig cleverly suggests I arrange to play a big, $3,000-a-hand poker
match at the Mirage, where both he and I know the manager, Niall
Nokes. "If you're trying to pass yourself off as a big poker player, eventually some sportsbook guy is going to call Niall. And Niall's going to tell
them what he knows, that you're a writer, a guy who writes gambling articles. Why don't you tell him you've come into a lot of money and you
want to play high? Then bring a buddy and stage a game. It'll only cost
you a couple hundred dollars for the rake, and it will buy you a lot of
cover."

I agree that it's a fine idea. And fun.

After dinner, we all return to the Hilton for a nightcap. I observe several casino employees hanging around the bar, hawking me from a safe
distance. Perhaps I'm only imagining this rank surveillance, or maybe
Craig's cautionary advice is particularly appropriate here at Super Moe's
house.

Am I inebriated, or has someone been in my room? My papers, which
include a full schedule of football games and my Brain Trust marginalia,
seem to have been rifled. My briefcase, which contains, among other
things, Rick's telephone number, notated as "BD," is securely closed—
which worries me, since I could have sworn I left it open. I look around
the suite. A maid has turned down the bed and left chocolates on the pil-
low. But something else is different, too. I can't say what, but I can feel it.
I tiptoe toward the bathroom, half expecting to find someone hiding in
the shower, half laughing at myself for being suspicious.

No one's there.

Vivian would provide immediate comfort right now. She'd say

something reassuring, something sober. I call her at home. She doesn't pick up.

I bolt the door, lock my patio window, and go to bed with the phone tucked beside me, predialed to 911.

On Sunday, Big Daddy has five orders off the NFL menu. Problem is, none of the point spreads the Brains seek are currently available. He wants me to go downstairs, camp out near the counter, and pounce like a feral cat when the lines move to our desired number. My instructions: Bet what I can and sneak back to the room thirty minutes before the 10:00 a.m. kickoff time to check in for further directions. And make sure no one's following me.

At 8:45 a.m., when I enter the Hilton SuperBook, which like the sportsbook at Caesars is as cavernous as a medieval dining hall, the place is already abuzz with bettors diligently studying their tout sheets and handicapping forms, searching for a winner. I take an empty seat in front of the giant television screens, broadcasting pregame shows. Perhaps it's my newly formed paranoia, or maybe I've simply become acutely aware of the environment around me, but out of the corner of my eye, I catch one of the mid-level supervisors snooping on me, trying vainly to blend into the crowd. Since I'm carrying neither a beeper nor a cell phone, I'm cool. But still, I know I'm being watched, and I need to be especially careful.

Am I hallucinating, or do I recognize two other familiar faces in the crowd of bettors? No, that's them: a young woman with wild red hair, like an Irish fairy; and an older gentleman with a baseball cap and a leather fanny pack. We never say anything to one another, but I'm sure Flame-head and Packman notice me, too. For all I know, they're paid (by either the Hilton or the Brains) to keep an eye on me.

Shortly after nine, the San Francisco–St. Louis line goes from Frisco −14 to −14½. I leap into action, betting the Rams +14½. The number immediately goes back to 14, a point spread that Super Moe and his deputies hope will attract a legion of San Francisco supporters to balance my $55,000 wager on the underdog.

None of our other numbers come up. So I return to the room and check in with the boss. He amends some of the orders, telling me to go ahead and bet Detroit +6 for up to $75,000. Since our limit is $50,000, I figure Big Daddy must be getting me confused with another of his operatives. I return to the counter and bet the game for my limit. The line moves to 5½. Ten minutes later someone—or a lot of someones—lays the 5½ on Tampa Bay, and the line bounces back to 6.

After kickoff time, when I call Big Daddy to report my wagers, he asks me why I didn't bet $75,000 on the Lions. I immediately realize I was supposed to bet an additional $25,000 when the line moved back to 6. And I didn't.

Instead of making excuses, I tell him bluntly I made a mistake and I apologize. Big Daddy gives me a brief lecture, explaining that anytime the line moves, even if I've already bet the game once, I'm entitled to bet it again at the new number. I tell him I understand and that I won't make the same mistake twice—though I know it's exactly this kind of betting that will bring major heat down upon me. The average gambler doesn't exceed his personal limit because the line returns to a point spread he likes; only wiseguys do.

"All right, then, 44. I'll get back to you," Big Daddy snaps. An hour later, he instructs me to bet up to an additional $100,000 on the Rams—if the number moves to 14½ again. (I'm praying it doesn't. Making that kind of wager would be wearing a sandwich board that says, "Hi, I'm part of a betting syndicate with unlimited resources. Did you think I was just some fool from Los Angeles? Think again!") I'm supposed to hang around the sportsbook and wait for the line to pop.

This gives me an opportunity to visit the SuperBook's Hall of Fame Room, where invited suckers (i.e., people who bet large and usually lose) can watch the games in soft-armchair comfort. Again, I know I'm being spied upon—but so what? I've got nothing to hide. I spend the next hour chatting with a couple of other big bettors—"squares," as management would call them—about the football games. They ask me who I have going in the morning games, and I tell them: Miami and Detroit.

"You're looking real good in both those games," they say.

Detroit, the underdog, is soundly whipping Tampa on the Buccaneers's home field. The Lions will definitely come in under the spread. Now I feel really bad about not betting the additional $25,000. My cut of the extra money would have been $2,500. And I'm sure the boss isn't too pleased, either. Nonetheless, we're now up $110,000 for the weekend.

The Rams' number never moves the half point I'm looking for, so after the 1:00 p.m. kickoff, I return to the room to report. The first thing I tell Big Daddy is, once again, I'm sorry. I apologize for screwing up, and I tell him I feel terrible about letting him down.

The gracious southern gentleman has returned. He says, "That's all right, pards. We coulda lost the game, too. Don't worry about it. No big deal." Big Daddy strikes me as the kind of man who values an associate who can take responsibility for his actions, although he also strikes me as the kind of man who wouldn't come out and say so.

We're done for the day, Big Daddy says, but I should ask Deputy Nick if I can bet my games for next week tonight, since I'll be away in Hawaii the following weekend, working on a magazine story about the Ironman Triathlon.

Nick tells me I can bet, sure. But at low limits. "We put up the line Sunday night more as a courtesy than anything. I'll have to ask Moe, but I know the limits are going to be pretty low." I say thanks but no thanks and go to the gym, where I work out in front of the television, watching the Rams get waxed by the 49ers. It looks like we're going to finish the week with a $55,000 profit. Good, but not spectacular—which is probably the best result to encourage longevity.

Sarge arrives promptly at 4:30 to pick up the phone and money. "How'd we do?" he asks, in the loud voice that always makes me feel that an eavesdropping security officer could easily make us. I tell him it was a good week. "Yeah, anytime it's positive instead of negative is a good week," he says, tossing the bricks of hundreds into a duffel bag. When Sarge calls Big Daddy, I can hear his voice projecting through the earpiece speaker in Sarge's cell phone. "All right, Sarge," Big Daddy says. "Deposit the money in an account at the Union Plaza. Name of Kelly Josephson."

I smile to myself. The Brain Trust door has opened a crack. This

Josephson fellow happens to be the manager at one of Big Daddy's restaurants.

Before I check out, I make a point of shaking Deputy Nick's hand, complimenting him on what a fine shop he's running, with cheerful, helpful employees who couldn't be nicer. I tell him I'll look forward to coming back, if only for the chance to meet Super Moe Farakis. "I guess you've got to play much higher than I do to shake his hand, huh?" I say.

Nicky chuckles nervously and says how much he appreciates my living up to the action I promised. He's pleased. Super Moe, he says, will evaluate my play from this weekend, and if he likes what he sees, Nick is sure we'll be able to continue our nice relationship in the future. This last comment disturbs me—the bit about evaluating my play—but I just say thanks again and tell him I'll look forward to seeing everyone in two weeks.

In the limousine to the airport, feeling naked and depressingly average with only a hundred dollars in my pocket, I silently pray my adventure hasn't ended.

When I'm away from Las Vegas, I continue to work as a journalist. I vainly try to be a good boyfriend to my aggrieved partner, who reconciled with me in time to fly off to the Kona coast for a long weekend of sunbathing and swimming. Upon my return from the Hilton, I rededicated myself to improving my relationship with Vivian, who confessed she missed our Las Vegas extravaganzas (among other things). Over dinner in our dining room, away from my computer and the television, those conduits of news and odds and all things sports related, I reassure her, "When we're away from Las Vegas, I'll forget about the gambling. That's just for the weekends."

"Because it's not like three days a week isn't enough time for football games," Viv reminded me. "There's more to life than point spreads and Rick Matthews, right?"

"Of course," I agreed. "Music. Art. Literature—all way more compelling than some stupid college football game."

But, honestly, after what has seemed like an eternity away, I'm raring to go, eager to rejoin my other life. I try to be Michael, the normal guy who walks the dog, goes to the gym, writes all day, and takes his girlfriend out for dinner when she's not too tired from ten-hour days at the office. But I miss the action.

Before unpacking my luggage from Hawaii, I call Nick Cerruto to confirm my weekend reservation—and to make sure everything is still cool at the Hilton. Nicky asks me how Hawaii was, and if I competed in the race—"I know how much you like to work out," he jokes, referring to my insistence that the sportsbook comp the on-site health club as well as my RFB. We chat about sports, how I missed some good games, how his book did over the weekend. He's surprisingly candid—"We lost on college football, broke even on baseball, and won a little on Sunday football"—which, I infer, means the Hilton's not scared of me.

Deputy Nicky and I go over the particulars of my upcoming visit, including a special request I've made for the casino to take care of an additional room for my neighbor, Rex, a Hollywood actor–model–dancer–nightclub bouncer who's coming to town for some classic Vegas debauchery. We agree to talk again in two days, on Thursday, when Nick knows his key games.

I'm feeling good about this place. Everyone seems to like the other guy, as if we're all frat brothers, not financial competitors fighting over a pot of gambling gold.

I haven't spoken to Big Daddy for almost two weeks, during which time I've followed the movement of the lines, keeping track of what I assume are Brain Trust positions. I've missed him. And I secretly hope he missed me a little, too.

Rick Matthews sounds genuinely pleased to hear from me. But he's perturbed that I didn't ask Nick exactly how much I'm allowed to bet on circled games. I figured I'd just find out when I went to make a play. "Ask him, 44," he instructs me, "so there's no fooling around with your limits once you get there." I tell Big Daddy I can call back right now to clarify, but the boss man thinks I shouldn't make a special entreaty—too obvious. But if I happen to talk to Nicky on another occasion, I ought to ask.

Big Daddy, I've come to realize, gets exasperated quickly with anything that remotely resembles incompetence. You don't earn millions of dollars while everyone else loses without doing everything right.

. . .

Minutes after checking in at the Hilton, I call the boss from a pay phone. He says Sarge will be here with a delivery within fifteen minutes and that he'll call my room in five minutes with a bunch of plays. We could probably find a less conspicuous place to transfer the money, but probably not a safer one. I hang up and grin: It's good to be back in action, back on the furtive mission of beating the casinos at a game that shouldn't be beatable.

When Big Daddy calls with the plays, three of them are added games, the lightly bet, untelevised contests between teams like Southeast Louisiana and Troy State. Rick asks me, "How much are they gonna let you bet?"

I tell him, "Almost nothing. Six thousand." Funny how $6,000 has suddenly become almost nothing.

Then Rick asks, "Now, 44, do you think betting any of these games is going to wake them up?"

I haven't felt any heat up to this point. But the added games were what seemed to raise suspicions with Pencil Stevie over at Caesars Palace. So I tell him it's likely.

I can hear him chewing on a lollipop. "Tell you what, go on down there and bet two of these games. Mix 'em up with the television games. It should be all right." I like that we're betting the big Michigan vs. Michigan State game. And I like that we're playing New England vs. Miami, an NFL game, on Friday night. But I'm wary of wagering on the University of Alabama–Birmingham. I don't like fooling with anything that might stir suspicions and blow my cover.

Sarge shows up at my suite minutes later with $300,000. But he has no phone. "Rick never gave me one," he says, an unlit cigarette dangling from his lips. "Let's call him." He heads toward the phone on my bedside table.

I stop him. "The numbers show up on the hotel bill." Sarge nods and starts to leave for a pay phone downstairs. Then he realizes he's got his own personal cell phone in his jacket pocket. He laughs and launches into a smoker's coughing fit as he dials Big Daddy's number.

The boss says he'll personally deliver a secure phone in twenty minutes. I should look for him at the hotel's back entrance, in a red Lincoln Navigator. The $300,000 in cash slung over my shoulder in a carry bag makes me feel like I'm toting a small child. I wait in the Hilton's rear parking lot, like a CIA operative waiting to make a microfilm drop.

Big Daddy arrives as promised—with his sister Kathryn and her nephew Eric. They're on their way to dinner. Mrs. Matthews-Reynolds is a real beauty, a well-preserved southern belle of fifty, with a bright smile, a smashing figure, and a plumbing contractor husband with no interest in gambling or sports. He plays chess for amusement and can't understand why his wife and her big brother derive so much enjoyment from betting on football. Nonetheless, the tolerant Mr. Reynolds allows his spouse her unusual hobby in the interest of keeping the whole family happy. Eric, clean-cut and handsome, seems about my age, in his thirties. I say polite hellos to everybody, as if I'd just run into them in the grocery store. Big Daddy hands me a phone and several batteries. "Knock 'em dead, pards," he says, smiling.

I watch the luxury SUV roll away, and I wonder what Big Daddy is telling his loved ones about the young fellow holding $300,000 of his organization's money. Trustworthy, probably. Or maybe naïve and ignorant. I wish Big Daddy were telling his family that I'm super sharp, a real wiseguy. That I put the smart in smart money.

When the cage personnel count the cash, I'm $100 short. I have $299,900 to play with. When the cashier asks if I want to add another hundred to round it off, I reach into my pocket and discover I have only $78. That's me: Mr. High Roller.

I make my football bets without incident. Indeed, when I'm done wagering, one of the clerks says cheerfully, "Enjoy your dinner, Mr. K." I do. And also going with Viv to the stripper bar afterward. And dancing in the lounge. All of it. Las Vegas is a hedonist's paradise when you're rich. Even if the money's not yours.

Everything starts to unravel.

I bet on seven college football games, winning six of them, including the big Michigan contest. Most of my bets, Big Daddy assures me, are cool plays, the kind of bets "they'll love you for." But the bursars of Vegas, especially the actuaries in the sportsbooks, don't like anyone who shows any hint of expertise. You're not supposed to go 6–1. You're not supposed to come out on top. Period.

Deputy Nick, his boyish features arranged into a pensive scowl, approaches me in the Hall of Fame Room late in the afternoon, when I'm up about $125,000. He tells me he's going to have to cut me back from $25,000 to $20,000 on college games and from $50,000 to $40,000 on pros. "That's still double the normal counter limit," he explains. "But management wants to see some casino play out of you. They'll extend the limits as a courtesy to big casino players. But we haven't seen any play in the pits from you. So . . ." He holds out his palms. "That's the deal."

I don't protest. "But I can finish out my weekend at the limits we agreed upon, right?"

"No," Nick says. "Effective immediately."

When I report the news, Big Daddy laughs bitterly. "You're not allowed to win, pards. You just broke the rules."

I remind him of a famous marketing campaign one of the casinos launched not long ago. The theme was "We Love Winners!"

"Oh, yes. Sure they do. Love 'em to pieces. Maybe you ought to go visit Moe Farakis right now, 44, and see if he wants to give you a hug and a kiss."

"Only if I promise to give back everything I won, right?"

"Now you're learning, son. This whole sports betting racket—pretty fun, isn't it?"

Early Sunday morning, while Vivian helps herself to Hilton spa treatments, I encamp in the SuperBook to wait for line changes on five NFL games. If a juicy number the Brain Trust wants suddenly appears, I'll bet. If not, I'll pass. In the meantime, I wager $44,000 on the Pittsburgh-Jacksonville game. Steelers –3.

After I make my play, I sit in the front row of the SuperBook chairs, with the rest of the gamblers, scanning the board for my key numbers. Then Nick Cerruto appears at my side. "Mike, I gotta talk to you again. We're cutting you back to normal counter limits. We know you're getting your plays from somewhere. It's no coincidence that every time you bet a game it moves all around town within five minutes."

I act flabbergasted—partly because I am. "Nick, I have no idea what's going on at other casinos." I really don't. "If I make a bet and the number moves someplace else, that's none of my business. I really don't know what you're talking about."

"The Pittsburgh game," Nick says. "You bet it two minutes before it moves to three and a half in every place in our industry."

I tell Deputy Nick that it makes no difference to me. I could have bet the game last night, or two nights ago. This is, indeed, all a coincidence.

"Well, why didn't you bet it then?" Nick's youthful features grow dark.

"Because I was hoping it would go to two and a half," I reply, logically.

Nick shakes his head. "We're not stupid, Mr. Konik. We know what you're doing."

I tell him what I'm doing is winning. That's my real crime.

Nick says, "If you can beat us on your own, god bless you. But we know you're getting help from somewhere. You know it and I know it. Now you can deny it, but we both know the truth."

"Man, I didn't know the Hilton was in such weak financial shape. I better short the stock," I hiss, getting up to go. "Careful, fellas," I announce to the congregation of football fans eavesdropping on my dispute, "the SuperBook might be insolvent."

Of course Big Daddy is furious when I report the latest developments. "That's just an excuse, 44. Go over the list of plays you made in the last two days. Read 'em to me." I do, and he comments on each one: "That game never moved off the number"; "That one closed right where it opened"; "That one they needed your bet!"—culminating in a big laugh. "What a bunch of pussies. I tell you what, pards. If it were me, I'd be sending a limo full of hookers to chase you down, the kind of business you bring them. But these dumb asses, they want to run out a good customer. This whole deal about the lines moving when you bet is total bullshit. They just can't stand that you're winning."

Big Daddy is right. But so is Nick. I have no way of knowing how the lines are moving all around Vegas—Nick and Big Daddy know; their computers show them that information. I'm sure some of my bets have been hot ones. But others, I know, are totally cold. Nick's claim that every bet I make coincides with a major line move has got to be false. But, on the other hand, I'm sure it happens occasionally, despite Big Daddy's blanket denial. The bottom line is this: Of course I'm getting my plays from someone else. The best sports bettor in the world, in fact. But if I were losing, the casino boys wouldn't mind one bit.

Big Daddy tells me to forget about betting the five other games he's ordered. We're through at the Hilton. In fact, he wants me to write an outraged letter to the president of the company, outlining how I've never received such shabby treatment. I can't really see the point, but Rick's got motives that extend beyond me and my fleeting ability to bet on a few football games in the sportsbook.

I return to my suite, depressed. "It's over," I announce to Viv, who's lounging on the bed in her panties. "We don't have anywhere else to play."

"We've made a lot of money, and who knows, Big Daddy might have some other plans for you," she consoles me.

"Not if I can't make any bets." My tenure with the Brains has lasted less than two months. Five weekends of betting.

I spend the afternoon figuring my total take for the season. I feel like there's been a death in the family and I'm straightening up the odd personal effects. I'm also rooting madly for my two outstanding NFL games to come through. If I'm finished, I want to go out $10,000 richer. For one of the few times all season, I feel the heart-pounding, sweaty-palm excitement of having thousands of dollars of your own money riding on the outcome of a football game. The Pittsburgh game is an $84,000 decision. I *need* this game.

The lead seesaws from a point-spread loser to a winner several times. On their final drive in the fourth quarter, the Steelers kick a game-tying field goal. We're going to overtime. I explain to Viv that probably the best we can hope for is a tie, in which case we'll get back our $44,000 bet. In sudden death most teams march down close to the opponent's end zone and kick an easy field goal. If the Steelers do that, minus the three points we had to lay, the game's a push, a point-spread tie. If Jacksonville scores first, we lose.

Pittsburgh wins the toss and promptly advances to the Jacksonville seventeen, where the inevitable field goal lurks. But then one of the least likely outcomes unfolds before my disbelieving eyes: On first down, Jerome Bettis, known to his fans as the Bus, rumbles into the end zone on a nifty little shovel pass play. Steelers by 6. We win!

I'm jumping around the bedroom like a kangaroo, high-fiving Viv and pumping my fist. "Eighty-four grand! Eighty-four grand!"

I'm still not sure how or when I'll collect my percentage. Now? When Big Daddy says so? But I'm glad to go out a $269,900 winner. My cut comes to more than $5,000 a week. And who knows how much in suites, limos, and gourmet meals?

Downstairs I collect my cash and shoot a dirty look at Nick Cerruto, who silently oversees the payout. Super Moe finally emerges from his back office. I assume he wants to get a good look at me. Short, round, with a head crowned by a fringe of curly gray Three Stooges Larry hair, the so-called Superbookie looks more like a ladies' shoe salesman. I flash him my warmest smile and resist the urge to blow him an appreciative kiss.

Twenty minutes later Sarge meets me in the suite.

It's over.

Four

CLOSE CALLS

Twelve hours later, on the Monday morning following my banishment from the Hilton, Big Daddy suggests I contact the Mirage's junket office in Los Angeles. He also tells me to call back our buddy Pencil Stevie at Caesars and see what he'll do for me. "Come on now, pards," Big Daddy urges, laying on creamy dollops of southern charm, "you got too much gamble in you now to quit. Hell, player of your reputation ought to be getting invitations from every joint in town, don't you think?"

"You think my name is any good anymore?"

He grunts. "Only one way to find out."

The Mirage is "eager" for my business, but they'll have to call me back later in the day. (Probably after doing some checking up on me.) They never call.

Stevie at Caesars says he can give me a nice room, full RFB, and the same $30,000/$15,000 limits as last time I played. "That's the best I can do," he tells me. I'm sure he's talked to Deputy Nick and compared notes. I ask him if I lose, will he raise the limits. "No, it's not whether you win or lose, Mike. You're always playing the sharp side. I just can't fade fifty-thousand-dollar decisions on every game you play. These limits we're offering you I can fade, whether you win or lose. They'll have to stay where they are."

"Sign me up," I tell him. "I'll see you Friday."

When I report the news to Big Daddy Rick, he delivers his usual lengthy diatribe about how badly these people run their business, etc. But ultimately he instructs me to get on a plane. "We'll give 'em some action."

It's not over yet.

While Vivian unpacks our bags in the suite, I deposit $300,000 into my account and chat pleasantly with Dina at the Caesars Palace sportsbook. She might be just an accomplished glad-hander accustomed to massaging the egos of big-time gamblers, but I play along with her genteel flirtation anyway. We're all actors in other people's high-dollar dramas. After the cash is counted and bundled, I give Dina seven plays, a mix of televised college games, added games, and an NFL game, Chicago vs. Detroit.

Afterward, when I confirm my bets, Big Daddy and I have a lengthy talk about the business of sports betting. If he were on the other side of the counter, he tells me, he'd steal away all the customers from places like Caesars and the Hilton. "These guys are a joke," he chuckles. "I'm looking at the lines right now," he announces. I imagine a monster computer with a live feed of the point spreads and odds offered at casinos around Las Vegas and the world. He laughs louder. "Caesars made Miami a favorite now—they were a two-point 'dog ten minutes ago! And the Bears are plus two and a half now."

"I suppose that's to be expected," I say, as though I know what I'm talking about.

"Actually, 44, it doesn't make real good sense." Big Daddy starts to share some secrets about the significance of the number 3 in football spreads, but stops himself in the middle of his homily. "You'll just write about it, and I don't want to wake up too many people."

This is the third time since I've known him that he's acknowledged that one day I'll chronicle my adventure. I'm sure it's part of Big Daddy's agenda: expose the casinos for the wimpy frauds they are. And someday I'll make the perfect mouthpiece.

We agree that I should research betting opportunities at several other casinos. In the meantime, we'll give Caesars some more plays—if he can find them. "Sometimes there's not much to do. Sometimes they make a good number. We're not going to manufacture games that aren't there. Of course, we could always get lucky." He laughs broadly again and says good night.

The next morning, Rick calls uncharacteristically late, with only one play. When I go downstairs to bet, the first thing I do is walk over to the Pencil and shake his hand. "Thanks for taking care of everything."

"Everything all right?" he asks, scribbling on an old racing form.

I tell him yes and make some more small talk, offering to bring some cigars over from a VIP party I plan to attend later in the evening. He says that would be nice.

Let's all be friends, I'm thinking. As I'm studying the board, Stevie tells me he'll be happy to take some more action on the Notre Dame–Navy game, if I want Navy +16. I nod and pretend to be mulling the proposition. What I'm really thinking is how amusing this has all become. Soon the bookies will be telling me which games I can and cannot bet.

The sportsbook is unusually quiet for a Saturday. Business is slow, since next weekend is the Holyfield-Moorer heavyweight title fight as well as the Breeders' Cup horse races, when all the hard-core gamblers in America will be swarming into the Vegas casinos like so many flies at the city dump. This lull before the action storm gives the Caesars Palace executives more time to scrutinize my every move, to analyze every bet I place. I can feel the tension.

Stevie and I engage in some more idle chatter before I slink off to the room. I've got $125,000 in play this weekend, and it feels like hardly anything.

Big Daddy doesn't deliver any other Brain Trust orders the whole morning. While Vivian enjoys the spa, I do "real" work on my laptop, writing a story about a former nun who now runs a porno Web site, and desperately hope the phone will ring. If I don't bet, I can't earn any money. At 2:00 p.m., exasperated, I call Rick and ask if he'll be needing me anymore, because I'd like to go out and do a fact-finding mission at some of the other casinos he and I have discussed.

He tells me to go. "Call me back around four for a check-in."

I walk down the street to Harrah's. Long a low-roller slot joint, the casino, which looks from the outside like a Mississippi steamboat run aground, has recently completed a much-publicized $250-million renovation, and management has stated publicly in gambling trade publications and through a costly billboard marketing blitz that Harrah's wants to attract a "premium" level of customer. So I march into the executive host office and say I'm an RFB player across the street at Caesars and I've heard about Harrah's push for big players and want to know how serious it is.

A perky young female host lights onto me like a vulture on carrion. I do my usual song and dance—blackjack and baccarat sometimes, sports for now, want to be taken care of, etc.—and she escorts me over to the sportsbook, where I'm introduced to Irving Rosenbaum, the manager. His greasy comb-over and fishy handshake say *putz;* his steely eyes and capped teeth say *macher.* My deceased grandmother, the one who peppered her English with Yiddish, would be happy I'm making deals with Irv. She would say, "He's one of us."

Mr. Rosenbaum quickly sizes me up as an ignorant sucker, an evaluation I reinforce by telling him what a supremely great handicapper I am. "Sure you are," he says, smiling solicitously. "Or else you wouldn't be betting, right?"

To my astonishment, Irving says he'll be able to offer me $30,000 limits—on everything! NFL, college, and, incredibly, totals. Whatever I want to gamble on, he'll book my action at thirty large a throw. As nonchalantly as I can, I tell him I'll certainly be giving him some business. Maybe as soon as tonight. We shake hands and exchange pleasantries, and I get back in my room as quickly as possible to report the astounding news to Rick Matthews.

He admits he's surprised. "The limits are a little higher than I expected," he says, restraining his glee. Thirty thousand on totals is more than five times what we're getting anywhere else.

Big Daddy wants me to bet a college game, but I can't get back over to Harrah's before kickoff. So I'm to withdraw $100,000 from my Caesars account, walk across the street with my phone, read off Irving's lines to the boss—Harrah's is not on the Caesars-Hilton-MGM computer line-reporting system to which Big Daddy subscribes—and be prepared to bet two or three games.

Before I go, I remind Rick how smoothly everything has gone at Harrah's, and I ask him as nicely as I can not to burn me out.

There's silence, then Big Daddy says, "Listen, 44, you have no fucking idea how hard I work to keep you cool as a well-digger's ass. I give you the coolest plays I've got. Them guys, Nick and Stevie, they're not choking on you because of your plays, it's because you're winning. Believe me, if they knew you were moving money for me, you'd be out on your ass in a second. They wouldn't take a dime from you. And if any of them runners for the other groups knew who you were connected with—well, they're liable to shake you down for information. So don't you worry about staying cool. I only give you the coolest plays. It's in my best interest, as well as yours."

I'm genuinely shocked. "You mean they would threaten me?"

Big Daddy pauses.

"Rick, are you saying people would hurt me just to get the Brain Trust plays?"

"People do crazy things, 44. You know, when money's involved, people get . . . let's just say sometimes it brings out the worst in people. These casinos, the other betting groups, they all act like you got a key to the cashier's cage. Like you somehow know in advance who's gonna win. Now, you and me, we both know that ain't true. It's just gambling. But greedy people don't recognize that, see? They believe you're some kind of walking cash machine. So if they got the chance to stick you up . . ."

I try not to let my fear cloud my judgment. "Look, Rick, if you keep me cool and I never tip my identity to anyone, no one is going to hurt me, right?"

"That's right. I wouldn't put you in that position, 44. It just ain't worth it to me."

I want reassurance. "So you're not going to read about me in the newspaper one morning: 'Sports bettor's body found in the Mojave Desert, hot football picks stolen from his pockets.' "

Big Daddy doesn't answer me directly. "I'm doing everything in my power to keep you cool and keep you safe."

I hang up, shaken.

The truth is, I don't really know what's hot and what's cold. I have a vague idea, yes, but this valuable information is known only to the true insiders who can track every dollar bet at Vegas sportsbooks with expensive computer software. I feel like the average private investor trying to make a killing in the options market: He thinks he's privy, but really he's as clueless as the next chump. Now I remember all the times I felt the gaze of familiar faces upon me at the sportsbooks. Was it my imagination? Or was I being watched by other syndicates, or casino management, or the Brain Trust itself?

When I go to the Caesars counter to draw down $100,000, the Pencil pops out of the back office to ask where I'm going. (He does this as offhandedly as humanly possible.) I tell him I might play some poker tonight.

"Oh, yeah?" he says, eyes widening. "Down at the Shoe?"

I shake my head.

"Next door? The Mirage?"

I tell him yes.

"Wow. No kidding? I tell you what, Mike, my opinion about you is changing. Maybe I was wrong about you." I have some idea what this means, and I don't want to encourage more conversation. So I mumble something nonsensical and shuffle away.

At five o'clock on a perfect autumn afternoon, I walk across Las Vegas Boulevard with a cell phone in my pocket and $100,000 cash in Vivian's purse, which I've borrowed while she lounges at the Palace's European pool, tanning her breasts. When I amble into the Harrah's sportsbook, a modest but bustling pit replete with television screens and shouting bettors, Irving makes eye contact with me as I approach the counter. I nod to him as I copy down the point spreads for the NFL games, as well as the day's two remaining college games. Then I take a seat in the back of the room and pretend to study my notes. When I'm sure nobody's paying attention, I glide away, looking for a secure place to call Big Daddy.

A nearby men's room is too busy, so I take an escalator to the third floor, near the showroom, and find a quiet corner, near a service elevator.

I call Rick with the lines, sotto voce. "These numbers don't have any opinion in them whatsoever," he says. "This guy's probably just getting his point spreads off some screen, from a computer service." He pauses a moment to consider the data; then he instructs me to make two total bets for $33,000 apiece. "And I guess we should give him an NFL game, too, don't you think?"

"Yeah, he would probably like to see that."

"I'm sure he would, pardsy-wardsy. Well, we'll give him something that looks real good. Go bet him the Monday night game. Pittsburgh getting three. He'll love that."

When I return, Irving and his staff couldn't be more cordial, if slightly flustered at the sight of $100,000 in cash. To my delight, nobody blinks at my bets, especially since the first one I make is the Monday night game. Indeed, as soon as I've received my betting tickets, the supervisor on duty asks if there's anything he can do for me. I tell him my girlfriend would love to visit the spa tomorrow. "She can't get enough of that seaweed," I joke. He immediately writes me a comp ticket, the currency of personal worth peculiar to Las Vegas, the drab little slip of paper that says, "You're important."

After attending the VIP cigar event, I return to Caesars and hand out pricey samples to several of the sportsbook staff. As Big Daddy has suggested, we want to remain friends with as many betting outlets as possible. And if a fine stogie can buy some much-needed goodwill, I'm happy to oblige. In this business, your "good friends" can turn baleful more quickly than you can say "wiseguy sports bettor."

On Sunday morning, Big Daddy calls later than usual—only forty minutes before the 10:00 a.m. kickoff of the East Coast games—and asks me if I have the Harrah's lines.

I tell him no. I've been waiting in the hotel room, a loyal soldier anticipating the order to go into battle. He sends me across the street to check on the numbers, after which I'm supposed to call him on the cell phone. I hustle across the Strip, jaywalking and jumping through a row of hedges. After scribbling down the current point spreads, I return to my service elevator alcove on the third floor. While I'm in the middle of reporting the numbers to Rick, the elevator door starts to open and I'm forced, mid-sentence, to shove the phone in my pants. When I return to Big Daddy a few seconds later, after a maintenance man walks past with a broom, he instinctively understands my situation and says, "Everything all right now, 44? Can you talk?"

"Yes, but I better make it fast."

"Well, don't do anything suspicious. Somebody will call security on you if anything looks funny. Anyway, let's play the Baltimore game, plus four and a half. You might as well give it to Stevie at Caesars; you probably need to give him some action, right?"

I dash back across the Strip. When I return to Caesars to bet the Ravens game, the tension there contrasts starkly with the eager, accommodating attitude at Harrah's. Jaws set, lips pursed, eyes unwavering. It's the difference between a place that wants to gamble with you and one that's scared.

Between the early NFL games and the start of the late games at 1:00 p.m., Big Daddy instructs me to alternate back and forth between the two properties, shopping for three particular numbers. If they come up, fire away; if not, I'm done for the day. After a peripatetic morning of Vegas Boulevard commuting, interrupted only by a brief poolside lunch with an increasingly brown Viv, they never appear.

The Brain Trust gets buried in two games—we're never a contender after the first ten minutes—and benefits from incredible luck in the third. Our team, Kansas City, returns the final kickoff against Washington for a "meaningless" touchdown that covers the spread as time expires. For the weekend I end up $4,000 to the good, with another $33,000 pending on the Monday night tilt.

When Sarge comes to retrieve the money, I get further confirmation of what I suspected all along: the former Las Vegas Metro detective isn't just packing for show. While he uses one of the two bathrooms in my suite, I surreptitiously inspect his pistol, a little silver snub-nosed thing, which he usually keeps in the waistband of his pants. It's loaded with six bullets.

When he returns, Sarge asks how we did. I tell him we made a small profit.

"That's better than losing," he says.

I shrug. "Maybe not." At this point I'm more concerned about long-term relationships. I can't win if I don't have anywhere to play. A week after it all seemed to come crashing to an end, it looks like now I've got several places to bet. And thus, the money, I'm beginning to understand, will come, as certain as the rising sun. I don't know how it's done, how we end up with a slight but definite edge, but it will come.

In less than two months I've gone from doubtful skeptic to true believer. I've seen the fear in a bookie's eyes; I've felt the paranoia. The Brain Trust makes otherwise strong men, powerful managers who are used to bullying the weaklings, tremble with trepidation. The bookies are accustomed to winning. So are the Brains. Something's got to give.

In preparation for another Vegas weekend, Irv Rosenbaum says he'll see what he can do about sending me and a guest to the big Holyfield fight. "It shouldn't be a problem," he tells me cheerfully. "We'll take care of you, sir." I like Irving. He's committed to pampering his new sucker, and he doesn't seem to mind gambling—so long as he thinks he's taking the best of the proposition. Jew, Italian, hillbilly—none of the stereotypes matter in the sports betting world. *Everyone* is trying to empty the other guy's pockets.

I've got three gentlemen on my call list. Someone's going to send me to see Evander. And maybe all three will get a piece of my business. Irv Rosenbaum is the first to call back to say he's procured two tickets to the fight for me. I immediately book a reservation at Harrah's and thank him for taking such good care of me. Terry Roberts, the boss man from Sunset Station, a new off-Strip property, calls to say he can offer me only $5,000 to $10,000 limits, but if I play at that level he'll have no problem comping everything for me. "And for the lady in your life, we're near a great shopping mall," he reminds me. Stevie the Pencil calls to say he can't get fight tickets for me—not for anybody. He can set me up at full RFB, but "they" won't give him any tickets for his big players. I don't complain. "Thanks for trying," I say.

He asks me how I did this weekend. "About break even?"

"Yeah, it's tough laying eleven to ten," I say.

"That's why nobody can beat it, why everyone ends up losing eventually. I'm telling you, the vig gets you in the end."

"Maybe you're right. But I'd like to take my shots and see what happens."

The Pencil steers the conversation around to what he calls "working for a living." He keeps repeating the word "workingman." Then he springs his big revelation on me: "Hey, Michael, you mind me asking what you do when you're not gambling?"

I tell him I'm a writer and that I'm in the movie business, that I've sold a couple of big scripts this year for some serious ching-ching.

"I thought so. In fact, I've read some of the things you've written. About gambling, I mean." He pauses to see if I'll react. "They were very good. You're obviously no dope. You know what you're doing."

"I told you I was smart," I retort. "I told you I knew more about gambling than ninety-nine percent of the people in your sportsbook, and that if anyone had a shot at winning it was me."

"Yes, you did say that. Anyway, I just wanted to let you know I enjoyed the stuff you wrote."

What he really means to say is *"I know who you are, pal."*

"I still think you're probably moving money for someone," he says. "But leave off the first week's results and you would probably be stuck for the season. So, I don't know."

"Stevie," I say, "I don't know which games are hot. And I don't know what the wiseguys are doing. I really don't. I just know what bets I want to make. I read *The Gold Sheet,* like everyone else. I do a little homework. And then I put my money behind my opinion. If I'm wrong, I'll pay the price. If I'm right, it's party time. In any case, I'd like to think the casino would appreciate my business. I expect to be taken care of." This is a theme I stressed in my letter to the president of the Hilton, decrying my rough treatment there. I'm getting annoyed with the belligerent attitude toward a good customer. "I expect the casino won't act like they're doing me a favor taking my action."

"All right, all right, Mr. Konik," Stevie says. I can tell he isn't completely convinced I'm as benign as I claim. But he's still having me as his guest for the coming weekend. I reckon he's afraid of getting beat but equally afraid of losing a pigeon who could be contributing mightily to his bottom line. So, in the end, I'm still welcome to play at Caesars. "But be forewarned, Mike," he informs me, "your comp privileges might get yanked at any minute. In fact, I've suggested to my superiors that they cut off your comps and raise your limits."

I sense this is a test. "I would be *very* unhappy with that arrangement. I expect to be treated like a valued customer."

"I hear you, sir," Stevie says. But I can tell the end is probably near at Caesars Palace. The Pencil and I have reached a new level of frankness. And I know things will never be the same, now that he knows that I write about gambling.

When I report the latest developments to Big Daddy, he laughs and suggests I tell Stevie that, yes, indeed, I'm going to be writing a big article about my season of sports betting, and it would be an honor if I could mention that the world-famous Caesars Palace sportsbook—run by Mr. Stevie Masters—barred me from betting. "Tell him you would love to write that you had Caesars trembling in their boots. And by the way, would he put it in writing how scared he is of you, so you could add it to the article. Tell him you would like the whole world to know that you were good enough to scare off a place like Caesars."

I chuckle. "Would you really like me to say that?"

"Hell, yeah! All this talk about moving someone else's money. He's bullshitting you. Well, throw it right back at him."

Big Daddy's response rolls over me like an enormous wave of relief. I may be on the verge of getting run out of every joint in town. But I'm sure of one thing: It's going to be fun.

I check into Harrah's hotel for the first time, on a Friday afternoon, traveling with nothing but a six-figure bankroll to keep me company. Vivian and I are fighting again. Although we're allegedly committed partners, living together, she's "starting to see" an unemployed actor-model-dancer-waiter she met at her gym. It's her unsubtle protest against what she perceives as a lack of attention—"All you care about is betting on sports!"

I'm in a melancholy mood. The management at Harrah's is not. Harrah's glee at my arrival is obvious: limousine at the airport, big suite, personal greeting by key-bearing host, tickets to the Holyfield fight.

Sarge arrives promptly with $350,000. I expected more, since I thought Big Daddy wanted me to play Harrah's and Caesars simultaneously. When I call Big Daddy to acknowledge receipt of the cash, he instructs me to cancel my reservation at Caesars. The Pencil, he thinks, will be happy to have me bet some games without having to comp my room and meals. "Just tell him you're playing at the Mirage, where they're taking care of you. He'll thank you."

Big Daddy has cautioned me not to mention a word about Harrah's to anyone. This is too good a situation to jeopardize. I'm not sure if Rick's analysis is correct, but it's not my call. I do as I'm told.

After placing $165,000 worth of bets under Irving's watchful and approving eye—of course he approves; I'm playing what seem to be "square" games on the wrong side—I trot across the Strip to Caesars, with $50,000 in my bag.

The Pencil, to my surprise, is there behind the counter. I make my bets, two lukewarm college games, and pay in cash. Instead of putting my usual $300,000 on deposit, I motion to Stevie and ask if he'll meet me down the counter at a closed betting window. "What's up, Mike?" he asks fraternally.

I tell him he can cancel my reservation, that I'll be doing most of my play elsewhere this weekend, but that I'll come by and give him some business when it makes sense for me. The Pencil says he understands completely and offers to buy me dinner anyway, since the bulk of my expenses will be covered by one of his competitors. Then something nice happens: Stevie and I chat for about fifteen minutes, relaxed and comfortable. I tell him I'm glad he enjoyed my articles, and, as he must know, I'll be writing one about my sports betting experiences—and, by the way, I'll make sure I spell his name right. And, oh, one more thing: Does he mind if I characterize mighty Caesars as being so scared of me they were "shaking in their boots"?

He grins and asks that I just be fair. "I got an idea for the title of this article," he says, writing two words on a piece of Caesars letterhead. "The Front."

I scowl disapprovingly.

The Pencil smiles broadly. "I'm kidding! I thought I could joke around with you."

We talk more about my "smartness," what a tough player I am, and how players like me make life difficult for bookmakers like him. "Can I be candid with you?" Pencil Stevie asks.

Before I can answer, he says, "Whenever the line on a favorite starts to drop, I know my book is about to take a hit. I know it. When all the sharps start betting the underdogs, I know we're in trouble. Believe me, Mike, I realize that guys who bet as much as you do usually have extremely sophisticated information."

"Well, I don't know, Steve," I mumble. "I'm just, you know . . . trying to pick—"

"Listen," he interrupts. "I take back what I said about you—the part about being unable to win laying eleven to ten. I was wrong."

"Serious?" I say, sensing a trap.

"Seriously. Your magazine articles, the ones you write about gambling, they're very sharp, just like your handicapping. Since I met you I've hung on your every word, waiting for you to trip up. I listen to everything you say, and you're always right there, saying the right thing."

Stevie also tells me what a regular guy he is, how he likes to kick back with the boys, have a beer, and play the guitar—he's got a Les Paul and a Stratocaster, and he's really into Zeppelin. Stevie's New England accent, I notice, comes on a bit stronger when he's acting less than corporate. He tells me how the pressure of answering to management, of always sweating one bad week, even if he has twenty good ones, sometimes clouds his judgment. "Hell, I don't even know if I'll be around for long."

I feel for him. He's been at Caesars for three years expertly managing the top sportsbook in Las Vegas, and any week could be his last. The Pencil is a decent guy doing a hard job. And having a weasel like me in his face, betting huge amounts, asking for big comps, doesn't make things easier. I genuinely like Pencil Stevie, and I appreciate his candor. It bothers me that I can't reciprocate.

Before I go, he confides that Super Moe Farakis from the Hilton called a few times. "I told him I thought you were pretty sharp, but that I was going to play with you anyway. You don't have to tell me what happened over there. I know. He's a total pussy."

We share a laugh and I scurry off to Harrah's.

• • •

I spend a sleepless night worrying about Vivian. When Rick Matthews calls at daybreak with the early morning Saturday plays, I'm bleary-eyed and grouchy. My mood further dims when, to my surprise, he sends me to Caesars to bet a single college game.

The Pencil is there again. I wave to him, approach a window, and proclaim proudly that I want Maryland plus 18. I *know* this is a square play, and my sureness is confirmed when Stevie bounces over and asks me, what I want—$20,000? Since I have only $17,000 in my pocket, I make a quick joke: "Now I know I really picked the wrong team." We both laugh. I pretend to check the board for a few seconds, looking for that one special point spread calling my name, and dash back to Harrah's.

I bet Rutgers getting two touchdowns from Boston College, which I've previously played across the street. Now the Brain Trust and I have $49,500 on this otherwise inconsequential game. I make some small talk with Irving—"You got a horse for me in the Breeders' Cup?"—but I can see he's starting to sweat the money a bit. I don't blame him. If I destroy his lines for a couple of weeks straight, the sportsbook's entire quarterly earnings will be obliterated, and Irv could be out of a job.

For the moment, Mr. Rosenbaum doesn't have to worry. I lose my first two games of the day, putting me in a $66,000 hole. Happily, the Rutgers game comes in, easing the sting momentarily. The other games in progress look bad—right until the end. Then I get lucky, as any gambler is entitled to every now and then. An interception returned for an improbable touchdown. A seventy-four-yard run out of nowhere. A terrible penalty call that goes our way. My teams start coming in from all directions. All three of my Caesars plays are winners, and most of my Harrah's games, too. While I'm at the heavyweight title fight, watching Evander Holyfield dismantle Michael Moorer, Arizona, my last side of the college day, covers its 16-point impost.

I go 7–2 and win $99,000.

Luckily, my two losses come at Harrah's. As tremendous as my current arrangement is at Irv's joint, I'm wary of burning it out by winning too much too soon. On the other hand, Harrah's makes money off legions of deluded people, many of them so sick they can't help themselves. Fuck 'em.

Early Sunday morning, Big Daddy orders four NFL total plays. Before most of Las Vegas has had breakfast, I've bet $132,000. On the phone he says, "Let's see, buddy boy, what do we have for ol' Mr. Caesars?" He chuckles to himself, and I imagine he's looking over his shopping list of games. "So Stevie says he's not scared of you. He's got to be *cautious.* Yes, sir, you can never be too careful when you're trying to take people's money."

Big Daddy Rick gives me a list of NFL numbers I'm supposed to look for. He tells me to hang around the Harrah's counter. "Is that place crowded?" he asks.

I tell him no, not now. During game time, yes. "It's packed with people sweating their twenty-dollar parlay card."

"All right, pards, you be looking for those line changes. Over and out."

Actually, I'll be playing a little guessing game, seeing if I can figure out which of the anonymous gamblers studying the toteboard are Big Daddy's foot soldiers. In the afternoon, I'd like to avail myself of some high-roller amenities. A brisk workout. A massage. Hell, maybe I'll try something I've never done before: get a pedicure. I'd also like to bet a few games at Caesars to maintain my relationship there. And I should do a fact-finding mission over at the Mirage, to see if there are any fresh fields to be sown.

My morning expedition in search of hot point spreads proves fruit-less, as Irving seems to be reluctant to move his line much. Whereas at Caesars my $33,000 bets would warrant at least a half-point adjustment, at Harrah's the lines don't budge. Big Daddy, I know, will probably ex-ploit this tendency by sending in an army of thousand-dollar bettors to pound the book at a choice number. If that happens, it won't take Irv long to catch on: He's going to have to move the line if he wants to attract balanced action. Then again, maybe he likes to gamble.

My poker pal, Spanish Jack, joins me for brunch in my suite. Over bagels and fruit smoothies, Jack rubs his triple chin and wonders out loud if I would get in trouble for telling anyone—him, for example—which teams the Brain Trust likes in the afternoon NFL games.

"Jackie, Jackie," I moan, shaking my head. "I'm shocked."

"I'm just saying," he shrugs.

"Come on now, brother, don't put me in that position."

"Just a thought."

The thought has indeed crossed my mind. What harm would it do if I told a friend or two which games the Brains liked, aside from breaching Big Daddy's trust? No one would ever find out.

Or would they? I get the sense that Big Daddy somehow knows about every bet being made at every bookmaking shop in Nevada, that he's an omniscient wizard controlling the action. I've observed firsthand how a point spread can move when "the steam"—a hurricane of bets, led by the smart money and reinforced by thousands of faithful followers—starts brewing. If one of the Brain Trust games went rocketing out of control because one of my friends bet on it—and told one of his friends, who told one of his friends—I'd be out of a weekend job, not to mention the good graces of a man I've quickly grown to admire.

I send Spanish Jack away without uttering a peep about the magic numbers and return to the sportsbook.

The afternoon games start without any of my key point spreads appearing. We've split results in the morning games and have two more bets in the afternoon, as well as one on the late ESPN game. I can either sit around Harrah's and sweat the scores or do some more digging. I call Big Daddy for permission to leave. Permission is granted.

My first stop, the Mirage, yields a vague promise from Julie Jimenez, the assistant sportsbook manager, that if I bet as heavily as I've suggested I do, she'll be happy to see what she can do for me. "But first we need to know who you are and how you play. We have to make sure you're not one of Rick Matthews's cronies," she says, laughing. I laugh with her, realizing instantly that the Mirage is going to be a tough spot to play. To help the cause, I pop into the poker room, where I know the manager, Niall Nokes. He's out, but I leave a note, telling him some exciting things have happened in my life, some of which might involve poker. Very high stakes poker.

Passing Siegfried and Roy's white tigers on the way out of the casino, I take the *Rain Man* people-mover into Caesars Palace. Little Mikey Brown, who could play Evander Holyfield in the movies, is behind the counter and, as always, greets me warmly. As he dabs his ebony forehead with a silk handkerchief, I tell him I want to cash some winning tickets, about $100,000 worth. He says it will be a few minutes. In the interim we chat about the fight, about sports, about girls. Then Pencil Stevie comes out. To my relief, he's chatty and all smiles. He comments that it looks like I had a good weekend. I tell him I did great yesterday but I'm losing the juice today. He confides that he's heavy on certain games—"we really need Baltimore"—and asks me how I did "over there," meaning the Mirage. I tell him I didn't play much, that I did most of my betting at the Horseshoe. (I can't mention Harrah's.) While Stevie draws what looks like a cubist still life on an odds sheet, we talk sports, specifically the difficulty in beating it, and even after I get my money, I stay and talk for another ten minutes, continuing to raise the comfort level between us. Stevie mentions a story I wrote, about Jox Brijox and his Vegas line. "As you said in your article, we tweak his numbers all the time. They're just a starting point. I got regular players in here who I *know* which way they're going to bet. So I put up the right line."

Before I go, Stevie promises he'll be happy to take care of dinner for me tonight, or next week, or whenever. "I've got a record of every single one of your plays, and you've definitely earned it," he says. We're officially pals, Stevie and me.

Hiding in a men's room stall, I stash the hundred large in my pants pockets and my underwear, $10,000 at a time. Then, as nonchalantly as I can manage with my currency codpiece, I walk through the casino and out the front door, into the light. Although Caesars and Harrah's are directly across from each other, crossing the street legally requires a detour to the corner of Flamingo and the Strip, or to another crosswalk several hundred yards to the north. Preferring to spend as little time as possible out on the sidewalk with cash in my briefs, I decide to jaywalk across Las Vegas Boulevard. I force myself through a low hedge and dash across the last two lanes before a barreling tour bus can flatten me. As soon as I arrive on the Harrah's side of the boulevard, two Las Vegas Metro cops roll up to me on their bicycles.

Clad in Tour de France yellow jerseys embroidered with POLICE on the spot where the bank sponsorship would normally go, bearing significantly more heft around the middle than Lance Armstrong, they both scowl at me disapprovingly through mirrored sunglasses. "What are you thinking?" one of them asks.

"You know we got crosswalks in this town," the other says. "Let's see some identification."

"Sorry," I say, fishing through my crowded left front pocket, searching with my fingers for my driver's license among the bills. "I was just trying to save a little time. I know it was stupid."

"What's the hurry?" the first cop queries.

I look him in the eye. "Honestly? I got a hot tip on a football game. I got a whole bunch of money in my pocket, and I wanted to run over here and bet it before the line moved." I hand the officer my license.

The bike cop looks it over and hands it back to me. "So, what's the hot play?"

"Pittsburgh, baby. Steelers all the way!" I say, nodding confidently.

"All right, then. I'll remember that. But it ain't worth getting killed over, is it? Next time, use the crosswalks like everybody else."

"Yes, sir."

"Be safe," they say, starting to roll off. "And good luck, dude!"

Making sure nothing has fallen out of my pockets—like a bar of hundreds, for instance—I start to make my way into Harrah's and nearly trip over Irving Rosenbaum, who's walking with a cell phone pressed to his ear. For a moment I panic. But then I realize I've got nothing to hide. He knows I'm going to make an occasional bet at Caesars. And while I'm not sure why he's outside his property on the sidewalk in the middle of a game day—maybe he's making renegade bets for himself!—I've got nothing to keep secret. Except, of course, the stuff that could get me thrashed by hired goons.

"Hi, Irving," I say cheerfully as I skip past him. He barely looks up.

Depositing my Caesars winnings at the Harrah's cage takes an inordinate amount of time. First I have to dig the money out of my trousers. It's clear they're not used to handling so much cash. Indeed, some of the tellers look up from their transactions to see who's playing. I try my best to act like this kind of deposit is normal for me—which, at this point in the season, it almost is.

After a massage and a manicure in the spa, I withdraw my entire bankroll from Harrah's and arrange a rendezvous with Sarge. He takes away $402,500 in cash. Before the late game, I'm up $93,000 for the weekend.

To pass the time until my limo leaves for the airport, I sit in the sportsbook with the other howling gamblers, eat some unhealthy sports-bar food, and root for the Steelers and the Ravens not to score. (I have the under.) It's fun to listen to the theatrical emotions generated by the guys around me—the impassioned curses and plaintive pleas, all inspired by a $40 bet. If they only knew the guy sitting next to them had $63,000 riding on the outcome.

Before I check out, my perky and over-cosmeticized host, Janelle, confirms arrangements for the following weekend. She wants me to know I can expect another executive suite next time, as well as a good window table at Harrah's spectacular steakhouse overlooking the Strip and a full day of spa activities for my girlfriend. Should I still have one.

I'm thinking life is good. "Life is good," I tell Janelle.

"Yes, sir," Janelle agrees, nodding her head so rapidly I'm fearful she'll hurt her neck. "You bet it is!"

When I leave Harrah's, the Steeler total is 23 points. I need the game to go under 44½. After checking in for the flight, I find an airport bar. The total is 30. On board, shortly before takeoff, the pilot says the score is 37–0, with six minutes to play. When I get home, I switch on ESPN and learn that 37–0 was, in fact, the final score.

It's a $123,000 weekend.

Niall Nokes, poker manager at the Mirage, calls on Monday afternoon. I do my song and dance about coming into a lot of money (movie scripts, Spielberg, possible television series) and I confess I want to take a shot at the big poker games. I ask him serious-sounding questions about game security and my short- and long-term expectations. But, really, I just want to find out if I can somehow stage a match (for show purposes).

Also, in case executives there are talking about me, I want him to be able to chime in with something helpful.

We talk for fifteen minutes, and when I hang up I feel like a heel. Niall is a good man, a cooperative casino executive with whom I've worked in the past. I hate lying to him.

Six days later, on a dull Sunday afternoon, the Harrah's hotel suite feels more like a torture chamber than a sanctuary. Vivian and I are enduring a civil détente, the main components of which are repeated apologies and solemn vows meant to ensure a mutually bright and faithful future. She swears she's stopped seeing her "friend" from the gym, and I swear I'll be more solicitous of her needs, especially the ones that don't involve her sexual appetites. Still, the tension between us is almost unbearable, and when she shows no inclination to leave our hotel room I have the urge to grab my Brain Trust phone and dive into the jangling distraction of the casino. This, I learned yesterday, is not a good idea. Indeed, when it becomes increasingly clear that the Brains have no action for me on this Sunday—the 10:00 a.m. kickoff passes without any word whatsoever from Big Daddy—I start to worry.

Perhaps he's had me shadowed and discovered that yesterday afternoon, desperate to escape Viv and the morose room, I withdrew $1,000 from my sports account to play blackjack (and lost) and then made a renegade bet on San Diego State for $2,200 to try to recoup my deficit. I'm not sure if this last bit was against Big Daddy's wishes—I strongly suspect it might be—but I didn't bother to tell him in any case.

When it became manifestly clear that San Diego State was going to be a loser, I realized I was now responsible for $3,200 of missing Brain Trust money. But instead of telling Rick or taking out a cash advance against my credit card, I went across the street to the Flamingo and bet the New York Jets for $4,400—the largest sports bet I've ever made on my own behalf.

The scariest part was this: The Jets were not a Brain Trust special. They were my play, my choice. The line early in the week had been Jets −3, and the public (and the wiseguys, no doubt) had bet the line down and down and down, until the game was pick 'em. I figured that my old interview subject Jox Brijox, the nation's linemaker, couldn't have been three points off in his reckoning. There had to be *some* value at this point in betting the disfavored Jets. Plus, *The Gold Sheet,* the handicapping service for quasi-sophisticated bettors, was calling the Jets' opponent, the Vikings, its key release of the week. So everybody in the world was on Minnesota. I figured I'd go the other way.

A defeat would mean I'd lose $7,600 of Big Daddy's money. My options then would be to tell him the humiliating truth and have the amount deducted from my commission, borrow the funds from a Vegas gambler friend like Spanish Jack, or chase my losses with another bet in the afternoon, this time for $15,000. Every time I thought about losing the Jets game I felt my heart begin to race and my stomach churn, and I'd realize I was no better than a million other piteous gamblers. It's a wonder that I slept at all Saturday night.

When Big Daddy doesn't call Sunday morning, I figure I've been busted. Maybe whoever he's paid off at Caesars is reporting my bets to him. Or maybe I'm being paranoid. Maybe there's simply nothing for us to bet on this NFL morning.

Since I must stay in the room for Rick's expected call, I can't watch the Jets game, which is being televised only regionally. It's probably for the best. Every play would most likely send me into joyous hysterics or incurable depression. Instead, I tiptoe around Viv, who has no idea what I've done, and check for updates every five minutes or so on ESPN's sports ticker.

To my enormous relief, the Jets never trail in the game. At halftime they lead 17–7. And well into the fourth quarter they lead 23–7, meaning the Vikings would have to score three times unanswered for me (and the Jets) to lose.

With a few minutes left in the game, Big Daddy finally calls. "How ya doin', pards?" he says breezily, as though he somehow knows I'm sweating out a crucial win.

"Ready and willing to work," I reply firmly. "You got any business for me?"

Big Daddy tells me it doesn't look like we're going to have any plays for the afternoon or evening. "So as soon as this Detroit game is over, let's rack up the money and see where we stand. I'll arrange for Sarge to pick it up in a couple of hours."

There won't be any chasing opportunities in the afternoon. Big Daddy wants his money.

When I leave the room, the Jets are leading 23–15, having allowed the Vikings a touchdown and a two-point conversion. Another touchdown and two-pointer would mean a tie game, which would force a sudden-death overtime. The symbolism of that concept is not lost on me.

As Viv and I make our way through the casino toward the sportsbook, we pass a bar where several games are being broadcast on large-screen TVs. The first image I see is Bill Parcells, the Jets' coach, raising his fists in triumph. The next image I see is a slow-motion replay of a Vikings running back being stopped two yards short of the end zone. "What happened?" I ask a happy barfly.

"Jets won. Vikings missed their two-pointer."

"That play was to tie the game?" I ask expectantly.

"Oh, yeah. Real nail-biter."

The Vikes had somehow scored another touchdown in the final seconds and with no time remaining went for the game-tying two-point conversion. And the Jets stopped them.

I'm glad I didn't see any of this. Vomiting all over myself would have been embarrassing.

How does Big Daddy deal with million-dollar decisions every weekend? How can he sleep at night knowing a small fortune was won (or lost) on the fickle bounce of a ball or the call of a myopic line judge? Funny as this sounds coming from someone wagering hundreds of thousands of dollars on football games, if I've learned anything from this renegade escapade, it's that I'm not cut out for high-stakes gambling. It doesn't thrill me. It nauseates me.

Luckily, as in a fairy tale, everything turned out happily ever after. That's when I tell Vivian the details of my near tragedy. She thinks I'm making it up. She can't believe I would do something so stupid and reckless. I can't either.

Following a celebratory glass of champagne, Vivian and I skip over to the Flamingo, where I cash what I anticipate will be my final ticket there. I make a big production of how my winning Jets pick was definitely not a wiseguy move. "Guess what, fellas," I crow to the counter personnel, "those so-called smart guys aren't always so smart, are they? I got news for you: There's a new smart guy in town, and you're looking at him. Those brilliant smart guys," I mutter. "They don't know everything, do they?"

I'm secretly hoping that with enough idiotic ranting and raving the Flamingo will install me at my preferred five-figure limits. It's a long shot, but in the meantime I'm having a great time being a lunatic. It's not hard to howl like a fool when you've just snapped off a $4,000 win that gets you out of serious trouble.

As I cash out my winnings at Caesars, a handsome gentleman dressed in a black double-breasted blazer and neatly pressed tan slacks emerges from behind the counter with a manicured hand extended in greeting. He introduces himself as Gino Miceli, vice president of something or other—the Pencil's boss. "Just wanted to shake your hand and thank you for your patronage. We appreciate your business. Thank you." As he turns to leave, he says, "By the way, Mr. Konik, I really enjoy your articles about gambling. They're great."

I tell the Suit he's really going to enjoy the story I'm going to write about my season of football betting. "You never know, you might get a mention."

"Oh, I'm going to look forward to that one!" he says, flashing a polished white smile.

At this point I don't know what I'm going to say about my experiences as a high-rolling sports bettor. Maybe this double life will go on forever. Maybe my fantastic secret will be known only among my closest friends. Maybe my life has been irretrievably changed. Maybe the hours previously spent constructing sentences and paragraphs will forevermore be dedicated to finding exploitable point spreads.

Before the aroma of Gino's expensive cologne has dissipated, I huddle with Pencil Stevie to set up a reservation for the coming weekend—"No problem, Mr. Konik"—and to inquire about getting my limits raised. On that count the Pencil's undecided. "Just ask," he says. "We'll have to do it on a case-by-case basis. I can't promise you anything."

"Have a nice Thanksgiving, Stevie," I say, patting him on the shoulder.

"You, too, sir."

I know I will. For the season we're 71–44–1, an astonishing 61.7 percent success rate. We've won $602,900—that's $67,000 per weekend. It would take a downturn of catastrophic proportions for me to finish the campaign a loser.

And they say you can't beat sports.

Five

A MULE OR A MAN?

Vivian and I arrive in Las Vegas late on Thursday night, directly from Thanksgiving in North Carolina with my parents, whom I've briefed about my involvement with the Brain Trust. My father thinks being part of a massive professional betting ring is cool. My mother wonders why I'm not devoting my time to writing human interest stories. "Is it really necessary to be associating with such unsavory characters?" she asks.

"They're actually honorable people," I retort. Mom makes a face.

As soon as we're off the plane, I call Big Daddy, who sounds dead tired and slurry. If I didn't know better, I'd swear he was drunk. He gives me Sarge's cell phone number and directs me to call the bagman as soon as I check in at Caesars. "It's gonna be about seventy, eighty thousand," he drawls. "I'll call you in the morning and we'll get started."

Seventy thousand dollars isn't even RFB money, I'm thinking.

The Sarge arrives well after 11:00 p.m. When he steps into our plush suite, in the newly opened Palace Tower, he says, "Hey, kid, you've really moved uptown."

"Let's see if we can stay here," I joke.

Sarge cocks his thumb and forefinger at me, makes a clicking sound, and says, "If anyone can do it, my friend, I'm looking at him." He tucks his gun (the real one) in his pants and exits the room. But I get the sense he hasn't left completely. My heart beating rapidly, I tiptoe to the door and peek through the view hole. Sarge is still there in the hallway—lighting a cigarette.

The college season is winding down. Only seven games illuminate the uncharacteristically empty Caesars toteboard. For me to make any serious money (and retain my comp status) we're going to have to play most of them. Which is unlikely. On the other hand, the Pencil might let me bet more than my usual, as he has suggested, since all seven games are prime-time television events, with various conference crowns at stake.

Big Daddy calls at 7:30 in the morning and sends me downstairs with two plays. Per my agreement with Stevie, I ask for more on both games, knowing the chances are unlikely on the Georgia contest (the line hasn't moved all week) and highly likely on Virginia Tech (the line has moved steadily, and I'm taking the side the bookies need). Sure enough, one of the supervisors grants me $15,000, the usual, on the Georgia game and $20,000, $5,000 extra, on the Virginia Tech side.

When I call Big Daddy, he's mildly annoyed. "I didn't want more on that game," he mutters. "From now on, 'less I say something, assume you're betting the usual limits."

"Got it." I'm mildly shaken. I thought the goal was *always* to bet as much as possible. Is Big Daddy merely using me to hedge some of the Brain Trust's early week action? Am I betting the wrong side?

I'm too timid to ask.

The Sarge will come by in an hour with more money, Big Daddy assures me. In the meantime, stand by for further instructions. Before the delivery, he calls back with another play, an over-under on which the Pencil typically allows $7,000 to be wagered. So I grab a $10,000 stack from my room safe and leave the rest in my bag, with Viv guarding the balance. When I approach the counter, Stevie steps out to greet me. He's warm and friendly, so much so that when I announce my bet, Syracuse, over 51 points, he offers me a $10,000 limit.

Momentarily taken aback, I mumble something about not bringing enough money (getting in late, and all), but thanks anyway. The Pencil is going out of his way to be a nice guy, and, unfortunately, I can't oblige.

When I report the exchange to Big Daddy, he says that the Brains could have used more on Syracuse, but that I did the right thing. "I'll keep it in mind that he's letting you bet more." When Rick sends me down again for another total play, I politely ask for—and receive—a $10,000 ceiling. "Don't ever say I'm not nice!" the Pencil says, as though he's doing me a favor.

I tell Stevie I'll remember him at Christmas. "But don't expect anything that costs more than twenty-five bucks. I don't want anyone to think I actually like my bookie."

When I return to the room, Sarge is there, babbling to Viv about his favorite actor, Clint Eastwood. "They said he'd never work 'cause his Adam's apple was too big!" he says.

He gives me another $76,000 and asks, apropos of nothing, if I've ever seen the Brain Trust's war room, where this whole business starts. Sarge confides that it's basically a two-person operation—Big Daddy and his beautiful sister Kathryn, who's apparently just as sharp with figures as her legendary brother—with four phones, a few television monitors, and several computer screens. "And you should see Rick work it all—it's like he's on Wall Street."

Sarge also reveals that though he has numerous runners stationed around Las Vegas, I'm the only out-of-town guy Big Daddy uses. My heart begins to race. The door leading to the Brain Trust's secret world is beginning to crack open. "Rick doesn't bet sports for the money so much as the thrill of winning the game. During the workday, man, he's deadly serious. Very demanding. Everything has to be in its proper place. See, Big Daddy is probably the quickest learner of anyone I ever met. He's the last person in the world you would want to play any game against."

I want desperately to see how the legend operates his business. I want to spend a day with him in the war room. But I'm labor; he's management. Until I prove that I'm something more valuable than a smooth-talking actor capable of convincing greedy bookies to take my monster bets, I know Big Daddy won't have much use for me as a decision maker. I can be one of the Brains, but I can't be a brain.

The Wizard of Odds calls only twice more all Saturday, once to double-check the amount of money Sarge delivered and once to inquire about Caesars Palace's limits on college basketball, of all things. Betting on college hoops does not strike me as a great idea. According to Pencil Stevie, the public doesn't bet much on this sport until the national tournament. Until springtime, it's the exclusive province of smart-money wiseguys.

Rick doesn't bother to release his trained mule officially until the dinner hour, precluding a health club workout, recreational blackjack, or the diversion of mindless arcade games, which Caesars offers to the children of gamblers, possibly in the hope that those kiddies will learn from an early age that shoving quarters into machines is a great way to pass the day.

Outside it's a gorgeous November day, with the sun warming the red mountains that ring the Vegas valley. On what's easily the lightest-volume day of my sports betting career, I watch movies in my room, go 1–3, and lose $28,500.

On NFL Sunday, I bet two games in the morning and sulk in my suite as both wagers go down in flames. The phone rings. "How's the world treating you, pards?" Big Daddy asks.

"Besides losing this New Orleans game because of a penalty on an extra point try, things are fine," I reply glumly.

"Yeah, that's not enjoyable." I can hear him riffling through papers. "Well, let's see if we can't find something to turn it around. I'll call you right back."

Ten minutes later he directs me to bet Denver—the last game of the day—for our usual limit. When I go down to make the play, the Pencil and I chat briefly about some of yesterday's games—"Intangibles, Mike," he says, commenting on the freak extra point debacle that cost me $33,000. "How do you account for that?" I discover that Stevie likes all the underdogs today. "I gotta tell you, Mr. K, I really like San Diego"—Denver's opponent.

"If I knew that, Stevie, I would have bet you straight up and saved the juice."

"For ten, twenty bucks, sure," the Pencil says. Fact is, that's about the amount I would probably bet myself if I weren't gambling with Brain Trust money.

When I report my wager, Big Daddy asks me to inquire how much the

Pencil is going to let me bet on the upcoming college bowl games. "It's time to go bowling pretty soon. Tell him you're a winner and you want to gamble it up. Tell him you want to bet a hundred thousand a game. See what he says."

I'll have to find an appropriate time for such a request—which I'm sure will be denied. But maybe I'll get $50,000 a pop.

Six minutes before the 10:00 a.m. kickoff, Kathryn Matthews-Reynolds calls me with a play. I'm surprised to hear from her. I had imagined that she spent her Sundays aiding her illustrious brother with administrative tasks, not barking out bets. "We need Buffalo plus two, but the game starts soon, so you've got to hurry." I repeat the order and sprint to the elevator, thinking that a bet this late must involve a last-minute injury that the rest of the world hasn't yet heard about. Or maybe the line has moved so much in the last ten minutes that all of a sudden there's value in the wrong side.

I arrive at the sportsbook with about two minutes to spare. And despite a large line of gamblers, I get the bet in under the wire. Standing beside my window, the Pencil, drawing what looks to be Georges Braque's version of a football stadium, again offers me a higher limit. I thank him but decline. "I'm losing, Stevie. Let me win a few and we'll see."

The board moves from Bills +2 to Bills +1. Thanks to the service Big Daddy uses, the one that pipes in up-to-the-second odds from casinos around the world, he'll see on his computer screen that I've made my play right before the deadline. So before I return to the room to phone in my confirmation, I stop at the deli to get a sandwich. Fifteen minutes later I'm back in my suite.

Rick chews me out for keeping him waiting. I explain that I saw the number move and paused to get a sandwich. He chuckles. "Well, that's not gonna work, pards. I need to know right away."

"Got it. Won't happen again," I promise.

Then Rick admits that he did in fact see the number move and that "his people" at Caesars reported that they witnessed me making the bet. "*No problema*, 44. Good day, sir," and then he hangs up.

The call leaves me trembling. Who are these people? How closely am I being watched? Is the Pencil in on this?

Cautioning me not to share my information with a single living soul; phoning in bets at the very last moment; having anonymous runners report my actions—it all suggests to me that Big Daddy suspects I'm picking off his plays and then who knows what? Selling the information? Leaking it to a competing syndicate? Doing *something* wrong.

I think about my weak moment of renegade betting the week before. Rick, in all likelihood, knows about this.

Clearly I've got to do everything by the Brain Trust book. Or else.

Even after the Bills whip the Jets straight up, notching another $30,000 win in my account, I hear nothing from my handler. Trapped in the still-tense hotel room, Vivian and I spend the day watching movies, waiting. Indolent and narcotized from room service snacks, she doesn't seem to mind the enforced inertia. Shortly before 4:00 p.m., the second of my Brain Trust cell phone batteries goes dead, and since I haven't been provided with a charger, I have an excuse to leave my plush prison. I go downstairs to a pay phone and call Big Daddy to report the news. Almost as an afterthought, he instructs me to bet the under on the Denver game. "I want it under forty-four, but if it's at forty-three and a half right at post time, bet it at that number."

While I'm hanging around the counter, waiting for the number to move, Gino the Suit comes out to say hello. He asks if I've seen the *Racing Form* today. Seems there's a mention of my latest gambling story about a couple of local bookies trying to bring parimutuel-style wagering, which is more commonly found in horse racing, to Las Vegas sportsbooks. The Suit and I chat amiably about this innovation—Gino suggests that it was he who helped craft the regulations that made it possible—and the pros and cons of such a wagering system. I like the Suit. He's a smart fellow. And he smells good.

Fifteen minutes before the Denver game, an obese Mexican fellow bets the over—for $50,000. I'm standing at the counter when this happens, and I almost can't believe what I'm seeing. The Pencil's letting this guy bet $50,000 on a total?

"Did I hear that right?" I ask.

Stevie looks up from his cartography and smiles sheepishly. "You're one of our big players, Mike. But you're not the biggest."

"That's obvious," I say, bug-eyed. "Tell you what, Steve. I gotta believe you might want some action on the other side right about now. I'll take the under for ten."

"You got it."

When I tell Big Daddy about the fat Mexican, he says, "I wish I knew that. We could have bet 'em forty thousand on that under. How 'bout this: Go back down and bet up to twenty-five thousand more, if they'll give it to you at forty-four. If it's forty-three and a half, bet them up to twenty thousand. Now, go on. The game's almost starting."

I race back to the book, where I ask for some more at 44. Nothing doing. So I propose $20,000 more at 43½. Gino the Suit, acting as chief negotiator, tells me I can have $10,000 more. I take it, moments before the kickoff sails through the air.

So I have $30,000 on Denver to win and $20,000 on the game going under. This irrelevant contest has turned into a big financial decision. While I'm watching the action unfold, I wonder what sort of information Big Daddy has that inspires such heavy play on something like the under bet. What does he know?

In this case, apparently not much. Both Denver and its opponent, San Diego, score at will, putting up 37 points—*before the end of the first half.* This game, as they say, is "over." On the other hand, Denver is covering the spread amply.

Even more interesting than the game at hand is the action at the counter. For the first time all season, I observe the frenzy that envelops the sportsbook as the opening point spreads for the next week's games are released each Sunday afternoon around 5:00 p.m. A few minutes before the numbers are circulated to the general public, Pencil Stevie predicts to me which games will move. He explains to me that betting the underdogs gives you an edge right off the top, since most of the favorites are, in his estimation, overpriced. He also confides that if he were to let me bet first there would be a "war," since nobody is supposed to get special access to the opening numbers, no matter how very important he is to the casino.

Most revealing is Stevie's admission that the very first guys to bet—the fellows with the badly concealed earpieces and radios—are brokers trying to scalp the number. They buy a side at, say, −2½ points and sell it to their customers at 3. Indeed, the Tennessee-Auburn game opens on the Caesars board at Auburn +7. In the next morning's papers, the line will say Auburn +6½, thanks to the early action that moves the line, action that almost nobody in the world, save for those huddled around Vegas sportsbook counters, ever sees. In this way the bookies can free-roll—have a shot at winning without any chance of losing—for a half point, hoping Tennessee wins by exactly 7, producing a tie for the scalper bookies (who have Auburn +7) and a loss for their customers who have taken Auburn +6½. I'm not completely convinced that anyone at Caesars cooperates with this cadre of early-betting bookies—but like the indigenous rain forest dweller who gets his first dose of antibiotics from a missionary in exchange for mandatory Bible study, I'm slowly becoming converted.

For the weekend—a slow, rather boring one—I go 3–5 and win $1,800. It hardly seems worth the trouble.

When I call Big Daddy to see if he wants me to bet on any of next week's games, he tells me no. In fact, he says I should plan on taking next weekend off. "Doesn't look like there's much to it next weekend," he explains. But there's a full slate of NFL games, as well as four big college matchups. Is Big Daddy punishing me for some real or imagined infractions? Is my career as a sports bettor fizzling to an inglorious end?

Or am I just taking a break?

Without any action riding on the football games, I'm almost inspired to place a few renegade bets with an illegal bookie. I call my pal Hot Guy Zarefarb, who knows a bookmaker in New York who would be happy to take his (our) bets. Guy is a successful attorney who performs magic shows on the weekend, swallowing swords and eating fire, earning himself his nickname. Hot Guy doesn't know anything about betting sports (other than it's amusing), and he assumes I'm as clueless as he is. Without revealing my intensive training program, I assure Guy I've come up with a system for beating his bookie. Looking over the current numbers versus the opening numbers, I'm able to deduce where the smart money has landed. And I can almost convince myself that I can detect an edge in some of the games. This is folly, I know, but as I direct Hot Guy to bet if the line moves one way and to lay off if it moves the other, for a few moments I feel like *I'm* Big Daddy.

It's a marvelous feeling.

What's even cooler is to go 7–4 for the weekend and win $1,300. Sheer luck? Perhaps. I don't have the handicapping algorithms or scouting reports (or whatever else Rick Matthews uses) to distinguish a good play from a bad one. I'm not as smart as men like Jox Brijox; or my friend Timid Joe Corcoran, a professional Texas hold 'em player with a physics degree from Stanford; or the nerdy math genius from my high school, Andy Shubert, who ended up at MIT, working on supercomputers. But I do understand what separates a good number from a bad one. I know where value can be found. I don't know why Atlanta –2 is a good value and Atlanta –2½ is not, but after closely observing the Brain Trust at work, I can differentiate the hot sides from the squares.

Indeed, when I instruct Guy Zarefarb to bet Kansas City –8 against Oakland, I know it's not a smart-money play. There's been no movement at all on this point spread. But my Square John analysis—I've spent far too many hours in a Las Vegas hotel room watching football games—tells me that KC should probably be more like a 10-point favorite. Thus, I see value.

The three games where the wiseguys move the number dramatically—2½ points and more—by pouring so much money on one side that the bookies are forced to keep adjusting their line until someone will bet the other side, turn out to be big losers. If Big Daddy had a hand in this (and I suspect he did) he ended up getting crushed this weekend.

I'm sober enough about the difficulty of beating sports to realize that gambling on seven pro games in one weekend is the sign of a sucker. The linemakers just don't make that many mistakes on NFL football, where all the information is widely known to everyone in the universe. Indeed, Hot Guy's bookie tracked our bets and reported to Guy that about half of our wagers were smart-guy plays, a few were total square plays, and the rest were indeterminate. He judged our action as "above average but beatable," mostly because we played too many games. Still, the bookie admits to Guy, he wouldn't want to take bets larger than $5,000 from us.

It seems nobody wants to gamble. Not even the outlaws.

. . .

During the next two weeks, at home in my office, trying with limited success to work on a magazine story about golf, my mind wanders to the Brain Trust. Whereas I imagine most men sneak a look at pornographic Web sites while their woman is away, while Vivian is out doing errands I surf sports wagering sites dedicated to analysis of the line. I've got betting on the brain, but the Brains aren't keeping me in the information loop. After several unreturned phone calls, I fax Big Daddy an update, requesting that he advise me of my Brain Trust responsibilities. Should I plan to take off another weekend? Am I through until New Year's Day? (I'm holding airline tickets for every weekend in December.) He doesn't reply.

In the meantime, half convinced that I actually know something, and half convinced that even if I don't I'll still manage an enormous profit for the season, thanks to my $605,000 in Brain Trust winnings, I bet twenty-three college and pro games. Using Hot Guy as my clerk, I monitor the moving lines, noting which games the wiseguys have got their claws into and which ones might offer some intrinsic value. Sure, I can often predict which way the point spread is going to move. But I don't know when, and I certainly don't know why. Nonetheless, armed with a three-month crash course in sports betting—which is different from sports handicapping, and possibly more useful—I manage to go 14–9 and win about $1,000, $250 at a time. This translates to an impressive 60.8 percent success rate, virtually the same ratio that Big Daddy has achieved in the 1997 season.

I'm smart enough to know that I don't know anything. Still, the thrill of victory, of choosing the winners based on what I've learned about line moves and hot numbers, is almost sweeter than pocketing $5,000 on a winning $50,000 Brain Trust bet.

I don't dare tell Big Daddy what I've been doing during my three-week vacation from the Brains. He'd peg me for the ambitious sucker I am, just another fool who hangs around the sportsbooks, scouring the newspapers, analyzing statistics, figuring somehow he's got the best of the proposition when, in reality, he's going to end up losing at approximately the same rate as everyone else who gambles on sports.

So how does Big Daddy do it? Year in and year out, how does he beat a seemingly unbeatable game? That's the magic morsel of truth that only Big Daddy and his sister—and perhaps a trusted lieutenant or two—will ever know.

On Christmas Eve, the phone rings at three in the afternoon. I'm in the middle of wrapping gifts.

"Mr. 44! How you doin', pardsy-wardsy? How's life treating you?"

"Hey, Big Daddy," I reply. "Good to hear from you."

"When you coming to town? We miss you." Either Rick's a master of mendacity (as I strongly suspect) or he's astonishingly oblivious to the entreaties and messages flowing through his platoon of secretaries. He acts as though we've been in close contact for the past twenty days, not completely out of touch.

I tell him I'll make myself available whenever.

"Well, we've got a big play tomorrow, Christmas Day, as well the day after and possibly the day after that. I'd really like to get started as soon as possible," he says, turning on the charm.

I tell him I'll be in Vegas by early afternoon on Friday, the day *after* Christmas. Vivian and I are going to drive. I could be there tomorrow, but the prospect of Christmas in a Las Vegas casino strikes me as unrepentantly sociopathic—although I'm not remotely religious or holiday minded.

"I understand," Big Daddy says, misunderstanding. "Everyone should be with his family on Christmas." He instructs me to call as soon as I arrive in town; Sarge will come to my room with some money. "In the meantime," he says, "happy holidays, pards. Don't take any wooden nickels."

Two days later, four hours after pulling out of our Los Angeles driveway, Viv and I (and Pepper, our cat, hidden in a blanket-shrouded carrying case) arrive at the porte cochere of Caesars Palace. Our dog, Ella, a white lab mix, stays behind with a sitter. We're booked in for nine consecutive nights—my longest stay in Vegas ever—including New Year's Eve, at full RFB. The hotel is sold out and full of holiday revelers. These immense crowds distract the overtaxed valets and bellmen enough for Viv and me to smuggle the cat inside unnoticed. One Asian gentleman sees our pet, though, and turning to his companion shrugs and says, "High rollers."

The Sarge arrives with $300,000, bundled in shrink-wrapped bricks. I have the option of sitting on the season's profits—in fact, Big Daddy's assured me I can quit at any time. The old Michael probably would have been happy to play it conservatively, to take the windfall and run. But now I'm 44. I'm no longer skeptical or scared. I believe in Big Daddy's handicapping. I believe I will leave Las Vegas with more than I came with.

In exchange for the money, I hand Sarge two Christmas presents: a box of golf balls with his name emblazoned on the side and a VHS copy of *Dirty Harry*.

Before he unwraps the gifts, my pistol-packing associate gets a tear in his eye. "Aw, 44, that's just so nice of you. Come here, buddy!" He throws his arms around me, squeezing me so close I can smell the menthol smoke in his hair. "Come here, you!" he says to Viv, giving her a hug and a rather wet kiss. "You two kids are the nuts."

He tramps off with his gifts tucked beneath one arm and who knows how much in cash stored in a leather satchel.

"Sarge has definitely got the Christmas spirit," Viv comments, wiping her mouth with the back of her hand.

The Pencil is also filled with holiday cheer, especially after I arrive at his sportsbook with a new titanium-head driver as a token of my friendship. He seems deeply touched. Whether or not my gift affects his judgment on practical matters is unclear, but he suggests we talk about my betting limits. He says he'll take $40,000 on the bowls—all the bowls. This is a startling (and welcome) development. "And if you ever want more, just ask. We'll evaluate on a case-by-case basis."

I feel like sprinting back upstairs to give Big Daddy the news, but counting $300,000 takes a long time. So Stevie and I talk food and family and music, carefully avoiding the central question: What the hell am I doing betting this much money on sports? Maybe he knows. Maybe we're both just playing our part in Big Daddy's elaborate charade. Or maybe a season of gambling has turned me into a mistrustful misanthrope who suspects ulterior motives from everyone in the casino business.

Seems the Pencil won first prize (a Caribbean cruise) in the trade journal *Gambling Today*'s season-long sportsbook manager's handicapping contest, in which all the Vegas bookmakers make theoretical bets on the games. He averaged about 60 percent winners—which is eerily close to what Big Daddy and the Brains have accomplished. I try not to read too much into this lest my mind melt into a heated mush of half-baked conspiracy theories. Inevitably, as he scribbles what looks like horses with arachnid legs, he offers his opinions on some of the upcoming games. I'm careful not to tip my hand—mainly since I don't even know what my hand is at this point.

Upon my return to the room, I call Big Daddy on the two-way radio he's provided me with for the week. ("Copy that. Over!") He seems pleased to hear about the limits I've been granted. I'm pleased, too, since this could mean additional business for me: one-stop, buy-in-bulk shopping.

Ten minutes later the fun begins. Rick instructs me to go downstairs immediately and bet Colorado State –3, a game that has been at 5 and 4 for the past two weeks. Clearly, somebody has weighed in with a big bet on the other side and Caesars Palace is looking for some counterbalance on the favorite. If I can get there in time I'll be the casino's white knight.

Getting from my suite, down the elevator, and through the rows of twittering slot machines to the sportsbook takes approximately four minutes when I perform a mad dash that Olympic judges would still consider walking. The security guard I waddle past near the dice tables looks at me as though I stole something. The Colorado State Rams are still –3 when I arrive at the counter. Trying to appear calm, I tell the clerk my bet and, with the Pencil nodding approval, he punches up the ticket—only it's for the wrong team, the underdog, Missouri. "Hold it," I say, slightly frantic. "I wanted the other team, Colorado State."

"You want to lay the three, right?" Stevie says, peering into his computer screen.

"Yeah, that's right," I say, hoping this won't turn into an incident.

"No problem," he says. "A little mistake."

The clerk issues me the correct ticket. "Laying the three. That's more like it," Stevie remarks, obviously pleased. For a second he must have thought everybody in the joint was going to start betting Missouri, that there was some sort of vital information he didn't have. I can almost detect relief on his expressionless face: It's just good ol' Mr. K taking a good number on the side we need.

Still pals.

When I walk away, one of the clerks calls my name. My girlfriend, he says, is on the phone. There's some sort of problem in the room. Unfortunately, he can't let me go behind the counter, but there's a house phone I can use near the keno lounge. I thank him and dash off.

Vivian says Big Daddy had called to tell me I could bet up to "a hundred dimes" on Colorado State. Too late now.

My paranoia revs around my mind like a 600-horsepower V-8 engine. What the hell is going on here? Is Big Daddy trying to burn me out on the wrong side of a game? Am I some sort of highly paid stool pigeon?

I don't have time to find out. When I return to the suite, Big Daddy immediately sends me back to the sportsbook with another bet. Michigan State getting 11 big points from Clemson.

"Everything all right, Mikey?" Stevie wants to know.

I mumble something about an overflowing tub and make my play. The former prizefighter, Little Mikey Brown, one of the shift supervisors, has come on duty, and I have a Christmas gift for him, too. I tell him I've left it upstairs, but I'll go and get it. He tells me not to sweat it; he'll be here every day for the next week. "These are some of our busiest days of the year. That's why they pay us the big bucks," he jokes.

Again, almost immediately upon my return to the room, Big Daddy sends me back downstairs to bet Auburn, a team that's been stuck on 6½ for two weeks. Why the last-minute scramble, I wonder? "Go bet 'em at six, and hurry," he instructs me. I rush out the door, with Lil' Mikey's gift in hand.

The Pencil spies my present and says, "You're too much, MK." I reply that I may have gone a dollar or two over the $25 gift limit, but hey, it's Christmas. And just for good measure, what the hell, give me Auburn −6.

I report back to the boss, who gives me a rare compliment. "Good job, pards. Way to hustle," he says. "I'll get back to you." And he does. At 7:00 p.m. Rick calls to say that we're through for the day.

I've bet $132,000 on three games. Viv and I go to our Palace Court dinner feeling that the complimentary meal is well deserved. We even laugh a little together.

In the morning, a squawking two-way radio wakes me from Burgundy slumbers. "Come in, 44. Time to get to work. Over."

"It's 44," I croak. "Good morning."

"Get yourself downstairs and bet the under on tonight's game between Arizona and New Mexico." I look at my official schedule of games, with my point-spread notes scrawled in the margins. The total number's been stuck at 52; now, according to Big Daddy, it's at 53. "Go and bet whatever they'll take, up to fifty thousand," he orders.

Getting that much seems unlikely to me, but, of course, all I can do is ask. In fact, the Pencil grants me $20,000 on the game, which is $10,000 more than the usual limit.

When I report my bet over the radio, Big Daddy wonders out loud what Stevie's policy might be on betting the same game, only at a different number. I tell him I honestly don't know, since it hasn't come up, but I suspect the bookmaker would go for it, as long as I'm taking a worse number. "Go down there and bet him the under at fifty-two," Big Daddy orders. "Take whatever he'll give you up to fifty dimes. Over and out."

When I ask, the Pencil tells me he'll let me make such a play, but not necessarily for as much as my original bet. In the case of my Arizona total, he tells me he'll take another $15,000. Now I've got $38,500 riding on the game. If both teams manage to score less than a combined 52 points, we'll win $35,000.

At 9:20, ten minutes before the kickoff of the first NFL wild-card game, Big Daddy radios me and asks how quickly I can get down and make a bet. "A couple minutes," I say, knowing I can sprint if I have to.

"A couple minutes," he repeats. "All right, pardsy, I'll get back to you."

He never does. I find out later, from my friend Guy Zarefarb, that the line went nuts right before game time. This was one time, though, when I personally had nothing to do with it.

Big Daddy disappears for the next six hours, leaving me in my luxurious cell, where Viv and I enjoy room service and movies, waiting for my man to call me, like a high school girl hoping the phone will ring with an invitation to the prom.

When he finally radios again, it's to inquire about limits on college basketball. Though this sport isn't officially part of our deal, I suppose he figures I'm here, I'm available, and, if necessary, I can deliver a convincing enough explanation for why, after months of football, I'm suddenly betting collegiate hoops. Big Daddy gives me two plays and instructs me to bet as much as Pencil Stevie will allow, up to $15,000 per game. With a sour taste in my mouth, I trudge down to the book, anticipating a fiasco. Is Rick Matthews trying to get me thrown out of Caesars?

Surprisingly, the Pencil is as cordial as ever, allowing me to bet $10,000 per game. He doesn't even comment on my sudden switch in sports. Just gambling, he must reckon.

When I report my bets, Big Daddy says, "Good job. I'll get back to you." Five minutes later he's beeping me again. "That Arizona total was at fifty-one. Somebody must have bet it for a big number, because Caesars just moved it up a half point. Go bet the under again for up to fifty thousand."

When I arrive at the book, there's a line of several hundred people waiting to cash their winning NFL tickets. I approach the counter and ask the Pencil yet again how much he will take on my under bet at the new total. He checks his computer and says, "I'll take another fifteen." He motions me to an unattended counter spot. "Wait right there and I'll get someone to take care of you."

I make my bet—now I've got $55,000 on the game—and drift off into the crowd of gamblers. Now I'm hoping the teams score less than 51 points.

Then, a few minutes later, Big Daddy directs me to bet next week's NFL playoff game, San Francisco vs. Minnesota, for up to $60,000. Caesars Palace has just posted the line, and the head of the Brain Trust thinks it's off—off by enough, a point and a half, perhaps, that we're getting the best of the proposition.

"Get down there and bet the Niners before someone else gets to it!" he urges me. I hustle down to the book, where there's still a large crowd waiting to cash out. The Pencil is chatting with two elderly fellows who want to know how much they can bet on tomorrow's New England play-off game. They want $100,000. After Stevie tells them they can bet $50,000 (which they decline), he turns to me. "Which game, sir?"

I tell him. "You want to lay the twelve and a half on San Fran?" he asks. "I don't blame you. You think it's too low, right? Should be thirteen and a half."

"Fourteen," I say with mock assurance.

He scans his computer screen, upon which I assume the sportsbook's accounts are compiled. "Okay. Fifty thousand."

As the clerk processes the bet, I ask the Pencil what the send-out was, the recommended line posted by Jox Brijox's organization.

"Ten and a half."

"Come on, you're joking," I say, feigning incredulity. "And you were smart enough to tack two extra points on?"

"I got lucky," he says. "But at fourteen, I play the other side."

"Sure, but not at twelve and a half."

"No, you're right. But it's not twelve and a half anymore, Mike." We both look up at the electronic toteboard as the line changes to 13½.

When I report my play to Big Daddy, he asks me how I feel about betting the under on the Arizona game one more time, at 51. This doesn't seem like a good idea to me, and I say so. I mean, what kind of casual sports gambler feels like *$50,000* isn't enough action on a frickin' over-under? To my surprise, he defers to me on this one. "You've got a better sense of how they're feeling down there in the trenches. We'll just leave it alone."

I'm pleased that he hasn't pressed the issue, but I'm also crazy with curiosity. What's going on that he's so confident about the total in tonight's bowl game? What does he know that nobody else does? When Big Daddy calls back to release me for the evening, I can't help myself. Knowing I might be way out of line, I ask Big Daddy, What's the angle? Why is he so confident that these two teams will score less than 53—and 52 and 51½—points?

"There's no angle, pards," he tells me. "Me and my boys, and our computer, well, we made the game a much lower number than the bookmakers put up. So we bet it. Simple as that."

Is it really that simple? I know I could never program a computer to analyze football games, and there's no one in my circle of friends, only people from my distant past, capable of reducing thousands of data bits into millions of ones and zeroes.

Though Big Daddy's handicapping methodology remains a mystery to me, his results do not. The Arizona game, per his prognostication, turns out to be a resolutely low-scoring affair (20–14) and we win all three of our under bets. Both basketball games come in for us, too.

We're up another $70,000.

At daybreak, hours before the NFL's 10:00 a.m. kickoff, the first words out of Big Daddy's mouth are, "Good morning. Find out if Stevie will let you buy half a point—and for how much." Since Rick doesn't want me to make a special trip for this information, he says he'll "try to find something" for me to play, and when I'm downstairs I can do my fact-finding. Nearly three hours later, ten minutes before the kickoff of the New England–Miami play-off game, he orders me to bet the over—and to find out what the half-point policy is.

When I arrive at the counter, the Pencil tucks his graphite #2 behind his ear and proposes, "New England? Laying the five?" anticipating my play.

"No. Over forty."

"How much did I say you could have, Michael?"

"Fifteen."

"All right, fifteen," Stevie agrees. "That's all I want."

I query him about the half-point policy, and he explains his terms. "Which game do you want?" he asks. I tell him I'm not sure, but that I'll be back later.

When I tell Big Daddy that buying a half point will result in my limits being cut in half, he launches into a classic Rick Matthews monologue about the debased Las Vegas mentality. "When you write your book, remember this. Obviously it's beneficial to them to sell a half point, or else they wouldn't be doing it. Yet they don't want to take any money in bets. Is that a good way to run your business?"

"Um, well—"

"No, it ain't!"

Shortly before noon, Big Daddy radios to confirm that I'll be available at the end of the playoff game. (As if I'm permitted to go anywhere.) Caesars will be putting up the point spreads for next week's games, and he wants to make sure we get first crack at them.

Predictably, he doesn't call back as planned. So I spend the rest of the afternoon alone in the suite while Vivian enjoys the pool, waiting again, feeling as my dog Ella must when she sits at the window, watching me drive away, uncertain when her best friend will return. Finally, a little after 3:00 p.m., Vivian returns, titillated by the pool scene and hungry for sex. Unfortunately, my master directs me to go downstairs and look for a number: Notre Dame +7 in this evening's Independence Bowl, vs. LSU.

I hate this particular play, and not just because it takes me away from my naked girlfriend. LSU seems to me the right pick, for a bushel full of reasons I would gladly articulate if I didn't think I'd get laughed at for paraphrasing the wisdom of ESPN pundits. But he's the boss, and I'm merely a well-paid amanuensis. Before I go to the sportsbook, Big Daddy requests that Viv be available to take radio calls if he needs to get me an important message. She'll come down if there's anything urgent.

Thirty minutes later, as I'm keeping one eye on the board and another on Little Mikey Brown, who's chatting with me about point spreads and such, Vivian appears at my arm. After exchanging pleasantries, I lead her away from the counter, toward my reserved seat in the crowded viewing area. Making sure we're not arousing suspicion, that we're not being eavesdropped upon, I mumble, "What's up?" She whispers that Big Daddy wants me to bet the Steelers at –6, for up to $55,000. I kiss her cheek and amble back to the counter, where I make my bet without incident.

She returns to the room to call in a confirmation. Minutes later, she's unexpectedly at my side again. "San Francisco minus thirteen and a half for up to sixty dimes," she says quietly. "And he said to hurry up before it goes."

Hundreds of gamblers are in line to cash winning tickets from the afternoon play-off game, and I start to fret that I'll miss the number. I don't recognize anybody as a big bettor, the kind of player capable of moving the number. But, just as at the neighborhood grocery store, my line seems to advance slowest. To my horror, I overhear a guy in a black baseball cap standing in the adjoining line, a guy I've never seen before, tell the clerk that he wants to bet on the San Francisco–Minnesota game. My game.

"I'll take Minnesota for five thousand," he says. He's taking the *other* side.

With a relieved grin on my face, I get to the front of my line and make my bet. The Pencil decides to accept only $30,000 of my action. "You already bet a bunch before. Come on, Mikey, don't beat me up on this game."

I don't argue.

Before I get five yards from the counter, Stevie calls out, "Notre Dame plus seven! Anybody?"

Spinning on my heels, I raise my hand. "Sold!" I say. "I'll take it."

"We have a winner, ladies and gentlemen," Little Mikey announces. Then he gives me a commemorative Caesars Palace baseball cap. "Thank you, sir, for your patronage."

I try to get the Pencil to sign it "From the Las Vegas Handicapping Contest Winner," but he steadfastly refuses. He thinks I'm teasing him.

Late in the evening, after our $44,000 Notre Dame game is under way and we're already enjoying the second course of a sushi extravaganza, Big Daddy radios back to find out how much money I have left in my Caesars account. I tell him around $30,000, with another $84,000 pending on tonight's game. He decides I'm going to need "some more bullets" to fire. "We need to keep you in money, son. Probably another two or three hundred thousand." He says he or Sarge will come to Caesars within an hour.

Realizing this transaction might look suspicious to the Caesars Palace management, I buzz Big Daddy back and ask him to consider the credibility issue. He comes up with a good solution: "Call Stevie and ask if he'll arrange a limo for you to Binion's. Tell him you want to go down there and pull out a whole bunch of money, because you're happy with your home at Caesars. Or something like that. Even if he won't send you, he knows that you're intending to get a bunch of money."

I like Big Daddy's idea, but after I call the Pencil on a house phone, I don't feel so great about the whole proposition. Stevie tells me that, in fact, he won't arrange a limousine for me. When I profess mild surprise, he tells me edgily that all the money I'm betting doesn't help him because I'm playing all the "computer sides." And he doesn't sound as though he's joking.

"All right, Stevie," I say, trying to remain nonconfrontational. "I can get down there myself."

When I report the exchange to Big Daddy, he assures me that the Pencil is either bluffing or guessing. "I promise you, there's nothing you're doing that would connect you to me in any way. He's just bluffing you, 44, because he's mad that you picked a few winners. This whole computer deal is bullshit."

Big Daddy says that he'll personally be making the drop-off at the side door. I should be there in fifteen minutes.

"I hate this," I tell Viv. "I've suddenly lost my appetite."

She waves a piece of unagi under my chin. "It's all part of the business, Mr. 44," she says. "Just laugh at it."

When I climb into Big Daddy's Navigator, his sister Kathryn Matthews-Reynolds and their brother-in-law Jerry are there with the man himself. Rick is all business. "Two hundred ninety-two thousand," he says, as Kathryn hands me two bricks of money and some Caesars chips. "Two hundred cash, ninety-two in casino sportsbook chips." We drive around the hotel's entryway in slow circles while he talks. "You just leave the strategy to me, 44. I'll make sure we cool you off tomorrow. I'm going to send in my runner girl, someone Stevie associates with me and my plays. I'll get her to bet twenty thousand on a side and have you come in and bet the other way. That way there's no connection in his mind whatsoever. He's bluffing you anyway, 'cause there's no way under Christ's sun that he wouldn't have run you out of there by now if he had made any connection between you and me. Ain't no way. So don't sweat it, pards. We'll cool him off."

He parks near the door, wishes me good luck, and warns me to be ready for him at 7:30 in the morning.

I'm praying the Pencil isn't there to watch me deposit the money. I feel weak, tremulous, like a liar caught in an inescapable trap. Thankfully, Stevie is gone. My buddy Little Mikey Brown is manning the counter, and without any innuendo he merely asks me, "How much?"

I'm about to say "Two ninety-two," but I have a sudden, chilling premonition: *Don't say that.*

"Two hundred," I say, pulling the bricks out of my bag and leaving the chips inside. I realize, just in time, that Caesars has never paid me a single dollar in sportsbook chips. Caesars tracks all my bets, all my deposits, and all my withdrawals, and somebody is bound to notice that I've never bought or received sports chips from the hotel. Which would raise the obvious question: Where did they come from? I can't think of a suitable explanation.

I'm dreading having to report my decision to Big Daddy, for he can be churlish when one of his deputies is too dim-witted to keep up with his blazingly fast problem solving. I'm convinced my call on the chips is the right one. But I could be wrong.

When I call with the news, Kathryn answers the phone. He's inside Bally's, she says, making some bets. (This I'd like to see.) I explain the situation and, to my relief, Kathryn agrees with my decision. She instructs me to put the chips in a lockbox. We'll deal with them tomorrow, if necessary.

We would have to lose an awful lot of money to dip into the chip fund. Of course, if Big Daddy insists on making plays like the Notre Dame one—which I hated from the start and hate even more when LSU crushes Notre Dame—I might be faced with a rapidly evaporating pool of profit. The Pencil and his cronies at Caesars Palace, I'm sure, wouldn't mind that at all.

I wake up with a cold, symbolic, I suppose, of my general malaise. I'm dreading having to talk with Pencil Stevie, dreading the air of interrogation that imbues all our transactions. My losing $44,000 last night on the damned Fighting Irish should put him in a cheerier frame of mind. Before I make an appearance, though, I have to wait for the metallic chirp that signals Big Daddy is about to grace my life once more. My radio rings three times, but it's not the boss on the line; it's three guys I've never heard of—Dawkins, Hutt, and Strother, according to my radio's LCD readout—looking for "Clarence," whose radio I'm using for the week. I discreetly tell them who I am without telling them who I am. When they ask how they might reach Clarence, I tell them to go through "the main man." They all understand whom I mean.

Finally, shortly before noon, Big Daddy calls with a play: the over in the afternoon college bowl game, Boston College vs. Washington. Rick says he's already sent in some of his known runners to bet the under, so the Pencil will be both appreciative and confused. I'll be betting against the computer. The only catch is, Rick wants me to bring my radio with me, with the speaker turned off, because he expects to give me further directions minutes after my play. I'll be walking into the sportsbook with incontrovertible evidence of my Brain Trust membership in my pocket.

Pencil Stevie is happy to book my $20,000 bet, since the wiseguys have just bet the other side. After a bit of small talk I slink away to the nearby video arcade, where I take a seat inside the cockpit of the *Lost World* game, shielded from casino surveillance cameras. With explosions and shrieking missiles blasting all about me, I buzz Big Daddy and report my wager.

"Is that you, 44? I can barely hear you."

"Sorry, I'm in a secure location, but it's a little loud."

He orders me back to the sportsbook to bet the over again at the new number. This time the Pencil takes an additional $15,000. I return to my video game to radio, surrounded by intrigued children staring at an adult interloper huddled inside one of their favorite machines. Then I retreat to my suite and turn on the television.

It's a scoring orgy. Every time Boston College posts a touchdown, Washington matches with one of its own. The game is "over" early in the third quarter. Later in the afternoon, Big Daddy calls to celebrate our total bet win. "Now what's Mr. Stevie gonna think?" he crows, giggling like a happy child. "Looks like them computer guys were going the wrong way, huh?"

I tell Big Daddy that the Pencil must suspect that everybody in his sportsbook is some sort of wiseguy, since two-thirds of the regular players wear earpieces. Rick laughs heartily and signs off. "Ten-four on that one!"

When he calls back an hour later, the joviality is gone. Again he's got a total bet for me, under in the Purdue game. Again I'm betting against the prevailing opinion. Caesars Palace should certainly appreciate my patronage. It does, taking $22,000 from me. The Pencil and I chat briefly about the Colorado State number—it's gone from 3½ to 2½, and I tell him I fear I've laid a bad number at 3. "I hope not, Mike," he says, nervously circling the game repeatedly on his schedule. "We've booked a ton on Missouri. I'm hoping you're right."

Shortly after I return to the room, Big Daddy sends me out with another total bet, on the Colorado State game. When I place my wager—again against the prevailing trend—Stevie makes a gentle (but snide) joke about going to check his computer to see if the number moves all around town after I bet. I don't react. When I report the remark to Big Daddy, he snorts acidly. "Of course it moves all around town after you bet, 'cause them guys are paying him off! Well, he's telling all those runners, the guys with the earpieces, that one of his sharpest customers is making a wager, and those runners turn around and start filling up every joint with five-thousand-dollar bets on the same team. So of course the number moves." Rick considers for a second and says, "I guess you probably don't want to say that to him."

Big Daddy asks me if I'm scared to bet a game that will, in fact, move all around town. I remind him that my official position is: "I'm completely ignorant of what's going on at other hotels. I only know what Caesars has on their board. If something moves someplace else, it's none of my business." This all happens to be the truth.

"Yeah, that's right," he agrees, fired up. "All right, then, I'm going to call you back with a pro play in about a minute. Hang tight."

The play is Green Bay—13½ against Tampa Bay in the play-offs. As I approach the window to bet, one of the earpiece guys is making a $500 wager on the same side. The Pencil grants me $50,000 without any sarcastic comments, but when he hands me a copy of my ticket, he says, "I can still void this if you want. It's not too late."

I tell him I'll stand pat. "You know what side I like," Stevie says.

"And at plus fourteen you should," I reply. "But at thirteen and a half, it's the Pack."

The crowd is light, and we have a quiet moment to chat, save for when an older high-roller gentleman, who looks suspiciously like the corporate raider and enthusiastic sports bettor Carl Icahn, sprints toward the counter. He's hoping to bet Missouri for $50,000, only to discover that the game has already started. The Pencil and I talk of betting angles—his theory is that deaths and serious injuries do not motivate teams—and of my writing career. I'm just beginning to explain how screenplays get polished by uncredited writers when he has to take a phone call, and I have to return to the room to confirm my plays. If we weren't on opposite sides of a rough business, the Pencil and I could probably be great friends. For now, though, it's mutual paranoia.

Caesars and I need the same side in the Colorado State bowl game. And we both need the under. This is how I like it: Stevie and me vs. the alleged wiseguys.

After dinner, Viv and I pop into the sportsbook, where we discover we've gotten lucky again. Colorado State and the under both came in. We're up $81,500 for the weekend.

There's only one bowl game Friday, at 5:00 p.m. The prospect of sitting in the hotel room for eight hours depresses me. I would so much rather be outside, in the desert's winter coolness, playing golf with Vivian. But when I get up the courage to ask for a day pass, Big Daddy's radio address registers as "target unavailable." I try again ten minutes later and get the same result. Just as I'm about to use the telephone, my radio beeps.

"Good morning, 44. We're going to make a play in about ten, fifteen minutes. Make sure you're available."

The play is Tennessee getting 14 points against Nebraska in the Orange Bowl. The handicapping on this one seems sound to me. But why, I wonder, didn't we take the Volunteers yesterday morning when they were getting 16 points?

At 9:00 a.m. the only ones hanging around the counter are the regular earpiece guys, runners for big betting groups, talking, as always, about point spreads and odds. They're tolerated because they're allowed to bet only the usual counter limits, and they know better than to ask for more. Besides, the casino likes knowing where the action is coming from. It helps them sharpen their lines.

Pencil Stevie, I'm told by one of the clerks, will be out until the afternoon, so Richard, the day-shift supervisor, has to call his boss to get the bet approved. He says it will be about five minutes.

Richard returns from the back office a few minutes later. "Excuse me, Michael," he calls to me. Apparently one of the regular earpiece guys is also named Michael: he and a dozen of his cronies make a mad rush on the counter, thinking Richard's releasing the day's basketball odds.

"No, no, not you. Sit down," Richard says. "The other Michael."

I approach the counter. "That was a near riot. It's like the provisions just came in on the bread line. Starving children in Somalia."

"It's sick. Anyway, Stevie said fifty is okay on Tennessee."

"Do these guys live here?" I joke. "I've never not seen them here."

"Yeah, they like it here."

"Do they sleep here?" I ask.

"Sometimes it seems like it."

I report the play to Big Daddy, who gives me a curt "over and out." Asking for time off seems out of the question. It's back to climate-controlled prison.

Vivian is out at the gym and spa, enjoying the perks of high-rollerdom. After an hour, I get up the courage to ask the warden for a reprieve. "I notice there's only one bowl game later this evening, so if you won't be needing me until later in the afternoon, I'd like to get out of here for a few hours."

He tells me to go. "But please be back by quarter past two. We'll be making some moves then." I nearly sprint out of Caesars. What a pleasure it is to feel sunlight upon my face and wind on my neck, to wander aimlessly. I blast Dean Martin on the car's CD player as I cruise down the Strip. Outside Caesars Palace I can be me, a (semi) regular guy who wouldn't dream of making $55,000 bets on college football games, someone who actually works for a living. As much as I enjoy the charade, being a richly compensated human mule taxes my psychic endurance. I feel like I'm addicted to the constant pursuit of *more*. It's what Las Vegas encourages in the most monastic souls. One brief afternoon away from the gambling mill reminds me that life as I know it still exists, and I still have a modest place in it.

An hour after I return Vivian is still out, though her gym clothes are piled on the floor. Big Daddy calls with a play for tonight's bowl game, Oklahoma State getting 4½ points. Earlier, on the way to my suite, I saw that we could have gotten 5 points, and I'm wondering what happened to our penchant for grabbing the best number. When I get to the sportsbook, the number has dropped again, to 4. I'm too late. I dally for a few minutes, hoping the magic half point will pop up again, but it stays stuck.

When I open the door to the room, the phone is ringing—and Vivian is still gone. I pick up the receiver and the line is dead. Then the radio beeps. It's Big Daddy, frantic. "I told Vivian to get a message to you. Virginia Tech plus eleven and a half. Hurry!" I race back down and find Viv searching in vain for her gambler boyfriend. I kiss her cheek and say quietly, "I know the play." After we bet and visit briefly with the Pencil we return together to the room. She tells me that the earpiece guys were talking about me. I can only imagine what they were saying.

"Do they have any suspicion who you are, or who you're playing with?" she asks me.

"I'm sure they do. But I never talk to those guys. Ever."

As I'm explaining our respective places in the sports betting universe—Big Daddy is the sun. I'm his moon, and the earpieces are distant asteroids—Rick calls back with a basketball play. I don't like it, but I don't complain. The Pencil looks at me slightly askance when I place the wager. Finally, fifteen minutes before kickoff time, I'm directed to play the under and the underdog. Oklahoma State, in tonight's bowl game. Now I'm taking 4 points. This is a horrible number compared with two hours earlier, but 2½ better than when the line opened.

To my surprise, Pencil Stevie not only lets me bet $50,000 on the side but also then leaves the number where it is, essentially offering to let me have more at 4. Since I haven't been given directions, I tell him I'll think about it and promptly slink off to the nearest pay phone. When I report the events to Big Daddy he says, "That's fine. Go ahead and return to the room." He sounds tired all of a sudden. Though he won't say it, I suspect Rick feels like he didn't necessarily get the best of this proposition. Though Caesars Palace really needed action on the Oklahoma State side, it got us to take a slightly worse number, simply by holding fast. In a sense, Big Daddy got bluffed. Or Stevie made a really good guess.

In the end, the half point makes no difference. Oklahoma State gets trounced by 13. On the other hand, the under comes in. When this is coupled with a small loss—if $11,000 can be considered small—on a college basketball game, I lose $46,000 for the day.

As night falls on Las Vegas, Big Daddy asks me to retrieve the Caesars sports chips and deliver them to him and Kathryn at the adjoining Forum Shops, where they'll be having dinner. At 6:00 p.m. I carry $92,000 in $5,000 chocolate chips and $1,000 banana chips to the Cheesecake Factory restaurant. On the way there, I nearly bump into Big Daddy and his sister, outside the Warner Brothers store. He calmly tells me to make the transfer with Kathryn and walks on.

She and I find a quiet gallery and slip in to admire some awful Thomas Kinkade–style art, mushy country scenes dappled with pointillist highlights. Certain that no one's watching I hand her the casino chips, which she deposits in her purse, uncounted. Just as we're about to blend into the holiday crowds. I look up and, as though I'm hallucinating, see Danny Gans, the "man of many voices" and Las Vegas Entertainer of the Year, whose ubiquitous face graces magazine covers, taxicabs, and billboards all over town.

He smiles at me and nods. I'm not sure if he's seen what's just transpired or if he's being polite.

"Hello, Mr. Gans," I say sweetly, "I'm a big fan. You're really an amazing talent."

He thanks me, speaking very softly—to conserve his voice, I suppose.

"Just out shopping for, um, art?" I ask.

"Out with the wife," he replies, nodding again.

"Me, too," I say, smiling at Kathryn, who titters nervously.

Danny Gans nods some more. "Well, you have a nice evening."

"Thanks, Mr. Gans. You, too." Then I put my arm around Kathryn's shoulder and lead her out of the gallery. We walk a few yards together and gradually separate.

When I head back to the suite, I walk past a lounge and spot Big Daddy sharing a table with a shaggy-haired fellow. We make brief eye contact as I continue on without breaking stride. What the hell is he doing? I wonder. Then I remember Kathryn telling me not long ago that Rick occasionally comes into casinos and makes bets himself, saving the runner's commission. He's able to do this because few people actually know what he looks like. And though the casinos are supposed to ask for identification on bets over $10,000, they seldom do when the player bets with chips.

I'd love to take a seat in the sportsbook and watch this little drama unfold. But I have a dinner date with a high-roller moll who's spent the day in the Caesars Palace salon.

The last day of 1997 is a gray one. Big Daddy calls at 8:30 a.m. to get an accounting of how much money I have left to bet. When I tell him $167,000, he says, "Well, that's not going to be nearly enough. I'm going to send Sarge over with two hundred thousand more. In the meantime, go down and play Clemson, plus six, for up to fifty thousand."

Just as I'm responding, the connection fizzles out. "Network Trouble" my radio readout says.

More like ethical trouble to my way of thinking. Big Daddy has just asked me to bet a game I've already played—on Auburn, the other side. At the exact same point spread. The only reason he would want to bet both sides of a game—with no middle or arbitrage opportunity—is because he really doesn't care which side wins. And the only reason he wouldn't care which side wins is because he's merely moving huge sums of money for other gamblers (bookies from around the country, perhaps) and collecting a commission. Just what I'm doing for him. Only he's collecting magnificently larger sums, I would assume.

The connection returns. "You know what? Don't fool with that game. Leave it alone. Over and out."

Either Rick Matthews has made an unfathomable reading error, or he's just exposed himself as a fraud. Now I worry that maybe he's trying to use me to dump off a lot of money, thereby erasing my profits. Vivian thinks this is highly unlikely: The Brains are still up $36,000 for the week and $650,000 for the year. I'm inclined to agree, but I don't know if I'll ever think of Rick Matthews the same way, no matter how courtly and well mannered he is when he thanks me for my holiday gift, no matter how sharp his gambling instincts seem, no matter how much money he puts in my pocket.

On the other hand, he could simply have misread his betting notes.

The relentless opacity of Big Daddy's operation is driving me crazy. I can understand why Rick and his chief deputies want to keep their secrets to themselves. On the other hand, making me feel like a fully vested member of the team, not merely a temporary worker, would do wonders for everyone's level of trust. If I can get up the nerve, I'm going to tell Rick all this.

Sarge delivers another $200,000. As I ride down the elevator to the sportsbook, I realize that in less than four complete months I've become immune to the fact that I'm holding nearly a quarter-million dollars in my hands. No longer do I reflect on the epistemological ramifications—not to mention the mechanics—of having this much cash lying around like so many old comic books. The Brains just have it.

The only question Pencil Stevie asks about my new batch of money is "Why didn't you deposit this last night, when I didn't have a line of thirty people trying to bet?"

I make a lame joke about thinking I was going to win my game last night and not needing the infusion, but after all the counting is through I apologize to him for the bad timing, and he shrugs it off graciously.

Back in the room I wait, expecting Big Daddy will have me bet the first bowl game of the day between Arizona State and Iowa, which has moved 4 points in the past two weeks. It's the kind of point-spread manipulation special we seem to thrive on. But he doesn't call. Instead, I'm ordered down minutes before the second game of the afternoon, the Southern Mississippi–Pittsburgh contest, to bet the under. Big Daddy stresses that

I'm not to bet the game until moments before post time. Thanks to long lines at the counter, I almost take his instructions too literally, placing my wager nanoseconds before the kicker's foot sends the football airborne. Three hours later, I'm glad I made it. We win both the under and the side, for a $60,000 profit. And just as the results become final, I bet Syracuse and the under in the last game of the evening. Per Big Daddy's advice, I bet the under again after Stevie moves the number a full point and a half. "You're too tough, MK," Stevie howls. I shrug modestly. He shouts, "The Mr. K Special is too tough!"

When I return to the room to report my bet, Big Daddy starts to wish me a happy new year and then suddenly sends me back to bet Washington State, getting 7 points, in the big Rose Bowl game against Michigan. Here's another case of getting less than the best number (7½ was available hours earlier). Paired with the Auburn-Clemson debacle, I'm starting to wonder. Then again, I'm up $95,000 for the week, so it's hard to complain.

Big Daddy reminds me to be ready to go at 7:00 a.m. "And, 44?" he says. "I just want to say: Thanks."

Following a night filled with champagne, the Temptations, and Vivian's usual drunken debauchery (this time involving an impromptu striptease for a table of intrigued partygoers), I get my morning call from the boss. My first bet of 1998 is the Wisconsin-Georgia game going under. My next is the North Carolina–Virginia game going under. And my next is supposed to be the Penn State–Florida game going under. Unfortunately, for the first time all season, I get locked out.

Big Daddy had instructed me to wait just until post time to make this play. As the teams line up for the kickoff, I announce my bet to a ticket writer. All the supervisors, who must approve my wager, are joking together in a small huddle. The writer calls for a key, an authorization, but nobody hears him. I call out "Key!" myself, but by the time we get anybody's attention it's too late. The ball is in the end zone; the game has started.

The Pencil and his deputies apologize. The computer locks up the game, so there's nothing they can do. I don't make a big issue of it, but I am concerned about what Big Daddy's going to say when he hears the news. To my relief he says only, "That's okay, 44. Just learn from this. Make your move just a bit sooner. Meanwhile, go play Texas A&M, plus fourteen and a half, for fifty thousand. Over and out."

I knew this bet was coming. And I know it's mathematically a good one, because of the magic half point that requires the favorite to score two touchdowns *and* a field goal to cover the spread. But I still don't like it. UCLA, I suspect, has the firepower to blow the Aggies off the field. Nonetheless, I do as I'm told. With five minutes to go before game time, Big Daddy radios me and asks, "Can you make a bet in the next five minutes?" When I tell him I can sprint, he orders me down to play Texas A&M again, this time for +14 points, for another $55,000. Personal history is made: The Cotton Bowl, UCLA vs. Texas A&M, is my biggest bet of the season, $110,000. I try not to think of the financial ramifications. I just sincerely—very sincerely—hope we win.

We do.

I almost expire from stress-induced hyperventilation, but we do. The $100,000 infusion puts us back on the positive side, up $50,500 for the week.

The fun, however, isn't over. I bet the under again—twice, on two different numbers—on the Rose Bowl. We have $99,000 riding on Washington State and a low score. The outcome remains unclear until the final seconds, but when the clock expires we've won both ways, pocketing another $90,000, swelling the week's cumulative profits to more than $140,000.

Big Daddy doesn't sit on the winnings. When the Tennessee number goes back to 14, he sends me down to bet another $55,000 on the underdogs. And minutes before the Sugar Bowl begins, he instructs me to camp out at the book and bet the underdog and the under if our numbers pop up on the board.

They don't. When I radio to report no action, Rick says. "Yeah, pards, I saw that. Doggone it, they never moved those numbers. I should have told you to bet 'em anyway. Well, we'll try to find some more winners tomorrow. You have a good night, sweet face."

. . .

In the morning, Big Daddy radios with a cheerful greeting and asks non-chalantly how much money I have at Caesars Palace. My figures show $488,600 in cash on hand and $352,000 tied up in future bets. "Here's the numbers, Rick," I report. "It's $840,600 total."

"Those numbers differ substantially from what our figures show. Hold on, please. Let me check something." There's a tense silence. "What do you have, 44?"

I repeat my figures. I keep a record of all transactions both in a ledger book and on computer accounting software, which I use meticulously to record every dollar that flows in and out of my gambling bankroll. My math is usually accurate.

"No, we have a substantial difference." I hear other voices in the background, saying things like "the two hundred thousand we brought him" and "six hundred forty." I can hear Big Daddy saying to someone. "Well, now I'm really confused." He says to me. "Hold on, 44. I'll get right back to you."

I can hear murmuring. "Tell me again what you have, 44."

I repeat the numbers again.

"That's a good number," he says, sounding relieved. "That's right."

"So we're in agreement on the totals?"

"Yes, we are," Big Daddy says. "I'll get back to you a little later if our numbers come up."

About twenty minutes before the start of the Peach Bowl, I get the call I've been expecting; surely it's time to bet the total, which has been plummeting all week. To my surprise, Big Daddy wants me to go down and bet the Pittsburgh Steelers for $55,000, at a worse number than earlier in the week. This strikes me as inexplicably strange—unless there's some sort of news (Drew Bledsoe sprained his ankle?) that the rest of the world won't hear about until the evening *SportsCenter*.

While placing my wager, I note that Auburn has fallen from a 6-point favorite to a 4½-point favorite. According to friends I've spoken to—people who have contact with the outside world—Auburn suspended a couple of its starting linebackers for team violations. So maybe when Big

Daddy wanted me to play the other side, Clemson, he wasn't actually exposing himself as a money-moving fraud, but rather he had gotten the information before everyone else and wanted to exploit his advance knowledge. As it stands, I'm stuck with a bad number (Auburn –6), hoping to get lucky. But I'm happy anyway. I feel like a husband who discovers that the suspicious late-night meetings his wife has been taking really *are* for business.

After I bet the Steelers, I notice several of the earpiece squad inching toward the counter. Apparently I've earned a reliable reputation: They all bet the Steelers before Caesars moves the number to 8.

Knowing I won't be needed for at least three hours—if not more—I request permission to take a respite from the room and spend a blissful hour hitting golf balls on a driving range. The walkie-talkie, my constant companion, lies beside the Astroturf mat. Then it's back to the hotel, where I watch a feckless Auburn squad fail to cover the spread. As expected, I lose $44,000. Big Daddy doesn't contact me until 4:30 p.m., a half hour before the Orange Bowl kickoff. He wants me to camp out and look for Tennessee getting 14 points. And he stresses that I should stay very close to the counter, since, he says, there are "other guys" looking to take the same number. I do as I'm told, but to no avail. Since no big square bettor plunks down his money on the favorite, Nebraska, the Pencil never moves his line. I have one last chance: Carlos El Gordo, a rotund Mexican, who, according to some of the gossiping clerks, is an owner of a Mexican soccer team and has been one of Caesars Palace's best customers for ten years, approaches the window. Unfortunately, one of the biggest suckers in the joint has suddenly been educated by the earpiece gang. Lately they've been hanging around El Gordo, sharing laughs and, it seems, plenty of up-to-the-minute information. According to one of the supervisors, El Gordo has suddenly started to play all the sharp sides—and has had a very big bowl week. Thus it's no surprise when he waddles up to the window and starts clamoring for the Pencil and the Suit to let him bet Tennessee at +14.

This is a revolting development. Because if big-betting squares don't take the "other" side, Stevie can't let me bet the smart side for the huge limits I'm requesting. He'd get slaughtered.

I'm fortunate not to have gotten any extra money down on the underdog Volunteers. Nebraska demolishes them—and a hefty chunk of my bankroll as well. The $110,000 loss is my biggest to date, and coupled with the Auburn debacle, adds up to the worst day I've had as a sports bettor: $154,000 down the drain. All told, who knows how much Big Daddy lost this day. Half a million? A million?

Despite the huge hit, I'm light only $14,500 for the week. With more than $250,000 on the line tomorrow, my season could still be tremendously good, depressingly bad, or disappointingly middling.

I just don't want to lose it all.

I bet $55,000 more on Pittsburgh just before game time, and my $110,000 worth of bets on the Steelers looks promising at first, with Pittsburgh scoring a spread-covering touchdown and generally paralyzing the New England offense. Then the underdogs mount an unwelcome comeback. Very unwelcome. I need this win. I tell the Pencil that when I win I don't gloat, and when I lose I don't whine. But if I lose this game I might start.

At halftime, Rick sends me down to bet a college basketball game. The $11,000 I wager somehow seems ridiculously inconsequential. I mean, it's only *$11,000.*

With less than three minutes to play, Pittsburgh has the ball first and goal at the New England seven-yard line. A touchdown will cover the spread. Three plays bring the ball within two feet of the goal line. On fourth and goal, Pittsburgh decides to go for the icing touchdown, a touchdown that will put $100,000 in my account. Instead of giving the ball to Jerome Bettis, their bruising, 260-pound running back, the Steelers call a quarterback sneak.

And get stuffed.

I've lost more than a quarter-million dollars in less than twenty-four hours.

I feel as though a virulent disease is coursing through my body, infecting my blood and destroying my organs.

Big Daddy calls with another basketball bet, and I can tell he's sick, too. He almost never comments on wins or losses, but this time he can't help himself. "We couldn't get that quarterback sneak, huh?"

Even the Pencil is sympathetic. "Don't worry, Mike. It'll get better." He looks at the San Francisco game, in progress on the amphitheater screens. "Right now, San Francisco wins by twenty. You can pencil it in." He starts to scribble the number "20."

"Can I get a towel to go with that guarantee? I need something to cry in. It's been a rough couple of days."

"Hang in there," Stevie says.

I try. Both college basketball games go down to the wire. One we win by a half point; the other we lose by 2 points. In the San Francisco football game, the 49ers lead by 16 with under a minute to play, but the Vikings drive, taking advantage of bend-not-break defense. A cheap, "meaningless" touchdown would mean a lot to those of us who bet the Niners at −13½. They hold on, pleasing both their fans and the gamblers. With the victory, we're down $45,000 for the week, but with $55,000 riding on the Packers tomorrow, we have a chance to show a small profit for the week—or a six-figure loss. This is not how I envisioned my season ending. But I'm learning. Losses are an integral part of being a winning sports bettor. One just hopes to encounter them infrequently.

Vivian consoles me in a way that only a talented woman can. For a few hours I'm not worried about tomorrow's games.

Go Packers! Twenty minutes before game time, Big Daddy Rick instructs me to camp in the sportsbook and play Green Bay for another $50,000 if the point spread goes down to 13½. It doesn't. Pencil Stevie, I suspect, is scared to move his number because he knows I'm hanging around, waiting to pounce. So I return to the room to root for my childhood home team. This has taken on a disproportionate importance: I don't want to have spent nine days in Las Vegas stuck in a luxury hotel room without showing a profit. Sure, I had hoped to clear several hundred thousand this trip. But now $5,500 seems like a good number.

The Packers, after much drama, cooperate with my master plan. In the final accounting, the bonus week, after 23 wins and 16 losses, ends up midly successful.

"Looks like we're done until the Super Bowl," Big Daddy tells me. "Unless you want to come in to play some college basketball next weekend."

Before we can finalize my schedule, Rick Matthews launches into one of his monologues about the hypocrisy and underhandedness of Super Moe Farakis over at the Hilton. Seems the Superbookie has played dirty with another of Big Daddy's soldiers, changing the line on him *after* he announces his bet. "It's like a three-card monte game over there," Big Daddy complains. "The guy's a con man." I empathize as best I can, but my mind is on another issue.

"Um, Big Daddy, how long is this arrangement going to last?" I finally stammer. "When, or how, does it end?"

"I'd like to see it go on forever," he says. "We'll do it again next season, I hope. For now, though, our arrangement extends through the end of the college basketball season. You're welcome to draw out money against your earnings at any time. But if you take it all now and we lose, you'll have to make up the difference."

I decide to take $50,000 of my $61,000, leaving room for an unlikely (but possible) $110,000 loss on the Super Bowl and March Madness. "That's fine, 44," Rick Matthews says. "No problem."

The $705,500 I withdraw from the Caesars Palace cashier cage weighs at least thirty pounds. One neat minibrick of five $10,000 slabs is going to stay behind. After all these weeks of sending all the money back to Big Daddy, the realization that some of this is actually mine is sinking in. I'm actually going to drive home to Los Angeles tomorrow with $50,000 in my luggage. I'm actually going to deposit this chunk of money at my neighborhood bank. I'm actually going to be able to do what I wish with this money.

The countless hours waiting for the phone to ring or radio to beep, the tension, the interrogations, and the subterfuge—they seem worth it now.

Six

SUPER BOWL

Super Bowl weekend, 1998! (You can't write the phrase without an exclamation point.) For bookies all over America, legal and not, it's the
biggest game of the year, attracting ten times as much wagering as any
other event, including the NBA Finals, the World Series, and the Final
Four. During the regular season, the Nevada books are usually concerned about keeping their accounts balanced, garnering equal money
on each side; on this game, they're scared to death. This is one contest on
which they don't want to gamble. Give them equal action and they're
happy to collect the substantial juice. This is why I know I might be able
to bet a huge amount of Brain Trust money—if our play is on the side
they need.

When Vivian and I check into Caesars, I can't reach Big Daddy
Matthews on his cell phone; I leave a message on his home phone. Three
hours later I still haven't heard back, so I call the cell again. When he finally answers, he explains that he's in San Diego with his football-loving
kid sister at the game. (Getting insider information direct from the Denver locker room, I suppose.) The Sarge has extra money and a new radio
for me, which he'll deliver to my room soon.

And he asks, almost as an afterthought, "How much they gonna let
you bet?"

"Six figures, for sure. If it's the side they need, could be just about anything we want."

"All right then, pards. I'll talk to you on the radio after Sarge makes the delivery," Big Daddy promises.

When Sarge arrives at my room, he unceremoniously dumps a quarter-million dollars, a radio, and his snub-nosed .45 on the bed. I'm again unable to reach the boss to confirm the delivery. He's got his radio and phone switched off. "Probably out to dinner," Sarge surmises. "He'll get in touch if there's anything important."

The transfer of $250,000 doesn't qualify?

When I go down to the sportsbook to deposit the cash, the place is already swarming with gamblers. And it's only Friday night. After noting that the line has dropped to 11—the Green Bay Packers have been favored by 12 for most of the week—I weave my way through the crowd and catch the eye of Little Mikey Brown, the imposing night manager whose shiny brown head is as recognizable as his girth. While we go about the formalities of counting a quarter-million dollars, Stevie the Pencil appears from the back office. He looks like a raccoon, as though he hasn't slept in three days. "Hey, buddy," he says, fatigue dripping in his voice. "I just wanted to tell you how much I enjoyed your article in *Sport*, the one about betting on the Super Bowl. Really well done. I read it from start to finish. It was great."

I thank Stevie, telling him how much it means to me that a real professional, a guy in the business, likes what I have to say about gambling.

"Great job," he repeats. "Listen, I'm beat. I gotta go home." Before he can get away, I ask him about the big game. "I see what's going on, and I don't like it," he says. "I'm not happy about it. The Packers are definitely the side, and even though all the money is coming in on Denver, I'm not sure we should be lowering the number. I think we'll get plenty of people taking the bad numbers—you know, eleven and a half through thirteen—so we don't need to come down. But it's not necessarily my call, if you know what I mean."

I nod. "I understand," I tell the Pencil. As he departs. I marvel that he's comfortable sharing with me, one of his biggest bettors, the straightest dope you can get. I assume it's because he takes for granted that I already know what he's confirming. I am a wannabe wiseguy, after all.

When the line bounces back up to 11½, I say, "You must have taken some big, big bets to make that move." I know the books need an avalanche of money on Green Bay to balance their accounts.

"I don't know," Mikey Brown says. "You would think so. But, hey, it's not my call."

"I mean, even if you booked a couple of six-figure wagers—is that enough to move the line at this point?"

"Let's put it this way: Not all big bets are looked at the same way," Mikey replies. "Some baccarat player bets us fifty grand, so what, right? You yourself, on the other hand—you make that same bet and we're going to take it a lot more serious. You see what I'm saying? We know you know something. A smart player like you makes a bet, we pay attention."

"Well, if that line keeps moving, you better start paying attention," I joke. In truth, since I haven't gotten instructions from Big Daddy Rick, I'm not sure what I'm supposed to do if the boys at Caesars *do* move the number drastically. I assume I'm supposed to bet the Packers at a good number—but, then again, Denver getting 13 might be my play. At the end of the day, like Mikey says, it's not my call.

Gino the Suit pops out of the back office. He's dressed impeccably in a tailored Italian three-piece, and his hair is coiffed with some sort of spray that makes it look wet and shiny. His teeth gleam as brightly as the diamond ring on his left pinkie. He's got some business to discuss, and he motions me to the end of the counter, away from curious ears. Having seen casinos bar blackjack players from their tables, I know when a manager is about to tell me he doesn't want my action anymore. My instincts tell me this isn't one of those times.

"Can I ask you a question, Mr. Konik?" Gino says. "Tell me honestly. My manager Mikey says you showed some interest in the Packers at eleven. Were you going to bet them before we moved them? Tell me the truth."

The truth is I don't have any marching orders. But Gino doesn't need to know this. "No," I tell him. "No, Gino, I wasn't. I was going to wait until tomorrow, see if you had any panic buys on Denver, people who thought the line was getting away from them. I figured it might go even lower. So even though eleven is attractive, ten and a half is even better. And ten would be pretty juicy."

"I appreciate your honesty," he replies. "And I'm going to make you a proposition. Obviously we need your action on Green Bay. How much did you deposit—two hundred thousand something? I'll let you bet a hundred thousand at eleven as long as you bet a hundred thousand at eleven and a half. What I'm saying is, I'll move the number down for you, but you've got to give me some action where it's at. What do you think?"

I can't accept Gino's offer without getting approval from Big Daddy. But I also can't reject the offer out of hand, if, indeed, this turns out to be a deal Big Daddy likes.

I think of Big Daddy, cool and collected under pressure. I feel myself getting strangely calm, as though I've taken a sleeping pill. And then I tell Gino that I'm going to gamble that the book is going to have to move its number lower as game time approaches. "I'd feel pretty stupid laying eleven and a half if I could be getting ten. I figure, come game time, you're going to be looking for a knight in shining armor to come to your rescue."

"I might need five knights. A whole Round Table," Gino says, laughing.

"You can understand; I don't want to lay a bad number," I say, relaxing.

"The only way you're not going to like laying the extra half point is if the Packers win by eleven," Gino says, smiling. He's selling hard. "And besides, I could be wrong, but I see this number moving back up, actually. This might be as low as it goes."

"We'll see about that. And who knows?" I say, planting some indecision in his mind. "If it goes high enough I might have to play Denver."

Gino the Suit tells me his offer is good until 10:30 p.m., when he goes home. "Think it over and let me know," he says.

I almost sprint to the room, Big Daddy's still unreachable. The Sarge is unreachable. The phone is off; the radio's off; nobody's home. I'll just have to let this deal pass.

Although I don't get a bet down, I learn a great deal about where my pals at Caesars Palace are at on this game, the make-or-break bet of the year. They need Green Bay. Badly.

In a short time, I should know if I need Green Bay, too.

Big Daddy Matthews remains unreachable on Saturday morning. It's nearly 10:00 a.m., and I've yet to hear from him. Though there are nearly a hundred college basketball games on the betting slate today, though Gino the Suit made a fascinating proposal for us to consider, though the Super Bowl is one day away, Big Daddy doesn't call.

I raise the Sarge on the radio. "Big Daddy still has his phones and radios turned off," I report. "What's going on?"

Sarge says he'll get back to me in a few minutes. "Doesn't look like he'll be needing you this morning. And I've relayed the information about the point spread. He'll get in touch if there's anything important. In the meantime, go out, have breakfast. It doesn't look like much is going to happen."

Indeed, Rick doesn't contact me all day. Vivian and I watch free pay-per-view movies, go to the gym, and, most rare, actually leave the room together for lunch. During my forays off the twenty-first floor, I periodically check the line. It stays stuck on 11½ all day. Either Pencil Stevie and his bookmaking colleagues are getting good two-way action or they're being stubborn. In any case, I'm on the sidelines until otherwise ordered.

Tomorrow, I sense, could be a very big day. Green Bay laying 10½? Denver plus the points? Only Big Daddy, it seems, knows the divine truth.

The leader of the Brain Trust finally calls Sunday morning at 8:00 a.m., seven hours before kickoff. He asks me if the line at Caesars Palace is still 11½.

"I haven't gone down yet, boss," I say. "But that's what it was last night."

"We're looking to take Denver, plus twelve. Denver plus twelve points. Over."

Dumbfounded, I repeat back the order. So much for being on the other side. If my number comes in—and the Pencil has indicated it will—I'm going to be betting with the public, the same public that drove the point spread down from 14 to its current state. Betting with the public is usually a good way to lose your money. But in the past seven Super Bowls, the public has been right six times. And the wiseguys have taken a beating.

Big Daddy instructs me to make periodic visits to the book. When the 12 comes up, he wants me to bet up to $220,000. I'm not sure the boys behind the counter will want to take that much, since such a wager will only make them more lopsided. Plus I'm going to have to invent a good song and dance to explain why I'm now on the square side. Making a bet this size, given the circumstances, is going to be a test.

On my first fact-finding mission, at 8:30 a.m., Stevie shakes my hand excitedly. This is a very big day for him. I look at the board and say, "Stevie, we can't stay at that number, can we?"

"No way," he says emphatically. "It's definitely going up."

That's reassuring, I think. Stevie the Pencil assumes he's going to get an avalanche of money on Green Bay. Which is what I need if I want to get Denver at the right price. Before I go, I ask Pencil Stevie for a favor. "I know it's against the rules, but do you think my girlfriend and I could take a quick snapshot in front of the counter, with the board in the background?"

"Sure, I don't care. Just do it before a security guard grabs you."

On subsequent fact-finding expeditions, the line remains stuck on 11½. But several hours remain before game time.

Around 11:00 a.m., Rick Matthews reaches me on the radio. "Hey, 44, we still got a few hours, and this number is going up everywhere. I don't think twelve is going to be a problem. Let's hold out for twelve and a half. Denver at twelve and a half only."

I copy his instructions. But when I go to check the number again, making my way through a sea of gamblers, studying their prop sheets, looking for a profitable bet among the forest of sucker plays, the line is still where it's been all morning, 11½. And it stays there through noon and 1:00 p.m. With two hours to go until kickoff, I still have no bet.

Early in the afternoon, I wander into the VIP Super Bowl party at Caesars Palace's Colosseum ballroom. There's a dizzying spread of food and beverages and pretty cheerleaders handing out official programs and hats. But most of all there are gamblers. Thousands of them. The casino's best customers. And wandering through the assembly, I get the same feeling I sometimes get milling about the sportsbook: Out of all these people, all these high-rolling, powerful people. I'm one of the biggest bettors in the throng. And certainly, thanks to Big Daddy's sports-gambling acumen, one of the best. It's a cool feeling.

What's not so great is agonizing over the line moves. It's bad enough to sweat out the result of the big game. Now I'm nervously anticipating the point-spread changes that will allow me to nervously anticipate the outcome of the game.

At 1:15 p.m., the line has moved to 12. I hang around the $10,000 minimum bet window for a few minutes to see if any whales drop enough on Green Bay to move it up another half point. The room is packed, with maybe five hundred bettors standing in line, waiting to get their action down. The $10,000 window is blissfully empty, beckoning like the carpool lane on a Los Angeles freeway at rush hour.

When I return to the room to update Big Daddy, my radio is beeping, with an "Alert!" message on the screen. "Go ahead, Big Daddy," I call out.

"All right, 44, go bet Denver plus twelve, to win up to two hundred thousand. Over."

I copy his instructions and dash back to the book. On the brief walk from the elevator to the counter, I can feel my breath increasing with a curious mixture of joy and dread. This is it. This is the year's biggest play. And it's at a number that seems, on the face of it, a bad one. Twelve points is less than two touchdowns (14), and less than a touchdown and two field goals (13). Twelve seems like a dead number. But this is it, nonetheless.

I approach the $10,000 window and tell the clerk I'm ready to gamble. Larry, a longtime clerk who's been promoted recently to supervisor, asks me what it'll be, like a butcher standing over his selection of fillets and chops. "Number one zero two: Denver, plus twelve."

"Green Bay minus the twelve?" he asks.

"No, Larry. Denver getting twelve. Do you want to call Stevie over for the amount?"

"I can just tell him," Larry says.

"Two hundred thousand," I say.

He nods. "Let me see." Larry walks over to Stevie the Pencil and Gino the Suit, who are huddled over a glowing computer screen. I can see (but not hear) their brief conversation, which includes what looks like a lot of affirmative head nodding.

Five seconds later, Larry walks back to the window. "Write it!" he orders.

The clerk is slightly flustered, since her machine only produces tickets up to $99,000. Larry calmly repeats the bet. "Two-twenty to win two hundred."

"I bet this much and I don't get a break on the juice?" I ask, smiling.

"Yeah, at Leroy's, the neighborhood bookie," Larry cracks back.

"I don't even get a free hat?"

"I'll see if I can't find something lying around in the back."

The Pencil ambles over. "So, Mikey, you were waiting for that magic number, huh? That magic twelve?"

"I know you hate the bet, Stevie. I had to go with the public on this one. You know which side has gotten the money the last few years."

"That's what I'm afraid of," Stevie says. "I personally have the Packers. This game could be a mismatch, a total blowout. It looks like it could go that way."

"Stevie, no offense," I say, shaking my head, "but I sincerely hope you're wrong."

He nods and shrugs. "Enjoy the game," he says. "I'll see you at half-time."

Gino the Suit walks past on the way to his office. He flashes me a thumbs-up. I know they're hoping I lose this game, and not just because of my $220,000, but because of the millions of other dollars they've booked on the Denver Bronco side. Pencil Stevie later confides that the nearly quarter-million I wagered was only in the top-ten bets they took. There's obviously some obscene money on this game.

When I return to the room to report my bet, Big Daddy tells me Sarge is on his way over with more cash. "We've got a play on the over-under," he says. "He'll be right over with another sixty thousand."

I'm already starting to breathe heavily. With a nearly $600,000 swing ($297,000 if we lose; $270,000 if we win), this single game could ruin my season. Or make it.

Big Daddy radios again. "The number just went from forty-nine and a half to fifty. If you go down and it's at fifty, bet seventy-seven thousand to win seventy thousand. If it's at forty-nine and a half, bet sixty-six to win sixty. We want the under. Denver *under* the number."

I copy his order and wait for the bagman. And while I do, the possibilities dance around my head: A win on both bets would put us up more than $800,000 for the football season; a loss would drag us down to near $300,000.

Viv finds much amusement in my feverish hand-wringing. "Baby, we've got to win this game," I say, almost pleading for her to intercede. She's suffered through a season of sports betting with me and now, it seems, I could lose so much of what we've worked to build. Suddenly I feel as though everything—money, love life, my very identity—is riding on this one stupid football game.

Viv smiles and giggles. "Don't worry, honey," she says. "It doesn't help."

The Sarge arrives at 2:30, forty-five minutes before the kickoff. He's got only $50,000 for me, so no matter what the number is, I'm going to be betting $66,000 on the under. I hurry down to the sportsbook, which, at this late hour, is standing room only. Gamblers are pressed shoulder to shoulder in line, hoping they'll get to the window in time. I've never seen a crowd like this in a casino, even on a heavyweight title night. The throng, I tell Stevie and Gino, is a tribute to how well they run their business. No other casino, I assure them, is doing nearly as much volume as they are—and that's because these wily managers have made Caesars Palace they premier place to bet sports in America. The so-called Superbookie over at the Hilton could learn a few lessons from these fellows.

I wiggle through the mob, eventually finding some elbow room at the

$10,000 window, where a security guard eyes me suspiciously. Perhaps he doesn't make me for a legitimate high roller. When I open my duffel bag and start stacking $10,000 piles on the counter, he nods and looks away, watching my back. A low roller from an adjacent line sidles over, asking me which team I like. "Who you betting, man?" he pleads. The security guard ushers him away.

I announce my bet to the clerk, who looks to the Pencil for approval. I make a thumbs-down signal, to express "under." He pantomimes "five," as in $50,000.

"Sixty!" I shout.

He looks at his screen and confers briefly with the Suit. "Okay," he says, nodding and frowning. "Under forty-nine and a half."

Stevie the Pencil comes over to the betting window. "Good luck, buddy."

When I report the bet to Big Daddy, he says, "All right, pards. Enjoy the game. Let's pull those Broncos in. Over and out." I've never heard him actually root for a team. But having—what? a million dollars, two million?—on a football game has a way of turning even the most sober analyst into a fan.

And for four hours that's what I become: A fan. A fanatic.

Green Bay takes the opening kickoff and promptly marches downfield, scoring a touchdown on its first possession. Brett Favre and the Packers look indomitable, awesome, an unstoppable force. I feel like I might vomit.

But then the Broncos come right back with a touchdown of their own, moving the ball effortlessly through the Green Bay defense. Maybe Denver is actually going to make a game out of what seemed like a romp. My nausea subsides momentarily.

The famous Super Bowl television commercials, which inspire viewership, commentary, and analysis of their own, bring me no amusement. They're merely thirty-second interruptions that delay the ultimate disposition of my net worth.

At halftime, with our team leading 17–14, I tell Viv we must leave Caesars' VIP Super Bowl party, because I can't handle being around other people at the moment. Every time someone cheers for the Packers, I want to slug him. Every time someone roots for my Broncos. I want to embrace him in appreciation. This is not healthy.

We retreat to our hotel room, where I throw myself around the bed like a spoiled child when a Bronco receiver drops a pass. I pump my fist like a welterweight contender when Denver scores. And I swear like a merchant marine when Green Bay does likewise.

It's $286,000 we're talking about.

Back and forth the score goes. Punch and counterpunch. Euphoria and despair. Though Green Bay never covers the spread the entire game—not once do the Packers lead by more than 12—I can't relax until Denver scores a go-ahead touchdown with less than two minutes to go. The score kills our under bet—so long, $66,000!—but it ensures our winning team bet. Hello, $200,000!

I hug Vivian and jump up and down. We've won $134,000 on the Super Bowl.

For the season, we're up $744,000.

Big Daddy calls shortly after the final gun to make pickup arrangements. He's back to his usual imperturbable self, as if nothing important has happened in the last four hours. The Sarge, we decide, will come to the room in ninety minutes. Before signing off, I say, "By the way, Big Daddy, congratulations."

"Thanks, 44. I'll talk to you later," he replies phlegmatically.

When I go to collect my winnings, the mood behind the sportsbook counter is solemn. The bookies got hurt. Given the almost guaranteed profit they reaped on the crazy proposition bets, the day was by no means a disaster for the casinos. But the players—like me—did well for themselves. Knowing this, I try not to celebrate. Instead, I thank the Pencil and the Suit for making this day so exciting and for handling a difficult challenge with aplomb. Gino tells me how proud he is of his staff and how, taking the long view, he figures this Super Bowl will do wonders for his industry. "The players are going to be happy to come back and bet some more," he says.

He's very gracious. And I tell him so. "Nobody likes to hear a bookie whine, Mike," he explains. "Nobody cares, including the bookie's mother. Because sometimes she bet the other side."

We laugh and shake hands, As I turn to go, Stevie the Pencil comes out of the back office to say good-bye. "When are we going to see you again?" he asks.

"Maybe next weekend, maybe in a few weeks. I might try to bet some college hoops," I say.

He says he would love to have me. Just give him a call.

I hope I will be seeing him—and all the boys—soon. Because I know I'll miss the action, the drama, the money, the gourmet meals, the tension, the fun, the uncertainty, the satisfaction. The game.

In the meantime, I'll content myself with my $75,000 share of the Brain Trust's winnings.

Seven

MARCH MADNESS

The month of February 1998 suggested to me what a drug withdrawal program must feel like.

When Pencil Stevie set my betting limit at $10,000 a game, Big Daddy Rick and I concluded that it wasn't worthwhile to use my peculiar services for the regular college basketball season. "If Caesars is going to let you play more like twenty thousand during the conference tournaments and so forth, well, then it's a different story," Rick said.

We agree to touch base in a few weeks. Until then, I face the harsh glare of real life. I'm back to walking the dog at daybreak, breakfasting over the newspapers, answering mail, and making phone calls to magazine editors about stories I'm supposed to submit. Unaware of my intimate connections, a monthly periodical assigns me an article on Las Vegas sports-betting syndicates, which gives me an excuse to talk with the Poker Players, Blair & Ferdinand, the IBMs, and a host of other groups that compete with the Brain Trust for the best point spreads. Pencil Stevie kindly arranges a few introductions with the notoriously tight-lipped gamblers, leaving out the bit about my being a big player at his casino. None of the boys have much to tell me that I don't already know from firsthand experience, but it's enlightening to know how admired and reviled my partner Rick Matthews is by his fellow wiseguys, none of whom will admit to being jealous of Big Daddy, though they are all grudgingly respectful of his accomplishments.

For a desolate series of fortnights, I'm back to being a writer. I feel suddenly that the allegedly romantic occupation of composing sentences on paper is the vocational equivalent of putting the same rivet into the same sheet of metal eight hours a day. Big Daddy calls me just once—to confirm that he won't need me until the start of the NCAA men's basketball tournament.

Then March arrives, that hopeful time of year when the stirrings of renaissance uplift both the natural world and the surreal one, when preternaturally tall ectomorphs from institutions of higher learning entertain us with their running, leaping, twirling, and, most impressive, astounding ability to throw an inflated orb through a distant ring.

The Madness begins.

For five weeks, I've felt depressed and distracted, longing to return with Vivian to our weekend rituals in this make-believe city, with its gaudy temples of acquisitiveness. Walking through the front doors at Caesars Palace, past the statue of Caesar, the banks of chirping slot machines, the dice tables, I feel as if I've returned to my other home, a weekend getaway that's an adrenaline-soaked engine of commerce, dripping with power and money and sex, hookers and action junkies and lonely desperadoes. My people.

It's good to be among them, but not truly one of them. I'm here to work, to filter as much money as I can through a machine with something like a 10 percent edge. I'm here to win.

Several hours before the start of the National Invitational Tournament, or NIT, the secondary contest for the teams that didn't get into the big dance, Viv and I settle into our familiar routines. She unpacks and makes restaurant reservations. I call the Boss Man.

He tells me Sarge will stop by shortly with "two-fifty, a radio, batteries, all that good stuff." In the meantime, I set up my "office" on the desk in our hotel room: computer, game schedules, ledger book. We're open for business.

When Sarge arrives at my nonsmoking suite, he courteously stubs out his cigarette in the bathroom sink. Then he offers an impromptu geography lesson at my panoramic window—"That there is Sheep Mountain," he says, pointing to the north, "lots of sheep and burros and such"—and hands me a quarter-million dollars in hundreds. Big Daddy is momentarily unreachable via phone or radio, so Sarge leaves, trusting me to report the delivery.

When I finally raise Big Daddy Matthews on the phone, he tells me to deposit the money and return to the room. "A guy named Brother Herbie—he might call himself Curt—is going to call you," he says. "I'll talk to you later, pards."

Unsure of who this mysterious Brother Herbie figure is, I head to the sportsbook for the first time in six weeks. The gang is all there.

Little Mikey Brown counts my money and Gino the Suit stops over to shake my hand and discuss limits. He offers me $10,000 on the lightly bet NIT games, although Pencil Stevie has previously promised me $15,000 minimum. We settle on an "ask for more" policy, with the understanding that I'll usually be able to bet $15,000 on NIT and $20,000 on NCAA. I don't press the point very hard. After the Super Bowl, these numbers seem comically inconsequential.

The Pencil, stopping in on his day off (the poor guy never leaves the sportsbook, it seems), greets me at the counter. "Just wanted to make sure you got in all right," he says. Which is another way of saying, "Just wanted to see how much money you brought and how much of it you want to bet, and on whom."

I give Stevie the Pencil a small gift I've been saving for him. It's a framed *New Yorker* cartoon of a football player telling an interviewer, *"It's a game of speed and power and grace. But most of all it's a game of points."* Vivian found a card to go with it that seemed appropriate: *"You just keep giving and giving . . . Keep it up!"*

I tell Stevie how much I appreciate all he's done this season. Mr. Pencil is not the kind of man to be deeply touched by anything except an accurate point spread, but I can tell he really likes my card and gift. "Fitting," he says. "Very fitting."

When I return to the room, there's a message from Brother Herbie on the hotel voicemail. A soft, southern-accented voice says he wants me to call him. He doesn't say why.

When I reach him, he says, "I guess Rick told you we would be working together, right?"

"Yes, he did. Will I be talking with you all weekend, or will I hear from Mr. Matthews again?"

"You may never hear another word from Rick this whole tournament," he says, chuckling.

I like this fellow, whoever he is. I don't know if Big Daddy is merely renting out my services to another syndicate, or if Brother Herbie is his basketball manager, or if the Brain Trust bankrolls Brother Herbie and extracts a cut of the profits, or a combination of everything. But I'll play along.

"Okay, young man, I've got some stuff I'm ready to go with," Herbie says. He gives me a couple of orders. Before I go, he shares a few other plays he'd like to make if the numbers move—Big Daddy, apparently, has informed Brother Herb that I can be trusted with the information. We review my camp-out-and-call-in strategy. I'll look for the numbers, bet if they appear, and report back at predetermined intervals for updates.

"That sounds good," Herbie says.

Since I'm making a fresh start with this new handler, I propose some schedule guidelines that I wish Big Daddy would follow more assiduously. I tell Brother Herb that I'm completely available to him from the start of the day until the last tip-off. But if he knows that he's done with me for the day, or for a chunk of time in the middle of the day, please let me know.

"No problem," Herb replies. "In fact, you want to take a couple hours for lunch, or whatever, just let me know."

I *really* like this guy. Big Daddy is brilliant and tough and easily displeased. Brother Herbie is *nice*.

He also seems to know a little something about handicapping college basketball. The two plays he gives me for the NIT are winners, as are his first two NCAA picks. It all seems way too easy. Which, I'm certain, means it *is* all too easy. Which means things must inevitably change for the worse.

The crowd in front of the Caesars Palace sportsbook counter is enormous—almost as big as for the college football bowl games. As usual, I feel anointed, *different*, waltzing into the horde of gamblers. I've got the secrets. I know something. Never mind that I'm playing with borrowed funds and rented expertise, that I'm an unclothed emperor hiding behind a façade of bravado and bullshit. I've been successfully transformed by that vacuous pop culture imperative, *Believe in yourself*. I know I'm just "44," an actor playing a role. I know I'm not Big Daddy incarnate. But the constant pretending, the believing in an obvious fiction, has made me into something more—at least when I prowl into a Las Vegas sportsbook. Just as a famous movie star with a fanciful stage name and an expensive publicist understands that when the lights are extinguished and the makeup's removed he's still just a farmboy from Iowa, I know who I am.

But I'm loving the charade while it lasts.

Bypassing the queues, I sidle up to the $5,000 minimum window and give the boys a $20,000 bet on West Virginia, getting 3½ from Temple. "Somehow I knew you'd be betting West Virginia," Adam, one of the supervisors, says to me as he takes my wager.

"How'd you know?" I ask, wondering if Brother Herbie has gotten me heated up early.

"Just had a feeling," he says, smiling.

Hot or not, the underdog Mountaineers win the game by 30 points. Clearly, something weird was happening with this game, and, as usual, I'm the only guy who has no idea what that thing is. Which, in a way, is perfect for my big-player image. Let the wiseguys trade in hot information; I just wanna bet.

An hour after placing another $20,000 wager on a team I know Caesars needs, I'm lounging in my suite, waiting for more orders, when Herbie makes a courtesy call, informing me there won't be any more action until at least 2:30 in the afternoon.

I tell him I'll be back in the room, ready to go, at that time.

"Thank you kindly, sir," he says.

With three hours free in the middle of the day, I can walk slowly, browse the overpriced boutiques filled with what Viv calls "slutwear," do nothing. It's fun. After checking on the sportsbook—it's still rocking with business—I walk over to the Mirage, hoping to find my poker player friend Spanish Joe. After an unsuccessful search, I return to Caesars Palace, have a low-roller salad bar lunch that fractionally offsets the 5,000-calorie high-roller supper waiting at the Palace Court, and pop back into the casino. It's still crowded. This is good. The more tickets Pencil Stevie and his boys write, the more comfortable they are fading my large action. As long as Caesars Palace is winning, they don't care if I'm winning.

Which I am. Halfway through day one, we're up $55,000. And the games Herbie has given me all seem to be sides Stevie the Pencil needs, or at least wants. I don't bet anything *with* a line move. All my wagers are *against* a line move. Stevie doesn't move his number unless he's trying to attract action on the other side. So, in effect, we're rooting for the same side. I win, he wins.

After lunch, Brother Herbie's next order is for an early game tomorrow. He urges me to see if the sportsbook will take more than $20,000. "The number has been moving down, so they might want it," he suggests.

When I make the bet, I propose going higher. Caesars doesn't want it. Twenty thousand is enough. I don't argue. I can see that dozens of gamblers hanging around the counters are watching what I do, hoping to get some hot tips from a young guy betting at the $5,000 window. The last thing I need is more attention.

When I report the bet to Herbie, I remark that Mr. Caesar might have been more willing to take more if we hadn't gone 3–0 on him. A comment like this would normally elicit a vitriolic diatribe from Big Daddy.

Brother Herbie merely says, "Thank you, sir."

As our afternoon game is coming to a conclusion—another $20,000 win—he sends me down to camp out at the counter. He—or is it the Brain Trust?—is hunting for three special numbers.

On the way to the sportsbook, I stop to get a frozen fruit bar. And I get an extra one for the Pencil. These little gestures—bringing him a snack, a small gift—are too inconsequential to be seen as an outright bribe, but friendly enough that when it comes time to make a tough call about my action, he might be more likely to be an advocate. For the same reason, I've invited him to lunch with me during an upcoming trip he has planned to Los Angeles, where he's going to see a few Yankees games at Edison Field.

As we slurp our frozen confections, one of the point-spread numbers I'm looking for pops up on the toteboard. I say to Pencil Stevie, "As long as I'm here delivering your lunch, let me make a bet."

Before I can announce my play, he says, "I know, San Francisco plus the ten and a half."

"You got it!" I say, smiling.

"Yeah, I laid that one out just for you, Mr. K."

How he can predict which game I'm going to bet I don't know. But I've learned not to sweat these mysteries. I don't even pretend to understand how Herbie and Rick Matthews handicap college basketball games, so, of course, there's no way I could know why San Francisco is a play at +10½. I'm like a devout religious acolyte. I just know it is because my gurus say so.

While I wait for my other numbers, a few heavy hitters, including Fat Carlos, the wised-up sucker from football season, approach the $5,000 window. I'm hoping they'll bet on the other side of the games I need. Unfortunately, one of them, a biker dude in a Harley-Davidson T-shirt, bets San Francisco, at a worse number than I got. I sense the Pencil eyeballing me, trying to discern if I know this bettor, if he's with me. I'm hoping my body language suggests I've never seen this guy before in my life, which is the truth.

Turns out Pencil Stevie ought to have adored all the action on San Francisco. It ends up getting buried by Utah.

My other two numbers don't come up, so I retreat to my room and await further orders. Shortly after 6:00 p.m., Herbie calls for the last time. "Let's wrap this thing up," he drawls. "Go play Nicholls State, getting twenty-six and a half."

"That's a good bet," the Pencil assures me, doodling what look like toy soldiers. That he originally opened Nicholls as a 19-point underdog might have something to do with his opinion. This line has soared 7½ points. "Tell you what," Stevie says, pointing his pencil at me. "I'll give you an extra half point if you can tell me Nicholls State's nickname."

I don't even know what state university system Nicholls proudly represents. Hoping this isn't a test, I say, "I honestly have no idea, Stevie. But I am sure of one thing. They're getting twenty-six and a half big points."

"The Colonels!" Stevie roars, retreating into his office. "Go, Colonels!"

"Go, Colonels," I mumble weakly.

Sadly, the Colonels suffer a string of battlefield casualties and get destroyed by 39 points. For the day we're up $31,000.

With dozens more games to come.

"Here comes trouble," Adam, the counter supervisor, says as I approach the $5,000 window, reaching out to shake my hand.

"Give me a hundred thousand on the Radford money line!" I jokingly bellow. At 50–1 odds against Duke, I'm looking at a $5 million score.

"Yeah, sure, we'll write that ticket," Adam says, playing along.

I know a seven-figure win is out of the question, but a nice six-figure one isn't. I anticipated the tournament would be a roller-coaster ride—with, I hope, more highs than lows—and I'm not wrong. On Friday we win two of three and pocket $27,000. Saturday afternoon I win two more bets, bring our profit to $67,000. And then, in the evening, we bet Illinois State getting 15½ from the number-one seed, Arizona. The line opened at 12½. I know Pencil Stevie is going to *love* my wager.

In fact, when I make it, he fairly begs me to take more. "Where you been? I've been waiting for you," he says.

"Your knight in shining armor, right?"

"We're buried on the other side. Take as much as you want," he offers. But since Brother Herbie has only authorized me to wager $20,000, I decline.

"The offer stands," he reminds me.

"We're on the same team, Stevie," I tell him. "You and me against all the wiseguys."

When I report my conversation to Brother Herbie, he tells me that the Illinois State number has actually moved up to 16 at some places around town. "I could never dream it would go that high. We might take some more a bit later. Stand by."

We end up standing pat on our original bet. Which turns out to be a good decision. Illinois State plays marvelously in the first half, staying within 3 points of mighty Arizona. In the second half, though, Arizona outscores Illinois by 30 points. What looked like an $87,000 weekend quickly disintegrates into a $45,000 one.

Ah, gambling.

Sunday morning I'm still asleep, Viv's dark tresses resting on my shoulder, feeling the aftereffects of a tasty Margaux from the night before, when Brother Herbie calls at 8:00 a.m. "Rush right down and take Florida State, minus seven and a half. You gotta hurry," he instructs me.

I don't tell him that I'm not dressed or wearing my contact lenses. To save time, I throw on pants (sans underwear) and put my shoes on in the elevator. When I get to the book, my vision is so blurry I can barely make out the numbers on the toteboard.

Since this game opened at 6 and has climbed steadily upward, I know Stevie the Pencil isn't going to be thrilled with my bet. I tell him I want Florida State almost apologetically.

"Fifteen thousand, Mike, That's all I want."

"No problem. I understand."

I leave quickly, hoping nobody noticed any drool stains on my chin.

When I tell Brother Herbie what transpired, he says, "I understand, 44. And I'm tickled to death to get fifteen at this number. Good job, partner."

This is clearly a hot game. Herbie rings back thirty minutes later and asks me to bet another $15,000 at 8 points. I tell him I'll do it if he really wants me to, but that I believe Stevie might be furious. "The guy is buried on this side, Herbie. If you want to take the long view, hitting him hard while he's down might cost us in the future when we want to bet a bundle on a side he needs. I'll do it," I say. "But it might not be good for our long-term health."

"I understand," Herbie replies. "No problem. Gotta run, 44."

Is he one of the Brains? Is he the leader of his own syndicate? Is he actually Rick's brother? (They have the same southern drawl and courtly manner.) Who is Brother Herbie?

"Why don't you just ask Rick?" Viv suggests.

"Just ask him?"

"Right. Invite him to dinner. Spend an evening with him. And ask him what's on your mind," she urges. "I'll go with you if you need your hand held."

"I don't know . . ."

"Why are you such a pussy when it comes to Rick Matthews? It's like you live in mortal fear of the man," Vivian observes. "Just call him up and make a date. Do it!"

I feel like I'm back in high school, trying to work up the nerve to ask out a girl I'm not sure really likes me. My finger trembles as I push the phone buttons. "Hi, Rick? It's me, 44, over here at Caesars."

He says he would *love* to have dinner with me. "Is it all right if I bring my sister?"

We agree to meet at a neighborhood Italian joint they like, a dimly lit place where the maître d' has Rick's favorite appetizer (fried zucchini) brought to the table as soon as he arrives. The four of us make small talk through the courses, but Viv's persistent kicking under the table reminds me I'm here for a purpose. "I was wondering," I blurt out, "are you and Herbie related? Is he your brother?"

Rick and Kathryn Matthews-Reynolds explode in laughter. Big Daddy howls. "I tell you what!" He breaks down in hysterics again.

"I guess not," I say, shrugging.

"No, I'm not making fun of you, 44. It's just funny, see, because we call him Brother Herbie because back in Arkansas he actually was a monk at one time."

"Stop it," I say. "Come on."

"No, really. I'm serious," Big Daddy Rick says, somewhat seriously. "His name is Herb Curtis. You can look it up probably. He was in the seminary, or the monastery, or whatever you call it. He was going to be priest, I reckon. Well, the only problem was, he liked to bet on football games."

"You're kidding," I say, looking to Viv for reassurance. Is this all a ruse?

"No joke, 44. The man's a degenerate gambler. Dice, horses, sports— he just loves to bet. He might have gone the religious route to, you know, find a cure. But—and this is the funny part—he ended up booking games, taking bets from all the other monks. Nice fellow and all, but not exactly the kind of man you want taking confession."

I wonder out loud if Brother Herbie is the head of his own organization.

"Shit, he couldn't hold on to the money long enough," Rick guffaws. "Herb Curtis works with me. He's part of the Brain Trust. Just like you."

"He's a beard? A front man?"

"Well, no. He's one of my primary associates. We go way, way back."

Kathryn Matthews-Reynolds interjects, "Herb Curtis is a dear friend. He's one of our most valuable associates. And so are you."

"And does he handicap the basketball games?"

Rick starts laughing uncontrollably again. "Hell, no. We've got professionals for that. We've got two basketball experts we rely on, along with our trusty old computer. Don't you worry, 44, you're not betting for Brother Herbie. You're betting for the Brain Trust."

"Who are these professional handicappers?" I ask impertinently.

"Come on now, 44, you don't expect me to give away the store just yet, do you?"

There's so much more I want to ask, so many more secrets I want revealed. But Big Daddy flashes me a look that says enough for now. So I refrain from further questioning.

Then we have dessert.

The next afternoon, while I'm waiting for further orders from the Defrocked One, my friend Timid Joe Corcoran helps me figure out my exact expectation on each bet I make. Aside from my high-school classmate Andy Shubert, Joe Corcoran is about the smartest guy I know. A fearless poker player accustomed to staring down the sternest competition, Timid Joe is a soft-spoken lamb of a man with the heart of a lion. Polite, quiet, and exquisitely well mannered around the ladies—his reputation as a lothario is legendary—the Timid One has a way of lulling his poker opponents into a willing trance. He's also a math expert. By analyzing a season's worth of bets with Big Daddy, we're able to derive what my edge is, on the basis of wins and losses over a 160-game sample period. The figure we come up with is an astounding 15.4 percent edge. In other words, for every $1,000 put into play, I should win $154. (Indeed, for the current week, I've put about $285,000 into play and won $45,000—which is almost exactly what my expectation says I should earn.) This is one of the largest advantages you'll ever find in the world of gambling, save for cheating or being the casino in a keno game. If our numbers are accurate—though they might not be, since one season might be too small to give an entirely accurate picture—Big Daddy and I have an almost 0 percent long-term chance of going broke and an almost 100 percent chance of making a pile of money.

"This is a gold mine," Timid Joe announces, looking over our calculations. "Actually, it's even better than gold."

None of the long-term expectation is possible, of course, if I don't remain in action at Caesars Palace. Which means I *must* remain in Gino and Stevie's good graces. Which is tough to do if I'm beating them for thousands of dollars every weekend while soaking up complimentary French wines and chilled lobsters delivered to my suite. When I see Gino the Suit at the counter, however, he shakes my hand and asks if there's anything he can do for me. I tell him everything is great, but if he'd like to put in a reservation for next Wednesday, when the tournament resumes, I'll be back.

Flashing a blinding smile, he says he'd be glad to.

I feel like a valued customer, and in a sense, I really am. Because when the boys need me to take a side for a bunch of money—as they do later in the afternoon—I'm the one guy who can step up to balance their books. This happens on the last game of the day, when Herbie instructs me to take Rhode Island and the points against favored Kansas for up to $30,000. The Pencil takes the wager immediately and tells me to hang around, because he might need even more. I'm done with my Rhode Island business, but I give him $30,000 more on Purdue, another side he desperately needs. Again, we're gambling partners.

To our delight, both sides prove to be winners. That I've won $60,000 doesn't trouble him. At the end of the day, as Stevie is tucking his #2 scribbler behind his ear and saying good night to his crew, he pauses as he walks away and says to me, "Hey, Mike, great day."

The NIT games don't begin until 4:30 p.m., but Herbie wants me to go down and check on a proposition bet. Seems he and his gang have already bet Purdue, at 8–1, to win its region for $10,000. They want to hedge their bet and lock in a guaranteed profit by betting the region's other remaining team, Stanford, at 3–1. Only problem is, Pencil Stevie has taken the future props for this region off the board, since the favorite, Kansas, is out of the tournament. "What the hell," Herbie muses. "See if he'll go for it."

The answer is he won't. And I don't dare push the issue, since alarm bells might start going off if the Pencil connects my bet to Brother Herbie's crew. So instead we chat and he almost talks me into making a few silly wagers on 50–1 Masters long shots. But I respectfully demur. "Best numbers in town, Mr. K," Pencil Stevie cajoles me, drawing dozens of crosshatched number signs on an old racing form.

"I don't see how you guys can make any money at these prices," I joke. "You're practically giving it away."

"No, we can't make any money," Stevie concurs, smiling. "Especially when the public bets Denver in the Super Bowl!"

When I report back, Herbie says, "So, Stevie's saving Stanford for himself. I guess that's his only out. Well, we better hope Purdue dusts them."

I say, "Stevie is the one sportsbook manager I've met in this town with an opinion. He's not afraid to make a tough call."

"Well, don't give him too much credit," Herbie says, chuckling. "He's got a handicapper working for him, a guy he lets bet first, before the lines are even up. That's where most of his opinions come from."

"Jimmy something?" I ask. "I heard about this." Big Daddy, in fact, had suggested that this was the case.

"No, not anymore. The guy he uses they call Brooklyn."

"Brooklyn Red?" I say, remembering a wee man with an ancient Red Sox cap who introduced himself to me one afternoon in the sportsbook.

"Yeah, that's him."

"Little guy. Wears a Red Sox cap. Has a strong New York accent."

"Yeah. Bug eyes."

"Sure, I see him down there all the time," I say. Brooklyn Red is something of a legend in the sportsbooks of Las Vegas. While researching my article about sports betting syndicates, I learned from two of my sources that Red's worked for most of the big groups at one time or another. And what makes him unusual in this modern age of parallel-processed algorithms is that he reportedly doesn't use computers or any other technological tool. He simply has what sports bettors call "feel." Vegas gamblers say that Brooklyn Red can feel the texture of a contest, that he can discern where the value hides. They say he's remarkably good. And now he's helping shape Pencil Stevie's lines.

Funny, when I met Brooklyn at the sportsbook, I figured he was a hundred-dollar-a-day runner.

After a couple of much-needed days off back home in Los Angeles, I return to the Vegas office with Viv in tow. Herbie has told me that I won't be needed until late in the afternoon, shortly before the NCAA games begin, so my girl and I spend the day outside, near Caesars Palace's new pool complex. The pale and pasty world of point spreads and line moves seems a continent away from this glowing land of frozen daiquiris and suntans.

Still, I'm compelled to have my Brain Trust radio tucked into Vivian's tote bag, and inevitably I'm wrenched back into the fray by a beeping alarm. Herbie instructs me to play West Virginia +5 against Utah. We've won twice with the West Virginians, and this suggests he's recognized some inherent value in them, but, on the other hand, we're getting a point less than we might have gotten if I had bet them two days ago.

When I approach the counter, I wave to the boys, Gino, Stevie, and Little Mike, but I don't get a warm feeling. And when I announce my bet, telling the clerk to ask the Pencil how much he wants—I've been authorized for up to $30,000—the decision makers huddle around their computer screen for what seems like a minute. I can't hear what they're saying, but Stevie the Pencil seems to be scribbling some figures on a notepad—which isn't out of the ordinary. But there's much solemn nodding. Finally Stevie holds up three fingers—signifying $33,000 to win $30,000.

I nod. "To win thirty thousand," I tell Monica, the clerk. She asks me for my player number.

I tell her, "Five, nine, seven."

"Blackjack," she says. And I realize all season I've been playing with an account number whose digits add up to twenty-one. If that doesn't guarantee success, nothing will.

When I report my bet to Herbie, I mention that Pencil Stevie didn't bother moving the line.

"Yeah, he outwaited me," Herbie says morosely. "I was waiting for the sucker to go to five and a half. But he never moved it." This amounts to a minor victory for the bookie. That extra half point, the seemingly inconsequential difference between a point-spread tie at 5 and a win at 5½, is probably worth around 2 percent in long-term expectation, or return on investment.

Herbie says, "It looks like we're done for the night, 44. If you could be ready around ten tomorrow morning, there's a few NIT numbers we're looking for."

I tell him I'll be ready. And before I sign off, I can't resist asking a handicapping question. "Hey, Herbie, what's going on with the Washington game? It's moved from seven to nine and a half. Is there some sort of news? Is it public money?" I'm trying to figure out why we're not playing this large point-spread jump.

"Well, we bet the other side at eight, and the public liked it at nine. That's basically it."

Funny, I know now which is the smart side, and I can't do anything to capitalize on my knowledge. The good number, as sports bettors say, is gone.

Since I've been relieved of my duties, I decide to make an informal visit to the sportsbook. I don't want the guys there to feel I show up only if I'm betting. I also want to see if there's some sort of tension I should be aware of. I'm in search of friendliness.

I find none. Nobody says anything to me, though I conspicuously hang around in front of the counter, looking at the toteboard. Nobody so much as makes eye contact with me. Plus, I see a couple of guys in suits I've never seen before. Corporate watchdogs, I imagine. One of them eyes me warily.

Something is brewing, or I'm just imagining things.

Despite my bad number, West Virginia escapes with another point-spread victory, raising my NCAA take to $117,000 for the week. If the Caesars Palace boys have a beef with me, I'll surely hear it now. When I go downstairs in the morning I don't sense any problem.

Later in the day, Brother Herbie wants me to bet Connecticut for up to $50,000. For this, I need to chat with the Pencil. Following some idle chatter about golf, I tell him I want to bet tomorrow's game—how much does he want?

He consults his screen, has a brief talk with Gino the Suit, and tells me he'll go $30,000.

"That's what you're comfortable with?" I ask, knowing not to push the issue.

"Yeah, I'm comfortable with that."

I ask him if I were to bet tomorrow's other game—Utah vs. Arizona—if he would be similarly comfortable with $30,000.

"I would think so," he says cagily.

Gino the Suit stops by to say hello. He shoots his cuffs repeatedly, and we get into an extended conversation about my play—or lack thereof—in the gaming pits. He says he understands why I don't regularly play roulette or baccarat in his casino, games that have a house advantage. "You're a very calculating guy. Very smart. You weren't even sure you were going to bet the Super Bowl, or college basketball. You don't want to bet on anything if you don't have an edge. Casino people are wary of that kind of player."

This raises the question, Why is the Suit letting me play in his sportsbook, especially when I'm winning hundreds of thousands of dollars? I don't know the answer, but as long as I stay in action, I can make money for everyone. In truth, Caesars Palace might not be the best place for me to play blackjack or any other beatable game, especially if the pit bosses know Gino the Suit, who will be likely to tell them what he told me: "Mr. Konik? Very smart. Very calculating."

This, it occurs to me, is how most people would describe Big Daddy, along with a warning. While talking on the phone with a gambling buddy, a world-class blackjack player, I'm told again that Big Daddy is the biggest snake in the business, a guy who would screw his own mother to make a buck. "He's a lowlife cheat, a scoundrel, a thief."

I don't doubt my friend's sincerity. But I've never experienced anything to support the accusations. Rick's most commonly mentioned offense—playing the opposite side of a game from his partners—is something he can't afford to do with me. I'm his biggest outlet. If there's any chicanery going on, I'm probably benefiting from it.

"I don't know what that guy is doing down there at Caesars," Brother Herbie tells me, shortly before the Utah-Arizona tip. "He moved his number down to ten, and there's eleven all over the place."

"Either it's a money move or Pencil Stevie's got an opinion," I surmise.

"Probably an opinion. Everyone is betting on Arizona. He's probably scared that if he moves it to eleven you'll go and bet him on Utah." Herbie chuckles. "And he's right."

"He knows I've been playing all the 'dogs." I also know the Pencil believes there's inherent value in betting against the heavily hyped favorite. And that I agree with him.

We never get any money down on the game. Utah, by far the underdog, wins by 25 points. For the sake of a measly half point, we miss out on the easiest point-spread win of the tournament.

On the other hand, for the want of a measly point, we lose $33,000 on Connecticut. We get ten points; they lose by eleven.

After the game, Herbie calls me to say we're done for the night, but that we're definitely going to have a play tomorrow. "If you see Stevie tonight, you might ask him if there's any chance Duke might go to one and a half or two. Let's try to put some reverse psychology on this guy. I'm thoroughly convinced the reason he didn't move the Utah number was because he was scared you would bet it. I'm sure there will be plenty of Kentucky money tomorrow, but let's get the ball rolling in the right direction."

So the play will be Duke. The only catch will be getting that measly, magic half point.

It's my last day of the season, the last chapter in my gambling adventure. I feel something dramatic should happen, something climactic to put a fitting exclamation point on what has been a stupendous journey. For this reason, I'm terribly disappointed that on my ultimate day as the biggest sports bettor in Las Vegas, our organization doesn't have a single play. Not one. Herbie has a couple of numbers in mind, but thanks to Pencil Stevie's stubbornness—he seems to have become obstinate about moving any lines until *after* I bet them—none of them come up. I spend my last day at Caesars Palace waiting impatiently, doing nothing, itching for action.

A runner I recognize from another syndicate joins me in front of the counter, waiting hopefully for Mr. Stevie to put up a bettable number. I've made it a practice not to talk with other gamblers in the sportsbook, but this guy I've seen all season, and I even know whom he plays for, an East Coast contingent known as the Yarmulkes. Of all the betting teams, they were the most candid with me my while I researched my sports-betting story. The information they volunteered deepened my conviction that the Las Vegas sports-betting scene is one big Kabuki theater in which everyone plays his role and pretends he doesn't see the other guy's costume. So when the runner chats me up about the toughness of Caesars Palace's line, I begrudgingly commiserate. "You can't bet into these numbers," I agree. "They're too good."

The Pencil sidles over to us, two high rollers in wait. "If you're not betting, Mike, I know I must be doing something right."

I'm depressed. I'm on the sidelines. I'm a watcher.

We only want Duke at pick—no point spread, "pick" the winner without giving or taking handicap points. The Blue Devils close at −1, so we have no bet. When they take a 17-point lead with nine minutes to play,

I'm feeling sick, like a guy who's just watched $3,000 of his money float away on a craps table. But Duke manages to blow its lead and the game, and I feel like the luckiest schmuck in the world.

When Herbie calls me to say we're finished, that there won't be any bets on the Final Four, I have a bit of time to do a final accounting before Sarge comes to take the money.

For the season we're up $828,000.

I've established a reputation around town as one of the smartest sports bettors in the business.

And I can only pray Big Daddy and Stevie the Pencil and all the rest of the boys will let me come back next football season and play some more.

SEASON TWO

Summer 1998–Spring 1999

Eight

PERSONA NON GRATA

All spring I work as a writer, flying around the country for interviews, meeting deadlines, being responsible. One of the stories I write—a fictionalized tale about the world's biggest sports bettor—will hit the newsstands in late summer. If anyone asks me about it, I plan to say that it isn't really any one guy's story, that it's a composite portrait of everyone and everything I know about how sports betting works at the highest levels. This is sort of true. I worry, though, that sophisticated readers will think Mr. Konik knows a bit too much about the inner workings of the world's biggest wagering syndicates to be just a mere observer.

If my magazine articles about gambling have awakened new suspicions in Stevie the Pencil, he's not saying. A few weeks after the college basketball season concludes, in April, when baseball becomes the object of America's sports obsession, Stevie and his girlfriend Judy are in Los Angeles to watch a few ball games. I've suggested lunch somewhere flashy, something Hollywood—Wolfgang Puck's place, perhaps—but the Pencil says that would make him uncomfortable. He just wants something simple. Italian maybe. "Nothing fancy," he requests. "That ain't me."

The four of us rendezvous at a cheerful Mediterranean café on the Sunset Strip, a few minutes from my house. How strange it is to see Stevie in mufti, away from the pressures of the sports-betting world. Looking at him in his Yankees jacket and T-shirt, you would never suppose he's one of the most important figures in the world of sports gambling, the man who sets the point spreads at the premier casino in Las Vegas. Throughout lunch I try to gauge how much he knows, how much he believes, how much I can continue to get away with. He *must* know I'm connected to Big Daddy by now. He must. But then how can he let me keep playing? A few more glasses of Chianti and I might ask him. *Yo, Stevie, what's the deal? Who's paying you off?*

Fortunately, I make it through the afternoon without any significant faux pas. Either he knows I'm Big Daddy's boy (and doesn't care for some reason) or he doesn't know (and isn't particularly curious). So I don't have to pretend I'm a Hollywood big shot, or a degenerate gambler, or the smartest sports handicapper in the Western Hemisphere. I just have to be me: a guy who truly enjoys betting enormously large sums of money at Stevie's casino.

A month later, however, when I'm back in Vegas for the annual World Series of Poker, my real and imagined personas collide. I'm a high roller. I mean, that's the role I've been playing. Thirty thousand dollars on a college basketball game? A hundred thousand on a football game? Two hundred thousand on the Super Bowl? No problem! So when I run into Stevie the Pencil at Binion's Horseshoe, where his girlfriend Judy works as a blackjack dealer, I have trouble explaining what I'm doing playing in a $220 poker tournament, trying to win a $10,000 entry into the Main Event of the World Series of Poker.

A meager ten grand is supposed to be hardly worth my time.

"I like to use it as a warmup for the real thing," I say, neglecting to mention that competing for an entry into the "real thing" is about all my heart can handle. The truth is, I'd considered simply buying in for the World Championship. I figured it would be a good tax deduction against my sports winnings. But actually plunking down $10,000—of my own money—was too frightening for my low-rolling constitution.

So here I am at the Horseshoe, with the other scufflers, trying to win my way into a game with the big boys. And here comes the Pencil.

We chat briefly while I play, and I can't detect any obvious surprise or confusion in his eyes as he observes my action. He knows; he *must* know. He's got to know I'm merely the spawn of a much bigger fish.

Then I win the tournament.

And when I do, I cry for joy. I've made it into the finals of the World Series of Poker. I'm going to be competing for the title of World Champion—and more than $1 million. I don't tell Pencil Stevie about the tears part, the elation the next day when he calls to see how the tournament went. "Oh, fine," I say nonchalantly. "I won it."

"You won it?" Stevie exults.

"Yeah," I say, like what else is new?

In July, when the sun scorches the Mojave and any sensible person is far away from Nevada, I'm in Las Vegas for writing-related business. Magazine article research. Real-world stuff. And I can't resist a trip to Caesars Palace to visit the boys. Not going would be like traveling to my hometown and not seeing my mother.

The Pencil is gone by the time I get there. (This particular day is possibly the first one in a decade that the man has left before 7:00 p.m.) But Gino the Suit is still at work, and in addition to setting me up for a comped sushi feast, he shares an unusually candid conversation he recently had with even bigger suits than he. The gist of which is this: The new owners want to run Caesars Palace, one of the great gambling joints on earth, like a motel, not a world-class casino. Thus, despite his best efforts at educating the paper pushers upstairs, Gino thinks he's going to have a tough time offering me the limits I enjoyed last year. "We could do record numbers," he laments. "But they won't let us."

The Suit is smart and articulate and charming. But I can read between the lines: Don't plan on milking Caesars Palace for hundreds of thousands of dollars in the upcoming season.

I haven't spoken to Big Daddy since March. I've been putting off calling him, procrastinating until just a few weeks before the football season starts. Truth is, he makes me nervous. Viv says she can detect this in my voice when I'm on the phone with him. She says I sound frightened.

Maybe it's because I can't quite figure him out. My theory is that while sports gambling is most certainly about the money, for Rick Matthews it's really not about the money. This is a game that measures its winners and losers by the amounts they add (or subtract) from their bankroll. But, more telling, it's a game that almost nobody can conquer. Big Daddy is the man who can beat it. He's the man who sends thousands of bettors and bookies scrambling for the phone when he releases one of his plays. He is the source.

And I think he *loves* it. He loves it enough to put up with the hassles, with the annoyances, with the rules being changed on him every season to make what he does even harder than it already is. He loves being a winner. And I suspect he'll never grow tired of that. Still, were Big Daddy to become disgusted enough with the state of his business—and I can sense, from his regular sermons on the transparent hypocrisy of his tormentors, that he is getting close to this threshold—he might just take his tens of millions, unplug his phones and computers, and play golf every day.

I just hope that day is not today. Like an infatuated teenager clinging to a distant object of affection, part of me is scared to hear that he and I might officially be over.

Not only is Big Daddy polite and engaging when I reach him on his cell phone—"Howya doin', pards?"—he's eager to continue our partnership. "I did great with you last year. Every week you didn't play we lost. You're my good luck charm, 44." He instructs me to confirm my limits at Caesars Palace and to get back to him soon. He says this season I'll be set up with a full-time radio and charger, so he can reach me at any time.

I ask if during the new campaign there might be any way of avoiding having to withdraw the money from Sarge and deposit it every weekend.

"Sarge is no longer with the organization," Big Daddy says matter-of-factly.

Lack of discretion? Or maybe something worse? I want to ask, but I know better. "We gotta have some way of getting at the money if something should happen to you. Maybe we'll set up some sort of joint account. Someone they would never connect to me in a million years. That way we could leave the money set. And we could make some plays early in the week, too. Before you get there."

I tell him I like that idea. Sure, counting half a million dollars is exciting the first two or three times. But I'd rather be spending the hour that it takes at dinner with my girlfriend. I come away from our phone call slightly giddy. Looks like we're still in business.

The following Monday afternoon, however, Big Daddy tells me he just got out of a lunch meeting with Bruce Loren, the president of the Tropicana. "He asked me if I was partners with this Konik fellow," Big Daddy reports.

Seems some people have been asking about me, especially since the magazine story came out. "I told him flat out, no," Big Daddy says. "I guess in retrospect we both sort of regret you writing that article."

I tell Rick what I've been telling everyone who asks: it's a composite, a pastiche of everyone. Big Daddy likes that explanation, but he thinks the Tropicana is going to be a bit too hot to fool with for now. "There may be an opportunity in the future," he says. "I just think we should stay away from them for the time being."

I give the boss man a rundown on our current relationships: cordial at Caesars, still good at Harrah's. "But I don't know if that will last if we keep having seasons like this last one," I remark.

"Now, 44, that's not necessarily so," Big Daddy replies. He says my perspective has been colored by my experiences at Caesars and the Hilton. Irv Rosenbaum at Harrah's, he explains, might not be as jumpy as Super Moe and Pencil Stevie. Irv might think he's got the best of it and figure he'll just keep letting me gamble until I destroy myself. "And besides, pardsy," Big Daddy repeats, "you have no idea what I'm doing on my end to keep you cool. No idea at all."

I tell Big Daddy I don't need to know—as long as he's satisfied with the results. Clearly, he's sensitive to the fragility of my situation and will do everything he can to keep me in play. I just want to stay alive for enough weeks, enough games, to keep the money mill churning and the fantasy wheel spinning. I want to live it up before I die.

Vivian packs her short dresses, the ones she wears only to dens of iniquity. I assemble my betting paraphernalia—the sports schedules and point-spread charts and ledger books. We're going back to Nevada.

How sweet it is: the stretch limo waiting at the airport; the charmingly overdecorated suite with a stunning view of the Strip; reservations for the fancy steakhouse. The 1998 football season and another spectacular Las Vegas weekend begin—except that, unlike the other coddled pigeons roosting in their gold-trimmed nests, I have a decent chance of flying the coop with more birdseed than I arrived with.

A new Brain Trust courier, a gentle older man with a mop of gray curls who, for reasons that remain unclear to me, goes by the nickname "Rhubarb," comes to my suite at Harrah's with a phone. Unexpectedly, Sarge, who I learn has been reinstated on short notice, arrives shortly thereafter with $300,000 in cash (and a half-smoked cigarette he leaves on my desk). Big Daddy has nine football plays for me—$297,000 worth of action. While Rick surveys what I imagine to be his notes, he mumbles a running narration: "Let's see here, pards. . . . What are we gonna give 'em? I tell you what, pardsy-wardsy, it's tough. . . . Course, that's why no-body can beat the game, right? . . . Let's see, Mr. 44 . . . hmmm . . . Here you go. They'll like this."

After Big Daddy has dictated the shopping list, I go down to the cashier's cage to deposit the money and buy "chocolate" chips, $5,000 brownies. As the ladies behind the bars count my money. Irving Rosen-baum charges through the swinging glass doors.

"We've got to talk," he says solemnly. He has the haunted look I've seen before in unhappy sportsbook managers, and I don't like it. He motions for me to follow him, but I indicate that my money is being counted and I don't want to leave. "What's up, boss?" I ask.

Irving tells me, in so many words, that I'm through. His frazzled ex-planation includes "a lengthy meeting with the vice president of opera-tions," "Harrah's not wanting to extend themselves too far," "Harrah's is not ready to handle the kind of wagers" I make, and so forth.

The truth is, I won. I won a lot. More than $200,000. And after investi-gating me, Irv Rosenbaum probably determined that the chances of my winning in the future were quite good. And casinos, of course, do not want consistent winners taking money out of their tills.

I'm genuinely angry, filled with the same righteous indignation I've heard from Big Daddy when he's sermonizing. They're kicking out the one individual in the whole joint who can give them a fair fight. Instead of subjecting the messenger of bad tidings to a philosophical rant, I channel my frustration into the kind of prosaic complaints a member of the service industry like Irving Rosenbaum might fathom. I tell Irv I can understand if this was a corporate decision—but the timing, *after* I arrive in Vegas with my girlfriend, *after* I've shunned Caesars in favor of Harrah's, *after* I've put $300,000 on deposit in his cage, that's just wrong.

He apologizes and admits the timing couldn't be worse.

I fume a bit longer. Harrah's is comfortable taking only $10,000 bets—and that's on NFL sides; it's $5,000 on college and $2,500 on totals. Reminding Irving that $300,000 worth of loose gambling money is about to leave his casino, I storm off to my room.

Big Daddy takes the news calmly. "I knew you'd stumbled into a good situation there," he says. "I knew it wouldn't last forever. But I'm a little surprised they shut you down so fast, before you even got out of the box. Someone must have told 'em something." He urges me to go back down and bet them at $10,000 a pop. Then I should proceed down the street to the Barbary Coast casino and see what it's willing to do.

When I return to the Harrah's sportsbook, Irving is gone. His assistant says he's in a meeting; is there something she can help me with? I tell her I'd like Mr. Rosenbaum to meet my girlfriend—another apology opportunity—and that I'd like to bet some games at $10,000.

The assistant calls Irving and informs me that, in fact, they don't want *any* of my bets. Not for any amount. "So they're that scared of me," I mutter, shaking my head in disbelief. Obviously this is less about Harrah's policy and more about Irving and his colleagues sniffing out my relationship with Rick Matthews.

I trudge up the Strip with Vivian on one arm and $300,000 in cash on the other. I'm so furious I'm almost hoping someone tries to mug me so I'll have legal cause to bash his face in.

At the Barbary Coast, a grimy joint on a prime corner across from Caesars and Bally's, I put on my comp hustler act, the one in which nothing matters more to me than scoring a hosted dinner at its famous gourmet restaurant, Michael's. How much do I need to bet for all the free Château Lafite and rack of lamb I can handle? The assistant manager, a fellow named Kevin, says I can bet $5,000 on college and up to $20,000 on pros, as long as it's not right before post time. I feign ignorance of that term. "You know, right before the game. We need time to move the line around, get some action on the other side, even things out."

"Oh!" I say, wide-eyed. "I get it."

For $35,000 worth of play, Kevin assures me, everything will be taken care of. Considering I'm expected to drop $1,750 in juice if I'm lucky enough to go 50–50—the vig on $35,000 is $3,500—a comped dinner (even in a restaurant where a chilled shrimp appetizer costs $32) isn't exactly giving away the store. I bet $38,000 worth of games. It's immediately apparent that the fellows at the Barbary Coast aren't used to seeing this much money in one pile. To me, after a season of perspective-skewing, Big Daddy–style gambling, it seems like nothing. All those games I just bet wouldn't equal even one wager at my usual Caesar-Hilton-Harrah's limits.

Viv and I find a quiet bit of lawn on the corner of Flamingo and Las Vegas Boulevard and call Big Daddy. He instructs me to put the rest of my money on deposit at the Palace, play two or three games off my shopping list, and investigate the opportunities at Bally's. "We'll get all your money in play, 44," he says, chuckling. "You're just gonna have to work a little harder."

Little Mikey Brown, charming as ever, welcomes me warmly at the Caesars counter and chats loosely while he counts the $250,000 I'm putting in my account. We talk of sports and casino hosts and Japanese restaurants. I'm only sorry Little Mike isn't running the show at Caesars. It would be a blissfully low-pressure deal. Of course, he'd probably get fired after a few weeks on account of a guy like me taking out a couple hundred thousand every weekend.

Mikey tells me he's spoken to the Pencil: I'm full RFB. I tell him thanks, but that won't be necessary, since I'm staying somewhere else. But if he'd like to write up a comp to the sushi bar, we'd enjoy that. He couldn't be happier to oblige.

Before a late dinner, we go back across the Strip, bet two more games at Barbary Coast, and do a fact-finding mission at Bally's. The prospects there are bleak: Bally's takes only $10,000 on pros and $4,000 on college.

But if I'd like to work out a special arrangement, a supervisor tells me, I should come in tomorrow and talk with the manager, Jay Muccio. Too bad, I think to myself, since Bally's has most of the games on my order list.

After an entire evening of bet shopping, I've managed to get only $100,000 into play. Given my profit-sharing formula—I figure that I'm good for slightly less than 1 percent of all the money I wager—it's been a lot of work for a not very large return.

And then I realize: My conception of money has gone completely haywire.

For the privilege of betting on football games, staying in swanky digs, and eating like I'm going to the electric chair, I'm getting paid more than the average American earns in three weeks.

I survey the neon glow along the Strip and say out loud to no one in particular, "Vegas."

"I need outs," I announce to Viv, who's in our suite getting ready for dinner.

"You need to get out?"

"No. I need outs. Outs: places to bet."

She gestures to the glittering lights outside our bedroom window. "Well, it's not like there's only a couple of casinos in this town. Why don't you just open accounts with all of them?"

"I wish I could. It's not that easy," I say, looking down the boulevard. "Most of these joints, even the big boys here on the Strip, they're scared to take a bet. I'd have to run around to ten different places to get down even a fraction of what the Brains want to bet on a single game. Plus, the point-spread number would get whacked out of shape, and our plays would get hijacked, and—anyway, it's impossible. Besides, I'm pretty sure Big Daddy already has local runners working in most of the casinos. He needs me for the big out-of-towner action."

"Have you tried them all?" Viv asks.

Actually, I haven't. We sit down at the living room coffee table with *Showbiz* magazine's complete list of Las Vegas casinos (and restaurants and cheesy shows). I make three categories: cultivating big action (four), scared of big action (twenty-two), and indifferent but possibly open to big action (four).

After dinner and before driving to the outskirts of town for a party, Vivian and I go on a fact-finding expedition to some of the joints that allegedly welcome high-rolling chumps. We stop first at the Rio, which is rumored to be attempting an upgrade of its class of player, looking for premium customers. We talk to a host who says this is true, but not in the sportsbook. "They don't take hardly anything. I feel like telling the boss over there he should put up a sign: 'No gambling allowed.'"

At the MGM Grand, a host introduces us to Lenny Dip, the sportsbook manager. He tells me that the limits I want to play are nearly twice what they normally deal, but that he'll talk to the casino manager and see if he'll make an exception. And by the way, he asks, when do I bet? And on who? And why? We leave after Lenny promises to call on Monday—which, I suspect, is about as likely to happen as my hitting fifteen out of fifteen numbers at keno.

Early Saturday morning, I stroll across a strangely deserted Las Vegas Boulevard to visit the boss man at Bally's, which made it onto our "possibly open to big action" list. Jay Muccio seems nice enough. The only problem is that he's the self-described "best friend" of Gino the Suit over at Caesars Palace. So I play it straight. "Ask Gino about me," I dare Mr. Muccio. "He'll tell you I'm a smart, winning player. Maybe I'm not the kind of bettor you want."

I tell Muccio that I can't bet enough at Caesars to satisfy my gambling appetite. "Plus," I continue. "I'm a very smart shopper, and sometimes the point spreads might be more attractive here at Bally's." I suggest that if we can build a good relationship, including the commensurate comps. I'll be happy to give Jay and his store some substantial business.

He says he'll have to run all this by his boss, the vice president, but if all goes as he would like, I'll be able to bet as much with Bally's as I do at Caesars. How Gino the Suit will handle Muccio's inquiries makes me anxious—but, as with the bulk of the Brain Trust operations, it's out of my control.

Big Daddy has nothing else for me the rest of the morning. Since I've bet only $60,000 worth of games at the Palace, I'm *really* glad I didn't take Stevie up on his RFB offer. The (unwritten) Code of Comp Conduct says that in return for all the free booze and furniture and grilled John Dory garnished with white truffles, you're supposed to give the casino a shot at winning a large serving of bankroll fillet. Even though I know Caesars Palace is going to end up paying me in the long run, at least in the short run I want them to feel like they have a reasonable expectation of busting me.

My friend and gambling buddy Timid Joe Corcoran stops by Harrah's for a late lunch. He's been playing in a backgammon tournament at the Riviera, bleeding money. While Viv naps in the bedroom, we sit in the living room of my suite, talking odds and probabilities, sweating the results of the few games I've got outstanding.

Timid Joe is originally from Wales, and he repeats what he claims is a common maxim in his homeland: " 'Tis better to milk your goat than roast it."

I recall his advice as the results begin to trickle in. Predictably, the Gods of Gambling play their usual perverse joke. For the day I go 5–1. If I were playing at my usual limits, 'tis I who might be roasted by my casino hosts.

The Barbary Coast, I know, can't be too pleased with the results. Nor can Caesars, I reckon, since Caesars would like to see volume above all. Big Daddy can't be too happy. And I'm not, either. Somehow the prospect of a complimentary $500 orgy of gastronomy, courtesy of the casino, makes it all seem a little better.

The next morning, two hours before the early NFL games commence, I dash across the Strip to Caesars Palace. I've got plenty of business—five potential bets—to give my new best buddy the Pencil, assuming the numbers are right. Only two of them are. But before I depart, Pencil Stevie tells me to hang around for a minute since he's going to move some lines. "You might see something you like," he says, doodling the letters "K" and "C" on an old newspaper.

Indeed, when he changes the Kansas City Chiefs from 4 to 4½, I tell him I'll take it. "Who's your best pal?" I joke. Stevie smiles and points at me, like the Fonz. I know he's glad to have a smart-money player taking the other side of a game on which he's clearly imbalanced.

We chat momentarily about the Hilton corporation's failed bid to buy Caesars; about Starwood, the new owners; about his faulty computer system. The Barbary Coast, Bally's, and Jay Muccio never get mentioned.

Across the boulevard at the Barbary Coast sportsbook I introduce myself to Dale Lutz, the top man there. Dale is small and older and, it seems at first glance, a bit rough around the edges. I don't get the impression he's particularly bright. He doesn't have the polish and shmooziness of the Caesars boys. Dull Dale, however, is perfectly cordial. He's pleased to meet me and pleased my dinner at Michael's was good and pleased I've come in to give him some business. Dale, in general, is pleased.

I tell him I want to bet the Lions game. He asks me for how much. I say the supervisor I originally met said I could bet $10,000, but more if the casino needed my team. Dull Dale says he's heavy on the other side, Minnesota, so if I want to bet $20,000, go ahead and be his guest.

Everywhere in Las Vegas the game is pick, meaning the bookies figure the game to be exactly even. There's no point spread. But Dull Dale is posting the game as Minny −1. Betting Detroit, I get an extra point that no other casino in town is offering. The bonus comes into play only if Minnesota wins by exactly one point, and the statistical likelihood of that is slim but not negligible. So this extra point gives me a couple of percentage points' better probability of winning a game that the line-makers figure to be a toss-up. Obviously all of the Barbary Coast's customers have been betting the Vikings. My large action on the Lions is not only tolerated but welcomed.

None of my other numbers are available. So I bullshit briefly with Dale before going back to Caesars to do some more shopping. Dale tells me anytime I need a room to give him a call. "We got some nice suites," he says, and he's serious.

Before leaving the Coast, I take a hotel elevator to a high floor and, after checking for surveillance cameras, find a dark corner to call Big Daddy. He's pissed that I took so long to contact him but pleased to hear the deal I got on the Lions. Although he doesn't say so, I know the head of the Brain Trust appreciates having an associate who is so steadfastly honest he doesn't report the bet as pick and keep the extra point for himself. A less scrupulous fellow would say he got Detroit at pick, sell his first-born in the hope that the Vikings would win by exactly one point, and pocket $22,000.

I have $165,000 worth of action on four games. After the first half I'm winning all three of the morning contests. At the end of the second half nothing has changed. I'm still winning. This is turning into a very big weekend. With one game pending—the 49ers giving 9½ to the Panthers—I'm up $138,000. A win would put me at $168,000, a nice haul to begin the season. A loss would still net a $105,000 profit.

Back at Bally's, Jay Muccio tells me politely but firmly that, upon further review, he doesn't want my business. Seems he read the article I wrote about expert handicappers, and he figures I'm in a partnership with the king of the sports bettors. "If I let you play here," Muccio says, "it would be like owning a grocery store where eggs cost me twenty-four cents and I sell them for twenty-three."

I don't protest vigorously—it's a hopeless cause—but I do save some face, reciting my practiced explanation that the article was a composite portrait of several big-time sports bettors and that it represents everything I've learned about how sports betting works in Las Vegas. Nonetheless, I tell Mr. Muccio that if I were in his position I wouldn't want my play either: At the end of the season I'm going to be a winner. "I'm the best sports bettor Las Vegas has ever seen," I announce pompously. "They're going to be dedicating statues to me."

Assuming Muccio will report our chat verbatim to Gino the Suit, I take the opportunity to lay a little cover, dropping unsubtle hints about the "neural networking computer" I'm supposedly using to beat the point spreads. He seems genuinely fascinated with my improvised hogwash and jokingly suggests that I report my inside information to him before he opens his lines. In the meantime, Muccio tells me I'm welcome to play at Bally's, but only for the house limits: $4,000 on college and $15,000 on pros. We shake hands and part as quasi-friends.

As we depart, Viv puts her arm around me and says, "My dear, you don't have much of a future in this town." I fear she may be right. I'm cursing myself for publishing a magazine article that paid me $4,000 and will end up costing me an incalculable amount more.

Back at Barbary Coast Dull Dale, upon further review, doesn't want to get too "extended." I'm back to five and ten in his joint. I'm sure it didn't help my cause that I went 7–1 for the weekend. Still, if I ever want a room, give him a call. I tell him I'll be back Friday night and walk out of the casino with $162,000 in cash.

At Caesars, Viv and I watch San Francisco squander our $33,000. Periodically I check in with Big Daddy for orders. To accomplish this, since I don't have a room at the Palace, I must find an empty bathroom stall, occupy it as though I am using it for its usual purpose, and have a furtive conversation. Big Daddy tells me to look for a key number (San Diego +3) on the late game. Otherwise I'm to get my money and meet Sarge and his pistol outside the side door at 5:00 p.m.

The kickoff passes without the necessary line change, so Viv and I leave the Palace sportsbook with $478,000 stuffed into my bag. (It's so heavy the shoulder strap leaves a welt on my trapezius.) According to my quick calculations on a cocktail napkin, this is $10,000 more than I'm supposed to have. But I'll have to double-check when I return to the room across the street.

We pile into Sarge's pickup truck, a battered Chevy stinking of stale smoke, and while we make the short commute to Harrah's, he regales us with a tale of being stuck in a casino elevator. The moral of this particular story seems to be, When a security officer asks for your name and identification, give him an alias. "Anyone wants to know, just think fast and come up with a name. Your best friend, or something."

Back in the suite, I triple-check my figures. Indeed, I'm $10,000 long. This, I deduce, is because of a simple clerical error at Caesars. They just gave me too much. Innocent, naïve bumpkin that I am, I don't even consider for a moment that I could put this found money in my pocket. Instead, I report the discrepancy to both Sarge and Big Daddy, both of whom think Caesars might ask for it back. But in the meantime, Big Daddy says he'll put an asterisk next to my running balance.

Once again I realize that Big Daddy and I have what biologists would call a symbiotic relationship. I love that he's introduced me to the adrenaline-drenched world of high-stakes sports betting, a milieu whose mythological secrets I would otherwise never learn. He, in turn, must love having an associate handling hundreds of thousands of dollars of his organization's money who is either too stupid or too honest to take advantage of a five-figure accounting error.

When we check out of Harrah's, Chicago George, one of the chief hosts, tells me he's read my article. I ask him which one, though I'm certain he means the one about the big sports bettor. George tells me he's seen a few of my pieces, actually, and he's enjoyed them all. "You definitely know your stuff," he says. "Not the kind of player this store wants, believe me."

We have a breezy chat about the gambling business. I do nothing to hide my sophistication; he does nothing to hide his contempt for the way Harrah's runs its operation. While we talk, I notice other casino executives loitering in the VIP lounge, pretending not to look or listen. I'm the big fish that evaded their usually reliable net. They want a vivid mental picture so they don't make the same mistake their colleague Irv Rosenbaum made.

As the limo glides toward the airport, leaving the garish lights of the Strip behind, I know that Vivian is right: My days in Las Vegas are surely numbered.

First thing Monday morning, the Pencil calls me at home, "Hey, Michael," he says, "we got a little problem."

Before he can finish his sentence, I tell him I know, they gave me too much money—I was going to call him myself.

He says he appreciates my being a good sport about it. Assuming I want to stay at Caesars during the upcoming weekend, I can make good when I arrive on Friday. I tell him that's fine with me. The Pencil says he'll put in my reservation—at full RFB. "And, Mikey," he repeats, "thanks again."

· · ·

A Mr. Jason Muggers from the Las Vegas Hilton calls my office. Seems he's the senior vice president of casino operations over there, and he's been passed a letter I wrote some time ago describing my unpleasant experience at his property. First he asks if I'm the same Michael Konik who writes about gambling in all the slick magazines. I tell him that's me.

"I'm a loyal reader," Muggers says. "I love your stuff. It's very smart, very sophisticated, very entertaining. You obviously know what you're talking about."

I thank him.

Muggers goes on to explain that I of all people must know that they're running a business and that they can't afford to gamble too much with a smarty-pants. Higher limits are typically reserved for longtime "good" casino customers, players who regularly blow off buckets of money at the tables. What Muggers means to say is that the Las Vegas Hilton will extend its limits only for suckers.

I repeat my usual mantra about how when I make a sports bet I'm taking the worst of it (laying 11–10 gives the house a 4.54 percent advantage off the top), relying only on my gut convictions. Funny, I remark, how a gambling house doesn't really want to gamble with me.

Muggers is polite—he invites me for lunch—but adamant: "We would love to have you back to the Hilton, Mr. Konik. But we can only offer you the regular house limits."

I thank him and explain that unless my bankroll takes an unexpected nosedive, that won't be happening anytime soon.

Since Sarge is preoccupied with "other matters," which I frivolously imagine involve gunplay and car chases, Big Daddy himself delivers my money when I arrive in Vegas early Friday evening. After I climb into the leather sanctum of Rick's luxury SUV, he uses the occasion to deliver an impassioned monologue on the state of sports betting in Las Vegas. The short version: The bookies are a bunch of pussies with the collective heart of a common flea.

Keeping an eye on the side entrance of Caesars Palace, where syndicate runners congregate to talk with their handlers on cell phones, Rick reveals that he's had to resort to an electronic voice modulator—a "voice changer," he calls it—if he wants to call a sportsbook on one of his phone accounts. "You want to see terror, 44," he says, shaking his head, "look at the faces of these sorry sumbitches if I try to come in their casino. It's like Qaddafi walked in."

The result of Nevada's ineptitude and inhospitableness, he claims, is that the Vegas sportsbooks will chase away all their business, primarily to bookmakers in the Caribbean, who have gotten licensed and bonded in countries like Antigua and Belize. "These sorry-ass Las Vegas sports-books have got a monopoly. They're the only ones who can take a bet in America without fear of going to jail, and the way they handle their busi-ness, they're gonna scare all the money away to these offshore guys," Big Daddy predicts. "It's no wonder their volume is off fifteen percent this year. They're killing themselves."

Big Daddy confides that John Trotter, the sports manager at the Mirage; and Super Moe, from the Hilton, have been spreading rumors about me. The story—an utterly false one—is that I've been seen playing in the casinos with Rhubarb, Big Daddy's shaggy-haired associate. Fact is, I haven't played any casino games; I've seen Rhubarb once, when he handed me a phone at my Harrah's hotel room; and John Trotter and I have never talked.

"Your name and face are all around town like you're a wanted man," Big Daddy tells me, chuckling.

In the old days, he explains, when Bob Martin was the linemaker in Las Vegas, the people who ran the sportsbooks weren't afraid of the so-called smart guys. Bob Martin, according to Rick Matthews, would post his opening line on Sunday afternoon and let the ten "smartest peo-ple on Earth," the best sports bettors in town, bet his line. This way he would find out how and why the wiseguys were betting and could subse-quently move his number to reflect his newly gleaned knowledge. Now, guys like Pencil Stevie and Nick Cerruto won't fool with big line moves—2-point swings early in the week—for one simple reason: "They don't have any guts," Big Daddy says. That the gentlemen running a gambling establishment are a bunch of spineless jellyfish is somehow repugnant to Big Daddy, who grew up believing that real men live by their wits and are willing to back their convictions with their bankrolls. By his code, if two people have a difference of opinion, the best way to settle the argument is to bet on it.

We watch limousines disgorging passengers. The sky is growing dark, and the neon begins to glow. "This is the only segment of the gambling business where the people who run it have regressed and the players have gotten smarter," Big Daddy explains. "You've got a bunch of not very smart people controlling a very large industry. Of course, their bosses don't know how dumb these people are. Don't ever forget this, 44. In the valley of the blind, the one-eyed man is king."

I nod thoughtfully. Rick Matthews nods back.

I nod again. "So, business as usual, right?"

"Yes, sir. Now go pick some winners, son," he says. I climb out of his truck and join the herd pouring through the Palace's doors, another gambler in search of a lucky streak.

Shortly after I arrive in my suite, the phone rings.

Someone from Caesars management is on the line. "Mr. Konik, we want to know if everything is agreeable with your room. Do you need any extra towels? Are you comfortable?"

Before I can mumble an affirmative answer, Big Daddy comes on the line, cackling like a hyena. "How 'bout that voice changer?" he howls. I laugh along with him. It's funny (and a little shocking) to hear the solemn boss of the Brains playing like a little boy.

"You ready for business?" he asks.

"Shoot."

Big Daddy gives me "a whole rope" of plays, twenty-four of them. "This is everything for the whole weekend," he says, seriously. "Not a word to a single human being."

I stare down at my messily scrawled notes. The entire Brain Trust game plan is staring back at me. This little sheet of notepaper, this rectangle of Caesars Palace stationery, is worth millions of dollars to bookmakers and bettors around the world. And it's sitting on my desk, as seemingly inconsequential as a reminder to meet Lee from marketing for drinks.

While Big Daddy looks over his list, deciding which plays to give to the Barbary Coast and which ones to "Mr. Caesar," he mumbles softly to himself: "Hmmm, yeah, we'll give him some business, see how he likes it"; "Yeah, they're gonna love you when you bet this one"; "Let's see if we can't give you enough to bust you tonight, 44." Rick ultimately decides to give twelve plays to the Barbary ($66,000 of business) and twelve to Caesars. If all the numbers are right, I'll bet almost all of the $250,000 Big Daddy's given me tonight.

First I go to the Barbary Coast, and I can tell immediately that they still love me, despite the lower limits. That love grows even larger when I bet eleven of my twelve games. Phil, the night manager on duty, tells me I'm the casino's biggest customer. "Well, there is one guy who bets $12,000 on a game—but only one game."

"Unlike me," I say. "The idiot who bets every game on the board."

"No, no!" Phil reassures me. "You did very well last week. And maybe your good luck will continue." How kind the bookies are while the word "sucker" is still emblazoned across your forehead in shining letters worthy of the Wayne Newton marquee. I thank the Barbary people for their encouragement and skip back across Las Vegas Boulevard, blending into the crowd of weekend revelers.

Back at Caesars I bet the other half of my rope—including five total plays, which always seem to raise suspicions—leaving only $14,000 for the next morning. Unless Big Daddy sends over some more dough, I'm not going to have much to do except order room service and sweat the games.

There could be worse ways of earning a living.

After a long night of carousing with Viv, I get an early morning call from Kathryn Matthews-Reynolds. I croak a recitation of football teams and point spreads from the previous evening, barely able to open my bleary eyes. After I finish, she says they'll get back to me when she learns "where they're at"—meaning her brother and the rest of the Brains—leaving open the possibility that more money might be forthcoming.

No one from the Brain Trust ever calls. In the meantime, I monitor my games, which seem to be falling about 50–50. As Viv sagely notes, having a modest losing week at this point wouldn't be the worst thing in the world. Indeed, it might be for the best.

Alas, fate—and Big Daddy's handicapping acumen—foils that scenario. We go 7–4 at the poor little Barbary Coast and 9–3 at Mr. Caesar. For the day I win another $72,000.

The Barbary has seen enough. When I pop in to check on its Sunday NFL lines, Dull Dale, the manager, informs me that the Barb can't take more than $2,000 a game from me. "They don't want to gamble," he says, referring to the corporate types who apparently make these decisions. "It makes me sick. You come in here and bet me eleven games on a Friday night and they don't want your business." I commiserate with him, professing disbelief. Of course, I believe it all too well. This is the true Las Vegas.

"So they ran up the white flag already," Big Daddy comments, laughing bitterly when I inform him. "How did you do over there, anyway?"

"Seven and four this week; seven and one last week."

"Well, good for them," he replies, chortling. "Now they can get all their money back two grand at a time."

"I guess I could write them a nice letter apologizing for winning."

"Oh, they'd appreciate that, I'm sure. Hey, 44, you want a title for a good book?" Rick Matthews asks. "I got one. *The Big Lie.* That's Vegas for you, pally."

At the end of the day, while I'm hanging around the sportsbook, watching the scores and waiting for Viv to get dolled up for dinner, the Pencil comes out from behind the counter to shake my hand. "Hey, Mr. K," he says warmly, "I just want to thank you again for last night. You dealt with our little mix-up like a real gentleman. No controversy or nothing."

This is how I handled the "little mix-up": I walked up to Little Mikey Brown, presented him with an envelope with $10,000 in it, and said, "I believe this is yours. Now, what's a guy gotta do to get a buffet comp around here?"

This gesture has earned me some much-needed goodwill from the boys at Caesars Palace. Gino the Suit comes down from the executive offices to lay a hand on my shoulder. "I just wanted to thank you personally for how you handled Friday night," Gino says. "That was a very classy, very honorable thing to do, and let me tell you, I don't see that too much in this business. So I wanted you to know that it meant a lot to me personally and to all the management at Caesars Palace."

"We both know I don't have to steal anything to break you guys. I'm going to win all your money on the square," I say.

Gino grins. "You may be right about that, Michael. But as long as we can pay the light bill, we still got a chance."

Perhaps. Of this I'm sure: My life expectancy at Caesars Palace has just increased by at least two weeks. With luck, I might even make it through the end of the football season. Stevie confides that his sportsbook did a lot of business today—and won a big number. He suggests that as long as his side keeps winning, he'll consider taking some bigger bets from me. "I don't want to commit to that yet," he says. "But we'll see. And don't be afraid to ask. I'll tell you straight up if we need it."

I get the sense that my business might actually be welcomed at Caesars, that the Pencil and the Suit aren't just my new best pals, but that they're imaginative enough to see how cooperating with the smart money could be beneficial to their bookmaking operation.

Nine

THE WILD FRONTIER

It's early in the 1998 football season and I'm trying desperately to get my limits raised back to where they belong, where both the Brain Trust and I can make a big score every weekend. No matter how I cajole, implore, and plead, I'm not getting anywhere. Stevie the Pencil is as cordial as ever. But he can't give me an answer until he talks to Gino the Suit, who can't give him an answer until he talks to *his* boss, a newly installed hotel man trying to run a casino. "I'm gonna tell you right now, Mike," Stevie says, glumly, "it don't look good." He says the Caesars Palace sportsbook could earn more than ever before if the executives would just let him run the shop the way it ought to be run. They could set a new standard for volume. But the accountants don't want them to. "And I gotta follow orders, you know what I mean?"

When I check back with him a few days later, from O'Hare Airport, between airplane transfers, the Pencil is cheerful and charming and friendly. He's the nicest guy in the world. But his news is terrible. I started out with a $50,000 limit on pros and college. Then $30,000 on pros and $20,000 on college. Now? "All right, Mike this is all I'm gonna be able to give you. Now, keep in mind, if we need more on a game, it could change. But for now, this is all I can offer," he says.

"Twenty-five on NFL. Ten on college. Sorry. That's all they're letting me do."

We agree that with numbers like these the only bookies getting rich this season are going to be situated somewhere in the Caribbean. We're both disappointed. I make a reservation for next weekend but understand that there's a good chance I won't be coming.

"We'd love to have you, Mike," he says. And I almost believe him.

When I report the news to Big Daddy, he's disgusted. "Ain't that basically what they give to any guy off the street?" he asks rhetorically.

"Pretty much," I say glumly. Any Guy Off the Street limits render me expendable.

"Nothing against you, pards, but you can understand, if they're not gonna go any higher, it doesn't make any economic sense for me to use you. I'd love to work with you, 44, but at those numbers, I can't give any piece up. There's nothing left over for you. I need all of it and more."

I understand. I'm being downsized, as they say in the corporate world.

"Now, if you can find any other outlets, we can still work together," Big Daddy says.

"Like the bookies here in Hollywood, the ones who cater to the entertainment business?"

"Well, there's a million offshore guys."

"England?" I wonder aloud, having seen betting shops in towns throughout Great Britain.

"Yes. And Australia and Costa Rica, and a bunch of islands in the Caribbean I ain't smart enough to pronounce. Maybe you want to investigate some of these shops. I can put you in touch with an offshore expert who handles that sort of thing. As long as he doesn't already bet with the same people you have, there might be something we can use. I'll have him call you if you like."

"And this is all legal?"

"Yes, according to the best lawyers on gambling law. Some of these shops are even publicly traded companies, listed on the London Stock Exchange. Of course, after we get done with 'em you might want to short their stock."

"All right, Rick, I'll investigate. I just don't want to try to build a whole bunch of relationships and find out I'm duplicating what your offshore deputy has got already."

"I'll give him your phone number. You two can talk about it. And if anything good happens here in town, we can still do something."

"Yeah, Stevie said the limits might change at Caesars," I say hopefully.

"Well, you let me know."

"Good luck for the rest of this season, Big Daddy," I say, stifling my disappointment. "Go get 'em."

"Thanks, 44," he says. "We'll try to get lucky again."

I hang up the phone and wonder if this will be the last time I talk to the world's biggest sports bettor.

Three hours later, the offshore guy calls me.

It's Brother Herbie. College basketball Herbie. Extraordinarily *nice* Herbie.

"Hey, 44, I understand from a little birdie that Caesars got tired of you beating them," he says in his gentle drawl. He asks me if I've got any other outs lined up.

"I may have a couple of small Vegas casinos that might collectively amount to maybe ten thousand of action," I say. "But what about the offshore places?"

"We've used a couple in the past. Maybe you should look into that. You know, find three or four outs, even for a few thousand, and it starts to add up." We talk for thirty minutes. He's easy and affable. I would be delighted to do business with him instead of Rick Matthews. And I wouldn't have to fly to Vegas every weekend, which would probably thrill my increasingly disgruntled girlfriend.

"Let me see what I can find and I'll report back to you," I tell the former monk.

"Good luck," he says. "It's a jungle out there."

My bodybuilder-actor-model-dancer next-door neighbor, Rex, knows a guy who knows a guy. He'll introduce me. Like, immediately.

We drive to a trendy nightclub on the Sunset Strip, where Rex's friend, Jon, is a doorman. A rather large doorman. Rex, a onetime Chippendales dancer turned club bouncer, explains my situation: I'm a heavy gambler ($10,000 a game, sometimes more) who usually goes to Vegas every weekend. New girlfriend doesn't want that. Looking to bet from home. Whazzup?

Doorman Jon sizes me up as though I'm a teenager trying to pass off a fake ID. As long as Neighbor Rex will vouch for me, he says, we can do some business. Seems Jon is an "agent" for another guy, the "head agent," who works for a big organization down in Costa Rica. He'll arrange an introduction. Like, immediately.

We exchange phone numbers and agree to meet the next day.

I spend the morning trolling Web sites on the Internet, compiling a database of potential offshore outlets. There are dozens. And though I've written on the subject previously in gambling columns, I've never been confronted with the predicament of trying to place $50,000 bets over the phone. Obviously, I need referrals. But how many people can you ask, "Hey, do you know a reliable place to bet fifty large?"

After several calls to the Caribbean, I identify two cyberbooks that, according to zealous sales representatives, will let me bet whatever I have on deposit in my account. *And*, as a welcome gift, they'll add a 10 percent bonus on top of the funds I deposit. Or, if I like, deal me an 8-cent line: $1.08 to win $1.00, instead of the usual $1.10. Very interesting—except that this would involve wiring hundreds of thousands of dollars to a stranger in San Jose, Costa Rica. Which I'm fairly sure Big Daddy will be loath to do. But it's good to know such opportunities exist in the world beyond Las Vegas.

The next day I meet Doorman Jon and two "agents" representing another Costa Rican sportsbook in Hollywood at the same Sunset Strip café where I lunched with Stevie the Pencil in the spring. Jon sits quietly as Seth and Derek, both of whom wear expensive designer sunglasses and gold necklaces, ask me a few questions to "get comfortable." What's my betting history? How did I hear about them?—and then they settle into a well-rehearsed pitch. After sizing me up as a world-class moron, they tell me I can bet as much as I like on anything. "I'm not going to limit your wagers," Seth assures me. "As long as you've got the coin, you can bet it. Our operation has like nine thousand customers. We can handle anything."

Seth owns a small casting agency. Derek choreographs nightclub stage shows featuring strippers in cages. They work as agents on the side, herding losers into the offshore pen—and collecting a commission on the revenue they produce. In their eyes I could be a gloriously fruitful contributor. They almost finish each other's sentences trying to sell me on what a wonderful home their sportsbook operation will be for a gentleman like me. The shop they represent, known as Nautica, is based in Costa Rica and can be reached twenty-four hours a day by telephone at a handy 800 number. Seth and Derek are curious, though, about how a writer has so much "coin." And they wonder out loud how we're going to find a mutually acceptable way to put the money on deposit. (Maybe a safe-deposit box that requires two keys, Derek suggests.) But of one thing they're sure: Sign up this chump immediately!

My utterly-impressed-with-how-smart-I-am-while-appearing-to-know-nothing act is by now so polished that by the end of our meeting Seth can barely contain his exasperation as he explains to me the difference between squares and sharps. There's one guy in Vegas who basically controls the bets, he tells me. This guy, Seth says, has like 180 people under him, who get out his bets as soon as the guy "comes" on a play.

"Wow," I say, impressed. "Who is this guy? What does he know?"

"I don't know his name," Seth admits, fiddling with his necklace. "He's like a phantom. But he *definitely* exists. Absolutely. He's the source for all the information. He creates it. That's what we mean by 'sharp.' The guys who have access to this information are sharp."

I look perplexed. "How would someone get this information? And what is this information?"

"Listen, it's out there," Seth says. He leans across the table paternally. "Once we get to know each other a little better, I'll tell you how this all works."

"You know," I say, "I don't want to brag too much. But there were lots of times last year when I made a bet and all sorts of people started betting on the same team as me, and they moved the line like you're talking about. So I guess *I'm* the sharp guy."

"Yeah, probably," Seth says, nodding. "You're gonna be tough to beat."

"I guarantee it," I promise.

Everyone chuckles solicitously and heads for his expensive car.

After our meeting, Doorman Jon just wants to make sure about one thing. "Your friend," he asks Rex, the one who vouched for me, "you sure he's not an undercover cop?"

I have misgivings of my own.

A professional gambler friend in Vegas tells me that Nautica used to have an online casino, a virtual gambling den where players could enjoy all the games usually found at a brick-and-mortar casino without leaving their homes. And before Nautica shut it down, they stiffed some video poker professionals he knows out of $220,000. He's not sure exactly what happened, but he'll look into it. While this revelation does not speak well of Nautica's business ethics, it gives me some quiet incentive to beat the shop out of as much money as Big Daddy will allow.

Actually, this time I'm desperate to stay employed. I've won tens of thousands of dollars on football games and would prefer to continue doing so without interruption. As another Sunday of NFL games unfolds, I'm on the sidelines. I look at the lines halfheartedly, trying to guess which games Big Daddy might be playing. And I make a few mental picks myself. (Predictably, I go about 50–50 for the day.) The adrenal charge, however, is gone.

I'm just another forlorn gambler dreaming of big scores in Vegas. And I'm determined that by the following weekend this will change.

Three days later, both Seth and Derek make calls to encourage me to get everything up and running. They tell me that their organization can offer me a 5 percent bonus on my initial deposit. And unparalleled customer service. And whatever else I want. Everything will be great!

I tell them I'm still doing my research.

I hang up and call Brother Herbie. He's encouraged but says he'll have to talk to "the other guy" to see if we want to play with Seth and his Costa

Rican people. An hour later, Big Daddy rings. After having me repeat the safe-deposit box scenario—"And what happens if one of you dies?" he asks nonchalantly—and deciding he can bear the risk vs. reward, he says, "Well, I think we better give these boys some business. How soon can you get here to pick up some money?"

Four hours later, I'm on a plane to Las Vegas.

Big Daddy and I have agreed to meet in the morning so I can proceed directly from his office to the airport to my bank, where the money can be safely deposited in the box. "I'll see you when you get here, pardsy," he promises. At which point I'll officially be back in the game.

After a sleepless night in a downtown Vegas hotel, I hail a taxi to meet Rick and the cash. "Big Daddy is expecting you," the security guard says as my cab pulls up to Big Daddy Enterprises headquarters. "Right this way, please."

Big Daddy Rick's office, housed on the second floor of the flagship restaurant in his burgeoning chain, is the kind of grand marble-and-mahogany place that has the proprietor's name wrought in some kind of precious metal behind the reception desk. The kind of place where you have to go through three secretaries to see someone.

"He'll be with you in a moment," secretary one tells me.

The anteroom reeks of success: framed commendations; gilt-edged photographs; leather and lacquer.

Big Daddy bounds through the doorway. "Hiya, 44, come on in." He looks tanned and handsome, dressed in a golf shirt and slacks. The man radiates charisma. "How's life treating you, pards?" he says, escorting me into his office suite, outfitted with a cooler stocked with his beloved Diet Dr Pepper. "Have a seat, have a seat." His desk is covered with phones. Cell phones, radio phones, old-fashioned phones that actually plug into the wall. This is a man who clearly spends much of his time barking orders over a wire. "So, we can bet this guy, what, up to twenty-five percent of what's on deposit?"

"No," I say. "*Whatever* we have on deposit."

Big Daddy chuckles. "Yeah, I guess we're gonna have to give this boy some business." He bends down and pulls a white canvas sack from underneath his desk. "Here you go," he says, handing me two $100,000 bricks. Holding another brick, he thinks for a moment. "Here's fifty more. Two fifty."

"So with our five percent bonus that's, let's see . . . ," I say, calculating.

"Another twelve five. You got two sixty-two five to play with. Now get outta here. Go get your plane."

No papers to sign. No dire warnings. No cautionary tales. Just take this quarter million and skedaddle. I think it's fair to say at this point that Big Daddy trusts me like a brother. Maybe more. "See you later, alligator," Big Daddy says as I leave. I briefly consider chirping, "In a while, crocodile," but it doesn't feel right when you're holding a bag containing $250,000.

My return trip is blissfully uneventful. I feel like most couriers must on their inbound journey: a dull and constant dread. *Just let me get there.* Sitting in the airplane, with the bag between my feet, I have visions of some sort of scheme out of an Elmore Leonard novel awaiting me in Los Angeles, some sort of airport fiasco, in which I end up either dead or relieved of my cargo. Guys posing as DEA agents or something. A traffic cop looks at me as I exit the baggage claim, but that's my only brush with someone packing a gun.

I drive directly (and rather quickly) to my bank on Sunset Boulevard, arriving fifteen minutes before my scheduled rendezvous with Derek, who has agreed to cosign the safe-deposit box with me. This gives me enough time to remove the paper wrappers from the bills—the ones that identify them as coming from a bank in Las Vegas—and replace them with generic Bank of America bracelets. Derek doesn't strike me as smart or experienced enough to check for something like this, but you can never be too cautious when you're attempting to pass yourself off as a Hollywood square. Even though I'm using my real name, these guys don't read. They would have never seen my byline.

Nightclub Derek arrives a few minutes late, wearing his usual attire of baggy muscle shirt and baggy workout pants. It must have been a few days since he last shaved, since I can see the stubble growing—on his chest. He's one of these guys who use phrases like "Whazzup, man?" and "Howya doin', G?" like a regular badass homeboy. I'm in a jacket and tie, so I feel like a legitimate businessman executing a transaction with a hoodlum. I stifle a giggle as Derek explains to me his system for betting on sports, generously offering some of his hot picks to me, his best new customer.

After completing the paperwork for our box, Derek and I retire to a cubicle, where he painstakingly counts every one of the 2,500 hundred-dollar bills. "Cool-cool," he says as the last bundle goes into the box. "I didn't think you were going to bring so much."

"I couldn't resist the bonus," I say. "I would have put a million in here if I could have come up with it."

After exchanging driver's license information and home addresses, Derek asks if he can follow me home to see where I live. "Sure," I say, hoping my modest bungalow won't trigger suspicious thoughts, reasonable doubts along the lines of "Why doesn't the quarter-million-dollar-cash man live in a Beverly Hills mansion?" And then I remember: Derek wouldn't know a sharp bet from a square one anyway. It's the bookie down in Costa Rica I've got to worry about.

Viv says all the right things about her gambling boyfriend—"I'll miss the gourmet meals at Caesars, but it'll be good to have my high roller home on the weekends"—and Derek gives me my 800 number and password. "You're good to go, G."

Seconds after Derek walks out my front door, the phone rings in my office. It's Big Daddy. "I called once before. Everything all right?" I tell him the money is safely deposited and that the agent has just this very moment left. We're in business.

"All right, pardsy-wardsy, Brother Herbie will be calling you in a few minutes. We've got a play for tonight on the Navy game. Might as well get the lines, 44."

I want to say something like, "Let's not burn this one out too quickly," but I know better. Big Daddy is the expert. Still, I'm flabbergasted that the first play he and Herbie want me to make, my first bet with this new bookie, is for $50,000.

Herbie orders, "Go bet 'em Navy plus the points to win fifty dimes." Apparently he and Big Daddy are not concerned about waking anyone up.

The only problem, I discover, is that although Casting Director Seth promised me unlimited wagering—no ceiling other than what I have posted to my account—this message was not communicated to the bookie in Costa Rica. When I tell the clerk on the phone I want to bet $50,000, he says, "How much?!" And when I repeat my order, he tells me he's not sure he can do that. "Can you hold for a second?" he asks. I can hear him conferring with his boss. "Okay, sir," he says, returning to the phone, "you've got fifty thousand on Navy."

Just as I'm completing my accounting with Brother Herbie, my other line rings. It's Costa Rica calling. Seems there's been a mistake. Seems the clerk shouldn't have taken $50,000 after all. Seems $10,000 is the maximum.

"I tell you what I can do," the manager on duty suggests. "I can approve twenty thousand."

"This is outrageous!" I scream. "Go listen to your tape. I had a bet. Since when can you back out of a bet?" The manager apologizes profusely, telling me it's going to be his ass on the line if he takes more than he's supposed to. When the big boss comes in—tomorrow morning—the situation might well change. But for now . . .

Seth, the agent, calls on the other line. I tell him I'm furious. "Imagine this happening in Vegas!" I yell at him. "I had a bet and then they tell me I don't? This doesn't give me much confidence in your service."

"I understand," he says, trying to mollify me. "It was miscommunication. I'm doing everything I can to straighten it out. Look, I work with another shop. I'll get them to take thirty thousand, so you'll have your total of fifty, only it will be split up in two places. I'm really, really sorry about this. I'll do what I can. Just give me a few minutes to get this all figured out, all right?" He's highly motivated. He and the other agents collect 10 percent of my losses.

Brother Herbie calls on the other line. I tell him what has just transpired. "Oh, shit," he grumbles. It is the first time I've heard him swear, the first time I've heard him sound anything but courtly. I apologize and tell him about Seth's promise to find the necessary outs. "Call me right away," he says solemnly.

I know this turn of events has caused enormous consternation for the Brain Trust. Timing is everything in getting down wagers of this size, since, inevitably, the line starts moving all over the world. While Seth is checking into what he can do, the bookie in Costa Rica will be able to see that my innocent $50,000 wager was a precursor to an avalanche of money pouring down on bookies around America, and everywhere else bets are placed. This is not good.

Seth calls. "All right, here's the deal," he says breathlessly. "The first place, Rio Sports, will take up to twenty thousand a game with you. I got another place, Nautica. They'll take thirty thousand. I've told them you're good for it. So please don't fuck me, all right? Call them right now"—he gives me another toll-free number—"and confirm your bet."

I'm sick with anger. "Seth, you told me all along that I was betting with Nautica, not Rio. You never mentioned this Rio shop. I don't know anything about them. Now I've got twenty grand of my money sitting in their hands? What kind of con man are you?"

"Relax, relax. I work with both shops. They're *both* great places. It's just a little mix-up, that's all. Rio, Nautica—they're both safe places for you to bet. You have my word. Now, please, Mike, call Nautica and confirm that you want the other thirty dimes with them. They're holding the point spread for you. I guess it's starting to move."

I don't have time to mull my options. I follow Seth's new instructions. And then I call Herbie. And while I'm telling him that our bets are down. Big Daddy calls, wanting to know what the hell is going on. I explain as best I can, and he mutters. "I don't want them sumbitches moving my money around." But then he relents. "Let's just see how this works out. We can always bet 'em twenty and thirty, I guess. But the more places you give the bets to, the more chance you're taking that they'll leak it out and start messing with the number."

During the game, Casting Seth, who I'm quickly realizing is a man of constantly shifting words, told me that despite the $250,000 I have on deposit, he's only willing to let me bet up to $100,000 of it. "I can't take the risk," he whines. "I'm not going to let you get on the hook for over a hundred grand. I've got to cover it if you stiff us and, believe me, it's happened before, so I gotta put a limit—"

I interrupt him. "If I lose this game, I want Derek to meet me first thing in the morning at the bank. I'll pay you your fifty-five thousand. And then either I close down my account or it's the last time you ever bring up this bullshit about getting paid. If the money, *my money*, is in the box, I'm good for it. That was the agreement. And I expect you to honor it. Or I'll find someplace else to do business."

He wants me to let him think about it.

"Take it or leave it, Seth. I'm serious." If Seth insisted on limiting my bets, I'm certain Big Daddy would order me to close down my offshore account.

He took it.

This is one night where, in retrospect, I wish I hadn't gotten things straightened out. Navy loses a last-minute heartbreaker. The Brains lose $55,000. Five minutes after the game is over, I call both agents. "Man, you got unlucky in that game," Seth says insincerely.

Does he think I believe he wants me to win? Does he think I don't know that I must lose for him to make money? "Yeah, it happens," I say, reinforcing the idea that the money truly means nothing to me. "Listen, meet me at nine o'clock at the bank," I say. "I'm going to pay you guys six days early, way before our agreed-upon pay-up date."

I haven't authorized this with Big Daddy. I don't know if he would approve. But I think it's the right move. I believe it will buy us the kind of goodwill and longevity that returning the overpaid $10,000 to Caesars produced with the Pencil and the Suit. And besides, I'm tired of being called a potential potshot artist by a couple of punks who don't know me from Jimmy the Greek.

Casting Seth arrives at the bank in his silver Porsche Boxter a few minutes late, cell phone attached to his ear. He parks near the entrance and I get in the passenger seat.

"Hey, man, I got it all worked out," Seth says, smiling contentedly. "You're up for a hundred thousand at one place and a hundred thousand at the other. So it's all in play. You just split your bets twenty and thirty, assuming you want to bet that much. And if you want to bet less, it's up to you. Play wherever you feel lucky."

This is a relief. My money, it seems, is good.

Derek arrives in his Lexus, empty briefcase in hand. We go to the box. I give him $55,000 like it's no big deal, and we leave. "Thanks, man," he says. "You're cool, bro. Sorry about all the hassle. It was way out of line."

"I understand. Let's not have any more problems in the future," I say.

"No, there won't be any problems," Derek says. "See you later, man. Good luck this weekend!"

The instant I return to my office, Brother Herbie calls. I wonder for a second if he's had me followed. No, I discover, he just wants some updated lines. "Good morning, Herbie," I say cheerfully.

"I guess you could say that," he replies glumly. "That was tough last night." He sounds pained. "But, like they say, I'm on the right side of the ground."

"And you've got your eyesight and hearing and all your limbs," I say unhelpfully. I'm not used to giving a pep talk to my teammates. We're almost always winning.

"Well, we got some more business today," Herbie tells me. After I read the lines to him, he instructs me to make three plays, each for fifty thousand. Minutes after I get my bets down, Seth calls.

"Man, that was a great move you pulled this morning," he says, laughing forcefully.

Oh, no. A "move" in gambling parlance is a gaffe, a trick, a shady play. I figure he's going to tell me I made a great move by passing myself off as an earnest square—and then turning around and sticking them with three super sharp bets. Instead, Seth says, "I just talked to Larry down at Nautica. He loves you. He thought it was totally class that you paid off so fast. And he's mad at me. He wants to know why I'm letting you split your bets. He wants *all* of it. All fifty."

"Well, let's see how it goes this weekend," I say, trying to conceal my glee.

"Yeah, sure. Just wanted you to know that was a good thing you did, bro."

"Thanks," I say. "I hope you guys show as much class when it's time to pay."

"Oh, we will. You can bet on it," Seth assures me. "Let me know if you need anything, man. And have a good weekend."

When I call to confirm my bet with Brother Herbie, he shares the kind of information that Big Daddy has seldom bothered dispensing to a minion like me. The first play, on UCLA, will look like the squarest bet in the world. Another team of wiseguys moved a bunch of money on the other side, Texas, and the number shifted by a point. We're on the wrong side. The second wager, on an anonymous team called Northeast Louisiana State, getting 44 points from powerhouse Florida, is another no-heat play. "You're the only guy in the world betting on it," Herbie reveals. And the last one, on UNLV, well, that one's had a little action on it from our team of sharpies. "So there's a mix of bets there, nothing your bookie can figure out."

Herbie's right. The bets draw no heat. In fact, Rio Sports likes my action so much that when I inquire how much I can bet on "overs and unders," Rio tells me the usual limit is a few thousand. But in my special case it would be happy to let me bet my standard $20,000. On college totals.

I report this to Big Daddy. "Perfect," he purrs. "Perfect."

As in most of America, a typical Saturday morning in the Konik household would include hours of lying around in weekend languor, getting out of bed late to let the dog out and bring in the newspaper. But this isn't a typical Saturday. It's late September. Big Daddy and Herbie usually start their workday around 7:30 a.m. I've already been up for an hour, eagerly anticipating their calls. I've been waiting six months for this day, my first Saturday of college football action offshore.

The bosses don't disappoint. Herbie's got a game for me, and Rio is the only sportsbook that has it at the price he's looking for. I pounce while he holds on the other line. "Got it," I report.

"Good job, partner," he drawls. "I'll talk to you later."

I don't hear from him for the rest of the day, a day I spend watching a small loser and a big ($54,000) winner with particularly keen interest. Which is another way of saying I swear much more vehemently when we lose and dance much more like a retarded stripper when we win.

Viv sometimes catches me in a celebratory shimmy. "Stop that, you fool," she says, laughing.

"Yeah, baby," I sing and dance. "Uh-huh, uh-huh."

She shakes her head and returns to reading her pagan witchcraft book. Vivian reads omnivorously, whatever someone she likes recommends. Her manicurist, the one who specializes in French tips and psychic predictions, suggested this latest title, *The Witch Within*. (I asked Viv to get the manicurist's predictions on a few games, but football point spreads, apparently, aren't her area of expertise.) After only a few hours of the new routine, I realize how much I like working out of my home instead of a Las Vegas hotel room. I can give my doggie a bath in the backyard. I can sit on my front porch and read.

And bet tens of thousands of dollars on football games.

Late in the afternoon, a few minutes before the end of the UCLA game, Big Daddy calls. "Hey, pards, how much money you got left?"

It's only a few thousand at each joint. But as soon as the UCLA game concludes, it'll be close to $125,000.

"I guess we'll just have to wait then, right, pards?"

I suggest making an "if" bet. If the UCLA game is a winner—and it surely looks like a winner—then my new bets are on. If I somehow lose the UCLA game, the bets are off. "Yeah, try that," Big Daddy says, giving me three hot plays. Two of them are total bets, of which the bookies are typically frightened. He tells me to bet as much as I can but not to "shove 'em down their throats."

Per his instructions, I bet every dollar I have on account at Rio, where the manager, Dave, kindly credits my account before the UCLA game is officially over: two $20,000 bets on college totals. Business hasn't been this good since the miraculous welcome I had at Harrah's.

At Nautica, Larry Houston, the manager, is wary of total bets. He tells me he usually takes only a few thousand, since there's a professional syndicate that's been beating totals for the past couple of years, and everyone, even his oldest customers, jumps on its plays, "If you're not following them, if you're making your own plays, I might let you bet ten grand on totals. Let's start with five for now."

"Sure," I say breezily. "Five is fine. Just make sure you tell me what those hot team plays are so I can get on board!"

He laughs. "Well, they don't *always* win." Before I hang up, Mr. Houston graciously offers me a $50,000 limit on the pros for tomorrow.

"Let's see how I do tonight," I say.

When I report back to Big Daddy, he's purring again. "Perfect. Thank you, 44. Talk to you later, pal." From his tone I know he's pleased with how I handled the situation. I know he's pleased at how cool I'm remaining. And I'm pleased that Big Daddy seems to be doing his damnedest not to heat me up. It's a challenge to look like anything but a smart-money wizard when, for instance, you bet over 41 in the Notre Dame–Michigan State game and the teams eclipse the target halfway through the second quarter.

One of Rick's methods is simple. "That Rio place, I've been betting directly with them—on the other side! They take two thousand a game from me," he chortles. "So, yeah, they're real comfortable with you right now." And as far as Larry Houston goes, "He used to move money for me. He used to be another 44. Damn right he's scared of taking big bets on totals," Big Daddy crows. "Them guys would shit their pants if they knew where these bets were coming from."

Rick encourages me to continue researching other outlets, even though we're currently getting three times as much as Caesars would allow. "We're in pretty good shape right now, brother," Big Daddy says. "But we could always use more." Our day ends with two depressing losses that transform a hugely profitable day into a marginally profitable ($30,000) one.

Yes, we could always use more.

Herbie has two NFL plays, both of which, he predicts, won't become available until shortly before game time. "These games are going to move in our favor." He wants me to "oversleep" and groggily ring up my boys in Costa Rica ten minutes before kickoff and see where all the lines are. The game I'm looking for—St. Louis Rams getting 8 from the Vikings—will be available then, he assures me.

I end up making a total play as well, and after my business has concluded for the morning, Herbie and I chat. He's slightly irked about a pattern he's noticed.

"One thing that's bugging me," he says, "is that every time we make a bet with the Rio outfit, the Excalibur moves their number. It's happened a few times." Herbie figures the manager at the Excalibur casino in Vegas has access to the Rio's lines via an instant odds computer, just as Herbie does, and for some reason feels compelled to match the Rio's line moves. The motive, for now, is a mystery. But I know one thing: I've got nothing to do with the leak. All I do is wait by the phone, bet up to $100,000 a game, and revel in the results. We go 3–0 for the day, winning about $110,000. It's a five-figure weekend for 44, Inc.

God, it's good to be back.

Monday morning, Big Daddy calls to get the Costa Rican opening lines.

Seth the casting director/agent calls to "congratulate" me on my successful weekend. He also wants me to know that the money will be delivered, as promised, on Wednesday.

Derek the nightclub producer/agent calls to confirm that he'll meet me Wednesday. He also wants me to know he'll be going out of town next month for four days on a cruise, and he wanted me to have the courtesy of advance notice.

Dave, the manager of Rio Sports, calls to confirm my ending balance for the week—and to thank me for my business.

Everyone, it seems, is happy. And that's the way I like it.

Then Big Daddy calls back with some hot Brain Trust plays. "We're gonna light 'em up down there, pards. Give 'em a whole rope of bets." I can hear him looking over his notes as he talks. Could he possibly be making his betting choices as he chitchats with me? "Let's see here . . . hmm . . . give 'em game three-thirty-six . . . no, no, scratch that. We'll wait on that . . . give 'em, let's see . . ." This goes on for a few minutes until Big Daddy makes up his mind on a couple of early plays he wants me to make with "those cats."

And then he does something he's never done since I've known him: He asks me my opinion on a game. "How'd that backup quarterback for Dallas look to you, pards? He look all right? . . . This line's got to keep going up, don't you think? Can't go any other way, right?"

I'm stunned.

I admit to Big Daddy that I don't really have a strong opinion. Perhaps he's patronizing me; perhaps he's testing me. Or maybe he's just making a nice gesture, helping me feel more included in the team.

Big Daddy knows I don't have access to the computer algorithms he possesses. He knows I don't have an injury man on salary to keep me abreast of the latest sprained ankles and twisted knees. He knows that my single year of sports-betting experience hardly qualifies me as the smart money. But Big Daddy also knows that I want desperately to learn the secrets, to own the magic.

He knows I want to be one of the Brains.

Herbie calls late in the day and keeps me on the line while he moves money all around Vegas and the rest of the world. From what I can gather, he has dozens of people stationed at casinos around town, as well as several dialers who place smallish bets (a couple of thousand dollars) with the offshore operations. "Stand by, 44. Get ready to call. We're gonna see if we can't get them to move their number."

For forty-five minutes, as the *Monday Night Football* kickoff looms, Herbie and I try to get our money down in Costa Rica on the Redskins and the under. But the bookies at both my shops are either stubborn or smart. They won't move. After nearly a dozen calls, I finally get the number we're looking for, and I'm able to bet $30,000 of the $50,000 I want to wager. We end up getting crushed.

Halfway through the debacle, Big Daddy calls, wondering if I might have some additional outlets, other offshore books that might want some of my business. Never mind that I'm already betting $50,000 and up each game; he always wants more. I tell him about a few leads I've turned up, none of which will allow me to use the agent-in-L.A. method for handling the money. They all want me to post it in their bank, somewhere in the Caribbean.

"Well, that's fine. But we need to get some sort of bank reference, some sort of letter of credit," Big Daddy says. "You know: We put up, they match it. Something like that."

I tell him I'll look into it.

Rick Matthews tells me to do it now. Don't wait. "Let's see what we can manage. And if it works, I'll wire you some money tomorrow morning and you can wire it down there and we can get things going."

I talk to several managers at bookmaking shops in Antigua and Costa Rica who give me the usual sales job and security assurances, including bank references. They even offer me sign-up bonuses as high as 10 percent on my money and a two-cent break on the juice. But as far as matching bank accounts goes, I'll have to talk to the owners in the morning. When I tell Big Daddy this, he says, "That's fine. Call them bright and early, and then call me. And, 44," he says, "have your bank information ready. I'm gonna be sending you some money."

The next day, $300,000 shows up in my checking account.

"Man's gotta have some money to play with," Big Daddy says blithely.

We've reached an unprecedented level of trust. And, frankly, it scares me a little. I'm no longer a richly remunerated courier, I'm the conservator of a small fortune.

The funds, of course, aren't meant to sit in Los Angeles collecting interest. The next morning I open two new offshore accounts in Costa Rica, wiring $100,000 to each operation. Big Daddy has approved the transaction, saying, "We'll take a little shot with these cats, see if they're any good."

I've entered a world where $100,000 is a little shot.

I have also unofficially become a lieutenant in Big Daddy Enterprises. Late at night, Rick Matthews calls and patches me in with Brother Herbie. We have a three-way conversation among "the crew," as he calls it, evaluating where our money is, which shops will take what, and how we want to handle tomorrow's bets. Again Rick Matthews actually asks my opinion. (And concurs with it.) Though the key decisions rest solely on Rick's judgment, I *feel* like a trusted advisor. Matthews could probably replace me with another curious journalist without the Brain Trust suffering more than a momentary operational hiccup. But in my fantasy world, suddenly Mr. 44 is an indispensable asset. If I'm not Big Daddy's right-hand man—that would be the implacable Brother Herbie, I deduce—I'm getting to be the left-hand one. I feel like a made guy.

· · ·

On an otherwise unremarkable Thursday, when I'd normally be pecking away at my keyboard, composing magazine stories for two dollars a word, four things happen:

1. Nightclub Derek pays off my winnings.
2. My two new Costa Rican outs take my first bets graciously.
3. The Brain Trust wagers close to $250,000 on five different college games, including more than $100,000 on the evening's nationally televised Air Force game.
4. Big Daddy wires *another* $300,000 into my account. "We gonna do some business this weekend, Johnson," he says in his thickest drawl.

I've now got more than $900,000 at my disposal. We have $150,000 riding on the Washington Huskies game, a wager that approaches the size of my Super Bowl bet—and it's only the fourth week of the college season. I'm finding it increasingly difficult to work on my "real" job. When your bankroll is rising and falling by tens of thousands every weekend, mustering interest in grinding out a magazine story on, say, golf courses in Michigan requires the concentration of a yogi. Which is not what you'd call someone who considers watching ESPN's *Sports-Center* his chief religious sacrament. I've been infected with the action bug.

My newly acquired nonchalance about money allows me to back my opinions with a conviction born of an ever-fatter bankroll. Oscar De La Hoya is fighting Julio Caesar Chavez in Las Vegas. I feel certain that Oscar should be about a 20–1 favorite, that there is almost no way, save for a disqualification or a freak sucker punch, Chavez can win. Yet the Golden Boy, thanks to the efforts of many Mexican bettors in town, has been bet down to 8–1. (My pal Stevie the Pencil at Caesars confirms this when I call.) I decide this requires an investment.

Normally I might bet $800 on a proposition such as this, $800 to win $100. But, hey, it's only money.

I bet $27,500 of my own money.

Knowing the odds will continue to plummet, I wait until shortly before fight time to make my wager. And instead of taking a bad price from one of the offshore bookies, I call my partner in Las Vegas, Brother Herbie, and see if he'll get one of his runners to check on the price at Caesars Palace, where gamblers get the fairest spreads. It's down to –550, meaning a $550 wager wins you $100.

Brother Herbie is the ultimate money mover. So I ask him to spot me the dough. I tell him I'm coming to Vegas Sunday night for a party; if I lose I'll pay him then.

He asks that we keep this arrangement secret from "the other guy," as he calls Big Daddy, but, otherwise, he has no problem getting the bet down for me. "You really like De La Hoya in this one?" he asks, making sure I truly want to bet as much as I say I do.

"Yes, sir," I say, as confidently as Big Daddy picking a football team.

Brother Herbie calls me back a short time later. "You're down. Good luck!"

I'm not nervous. I know I'm going to win. And even if I don't—well, $27,500 is only a few football bets.

I win $5,000 on the De La Hoya fight and lose more than $8,500 (my share of the Brain Trust's $85,000) on NFL games.

All in a day's wagering.

Eight days later, I'm in the parking lot of the Las Vegas Hilton, directly across from where Brother Herbie lives—a penthouse apartment in a defunct casino, converted into residential condominiums. In town for the Blackjack Ball, a gathering of elite twenty-one players, I'm also going to pick up my Oscar De La Hoya winnings and meet the gambling monk for the first time. Listening to a freaky radio station specializing in the music of an indeterminate Central American country, I feel like a character out of a Carl Hiaasen thriller, someone shadowy and slightly mysterious who's constantly making large cash transactions. This is not the way a nice Jewish boy from suburban Milwaukee usually feels.

Herbie arrives twenty minutes late, wearing the white Caesars Palace hat he promised he'd be sporting. "You'll recognize me right away," he predicted. "Awfully good-looking gentleman, 'bout forty years old. Resembles Kevin Costner." The man parked beside me I would guess is closer to fifty and definitely movie star material—a dead ringer for Ernest Borgnine.

His modest Nissan sedan is redolent of cigarettes. An empty wineglass sits in the cup holder, with a ring of purple wine floating near the stem. "Mr. 44, I presume?" he says, handing me a winning ticket from the Caesars sportsbook.

"Pleasure to finally meet you," I tell him. And it is. Brother Herbie is a guy who makes me think reformed Christians aren't all bad. He's clean-cut and robust, with the belly paunch Las Vegas residents seem to acquire when gambling on the golf course becomes their most strenuous activity—remarkably like the way I had pictured him. I wonder if he thinks the same about me.

Our brief exchange of pleasantries (and money) turns into an hour-and-a-half discussion about the finer points of betting on sports. Brother Herbie gives me the kind of information I'm certain Big Daddy wouldn't want to share with an inquisitive novice. And I drink it all up.

He reveals, for instance, that Big Daddy owns "the computer," the magic box that consumes reams of raw statistical data, runs millions of simulations, and spits out a point spread that's accurate to a tenth of a point. I knew this, but having my belief validated by someone who has actually seen it makes me feel as though I haven't been a gullible lad swallowing a good story. The computer is *real*.

Brother Herbie reveals that, as a complement to the proprietary technology, Big Daddy employs four handicappers—two regular guys who predict the final score of each game, an injuries and weather guy who specializes in late-breaking news, and a psychological and matchup guy who doesn't predict scores but has a great feel for which team will have the upper hand. Brother Herbie doesn't reveal how many operatives work for the Brains. Herbie does reveal that when Big Daddy really likes a game, it seems as if he (and people like me) can never find enough places to bet enough money. "When Rick Matthews wants to get down," Herbie says, chuckling, "he's like a bulldog."

No kidding. This is why, despite Big Daddy's intention of keeping me "cool as a cucumber," he goes for the jugular as frequently as possible and risks bookie burnout.

"Seems like sometimes it's never enough," Herbie says, shaking his head.

Before our visit is over, Herbie recounts tales of gambling with Big Daddy on golf, gambling with the casinos at the dice table, and gambling with bookmakers on sports. (Herbie, I immediately recognize, never had a prayer of making it through theological training. The man loves gambling more than his Lord.) I endure his lengthy explanation of how he consistently beats the dice game, a proposition that anyone who's been around casinos knows is impossible. But who am I to disagree? A year ago I would have said the same thing about sports.

Back in Los Angeles on Monday, I pay Nightclub Derek $97,500 to cover my losses from the weekend. I won $84,000 at Nautica but lost $181,500 at Rio. My debt isn't due until Wednesday, but I want to clear the books immediately for goodwill purposes. Derek pronounces me "super cool" and promises that this kind of fast-pay gesture will mean a lot to everyone involved. "You're cool, bro," he says admiringly. "You're good for whatever amount."

My bank takes the opportunity to tell me that it will no longer allow me to withdraw the previously approved $50,000 a day, effective immediately. The bank manager, a stout woman who wears running shoes with her pantsuit, says that while she hates to lose a customer, she can't accommodate my "special needs" and suggests I start looking elsewhere for someplace that can.

"So, if I understand you correctly," I say, "you're happy to take in as much money as I care to deposit. But you're not willing to give my money back to me when I want to withdraw it?"

"Not in cash," she says, officiously. "It puts my branch at risk. Something reasonable—ten or twenty thousand—I can do. But I've instructed the tellers to stop with these large transactions."

When I break the news to Big Daddy, he's predictably livid. He doesn't realize that regular people in regular cities don't handle $200,000 in cash like irregular gamblers in an irregular city like Las Vegas. Incredulous, he asks, "You mean they won't just slide the money across the counter?"

Derek, on the other hand, understands. "That's fine, bro," he says. "Cashier's checks are cool."

So the next day I deposit $335,000 in cashier's checks, made out to me, in my safe-deposit box.

Later in the week I lunch on the Sunset Strip with Derek, Seth, and Ron Blutstein, the owner of Rio Sports International in Costa Rica. By the time the check comes, Ron, a young Jewish fellow from Chicago who claims to have formerly been an illegal bookie in Las Vegas—an occupation that seems to me as useful as a surfboard salesman in Uganda—is completely comfortable with our relationship. He tells me he has a good feeling about me. Of course he does. I'm the kind of excellent customer—someone who bets a lot of money, loses, and pays promptly—any bookie in his right mind would want to do anything in his power to keep. "What can I do to keep you happy?" Ron asks sincerely.

Rio Ron is a self-confessed degenerate gambler, a guy who likes to make $50,000 sucker bets such as five-team parlays, in which all five selections must win for a big jackpot. He understands intimately that some of us nice Jewish boys like to play real high. So I suggest he might raise my limits a little. That way I would bet more with him and less with his competitors.

"You got it!" he exclaims. Rio Ron says that as of this moment I'll be able to bet $50,000 on NFL sides, $40,000 on college sides, and (unbelievably) $30,000 on NFL *and* college totals.

And why not? I've just blown $181,500 in his shop.

Everyone is happy. The greedy bookie, his greedy agents, the greedy customer—everyone is licking his slavering chops at such an arrangement.

"I'll tell you what, Michael," Casting Seth says, laying a hand on my shoulder, "I've never met anyone like you. I wish there were more."

"No you don't, Seth," I can't help saying. "Believe me, you don't."

"I'm just saying. You're a great guy."

"Sure. But I'm going to win back every dollar I lost and make you guys cry." All three of my hosts laugh solicitously. "I'm not kidding, boys. I'm the best."

"Yes you are, sir," Rio Ron says, patting me on the other shoulder. "You sure are."

Ten

RIPPED OFF

I rapidly expand my international operation, opening accounts with three other giant bookmaking shops, all of which advertise in men's magazines, during the Howard Stern radio broadcast, and on Internet portals. These "big three" are the most reliable and trustworthy of the offshore bookies, according to watchdog groups that claim to monitor this burgeoning (and unregulated) industry. With Big Daddy Rick's approval, I wire hundreds of thousands of dollars to faraway financial institutions, simultaneously raising my risk of a gastric ulcer—I'm on the hook for all the cash should it disappear—and further convincing my suspicious bankers that I'm a successful drug dealer, even though I've explained in detail what I'm doing with the money.

According to a leading gaming lawyer in Las Vegas with whom I've consulted, betting on sports with bookmakers doesn't violate any laws. But when I told my bankers the truth, they didn't understand, because no one wins at sports-betting.

On a Sunday morning three weeks into my offshore betting career, the morning after a $65,000 win, I come out firing a string of bets. Some of them aren't as chilly as Big Daddy would have me believe. As I'm placing my wagers with an offshore operation called Premiere, based in Curaçao, the phone clerk puts me on hold for several minutes—which is never a good sign. His boss, a rough-sounding thug with a New York accent, gets on the phone and says gruffly, "Look, I know you're moving money for Rick Matthews, so I'm cutting you back to ten thousand a game. Take it or leave it."

I tell him I've never been treated so shoddily, etc. But what can I do? He's fingered Big Daddy by name. I can deny all I want, but he's not going to take big bets from me. I report the conversation to Rick, who, predictably, lets loose a torrent of invective about this particular bookmaker, another guy, Big Daddy claims, who once moved money for him and would scalp his mother if given the opportunity. He instructs me to close my account with Premiere and continue making bets with my other outs.

The North American Sports Association, known as NASA before the space agency's lawyers suggested it would behoove the renegade bookmakers to cease and desist (and find a different name to sully), is allegedly the world's leading offshore bookmaking operation. Using the Internet address Betonsports.com, this shop, run by a former Brooklyn street bookie, is marketed as the safest, biggest, and most trustworthy place to bet offshore. That is why I'm more than a little taken aback when NASA's owner, Gary Kaplan, who goes by the noble moniker "Greg Champion," gets on the phone and tells me my account is hereby closed. "I told you we don't take smart-money play here. I made that very clear. And I have a pretty good idea who you're moving money for," Mr. Champion informs me. "And I'm a little bit pissed, since I told you—"

"Hold it!" I yell. "If you're going to insult a customer like me this way, I don't want anything to do with you." This is what Big Daddy has instructed me to say when I get shut down. Act indignant and don't cop to *anything*.

Mr. Champion informs me that my account balance will be sent back to me on Monday. When I point out to him that I have bets outstanding, that I've already bet on three games for Saturday, he tells me that those bets have been canceled and will be considered "no action." I protest mightily, but to no avail.

"I'll be sending you a fax to confirm the figures," Mr. Champion says.

"And I'm deducting the bonus for administrative costs. You forfeited it by playing sharp sides."

"That's absurd."

"Look, you're lucky I don't keep all of it. Keep complaining and maybe I will," the King of the Offshore Bookies threatens.

When Big Daddy learns of *this* development he goes berserk. "I've been gambling since I was four and betting on sports since I was seven. And I think it's fair to say I'm the biggest sports bettor in the world. And, 44, let me tell you, in all my years, I have never—*never*—heard of anything so chickenshit in my life. It takes two to make a bet and it takes two to cancel it. Some of the old-time bookmakers, I guarantee you, if they heard this they'd be spinning in their graves."

Even Brother Herbie, who's usually unflappable, swears like a truck driver when I break the news to him. He's outraged at the principle, sure, but on a more practical note, he's now got to find approximately $60,000 worth of outs for each of my canceled bets. And at this late date in the week, the numbers are going to be way off.

With only a few weeks gone in the season, I'm hotter than a jalapeño.

How hot am I? Halfway through college football Saturday I'm winning everything. Not some games, not most. *Everything.* And since I'm betting up to $125,000 on a few of the games, the bookies are getting buried. With four games yet to be determined, I'm up more than $500,000 easily the biggest one-day win of my sports-betting career.

I'm dancing around the house in my underwear, barking at my dog, cooing at my girlfriend. The fellows on the other end of the telephone (the ones who have to pay me) don't feel so swell. They all like to talk big, about how many customers they have and how much money they make and what prime-time high rollers they all are. But the truth is, there aren't many players like me. Forget about what all the thousands of other customers do, wagering $50 and $100 a game: If I win, the bookies lose; if I lose they win. Period.

On this day, the bookies get crushed. For $434,000.

The first to start whining is Larry Houston, from Nautica. When I call to make a late bet, he snatches the phone away from his clerk and accuses me of being a beard for someone really smart. "And frankly," he sniffs, "I'm not real happy about it." My limits, he informs me, have been slashed. Forget about $30,000 wagers; I can bet $5,000 on a college game.

I tell him he can kiss my ass, and hang up.

While I'm on the phone with Brother Herbie, relaying the bad news, Larry Houston is undoubtedly on the phone with all the other bookies he can think of, including my other major out, Rio Sports, telling them who I "really am."

When I call Rio to make a few more late bets, the clerk informs me my limits have been cut in half. When I inquire why this might be, he tells me because I'm betting "very close to the kickoff."

"Fine. I'll make a point of calling earlier next time," I say, and hang up.

When I call back to bet two other games, both of which don't begin for another ninety minutes, the manager, Dave, gets on the line to tell me he's been instructed not to give me more than $20,000 on anything until I speak directly with the owner, Ron Blutstein—the glad-handing big shot who lunched with me only two days earlier. "Sorry," the manager says, "I'm just taking orders."

Twenty minutes later I get a frantic call from Casting Director Seth, my agent, the intermediary between me (his customer) and the bookies (his stores). Only today Seth won't be getting a commission on my losses, because there aren't going to be any losses. At the end of the season there will never be any losses. Perhaps realizing this now, he may not cherish me as he once did.

He says, "We got a problem."

"Damn right we've got a problem." Before he can give me the speech I know is coming, I tell him that I don't want to do business with Larry Houston ever again; that the man has treated me, a good customer, like shit; and that I want to pull all my money from the Nautica account.

Seth claims he understands my position, but that all the bookies have been calling him, screaming about me being a beard for some big guy in Las Vegas, something about wiseguy money. "This is the first I've ever heard about anything like this," he confesses. "I don't even know what they're talking about. But I know they've been checking up on you and they seem certain that you're fronting for this guy. They seem really mad."

I tell Seth I'm mad, too. I tell him that this is not the way I'm accustomed to being treated and that I have a mind to yank my business and gamble someplace else. "Nobody seemed to mind my action when I *lost* a hundred and eighty-one thousand last week! But when I win—that's when all the whining starts."

I can hear Vivian outside my office door. She's probably concerned by all the yelling, but she knows not to intercede when her volcano of a boyfriend is about to erupt.

"Look, I think you should talk to Ron directly. He feels like you set him up."

Herbie has dealt with this kind of situation before, maybe a hundred times, maybe more. "Yeah, it's no good," he says when I call. "Don't worry about it, 44. It happens. Just let 'em cool down a bit. They're just mad right now because they've got no shot to win their money back. You buried them today. Don't worry about it."

I begin to vent my frustrations, but Herbie tells me, as politely as possible, that he's got to get some bets down and that we'll have to talk later.

Big Daddy rings some time later to get a report. "I promise you, 44, some of those games you won, you were the only guy in the world betting them. All this talk about steam, and smart money, and all that bullshit is just a bunch of crying. They're bluffing you. Any time you beat 'em, they start crying." He chuckles bitterly. "You lay the man eleven to ten and he starts crying when you win. And this is after you blow—how much?—hundred an eighty something? I tell you what . . ."

Big Daddy decides to "chill these assholes out" a bit. Don't give them any business for a few days. See how they like losing a customer like Mr. 44. "And I guarantee they'll be eating out of your hand come Tuesday."

The next weekend I make no bets. I have no place to play.

Since the weekend slate of Brain Trust picks contained mostly losers, it turns out the bookmakers probably saved me $200,000. But I'm still out

$287,000. Rio Ron, who days earlier wanted to be my best friend in the world, gives me a dozen excuses about why he's not going to pay me the winnings Rio Sports International owes me.

"My business partners want to talk to your boss before anything further happens," Ron vows. "You played us for patsies. And we're not going to pay you a dime."

For the next five days, I barely sleep or eat. I'm in a constant state of nausea, disgust, and rage. I'm being cheated.

Big Daddy handles this outrageous state of affairs with something like serenity. I'm the one who has to talk to the low-life, thieving bookie and his agent. I'm the one who has to enlist the help of several influential people in the sports-gambling business. I'm the one who has to threaten, insist, and fume. But behind the scenes Big Daddy is pulling the strings, guiding my every move. And he seems to delight in the battle.

Rio Ron offers to pay only $117,000 of his debt. This figure, he explains, represents the previous week's $181,000 he lost to me minus the first week's $64,000 he won, with the final week being called a wash. The agents, Derek and Seth, urge me to take what I can get. Settle for *whatever*, they counsel, and *then* go after the rest. But Rick Matthews and I will have none of that.

This is $287,000 we're talking about. But Big Daddy seems content to lose it all rather than tolerate extortion by a bunch of petty con artists. Indeed, I can almost detect a faint glimmer of glee in his voice when he tells me, "I promise you, 44, if these boys think they're getting heat right now, they have no idea what they're in for. Ol' Uncle Ricky will take care of that, don't you worry 'bout it."

He instructs me to withdraw all my money from the safe-deposit box, get the agent to surrender his key, and wire back everything I have in my account to his bank. He wants all the money back home in Vegas immediately. Which concerns me.

I ask Big Daddy point-blank, "Could these people hurt me?"

"I honestly don't know, 44," Rick admits. "But I want you to be careful. They might try to send somebody over to your house, rough you up or something. But, then again, probably nothing at all is going to happen. I just prefer that you err on the side of caution."

I feel a prickling chill on the back of my neck. "Do you want all the money back because you think you should get it before I get knocked off?"

"My friend, if I thought that, I'd have been there myself first thing Monday. Nah, the reason I want it is because it ain't doin' me no good sitting in your box. I got things I can do with that money, pards." He tells me to listen carefully. "You gotta hear this, 44: I'm not going to let anything happen to you. If I thought you were in any serious trouble, I'd have somebody by your side in ten minutes. Fact is, I've got an L.A. private detective I can call. Don't you worry, pards, I ain't gonna let nothing happen."

"Rick," I say earnestly, "you're my friend, right?"

"You got that right, pardner."

I believe him, but despite his reassurances, I borrow a shotgun from a friend and teach Vivian how to use it. And when Big Daddy sends a courier in a private plane to retrieve the $400,000 in cash I have remaining in my box, I survey the parking lot like a Brinks guard before I step out of the bank lobby with the money bag.

This is not how I envisioned my sports-betting career ending.

The agents admit to me that they don't have the money, that they could never possibly cover Rio Ron's monstrous debt. They say they'll do everything in their power to help me get my money back. Problem is, in Big Daddy's view, the agents *are* responsible for the money. "They guaranteed the bets, didn't they?" he asks me. "Well, then, they better get them guys at Rio to pay, or they can kiss their reputation in the bookmaking business good-bye."

When I repeat this to Derek and Seth, peppering my position with provocative references to other gamblers and bookies, they're understandably scared. But, they tell me, they really truly can't get the bookies at Rio Sports to pay their debt.

Nightclub Derek proposes opening a fictitious account and trying to win the money from them. "And if you lose, just don't pay them."

Seth suggests accepting the buyout offer—and *then* unleashing our wrath on them.

"I'm not negotiating with extortionists," I tell them. "I expect to get paid every dime I'm owed, or they and everyone connected to them is going down hard."

Rio Ron and his partners refuse to pay.

"It's time to draw a line in the sand," Big Daddy tells me. "You explain to these motherfuckers that they have until noon on Monday to pay you your money—or make some sort of acceptable arrangement to pay you—and then the talking is over. And we'll have to go to phase two."

I remind Big Daddy that if we toe the hard line, there's a strong likelihood that we may not collect our money. Not any of it.

He says calmly, "I think you're a big favorite to get your money. A big favorite."

In the midst of all this turmoil and controversy, I'm back to working, betting a meager $10,000 per game with the only bookie who currently will take my action, an outfit based in Curaçao known as Skybook. I'm doing pretty well, too, winning about $40,000. Simultaneously, I'm trying to dig up fresh outs. There are several that are eager for my business, including a couple in Costa Rica, home of Ron Blutstein's Rio Sports International and Greg Champion's Betonsports.com.

I tell Brother Herbie that I'm amazed Big Daddy can even think about betting more money with offshore bookmakers, given the outstanding $287,000.

"Once you get to know the guy," Herbie says, "you'll learn one thing. When the man wants to get a bet down on a football game, ain't nothing going to stop him."

I end up a loser for the weekend with my one offshore out. *And* I'm getting stiffed out of $287,000. By 6:00 p.m. Sunday, I'm muttering to myself like a deranged drifter. Vivian can't stand to see me like this. She announces she's going to a movie with a friend—and shuts the door a bit too emphatically on her way out. I pace around my office, considering my options: a long run in the Hollywood Hills or a pint of premium ice cream? The phone rings.

"Let me ask you something, 44," Big Daddy says. "What do you feel your financial responsibility is in this Rio matter? Don't you feel you ought to make good on this debt?"

"I reckon I should sacrifice my ten percent—twenty-eight thousand seven hundred." I can feel my voice wavering.

Big Daddy snorts. "Listen here, 44. I could get a million people to act as beards, million random names. None of them are any good if they can't guarantee the bets. You," he seethes, "said that our money was safe. You said the agent and the bookmaker were stand-up guys. You convinced me to play with these cheating, slimy thieves. And you think you're only responsible for ten percent?"

My grip on the telephone receiver tightens involuntarily. How long would it take me to earn $287,000 to repay Big Daddy—especially since my tenure with the Brain Trust seems to be concluding? How can I possibly amass that kind of dough without betting on sports? And what might the penalty be if I can't?

"Rick, I'm, I don't . . . Look, I apologize for my bad judgment. I feel sick," I stammer. "You put your faith and trust in me and I let you down."

Big Daddy, satisfied that his point has been made, says, "All right, 44. Don't beat yourself up too badly. Everyone makes mistakes. The smart people learn from them. It's like going to college." He thinks we'll be able to work this all out anyway. But there's a lesson to be learned. He says, "The most important thing in this business, the number one thing: You gotta get paid."

Minutes before the Monday 12:00 noon deadline, I get a flurry of telephone calls from the agents and, finally, Rio Ron himself. Seems I'm going to get my money. In full.

It's just going to take some time. Like six months. They propose paying me $10,000 a week until the debt is fully retired.

When I call Big Daddy with the news, he calmly says, "Yeah, I know all about it already, 44. Now you just see if you can't get these guys to pay you a little quicker."

I do, contacting Pat Colombo, who runs the Right Away Odds computer service (which the entire betting industry, including the Brain Trust, uses), and a consortium of bookmakers, all of whom press young Rio Ron to "do the right thing." Now Ron sees the light. But, Big Daddy reminds me, it's not because of a sense of honor. This isn't a decision based on justice. "This guy'll tell you he wants to do the right thing and all that, but that's all horseshit. He just figured out it'll cost him less in the long run to pay you off and make you go away."

I'm just thrilled to not be ripped off twice in one month. Losing close to $100,000 at Betonsports.com was painful enough.

After two weeks of clumsy avoidance, Rio Ron finally calls me directly to talk about paying me off. Per Big Daddy's instructions, I struggle not to shout or plead or browbeat. I stress to Mr. Rio that I want every dollar owed to me to be paid in full, and I want it as quickly as possible. He gives me countless equivocations about why he should be entitled to whittle away at his obligation for what amounts to twenty-nine weeks. ("You weren't as dumb as you made it seem," he meekly asserts.) I reject them all and, after much badgering, get him to agree to make a sizable down payment—$70,000—and pledge to pay more than the minimum $10,000 installment if he has a good week.

Rio Ron tells me he'll personally meet me at my bank tomorrow with his initial payment.

I briefly fear for my life—and then I tell him I'll be there.

I call Big Daddy. "You shoulda negotiated a better payment plan, 44," he snarls.

I apologize again. And I tell him we need to have a heart-to-heart.

"Go ahead," he says. "I'm listening."

I can feel the pulse hammering in my forehead, but I know what I have to do. "Rick," I say, "our agreement has to be clear, and I've been thinking about it this way. If we encounter any problems with payment, I agree to forfeit my ten percent. I won't, I *can't*, be on the hook for the full amounts of money you play for." I pause, waiting for him to tell me to go to hell. He doesn't respond. "Rick," I tell him, "I can't be on the hook for these monstrous sums, because I don't have that kind of money—and I'm not willing to work for free for five years until I pay off the debt." There's silence on the line. I see my high-roller life expiring. "If you require someone who will guarantee every penny of your money—which is not an altogether unreasonable expectation—you'll have to find someone else to work with."

My heartbeat has slowed some, but Matthews still hasn't spoken. "The truth is, Big Daddy, I haven't slept well for a week. I've been anxious and irritable and miserable. And while I love being your partner, and would like very much to continue being your partner, I can't reliably assume the responsibility you desire."

Big Daddy clears his throat. "That's fine, 44. You're a totally honorable, one-hundred-percent stand-up guy. And I'm completely comfortable working with you. We'll just have to be a lot more careful in the future."

"I'll work diligently to research our prospective outs. I'll gather as much information as I can. But ultimately, it's your call."

"Sounds like a plan. All right, pards, I'll talk to you tomorrow after you get the first payment."

When Viv returns home, I envelop her in a hug and apologize for my grumpiness. "Everything's all cleared up," I tell her.

She hugs me back, but I notice a hesitation, a faint distance between us. "Everything's all right now," I say, reassuring myself more than her.

The next morning, I wake with a sour stomach. Before I leave the house, I kiss Viv and say, "Let's hope I see you again."

"Don't joke that way," she says, frowning. "Do you want me to go with you?"

"No. Just stay by the phone. I've got my cell predialed to our number."

"Be careful, Michael."

Driving to the bank, I scan the traffic around me. It looks like a normal workday morning in Hollywood. When I pull into the parking lot, Rio Ron is already there in his black BMW, whose license plate number I commit to memory. He gives me $71,000 as an initial payment on his $287,000 obligation—*and* he signs a pledge I've drawn up, acknowledging his debt and his intention to pay it in full. This document, I remind him, will be sent to Pat Colombo at Right Away Odds, who will monitor Ron's behavior. Any shenanigans and Rio Sports comes down off the screen.

"I'm gonna pay you in full," he says. "Otherwise why would I even bother giving you this much?" He hesitates. "After this is all paid off, when it's all over, would you consider playing with my shop for small amounts?"

I'm so stunned at the absurdity of his request that I'm left momentarily speechless. In the silence, Rio Ron says, "Think about it. I mean, if it would make you more comfortable, maybe I could post up with *you*, so *you're* holding the money. And if you win—and you know you're probably going to—you'll already have the money."

A bookie posting up with a player? I've now officially heard everything.

Big Daddy enjoys a hearty laugh upon hearing Rio Ron's generous offer.

I'm filled with righteous rage. I want to tell Big Daddy that he is the most remarkable man I have ever met. He's a man who's figured out a way to beat an unbeatable game. A man whom the sports-gambling world fears and respects. A man who is constantly harassed, cheated, and extorted. A man who has every obstacle put in front of him. A man who, nonetheless, continues to succeed. I want to tell him I admire him and, frankly, stand in awe of him. But he's not the kind of man to whom one can say such things.

So I tell him we'll talk soon. And then I hang up without another word.

Another Costa Rican bookie, Don Sanchez, who has a shop called Majestic, pleads with me to give him my business. High limits, good customer service, eight-cent juice—whatever else he can do to earn my action, let him know. With only the word of a third-party reference to vouch for me, he says he'll let me play on credit for the first weekend. And after that I'll only be required to post-up half of my available betting capital. *And* he'll send bank records. I expect Big Daddy to jump on this one like a linebacker pouncing on a fumble. Instead, he's cautious. He wants to know who this guy is, who will vouch for him, what's his background. I tell Rick I'll dig up as much as I can. But I'm feeling for the thousandth time in my betting career that my usefulness to the Brain Trust might be expiring.

Brother Herbie calls shortly before the 9:00 a.m. early college games begin and directs me to place three different bets with Skybook and Nautica, the latter of which is back on my good list, since, on the advice of Seth and Derek, they're accepting my bets on credit. "Mr. Nautica has *got* to know you're with me if he's doing that!" Big Daddy jeers when I relay this information. "They're hoping to hijack our plays."

My only concern is picking a few winners—and, of course, getting paid if I do. For the second week in a row, the picking winners part proves difficult. We go 4–9 and lose $92,000. As Big Daddy is fond of pointing out, the bookmakers have done a fine job of managing my money for me; if they had let me gamble as much as I wanted to I would have bled off $250,000 or more. I watch some of the games on TV. Every missed field goal, dropped pass, and bad break rankles. Every malignant bounce of the ball sears. Every loss feels like a whipping and every win like a consolation prize. For a few hours, I'm feeling very much like the average gambler, resigned to losing and cursing his rotten astrology charts.

I sulk around the house, a nimbus cloud moving slowly from office to den to living room. Vivian tiptoes around me, avoiding any interaction. A little Château Lafite, courtesy of the casino, would be a nice salve at the moment. Instead, I bolt down a tuna sandwich alone while Viv busies herself with e-mail.

"Can we try to get a little luckier today?" Herbie asks when he calls me early Sunday. He, too, is in a bad mood from yesterday. I make a couple of $20,000 total bets with Nautica and a few smaller ones with Skybook. With only $97,000 in action, I have little hope of recouping yesterday's losses.

In fact, as the clock expires on the sixth week of the '98 football season, I recover only $4,000. This leaves me $88,000 to the bad.

This season hasn't been a dream come true. But I still believe in Big Daddy. I have faith.

Later in the week, Big Daddy asks me to pull all my dough out of my Skybook account. He's heard rumors of financial instability. He might be right. Skybook is "undergoing cash-flow problems because of a bank freeze" and is unable to wire me the $192,000 in my account. The owners propose delivering $100,000 in cash to Las Vegas, using a runner. Only problem is, none of the runners in town—professional money movers—know me, and Skybook will only drop money with people they know.

Even if it were indisputably clear that I'm just another crazy bettor, the problem persists: *I* don't know anybody willing to receive the drop. I can talk about guys like Lance Mars and Okie "Oklahoma" Spender, the Poker Players, but I've only *interviewed* these guys. I'm not their friend. They probably don't even know who I am.

The following day Herbie calls me at 8:00 a.m. and delivers four orders. No chitchat, no "Howya doin'?"—just pure transactional conversation. He calls me several more times throughout the morning, but all my bets, per Herbie's instructions, are to go to Nautica only. Skybook, because of slow payment, has lost our patronage. Unfortunately, this reduces by at least half the amount of money I have in action. At the end of the day, after three wins and two losses, I'm a big $7,000 winner.

At least I don't have any airfare and taxi expenses.

On NFL Sunday, the telephone lines at Nautica aren't working properly—something about a blown transformer—and I'm not able to get through to check on the morning lines until shortly after 9:00 a.m. By then, Brother Herbie has placed most of his orders with other outs, and I'm left with only two bets for the entire day, a total of $44,000 in action.

It's hard to get excited. Only four weeks ago I had more than $1 million in play.

Clearly, I need to develop a few more outlets. But Big Daddy has made his position clear: We play on credit or not at all. And we've got to be sure we'll get paid. It's this last part that I'm never certain about. Until then, I'm stuck with my one small account—and a mountain of debt from Rio Ron.

In the meantime we've got a business to run. Rick wants to know how much the various bookies owe me, specifically the creeps at Rio. When I tell him $193,000, Big Daddy says, "Well, maybe his conscience will get the better of him and he'll give you a hundred thousand this week and ninety next week and be done with it."

"If we have to rely on Rio Ron's conscience, we can expect to get exactly zero," I say. "He hasn't shown evidence of having one."

"No, he hasn't," Big Daddy says, enjoying a deep laugh. "No, sir, he has not."

Despite the slow payment from supposedly solvent and upstanding bookmakers, we've still got bets to sweat. The two morning games—a couple of total wagers—both fall perfectly, and I end the weekend a $47,000 winner. It's the first positive outcome in nearly a month. And it feels good.

Leaving Vivian at home, where she's hosting her women's reading group—they're reviewing something called *Submit! . . . to Success*—I take the first flight out of Los Angeles to meet Rick Matthews in his office.

I deliver $104,000 in cash and chat with him for a few minutes, assessing who owes us what and what we're going to do to get it back. I assure him that we'll eventually get every dollar.

"Oh, I got no doubt about that, pards," he says, laughing darkly. "You can bet on that, pardsy-wardsy."

We make plans for dinner later in the evening. I've offered to have him and his sister as my guests. But he immediately dismisses the idea and asks where he can take me. He is, after all, the boss.

I next go to the offices of Right Away Odds, where I finally meet Pat Colombo face to face. Pat is a good kid, a smart, genuine fellow with a good head for business and a decent heart. I immediately like him, and I feel I can represent myself as a big-time bettor out on his own, playing with and against the syndicate action as I see fit. Even if Pat *knows* I'm Big Daddy's partner, he's fully aware that I can't admit the truth. So he (and I) play along.

Pat says he'll help me with my ongoing Skybook problem. I tell him I appreciate his help and make a mental note to drop off some fine cigars for him as a token of my appreciation.

After some pedestrian business (researching a story on backgammon tournaments for a magazine) I meet Brother Herbie for lunch near his office. Without the baseball cap he looks slightly older. But he still sounds the same: good old charming Herbie. He talks with me candidly about how some of the other betting syndicates make huge errors in their timing. He also mentions which games we'll probably be betting later in the week. I love listening to him, and I learn a lot. I also discover that I *have* learned a lot: many of the games he suggests we'll be playing later in the week are games I suspected we would be playing. I'm starting to recognize patterns in our plays—nothing particularly clever or earth-shaking, but intriguing, nonetheless.

Most important, we discuss how I might open up additional outs. I'm keen to do this, but I'm wary of getting Big Daddy in more slow-paying or no-paying spots. Herbie suggests I might propose to Big Daddy something like personally putting up, say, 25 percent of the stake, and if we get stiffed, suffering the loss along with him. "Don't tell him it was my idea," Herbie counsels. "But I think he might be interested in something like that."

I know I am. Later that evening, at one of Big Daddy's favorite Italian restaurants, I discuss the proposition with Rick and his lovely sister. He listens intently, laughs, and summarily dismisses the idea. "I need to have one hundred percent of my money guaranteed, or it's not worth it." Rick Matthews says he would hate to see me lose my entire bankroll because some scummy bookie didn't pay a debt. If we're going to do business together, it will either be with bookies he personally trusts or with book-ies I personally guarantee. That's not a very large pool from which to choose.

Later that evening at Bellagio, I meet my friend Simon Cubes, a man generally considered among the top three backgammon players in the world. He's got something like a million-dollar bankroll, and he's known throughout gambling society—big players who know big players—as an honorable, stand-up guy, a man who wins graciously and pays promptly when he loses. The kind of guy you would like as your bookie.

Over a glass of hot sake, I tell Simon Cubes of my betting woes.

He tells me he might have a solution: He knows an offshore shop that accepts large wagers from so-called wiseguys, and he's so certain of its solvency and honorableness that *he'll* personally guarantee my money.

No post-up necessary, no square John act; just bet what you want and get paid if you win.

Only two hours after dining with Big Daddy, I find exactly what I'm looking for. This sounds almost too good to be true.

And I know what that usually means.

Eleven

MILKING THE COW

My editor from *Good Life* magazine has arranged a round of golf at Bel-Air Country Club, and although I'm outdoors in the floral air, trying with limited success not to stare at the celebrity clientele while chasing my little white ball around the links, I'm never far from the grimy world of sports gambling. Like a convict with an electronic ankle bracelet, I tote around a digital cell phone so Brother Herbie can contact me when the need arises.

Today, the need occurs a few seconds after I've hit my tee shot on the downhill, par-five opener. "Howya playin'?" Herbie asks.

"Just teed off," I tell him, hoping whatever college football team we'd like to bet on won't be terribly offended if I express my support in approximately four hours.

Herbie gives me two plays as I walk to my ball in the fairway. "Go ahead and hit your second shot and then give your guy a call," he says. I run a fairway metal up to the green, take out my cell phone, and bet $22,000 on Iowa State. I also tell Herbie about my prospective out, the one Simon Cubes can arrange. He says he may already be using Backgammon Simon's guy, and that I'll have to get a shop name and a telephone number for him. "Sure sounds good, though," he says.

I'm still on the golf course—the tenth hole this time—when my cell phone rings again. It's Simon, and he's got all the information I need. "The shop's name is Summit Sports. You'll be dealing with the top guy there, Jerry. Your code name is 'Hemingway'—I thought of that one— and this is the eight-hundred number."

I scribble down the information on my scorecard. "He's expecting your call," Simon Cubes tells me. "If you want to reach me this afternoon at my cabana, we can talk more. But you're all set."

Simon is awfully eager for my business. It's understandable: He's getting a 1 percent commission from the bookie on my action, win or lose. (I suspect he hopes I'll win, so I'll play longer before finally succumbing to the power of the juice.) That he hasn't grilled me mercilessly about my ability to pay strikes me as odd. He may somehow know that I'm connected with Big Daddy, and therefore that's all the credit I need.

Eager to start betting big numbers again, I call Herbie with the Summit Sports news.

"Wow," he says, "you threw me a little curve. I didn't think it would be this guy."

"What do you mean?" I ask, confused.

"This guy Jerry passes himself off as a bookie. But he's actually one of the biggest players out there. I don't think we can use this guy. If he figures out where your plays are coming from, he'll just go out and bet every place on the Right Away screen. You'll have to talk to the other guy," Herbie says, referring to Big Daddy, "but I don't think he'll go for this."

With visions of crisp hundred-dollar bills flying from my wallet and out of my life, I call Rick Matthews. Before I can finish an entire sentence, he stops me.

"Forget about Summit Sports, 44. We can't use them."

"But the money is guaranteed—"

"Forget about them, 44. Just put it out of your mind. I'll explain more when I see you, but just forget about them."

"Okay," I say, dejected. In twenty-four hours I've gone from having the perfect out to having nothing. And I'm not even sure why.

•   •   •

Today is one of those betting days when I'm devoutly grateful to have only one out. We get pounded. Four wins and nine losses, to be exact; $60,000 to the bad. Were I betting $30,000, $40,000, or $50,000, the figure might be a quarter million.

The only bright spot in my otherwise bleak day is when Brother Herbie calls me late in the afternoon to bet Southern Mississippi, a game I personally recommended as my best bet of the week. Seems someone with a track record agrees with me. "Here," Herbie says when he calls with the play, "this will make you happy." It makes me even happier when Southern Miss wins. For about twenty minutes I fancy myself something of a handicapper. But I'm careful not to get carried away. Big Daddy told me once that Brother Herbie doesn't have more money because his old friend is too opinionated. "The guy is always betting on a whole bunch of games based on his opinion. He ought to know better, but he doesn't."

Still, when the Brain Trust picks four winners out of thirteen, even a chump like me figures he could do as well.

Winners, I need winners! I need action in general if I hope to make any money. But I *really* need winners. Regrettably, Big Daddy does not oblige. For the week I drop a dismal $106,000—all of it to Nautica. And to make matters worse, I'm still owed a pile of money from the slow payers at Rio and Skybook. For the season, I'm up only $228,000. It doesn't seem like much.

I spend the early part of the new week doing what I like least about being a big sports bettor: tracking down money. According to reliable sources, the bookies had a monster weekend and should be flush—Big Daddy confesses he personally lost $1.9 million, his worst weekend in six years. Extracting payment, however, is a torturously slow process.

Rio Ron claims he had a bad week and can probably get me only $20,000. The con artists at Skybook say their bank is still freezing their money but that they'll probably be able to get me "most" of the $121,000 they owe me by tomorrow afternoon.

On the bright side, my former personal banker, Lucy Davino, has moved from her old bank to a new boutique institution hungry for business. This means it's willing to bend over backward to woo "important" customers. In the distant past I had a college romance with Lucy, who's about the best-looking forty-year-old woman since Sharon Stone. I trust she knows me well enough to understand I'm not involved in money laundering or drug profiteering, or anything more illicit than trying to beat a bunch of offshore bookies out of their money. Just to make sure, we have a long lunch, during which I meticulously explain exactly why I need to send and receive five- and six-figure bank wires on a weekly basis. (I also tell her a couple of hot plays for Sunday.) Lucy assures me that she understands completely, and that she'll educate her colleagues, making certain my special banking needs shall always be met. "You can expect no-questions-asked wiring services. We work with lots of Hollywood celebrities," Lucy reminds me. "Lots of them do business under a different name, a stage name. There's no reason you can't have one, too."

"I'd like a dozen of them," I joke.

Lucy nods thoughtfully. "I can work on that."

"Seriously?"

"As long as they're all connected to your federal tax identification number, I don't see why not."

Then I'm struck with an epiphany: Having a menagerie of "also known as" pseudonyms would come in handy if your real name were useless among the bookmaking crowd. I'm constantly trying to disguise my true knowledge, my real identity from suspicious bookies. If I started playing in their shop under a name they've never heard of—and with a mailing address new to their customer database—I could stay under the radar for precious extra weeks. And if I had enough accounts, I might not have to bet the limit on each game. I could break it up among a handful of surrogate 44s. To satisfy the bank, my social security number would be attached to all the made-up names, which would keep me legal with the tax man and anyone else in government curious about all the money flowing in and out of my accounts. But to the chaps booking the bets in Australia and Antigua, Costa Rica and Curaçao, it would seem as if a whole platoon of affluent gentlemen in Beverly Hills, California, had been infected with gambling fever.

The next day, after Lucy Davino confirms she can put through the necessary paperwork. I open eight new betting accounts with my old pal

Greg "the Extortionist" Champion at Betonsports.com. Trusting that Mr. Champion and his cronies spend more time reading the box scores than the cornerstones of western literature, I assume that fellows like "Sid Carton," "Gene Valejeen," and "Johnny Galt" are more than welcome to wager a few thousand here and there. So are "Nathan Adelaide," "Jules Masterson," and "Francis Loesser"—gambling-crazy Guys hoping to win enough dough to impress their respective Dolls. (My three-year old niece and nephew also open a couple of accounts on behalf of their Uncle Mike.) By the end of a long afternoon setting up accounts over the phone, I've heard the Betonsports.com sales pitch so many times I can practically recite it verbatim: *"Thanks for calling! How did you hear about us?"*

The clerks never grow tired of hearing my voice. Because it's not really my voice.

Big Daddy has given us each a state-of-the-art voice changer. Armed with the tone modulator and a repertoire of accents that are just convincing enough to trick a Costa Rican clerk speaking English as her second language, I open account after account without raising suspicions.

When I report my roster of identities to Big Daddy Rick, he's impressed. "Looks like maybe you figured out how to get back some of that money that piece of shit stole from us, huh?"

"That's the idea. We're going to milk this cow until it's dry."

"And *then* we'll carve it up and put it on the grill. Ol' 44 is working on a farm now. Farmboy 44, milking his cow. You know you're gonna need a new nameplate on your office door, don't you?"

"Really?"

"Yes, sir," Big Daddy wheezes, laughing as he exclaims, "director of milking."

"That's me."

"Ol' 44, director of milking. Now that's funny. Hell, I don't even care how much we take from this piece of shit. I just want to squeeze the udders a little bit."

I tell Rick, "That can be arranged."

"Let's get 'em, daddy rabbit," he exhorts me. "See if we can't pick us some winners."

"You know who I'm counting on for that," I reply.

Big Daddy laughs. "Set 'em up and I'll try to knock over some pins."

Considering that my Brain Trust bankroll is now more than $2 million—of which $200,000 is my nominal cut—yes, I'm rooting for a few winners.

And so we begin Operation Dairy Farm. Under fourteen different names, using eighteen e-mail addresses, three different bank accounts, and a $1,200 voice changer, I—or facsimiles of me—have nearly twenty outs, representing more than $250,000 worth of wagers on college games and more than twice that amount on the pros.

And still, I know that after just a few weeks of consistent winning I might not be able to get a bet down anywhere.

The primary problem with gambling offshore is that although the bookmakers in foreign jurisdictions are licensed and bonded, the gaming commissions that oversee these legitimate businessmen have little incentive to punish—or even scold—misbehaving bookies. In Costa Rica, for instance, shops like Rio, Nautica, and Betonsports.com employ hundreds of local residents and inject millions of dollars into the national economy. The stringent background checks and perpetual oversight found in, say, Australia, where prospective license holders must consent to fingerprinting, are absent in Central America. You might as well be applying for a license to sell hot dogs. The island nation of Antigua, however, has an official gaming commission that collects $100,000 fees and rigorously polices the casinos (or at least pretends to police them). It's allegedly the safest place to play in the Caribbean.

Which is why I'm guardedly excited about the newest outlet I've discovered. The shop is called World Sports Exchange (WSEX), and it comes highly recommended by a tout named Joe Schlockman, who calls himself "The Doctor" and publishes a Web page devoted to sports gambling called The Sports Cure.

I expect that spreading around a little bit of my good fortune should shield me from more NASA- and Rio-style debacles. Although Schlockman is essentially a fraud—he promotes some offshore bookmakers as reputable and dependable although he knows they've stolen money from gamblers—I figure he has enough of his personal reputation invested with World Sports Exchange, a place he says is the safest in the business, to do the right thing. Schlockman will personally insure my money in exchange for some small consideration. I propose 1 percent of my win; he counters with "Just tell me your plays after you bet them." Even the so-called professional handicappers, it seems, want my picks. Schlockman claims that he's spoken to the proprietors of WSEX. Supposedly they've heard about me, they know that I'm a minor legend in Las Vegas, and they'd be honored to have a player of my stature open an account.

This all sounds like a not very clever scheme to hijack the Brain Trust selections. On the other hand, you sleep a lot sounder at night knowing that your $100,000 bank wire (probably) isn't going to disappear into cyberspace. Or that a previously "solvent" bookmaker is going to take more than a month to pay off your winnings—minus whatever he feels like keeping for his trouble. Skybook, the Curaçao-based slow-pay shop, is indeed planning on paying me all my money—less my $10,000 sign-up bonus.

"You mean this guy holds on to your money for five weeks, doesn't pay you when you ask for your deposit back, and he wants to stiff you out of your bonus?" Big Daddy sneers.

"That's what he says," I reply.

"Yeah, I bet you get your ten thousand," Big Daddy says firmly. "You wanna bet?"

"You're the last person I want to bet against. On anything."

"Oh, you'll get it. I betcha you will."

"All right, I'll bet you a hundred," I say, figuring that I've just donated a hundred dollars to Rick Matthews, Inc., in exchange for some peace of mind. Big Daddy is the kind of man who will fight to win a wager until he can't breathe.

"You got it. A hundred. But you gotta help me on this, 44."

"I will," I say. And then I rededicate myself to opening accounts, including one at the venerable English firm William Hill, whose female clerks have the most fetching accents in all of gambling, as though a dozen Judi Denches manned the phones.

In between comical attempts to collect my money from the

scoundrels at Skybook—the excuses they come up with for not sending the funds have reached a level of complex absurdity only Sam Beckett could fully appreciate—I manage to make a few bets with my new bookmakers, none of whom hate me. Yet.

The one place where I suspect real trouble is at Nautica, where a clerk puts me on hold when I try to bet a string of games. I can't be certain, but I believe he patches his boss, Larry Houston, into my call—and Larry simultaneously bets my games with another bookie. If this *is* happening, Herbie will surely discover the chicanery and take the necessary steps. The Right Away Odds company offers an instant-update premium service (for $500 a month) that displays the point spreads at several dozen of the biggest and best casinos around the world, including Las Vegas and the Caribbean. Herb and Rick monitor this screen the way some people track the Dow Industrials. If there's a flurry of trading activity on Brain Trust games seconds after I bet them at Nautica, we have a costly poison pill remedy. The easiest way to discourage a renegade bookie from going out with our plays is to give a rope of wrong sides. That normally quells any lingering urge for larceny.

The Skybook situation is becoming intolerable. I've now heard nearly four dozen reasons, excuses, and equivocations for why I don't have my money after five weeks. When I explain to the gentlemen in Curaçao that it's probably time for me to ask Pat Colombo why Skybook remains up on the Right Away Odds screen, the bookies snap to attention. By the end of the day, they've got approximately $100,000 of the $121,000 they owe me lined up through various sources.

When the fine day comes that I've been paid in full by every bookie who owes me money, the day I can simply bet on football games and collect when I win (without bookmakers whining and sniveling), that will be a lovely day, indeed. Somehow, though, I know it will never happen. This is the enduring paradox of being a winning gambler: It's almost impossible to win over the long run, but if you've figured out a way how, the bookies, the casino—the house—will cut you off like a drunk who's had too much whiskey.

In other words, you can't win. And if you can, you can't play.

. . .

Greg Champion, the proprietor of Betonsports.com, makes a vitriolic posting on Schlockman's Sports Cure bulletin board. While his stated intent is to defend his shop's swindling, his larger (and obvious) motive is to reveal my full name, defame my reputation, and out me as a beard for a "specific betting syndicate known as the Brain Trust."

Although this does not please me, our repatriation plan is working nicely. A few thousand here. Another couple grand there. Maybe $5,000 if we're lucky. Each of my little dairy accounts at Betonsports.com produces a few quarts of winnings. No individual player earns enough to overfill the jugs. But when Nate, the guy with the Chicago accent, and Gene, the French-Canadian fellow, and pleasant Sidney, who sounds vaguely like Cary Grant, all pick more winners than losers, the cream begins to rise. Within a month I've won back all the stolen money, plus another $137,000.

Ideally, I'd like to toil in anonymity. I would like bookmakers around the globe not to talk about me. I would like my private business to be private. But Champion's announcement of my identity, available to anyone with access to the Web, requires a swift and telling response. After consulting with Brother Herbie, who recommends that I fire back, rather than ignore, I post a lengthy and, I daresay, compelling rejoinder to Champion's rant. I emphasize that no matter how Betonsports.com rationalizes its crime, at the end of the day it's still stealing.

Within minutes, several gamblers from around the continent post supportive messages, including two fellows who claim that they too were ripped off by Betonsports.com.

One of these bettors, Dick, from Toronto, sends me a personal e-mail and asks that I call him directly. When I do, he gives me the "inside story" on the relationship between Champion and the Doc. I'm made to understand that the highfalutin Doctor, who passes himself off as the gambler's best friend, is a charlatan who would rather forsake his supposedly lofty principles than risk a few thousands dollars in advertiser money. I'm also made to understand that Toronto Dick is "very sharp" in hockey and would be happy to share information with me—in exchange for my football picks.

I feel like a comely lady with shapely breasts and a firm ass. All the guys can wax poetic about my eyes and my profound comprehension of Yeats, but at the end of the night I know what they really want. Everyone, I realize, is after the Brain Trust's football picks. For if the smart-money plays are strong enough that a bookie getting 11–10 from me would stoop to cancel my bets, then these selections must be something terribly special.

And the truth is, almost nobody really makes his own selections anymore. Everyone wants someone else to make decisions for him. And a guy like Big Daddy Rick Matthews isn't a bad place to start.

Juan, a professional money mover for Ferdinand & Blair, pleads with me to have lunch with him. He's got some information that I might be interested in, he says. Eager to hear what this might be—and also because I'm amused to see how desperate and conniving other gamblers are to get my selections—I agree to meet him at the Sunset Strip café. Seems Juan wants my advice and guidance on how to be his own man. Specifically, he's tired of chasing numbers, following the smart guys. He wants to get someone to program a computer for him so that he might make his own selections. And he's wondering if, you know, I could help him. For a fee, of course.

Slurping up a strand of linguine, I tell Juan he'll have to figure this one out on his own.

He stares at me blankly, crestfallen. "I really admire you, Mike; you're doing what I always wanted to do."

Perhaps I've grown paranoid, or generally cynical about everyone connected in any way to the whole sports-betting industry, but I suspect at this moment that Juan is either an agent for one of the other big betting teams, or an agent for one of the bookies. An agent of some sort.

Or he's just like everyone else: a guy who smells money in the form of my weekend picks.

Brother Herbie still has a touch of the priest about him. But when I bet Cincinnati in the Thursday night game and Larry Houston, the bookmaker at Nautica, immediately bets Cincinnati with three other shops on Herbie's Right Away screen, which instantly registers the line changes at casinos around the world, the former monk goes berserk.

"That goddamn motherfucker Larry Houston!" he yells through the phone. "The second you bet him, he turns around and bets the world. Caribi, Grande, and your old friend Rio, they all moved the game right after you bet."

"It couldn't be a coincidence," I say calmly.

"Highly doubtful," Herbie says. "Well, now we know what Mr. Houston's doing, we're gonna have to teach him a little lesson."

A lesson, I know, means giving him a bunch of opposites. In other words, Mr. Houston will get plays on the wrong side, bet the world, and move the number, and we'll come in and take the right side. Only problem is, I'll have to blow off a pile of my money keeping the bookie in line.

But Brother Herb tells me not to worry, we won't be giving Mr. Houston opposites. "We just gotta be real careful with him, that's all," Herbie drawls. "Go out on stuff late, be real selective, confuse 'em a little. See, we can't have him hijacking our numbers. Sort of defeats the whole purpose of betting ten dimes with him if he's gonna go out and bet fifty himself."

Even the bookies want to be unofficial members of our team.

Juan the money mover calls again. Seems he wants to put me into a shop he's used forever. Says I can play on credit; he'll guarantee the money. Says I can get high limits.

As a gesture of friendship, he offers to share with me Blair & Ferdie's plays for the weekend. I tell him not to bother; I can guess what they are. If a game has moved two points and I haven't bet it, I can safely assume it's Blair & Ferdinand's syndicate. Before Juan can reply, I rattle off three or four of his supposed hot picks.

"Man, you're good," Juan says, chuckling.

And just then I hear a walkie-talkie in the background squawk out, "Florida State minus sixteen and a half. Florida State minus sixteen and a half."

"Order coming in!" I say, laughing.

"Gotta go. I'll talk to you later!" Juan hangs up to start chasing numbers.

I don't rush to make the bet. I already placed it two days ago in Australia.

Saturday we go fifty-fifty. Part of this, I suspect, is that, despite Brother Herbie's assurances, I've played several opposites with Nautica. I don't like playing the wrong side—and losing—but I'm amused anyway. How many guys can afford to throw up $33,000 smokescreens?

Big Daddy calls wanting to know how my relationship with World Sports Exchange is holding up. I tell him it's been perfect until now, although there's no telling how long WSEX's politeness will last if I continue to take $100,000 a week out of the shop.

"All right, sweet face," he croons. "Everything good with you? Your family? How's your dad doing?" Before I can answer, Rick muses out loud, "Maybe we should be using Summit"—the high-rolling shop that just two weeks ago he dismissed out of hand.

This is a curious development. If what I've learned is correct, Summit puts people on for enormous amounts, as high as $100,000 a game. But the bookies at Summit also have a reputation for being huge players, the kind who, if they think a customer is smart money, will bet ten times as much as the customer. This syndrome, as capably demonstrated by Larry Houston at Nautica, is anathema to Big Daddy. Even if I can bet, say, $50,000 on a college game with Summit, this one huge wager doesn't add up to much good if Mr. Summit goes out and chews up $250,000 of the Brain Trust's other outlets.

Nonetheless, Rick instructs me to find out what kind of limits I can get from Mr. Summit and to report back. "We have to be super-careful with this guy," Big Daddy warns me. "But don't get me wrong, a fifty-thousand out would be great."

I call Simon Cubes, my backgammon pal in Las Vegas, the one who is guaranteeing both sides of the money, and he assures me the limits I'm requesting shouldn't be a problem. Getting paid shouldn't be a problem. And being smart shouldn't be a problem. Simon, I assume, doesn't waste his time reading sports-betting chat sites, so he probably didn't see Greg Champion's exposé of my identity. The fact that it all sounds too good to be true sets off the usual warning sirens. But it doesn't stop me from calling "Jerry," the proprietor.

Jerry sounds nice enough—from near New York or New Jersey, I would guess. He tells me that the limit I'm asking for ($50,000 on both college and pro games) are acceptable to him. He just asks that I don't sit on the computer and try to beat him to the line moves.

I assure him that I don't follow the moves; I bet before them or against them. Occasionally, I say, my picks coincide with one of the syndicate plays—that can't be helped—but I generally won't be giving him the tail end of the steam games.

He seems satisfied with that arrangement, though he tells me, "I'm not interested in booking very large on college totals, maybe three or four dimes maximum."

"Fine," I say, making a mental note to not give this shop any of these bets.

We'll settle by wire whenever I request; his clerks will know what I'm authorized to wager; and he'll look forward to doing business with me.

"One more thing," Jerry says before ringing off. "Your code name, 'Hemingway,' didn't fit in our computer. So I changed it. We're calling you 'Papa.' "

Brother Herbie and I talk late at night—he's been out most of the evening living it up at the Las Vegas dice tables. He's excited about the Summit possibilities. This outfit isn't hooked up to Pat Colombo's premium service, and thus is slightly more anonymous than the shops on the Right Away Odds screen. But he's cautious about how we proceed. "I'm telling you, 44, we're gonna have to keep you super cool at this shop, because this man down there in Carousel"—that's how he pronounces "Curaçao"—"he'll bet the world if he knows where your plays are coming from."

A new chapter in my sports-betting life seems to be opening. With the amount of money I'll be wagering with Summit, I stand to earn a pile of money. "This is the time of year I look forward to," Brother Herbie explains. "The more information we can feed into the computer, the more accurate it is. These few weeks leading up to the bowl games are usually the best ones. The later it gets, the better we get."

I request a $42,900 withdrawal from World Sports Exchange. It's extraordinarily cordial for a shop that has lost $142,800 to me in two weeks. Big Daddy thinks the bookies there might be going out on my plays. But I think the bosses in Antigua, Sherm and Thomas, former traders on the Pacific Stock Exchange, are genuine straight shooters, old-fashioned bookmakers who try to attract equal action on both sides of the proposition and collect the juice from the losers. When they say they don't mind my action because they've got thousands of other players to absorb the swings, I think they're telling the truth.

When Brother Herbie calls to make sure my weekend figures match up with his (they do) and to make sure all my outs are paying me as they ought to (they are), I confirm that my figures are accurate except for one thing: A certain acquaintance of his lost a $100 wager to me. Seems this fellow bet me $100 that Skybook would pay me my $10,000 sign-up bonus. And we all know how that turned out.

"Don't get me involved in that man's silly wagers," Herbie says, laughing. "He'll try to make me pay a piece of it. I think you should wait until about January and mention something like, 'Say, pal, you've been carrying a figure with me for some time now. How do you intend on paying it?' "

We laugh like jackals and return to scouring the betting lines, looking for the magic half points that make all the difference.

While my stable of phantom players steadily squeeze Greg Champion's teats—I've extracted nearly $350,000 from the larcenous beast—I give my new out, Summit Sports, nearly $400,000 worth of bets on seven college football games. It takes them courteously and professionally. Almost too easily.

I ask Herbie, "So, is Mr. Summit behaving himself?"

"I'm looking at the Right Away screen as we speak," Herbie tells me. "He seems to be holding the bets, he's not laying off your action with other bookmakers—for now. I guess he's not sure what to make of you. He's still feeling you out, trying to get you figured. Of course, everything you gave him is stone cold."

That's exactly how I'd like to remain: stone cold. Big Daddy promises he's going to extraordinary lengths to keep me camouflaged, that the games he's listed for me are against what "everybody in the world" is betting. "This guy, 44, he's sniffing around you like a hound dog. And as long as he can't connect you with me we'll be okay. But as soon as he does," Big Daddy chuckles, "you never seen a man move so quick on a game."

The key is to keep Mr. Summit confused. "You're dealing with double sharp people down there," he warns me. "You know from playing poker, when you bluff you can't just wave at a pot. You gotta come strong. So we're gonna mix in plenty of opposites, keep this guy confused." Brother Herbie, Big Daddy confides, is "a super nice guy who does a really good job." But in this situation, according to Big Daddy, "Herbie's in way over his head. So I'm gonna try to handle this account personally, as much as I can."

That's fine with me. I like getting his calls, hearing the oddly endearing comments Rick makes as he goes through the schedule of games: "TCU. Texas Christian University, the Frogs, the ol' Froggies . . . hmmm, Wisconsin minus ten . . . Whiskey minus the points." As long as the cerebrum of the Brains keeps me icy—and mixes in about 57 percent winners—I'll be happy.

My first wager with Summit is a loser, a $55,000 loser, which hurts the bankroll but buys some goodwill. The old maxim that the bookie is happy when half his customers win and half of them lose—preferably on alternating weeks—is a laughable lie. Bookies want *every* player to lose, especially the ones like me who bet big.

Case in point: Sherm, the proprietor of World Sports Exchange, tells me that from hereafter, the point spreads I see on my computer don't apply to me anymore; they're for smaller bettors. Anything I want to bet has to be cleared through him. Those are the rules.

"Okay," I say to him nonchalantly.

"You're betting a lot of money," he reminds me.

I go ahead and give him a couple of wagers, and on one of them, South Carolina getting 32 big points from the Southeastern Conference bully, Florida, I joke that I should have to pay only five-cent juice on the wager, since the side I'm taking is so frigid. (Everyone in the world is on Florida.)

"No, we don't need to be giving you any sort of break," he says, laughing bitterly. "A guy who's picking eighty-five percent winners doesn't need any help from us. Hell, I'd be happy if you worked your way down to the fifty-five-percent level. I mean, if you play any college basketball with us, I know you wanted ten thousand a game. But I couldn't give you any more than five thousand, probably. You're too good."

I laugh along with him, but I get the subtext: *You're on probation, pal. And you had better start losing pretty soon or we're going to have to take drastic action.*

We'll see how my full slate of college games goes tomorrow. As Big Daddy says, there are only two sides to every game. It doesn't take too much luck to look like a certified genius. Or a hopeless sucker.

I have more than $500,000 in action on today's college football games. I'm actually nervous. A disastrous day would more than erase my profits for the entire season; a triumphant day would make me momentarily rich. (And probably an ex-client.) After three morning games I'm $170,000 in the hole at Summit. I'm discovering that the bookie there, New York Jerry, has his clerks give me one line and forces me to bet with him on a slightly different one. He's scalping points wherever he can. The only time he gives me the stated line—the going rate—is when he knows there's a slightly cheaper price out there that he can grab for himself.

If I ask Jerry for a rundown of the lines, he asks me which contest in particular I'm interested in. If I tell him all of them, he says he'll give me to a clerk, but that the point spread the clerk reads to me is good for only $4,000 or $5,000. For big bets I must talk directly with him. When I relay this news to Big Daddy, he tells me we're probably not going to continue being customers with Mr. Summit. "You're dealing with a super conniving guy down there, 44," he reminds me. "It's like being on the phone with a guy who has his hand in your pocket."

Big Daddy tells me that the next time New York Jerry attempts to scalp me, I should simply tell him I'm not interested in playing cat-and-mouse with him, and if the line from the clerks is good for only $5,000, then perhaps I should just bet $5,000 at his shop. "If he don't want your business, he ain't gonna get it," Big Daddy says. "Besides, 44, I'm not sure you want to keep giving this man your action. I think he's starting to kick out most everything you're playing. And that doesn't do us no good."

For the entire day, we avoid Nautica, since Larry Houston is most definitely kicking out all my bets to other shops. But on one game— Army vs. Tulane—we can't resist. Nautica's number (Army + 18) is a full point better than what any other outlets are offering. So I give him the play.

One minute later Brother Herbie calls me, swearing like a truck driver. "That rotten motherfucker! Never again! That cock-sucking piece of shit!" I check my Right Away Odds screen. The point spread around the world has dropped to Army +16.

Larry Houston isn't getting any more of my college business, that's for certain.

To mollify Herbie, I share with him my play of the day, the one I'm putting on my VIP 900 line. "Tennessee minus the points," I tell him. "And if this game doesn't win, you're gonna get the bowl games . . . ABSOLUTELY FREE!!"

He chuckles. And when Tennessee wins but fails to cover the spread, Herbie doesn't forget to call me later in the day to remind me that he'll be looking forward to getting his complimentary bowl game selections.

Given the pothole I started in, the day ends reasonably. I win $38,000, most of it from the scalpers at Summit. I win a little at Nautica and lose a little at World Sports Exchange (finally!). Mr. Summit won't get any of my pro business tomorrow. Mr. Nautica will—but he'll have to be handled carefully. And Mr. World Sports is probably resting a bit easier than he has for the past two weeks. I've learned two lessons today: A bookie will take advantage of a customer as long as he can get away with it. And, as Big Rick suggests, I will show far better results if I don't have an opinion.

.   .   .

On Monday, when most American men are figuring out how they're going to tell the wife that they've blown the mortgage payment on weekend football games, Simon Cubes, the backgammon expert who put me into Summit, calls to ask how I liked the shop. I tell him the truth: I think Mr. Summit is scalping me, and I don't like it very much at all.

He says the proprietor at Summit has admitted that he "fears and respects" me as a player. "He thinks you're very sharp. He's got a guy playing there who has won millions betting sports, and he's not at all impressed with the guy. But you," Simon Cubes assures me, "he's very impressed with."

I feel like saying, *I know he is. That's why he's going out and betting all my games as quickly and widely as he can.* But I don't. I just calmly repeat my complaint that the guy won't give me a straight line. And if that continues, he'll lose my business.

"I'm not even sure he wants your business," Cubes tells me.

No, it seems no one does.

But within days Big Daddy calls and asks, "You wanna give Mr. Summit some action?"

"You know I do," I reply, pen in hand, poised to take down his orders.

"Well, you go get you some numbers from him and get right back to me. And make it clear to him, there ain't gonna be no bullshit. If he's gonna play around he's not gonna get your business," Big Daddy declaims.

"Yes, sir," I say, knowing the gulf between Big Daddy's expectations and the reality of dealing with bookmakers on an everyday basis is wider than the chasm between a wiseguy and a square. When I call Summit I'm half expecting New York Jerry to inform me that my account has been canceled. But he reads me his lines without too much whining. I do owe him $25,000, after all. The amount I wager, Jerry says, forces him to give me "obnoxiously neutral" lines.

I call Big Daddy, who instructs me to wait until 5:00 p.m.—right

around the kickoff time for the Thursday night college football game—
and then be ready for a whole string of bets.

It's more like an industrial rope. Big Daddy gives me fourteen Brain
Trust games to bet at both Summit and World Sports Exchange. Ten
minutes later, with little controversy, scheming, or double-dealing, I've
wagered almost $600,000 on the weekend college football roster.

I report the bets to Herbie, who emits a small sigh. "All right, pardner,"
he says. "Now let's find us some winners."

One day later, the college basketball season begins.

"How much is WSEX gonna take off you in basketball?" Herbie asks. I
tell him: $2,500 for now, maybe more later. "And Summit?"

I tell him: $10,000.

"Call them up. Tell them you're only interested in the Big Ten games.
Get the lines."

I do as I'm told. Secretly, I'm hoping not to give any more business to
Summit for the time being. I've got nearly half a million dollars at risk
tomorrow on football games, and I'd like to stay as cool as I possibly can,
if that can be done while betting $500,000.

Ultimately, Brother Herbie instructs me to leave Mr. Summit alone.
He tells me we're also probably done altogether with Larry Houston at
Nautica. He's proven to be too adept a hijack artist. When I talk to Houston later in the day to confirm a figure he owes me, he staunchly denies
following my plays. "Well, some bookmaker out there is betting the
world and moving the number," I say.

"I guarantee you it's not me," he says.

"Well, next time you wonder why I always seem to bet and then the
number moves, ask yourself who's doing the moving: me or the bookies,"
I tell him. I want Houston to know I'm on to him, just as he's let me know
that he's on to me.

Everyone is on to everyone else. And none of it means a damn thing if
the sides don't come in winners.

Herbie gives me a string of bets to place with World Sports Exchange, including one on Kansas State vs. Missouri. I make the wagers and call him
to report.

"Kansas State, minus thirteen and a half to win—"

"Goddammit, 44!" Herbie screams, uncharacteristically using the Lord's name in vain. "Minus thirteen, not thirteen and a half!"

I look down at my notes, Kansas State –13.

"I must have—"

"Shit, there's some twelve and a half out there," Herbie hisses.

"Sorry. My mistake," I say, feeling terrible. "I'll eat the half point. You're down for thirteen. If it falls on the number, I'll be responsible for the ten thousand," I pledge.

"No, you don't have to do that," Herbie replies.

"Yes I do. I screwed up. I'll take the responsibility. Let's just hope the damn game doesn't fall on thirteen!"

"Yeah, I sure hope it don't," Herbie says.

With less than a minute to go, Kansas State has the ball in Missouri territory. They lead by six. A "meaningless" touchdown and point after would make the margin of victory exactly thirteen.

I have wagered $11,000 with World Sports Exchange that Kansas State will win by 14 points. For the first time in my sports-betting career, I'm devoutly rooting for one of my bets to lose.

Thankfully it does. Kansas State, doing the gentlemanly thing, takes a knee and runs out the clock.

"You escaped that time," Herbie says, shortly after the final gun.

"And I learned a lesson."

"Now you see how the bookmaker feels when he gets middled," Brother Herbie counsels me.

When the results come down as they do today, the bookies really ought to love me. Despite being up as much as $150,000 around lunchtime, I end up blowing more than $65,000 for the day, losing three big $70,000 games in a row. Mr. Summit is now up $58,000 on me—but he'll probably still whine and moan when I try to bet him on college football games. Maybe he's right. Maybe I really do have a big edge over him and all the other bookies out there. It just doesn't feel that way right now.

On Sunday, early in the morning, I bet Nautica on an NFL total, Detroit and Tampa Bay over 36 points. An hour later, shortly before game time, Herbie rings back and orders me to bet the other side—*under 37.*

I assume he's made some sort of clerical mistake. "You mean over, right?" I say.

"No, no, *under*," he replies. "Do it for fifteen thousand and buy the half point. Hurry."

I have no time to protest. Maybe he's gotten late word that Barry Sanders pulled a hamstring during warm-ups or a monsoon is about to hit Tampa Bay. In any case, I've already bet the game with WSEX in Antigua. Apparently I'm stuck on the wrong side.

Or maybe not. The Lions and the Buccaneers combine for 35 points in the first half.

I call Herbie. "Do you have time to explain to me what that whole deal was about, buying off of the over bet?" I ask him.

"Well, we were having some problems with one of our other bets. I thought Mr. Houston was moving out with the play, so I gave him this other one. But I guess I was wrong: he'll move on your college stuff, but he'll keep the pros."

"So it was an opposite you gave me at first?" I say.

"Yeah, I didn't want to give it to you, but we gotta keep Houston on a leash, see?" Herbie says. "The under was the right side."

"Thirty-five points in the first half?" I say, skeptical.

"Well, damn thing *was* the right side," he says, chuckling.

The afternoon slate is all losers, and I blow back most of my profits. This seems to be an alarming trend of late: win early, lose late. I'm perilously close to needing a fill-up on some of my smaller accounts in Australia and Gibraltar. Which would be fine if I were winning steadily with the big bookies. But I'm not.

I get a surprise call from Big Daddy, whose voice I haven't heard in nearly a week. He wants me to get the lines from Summit while he holds on the other line. When I come back to him with the information, he asks me, "Now what's the guy takin' off you in the pros? A hundred?"

"No, fifty thousand," I report. "But he said I could always ask for more."

"Yeah, I know about the ask for more business," Big Daddy says, the irritation seeping through his honey-coated drawl. "What's the stated limit?"

"Fifty thousand," I tell him.

And then he asks me a funny question. "That one percent you're paying the guy to guarantee your money, are you getting any of that?" He means Simon Cubes.

"No, I'm not," I say, truthfully.

"All right," he says. "I'll be back."

Big Daddy is always thinking, always probing, always searching for ways that he can get the best of a proposition or for ways that someone might be getting the best of him. When enough money is involved, anyone, he must assume, will compromise his principles. Even me.

We move strong on the USC–Notre Dame game, laying 6 on the Trojans. Then 6½. Then 7. Within a few hours I've got $88,000 riding on the backs of my local scholar-athletes. The thinking here is this: Notre Dame's starting quarterback, who single-handedly accounts for 55 percent of the team's offense, is out with a bad ankle. USC's run defense is superb. And Notre Dame's pass defense is not. Ergo, USC big.

When the point spread moves dramatically around several key numbers—6 and 7, for example—the astute bettor can often come back on the cold side later in the week and have a large middle working. Thanks to the legions of followers, who drive up the odds after I've bet, the point spread finally settles on USC –9.

Without waiting for Big Daddy's instruction, I take Notre Dame +9 points for a few thousand dollars. If Southern Cal wins by 6, 7, 8, or 9, I win (or tie) on both sides. Any other result and I win one side and lose the other. In other words. I'm getting approximately 20–1 on my money with four very commonly occurring numbers as my targets.

For a very small risk ($350), I'm virtually free-rolling for a large return on investment ($7,000). I can't wait for Saturday afternoon.

nksgiving Day, when normal people ought to be appreciating
1 friends, health and vitality, liberty and justice, the Brain Trust
holiday gambling. While Viv attempts to roast a turkey, I'm
1y office working the phones.

Big Daddy instructs me to bet Tulane minus the points at Summit. Distracted by the possibility that I'm wasting my life on mercenary pursuits when I should be engaged in secular spiritualism, I fumble the order.

The Tulane game is an added game, shown only on regional television and generally bet only by wiseguys, bookies, and complete addicts. On such games Mr. Summit normally takes $10,000 from me. Generally, Big Daddy always wants more than that.

When I call to bet the game, New York Jerry has the number I'm looking for (which is rare, since the guy is the most accomplished scalper I've ever dealt with) and, to my surprise, he offers to let me bet $20,000 on the game. I take it gladly, assuming that Big Daddy will be pleased with my decision.

"Didn't I tell you specifically ten thousand on that game?" he seethes over the phone.

"Yes, I just thought—"

"That play was an opposite, a curveball. The only reason he gave you twenty on it is because there's all sorts of shops out there with a half point better. So he's gonna just take your money and lay it off with them at the better number. So you see, my friend, you got screwed." Big Daddy chortles.

"I'll take responsibility," I say. "I'll eat the extra ten thousand."

"No, you don't have to do that. It'll all just get thrown into the pile," Big Daddy assures me. "But you gotta just do what I tell you. You bet the right games at the right numbers and we're gonna do all right," he says. "We'll do just fine. Now go pick up the latest numbers."

"Would you like basketball as well?" I ask. We've been popping off a few college hoops games here and there and having a good time of it.

"Nah," he replies, "I'm a football expert. Just get me the football lines."

I like it when Big Daddy gets a little cocky. It means he's about to get the best of the proposition.

When I bet the Arkansas-LSU game with Mr. Summit, he tells me it's the last $50,000 game he wants to take off of me in college. "I only want tens from you from now on," he informs me. "The pros you can bet whatever you want."

I don't point out that I'm losing; I don't ask him why; I don't plead my case. I know why this is happening. And this time I'm not even upset. I knew this would come to an end sometime, I had just hoped I could make it to the bowl games. Or win a half-million dollars.

On the heels of a good Friday, we have a very good Saturday, winning four of our five big college games. The hoped-for middle doesn't come in on the USC–Notre Dame game—the Trojans win by 10—but at least the right side wins. It's a six-figure day—the first in some time, and I momentarily feel like we have a chance to make a big score.

As long as I can find someplace to take my bets.

Simon Cubes calls to find out how I feel about getting cut back. He wants to know if I'll continue playing anyway. He also wants to know if I'm connected with Big Daddy Matthews.

I hate to lie to people I like. But if I can be connected to the Man, my sports-betting career will come to a quick halt. So I dance around the question, dropping names of other syndicates, admitting nothing.

"Bottom line is, they're scared of you," Cubes reveals. "Even though you're losing, they're scared."

"So if they don't want my business, they won't get it," I say.

"Sure, but *I* want you to keep playing."

Of course he does. He's already earned close to $5,000 for doing nothing. "Is there any sort of compromise we can work out?" he wonders. "Like, you'll bet the pros with them if they'll let you bet, I don't know, twenty or thirty in college?"

"No," I say flatly. I've learned from Big Daddy: I'm not negotiating with bookies. No one is doing me a favor letting me bet 11 to win 10. "No deal," I say.

On Sunday, about thirty seconds before the early NFL kickoffs, I bet Kansas City –3 against Arizona. When I report my wager to Herbie, he sounds genuinely enthusiastic. "You got it? Good work!" he says. "Go Chiefs!"

Go, indeed. And go Jets. And go Ravens. Go all of you, and I'll personally win $370,000 for the Brain Trust.

It's a blessed day. Every pick is a winner. For the week I net a near-record $372,000. Almost as sweet as the six-figure profit is this: I'm leaving Mr. Summit $39,000 in the black. And I'm continuing to drain Greg Champion's reservoirs, eight little bets at a time.

I officially bid adieu to shifty Mr. Summit, requesting that he wire me my entire balance and terminate my account.

"So we're through?" New York Jerry asks.

"Yes," I reply tersely.

"All right," he says, and he doesn't sound sorry at all to see me go. When the Summit funds arrive at my bank, they're short by $27. It's Jerry's poetic way of saying farewell.

Nearly $200,000 of profit arrives from my other accounts. Regrettably, I must keep my word with the Doctor, the wormish charlatan who runs The Sports Cure, and pay him his 1 percent commission on my World Sports Exchange winnings. Though he continues to tout bookmakers whom he knows to be scoundrels as "reputable" and "excellent"— including, most laughably, the slow-paying extortionists from Rio— I'm honor-bound to give the Doc his promised cut. It makes me nauseous.

Indeed, much of the sports-gambling business makes me feel this way. Though we're slaughtering college basketball, picking nearly 75 percent winners, I feel no joy in the victories. Every bookmaker whines, every one of them snivels, as though I should feel guilty for winning. When I ask if I might get my limits raised from the paltry $2,500 per game World Sports Exchange is offering me, Sherm, the boss there, says, "Not so long as you pick so many winners. Once you come down a bit closer to fifty-fifty we can talk about it."

For the sake of my bankroll, I hope that doesn't happen. But for the sake of longevity, I know eventually it must. Or I'll need to find another cow to milk.

Twelve

DEPUTY 44

November 1998. Championship Saturday in college football. I have substantial money riding on nearly all of the six contests, but I can barely muster the enthusiasm to watch. I'd almost rather join Vivian, who has zero interest in the games, on one of her forays to the mall to shop for bath gels and incense. After so many close decisions, so much drama—well, I'm worn out. I'd almost rather wait until the end of the day, check the scores, and tally up the damages (or, as is the Brain Trust's custom, the profits). And today, as on most weekends, they're substantial.

Despite a loss on my biggest bet of the day—$44,000 on Kansas State—I still win nearly $70,000. A big portion of my earnings comes from college basketball games, in which we're winning at a mathematically unexplainable pace. Eighty percent of our picks are correct.

It's called dumb luck, a statistical deviation, a positive fluctuation. It can't last.

I joke with Vivian that if I keep winning 80 percent of my college basketball games, I'll be barred from playing anywhere on Earth. No bookmaker will want my business. On the other hand, if I keep picking 80 percent winners, I could establish one hell of a 900-line tout service.

The next morning, when I go to bet my first college basketball game of the day, the clerk at Nautica informs me that management has cut me down from $5,000 to $3,000 per game. I don't argue. When a guy is on a streak such as the one I'm enjoying, if he proclaims Colorado State +4 points to be the Holy Truth, than it shall be. If he says lay the points on Indiana, than you shall, and you will revel in the glory of his wisdom. You do not understand what it is he knows, what gives him this sporting omniscience, but you do not contradict it. And you do not allow him to bet very much in your shop.

If I were able to bet as much on college hoops as I'm able to on NFL football, I would have won something like $600,000 over the past two weeks. But since I can't, we must return to the gridiron, where, in recent memory at least, we've been torrid.

Big Daddy and the Brains have found nothing to their liking—at least not anything Rick Matthews cares to share with me. For the first time in a long time, I don't bet a single Brain Trust NFL game. This won't sate the taste for action I've been cultivating over the past few months. So I do what I know I should not: bet a few games on my own opinion.

One of my selections is against the steam; one anticipates the steam; and another is based purely on my own handicapping, meager as it is.

All three games come home winners.

Two weeks ago, I was down to my last $6,500 with my personal offshore bookmaker in Australia. At the conclusion of today's action, my balance is $25,000.

The next Saturday we again go 4–0 in college basketball. The only force that can slow us down, it seems, is my unwillingness to completely divorce myself from the real world. I continue writing, working at my "other" job. The money I earn seems negligible, but the work keeps me engaged with the 99.99 percent of society whose lives don't revolve around basketball and football point spreads—like Viv, who's becoming increasingly unhappy with the amount of time I spend gambling.

One weekend, I travel to the Bahamas for business and thus miss one of our big moves on an NFL game. The Brains somehow learn, before anyone else, that Brett Favre isn't going to start for the Packers. Brother Herbie isn't angry at my absence, just disappointed. He suggests that to avoid situations like this in the future—times when I'm hard to reach and a game fairly begs to be bet—we should set up my phone accounts so that my "girlfriend" (actually his charming wife, Charlotte) can call in bets for me. This arrangement seems untenable to me and, I'm sure, to the bookies. But Herbie says it's no problem. I don't argue; I'm a good soldier.

But I know that this is another instance where the Brains will likely kill the golden goose for a shot at a few more eggs.

It's Christmas Day. A year ago this time I was in residence at Caesars Palace with my girlfriend, my computer, and my cat. For normal people, it's a time of the year that means family and gifts and peace on earth. For sports fans, Christmastime means the beginning of an interminable menu of college football bowl games. For sports *bettors* it means there's a big game (or three) to gamble on almost every day of the week between December twenty-third and the Monday after New Year's. This year Viv and I can snuggle on the couch by the fireplace, eat holiday treats, and pretend we're the average family on vacation from work and responsibility. Except every time the phone rings I'm back on duty.

Brother Herbie wishes me a happy Hanukkah (and a happy Kwanzaa) and reports that we have a couple of small plays on the two Hawaiian bowl games today. On the first one, Colorado vs. Oregon, I have no opinion. On the second one, Washington vs. Air Force, I have a strong opinion—and it's in direct contradiction to Big Daddy's view.

This has happened before, and normally Big Daddy's side is the right one and mine is the loser, and I'm left wondering, *How does he do it?* But today I feel particularly convinced that Air Force will bomb Washington, despite Big Daddy's recommendation to take Washington plus the points. Yet after I place $20,000 worth of wagers for our group, I call my bookie in Australia and after a moment's hesitation hang up. I can't make myself bet on Air Force. The Brain Trust has declared the team damaged goods. It's tainted.

Big Daddy's cautionary words are haunting me: *"Herbie's problem is he's got too many opinions."* And I do, too, I suppose. You can't help developing them after watching something like 200 football games and examining something like 2,000 point spreads and analyzing something like 5,000 results. Only question is, are they valid opinions or merely the musings of another sucker gambler? I've been keeping a tally of my picks in the college bowl games. (I'm 2–0–1 going into Christmas; admittedly, one of those picks was a Big Daddy special. In the tie result, I had the opposite of him.) Still, I tell myself, one does not contradict the Oracle, because in the long run he'll be right more times than you.

So I don't back the courage of my convictions: I back his.

And Air Force bombs Washington.

There's a lesson to be learned here, but I'm not sure what it is yet. I do know this: My personal record in the bowls is now 3–0–1. Too bad I don't have anything to show for it but checkmarks on a page.

The bowl game season turns out a tepid disappointment. The Brains envisioned making a giant score; instead, we more or less break even.

For 44 Enterprises, however, the bowl games are spectacular.

I discover that World Sports Exchange offers interactive betting on virtually every televised game. The market is fluid, constructed like a stock exchange. You can buy or sell teams while the game is happening. And while I'm no Big Daddy, I do know this: Compared with the thousands of action junkies who play the interactive game, I have a far better understanding of the values (expressed as odds and prices) of each team on offer. (And I also know the presumptive right side.) Armed with what I suppose is superior knowledge and judgment, I can often find prices that are just plain wrong, prices that present an attractive overlay to the savvy gambler.

Case in point: West Virginia is playing Missouri, and the Mountaineers are getting buried in the first half. With each successive Tiger score, West Virginia's odds plummet. By halftime, down 17 points, a West Virginia share that once cost as much as $54 can be had for the discount price of $12. Now, not only do I know that the Brain Trust and I have a hefty straight wager on West Virginia +3½ points, thanks to nearly two full seasons of observation; I know that West Virginia is capable of scoring every time it has the ball. Blessed with an explosive offense, a 17-point deficit (13½ with the point spread) is by no means insurmountable. Indeed, I calculate that West Virginia will come back to cover the spread at least one out of three times.

If I'm right—and knowing that West Virginia is the hot side, anyway—the share price for the Mountaineers should be something between 30 and 40 cents. At 12, it's a steal.

I buy several hundred shares.

The price barely goes up, so I buy more.

And even after West Virginia cuts the deficit to 10 in the fourth quarter, the price is still a bargain. (This is partially because the linemakers at World Sports Exchange aren't quite as sharp as they ought to be and partially because the public bettors aren't sharp at all.) So I buy more.

With less than a minute to go, my $3,600 investment is worth more than $16,000. Elated, I consider selling, reaping the huge windfall. But then I make the mistake of asking Viv what she thinks. Should I sell? Or should I hold out?

She says hold out.

Shortly thereafter, it looks like West Virginia is going to give the game away, thanks to several penalties and pressure-induced miscues. The share price drops like a computer monitor being discarded from a frustrated sports bettor's office window.

As I fume and rue what might have been, West Virginia recovers the football, and with a few seconds remaining, sneaks inside the point spread.

My shares are worth $24,800.

I tell Viv I really, *really* like World Sports Exchange's interactive betting.

When the Atlanta Falcons (+10 points) upset the Minnesota Vikings in the divisional play-offs, netting us another $90,000, my Brain Trust win for the season jumps to $884,000. If we perform as well at the Super Bowl and March Madness as we did last campaign, we might well eclipse $1 million for the year.

It's Super Bowl Sunday! The Biggest Betting Day of the Year! The Day When All Americans Become Sports Bettors! The Day When You Can Bet as Much as You Like on Almost Anything! Party Time!

And I don't have a bet.

Big Daddy and I play golf together, just as we did almost two years earlier. This time, though, we're (unequal) partners, fighting together for the same goal. On the first tee, as the early light bathes our faces, Rick dispassionately mentions that the line, Denver –7 points, correlates exactly with our computer line. Thus, unless there's a major move in the next eight hours (because, say, John Elway gets his hand caught in a juice blender), no bet. "No big deal," he says, striding down the fairway. "We'll have plenty of other games to bet on. It's all one big long game."

Perhaps to further motivate me, perhaps because he's just a nice man, Big Daddy announces that, for no particular reason, he's thinking of increasing my end of the Brain Trust business. Thinking of bumping up my percentage. Whether it's a loyalty bonus or merely a smart way to prevent me from going off on my own, Big Daddy is considering making my stake in each Brains bet I place 50 percent higher than it was last calendar year.

Am I being groomed? I don't know. But it won't be unusual for me to have more than $20,000 personally at stake on some games in 1999, assuming someone wants to take my bets. We're still more than a month away from March Madness, yet I can feel the adrenaline building. The surreal world of big-money sports betting continues to envelop my life.

Rick Matthews also mentions, most casually, that he's got a plan for future seasons that will simultaneously keep me "cool as a cucumber" *and* make me a whole bunch of money.

This I'm eager to hear.

"I'm working on it," he says. "We're gonna get everything all fixed up." He smiles and winks. "You did fine this season. But you're gonna do even better next time."

We play a carefree eighteen holes, betting $100 on the match. "You're getting to be a big gambler," he needles me. "Man, if I'm not careful, one of these days you're gonna want to play for *two* hundred!"

"Come on, now," I retort. "You know this isn't gambling. This is charity. I'm contributing to the Rick Matthews fund for elderly hustlers."

"And we appreciate that," he says. "Thank you, sir."

The match is close—I'm playing out of my mind, shooting in the seventies. We're all square coming down the stretch. But on the eighteenth hole, as if by force of willpower, Matthews plunks his approach shot to the green about two feet from the flag.

I shoot him a look of mock disgust. He shrugs and bites his lower lip, saying with his body, *Hey, it happens. Even an old hillbilly gets lucky every now and again.* Then he breaks into uncontrollable laughter, slapping me on the back and falling all over himself. "Man, if I only had a picture of your face, 44. Why are you such a competitive cuss? Can't stand to let an old man win a little golf game?"

I put my arm around his shoulder and walk up the fairway, giggling like a little boy.

When I return home, I feel strangely empty. Super Bowl Sunday and no bet? It doesn't seem right. Last year I was a VIP guest in Las Vegas, wagering hundreds of thousands on the game. Today I'm just another sports fan on the couch, armed with corn chips and beer.

Out of something slightly more wicked than idle curiosity, I check in with my bookies every thirty minutes or so before the kickoff, just to see what's happening with the number.

It's moving.

The over-under total is coming down and the price on the Broncos is climbing. And none of it, from what I can gather, is Brain Trust–related. A team of Vegas blackjack players, I hear from a well-placed friend, has backed Denver in a big way. But I'm not sure this team alone could cause such a large move. Just to make sure, I call Brother Herbie.

"It ain't us," he confirms. "Hell, I hope it stops, 'cause if it gets much higher, Rick might want to play the 'dog. And that's no good. Denver's gonna blow this Atlanta team out of the stadium."

"So why aren't we playing Denver?" I ask.

"Well, you can't go against the number," Herbie replies. He means that if the computer says the number is 7 you can't contradict it, even if in your gut you think Denver is going to win by 17. The algorithms are smarter than you are. "But I sure like Denver," Herbie reiterates.

I look at it this way: If the number was initially right enough to preclude a bet, then if it moves significantly in either direction (and the move is not the product of Rick's or Herbie's machinations) it must be mathematically correct to bet against the move. So when the spread climbs to 8½, I bet Atlanta. And when the total falls to 51, I bet the over.

To give Viv something to scream about, I grant her a 10 percent free-roll, a tenth of the profits and none of the losses.

Now we're like most other sports fans in the United States, yelling at the television, eating unhealthy snacks, and hoping to get lucky. Doesn't really matter the outcome; we're in the game. So we have only a couple thousand at stake instead of a couple hundred thousand. But it's Super Bowl Sunday. And now it feels right.

Big Daddy and I decide to take a little vacation, forgoing betting on college basketball until March Madness commences. While I rue the loss of income, I treasure the free time. It's been more than three months since I've had a full week, much less a weekend, to do whatever I want. For one month I'll be able to live my life free of bookies, bank wires, and big bets.

I just hope all that will be waiting for me when I return.

In the interim, while Viv is off at a hotel marketing conference in San Francisco, I spend most of my time playing golf in Australia and New Zealand, where point spreads and line moves rarely intrude on my idyll. I had almost forgotten what it was like to awake at sunup and not have to check the previous night's results, not have to audit account figures with Brother Herbie, not have to move money from one shop to another. I had almost forgotten what regular life was like. Less stressful, certainly. But somehow denuded and dull, too. My month of liberty is thoroughly refreshing and sometimes even exhilarating. But the truth is, I can't wait for it to end. I want to get back to the business of beating the bookies.

When March comes—finally—Brother Herbie wants me to figure out exactly how much I've got in outs, how much I can bet on a single college basketball game. "If you've got enough, we might be able to take care of some of these games just with you," he implies.

This would be ideal. If the Brain Trust doesn't need to bet a dozen different spots to meet Big Daddy's voracious quotas, there's little chance of my getting heated up from simultaneous line moves. Unfortunately, when I check with my old pals the bookmakers, they're not as eager for my business as they were before my hiatus. In fact, the bosses at World Sports Exchange confess that they're frightened of my action and, frankly, don't want my basketball bets. "Nothing personal," they say. "Take it as a compliment. You're the sharpest bettor we've ever seen. You beat us on football and we're sure you'll beat us on basketball, too. You'd probably beat us on any sport you bet."

"Golf?" I say facetiously.

"Sure, that too."

Amid the bad news—and this really is bad news, World Sports Exchange being about the most reliable, honest organization I've dealt with—there's some hope. Sherm, the proprietor, tells me he was talking about me with another bookie on Antigua, a guy who runs a much larger shop. He told him that I was super smart and that he didn't think he could beat me. The other guy, according to Sherm, told him to send me over. "He's not scared of anybody," Sherm reports. "He wants you to call him."

So I do, making no pretense of being a square. Curiously, this new shop, World-Wide Tele-Sports (WWTS), seems delighted to sign me up. Whereas most other places might let me bet $5,000 on the tournament games, WWTS says it will allow me $20,000. "We handle all the biggest bettors in the world," the boss, Buckeye Bill Scott, says to me. "We're used to taking big wagers." He then rattles off a list of the sports-betting luminaries whom he services, including, first and foremost, Rick "Big Daddy" Matthews.

And when Buckeye Bill does that, the beauty of this situation becomes clear to me. If WWTS is already taking bets from Big Daddy (albeit small ones, in the $3,000 neighborhood) it certainly won't be frightened of booking my action. The bookies there believe they already know the right side of every game.

When I brief Brother Herbie on the latest, he says he's not surprised about World Sports Exchange barring me, but he *is* surprised (and pleased) about the WWTS limit. I can almost hear his smile over the telephone. His glee increases when I tell him I've also arranged to bet $10,000 per game with Victor Chandler, a Gibraltar-based bookmaking shop with an impeccable reputation. It is publicly traded on the London

Stock Exchange and sponsors sporting events, like a European PGA Tour stop.

But the best news is this: My old buddies at Caesars Palace, Pencil Stevie and Gino the Suit, are laying out the welcome (back) mat. They say they'll be happy to take $20,000 wagers from me on game day. Anytime before that, probably $10,000.

"They'll give you twenty thousand?" Herbie asks, pleasantly skeptical.

"That's what they told me."

"Well, you best be makin' yourself some reservations!"

Since I can reliably deliver $50,000 worth of action per basketball game, Big Daddy wires me $500,000 to get started.

"We can always get you more in Las Vegas if you need it," he assures me.

When a clerk from my bank calls to say I've been sent a wire for half a million dollars, she sounds apologetic, as if she's expecting me to say there must be some mistake. But, no, this is the world of Big Daddy Rick and the Brain Trust.

And it won't be a mistake when all $500,000 of the deposit gets zapped overseas to a coterie of eager bookmakers who haven't yet figured out that my partners and I know more about point spreads than they do.

Since last March I've been in and out of Caesars Palace a few times, mostly to say hello to the boys or have a meal. But I haven't been an invited guest, a bet-the-limit sports gambler, for nearly a year. Working from home in my underwear, burning up the phone lines while my dog lies at my feet and my girlfriend pads around the house, has been a real pleasure, notwithstanding the occasional extortion attempt by low-life bookmakers in the Caribbean. I've genuinely enjoyed my weekends in Los Angeles, watching the money pile up without ever leaving my living room.

But there's nothing like Las Vegas on a big sports weekend. And on a big sports weekend there's nothing like the Caesars Palace sportsbook. All the crew members greet me warmly, telling me they've read my articles and bought my books and generally missed me. They ply me with the best seats in the house to view the games, and passes to the Holyfield-

Lewis fight, and all the other amenities bestowed upon high-rolling suckers, even though they know I'm probably going to win.

Milling in the overflow crowd jamming the book, I'm struck again at the curious thrill of being one of the few anointed ones among the hundreds (thousands?) of bettors poring over their odds sheets, searching for the sure-thing locks of the week, the answers to all their gambling questions. How peculiar it is to know those answers, to really *know* the right side. In this business that's half the battle.

The other half is getting the right price. Pencil Stevie, as usual, has put up a tough line. "There ain't much to give him," Herbie complains. "Not unless the public knocks him around a bit." I see a couple of bettable games (lines that mirror what I bet yesterday offshore), but Brother Herbie tells me to wait and see. They might get better. In the meantime, armed with a vibrating radio, I'm free to roam from the hotel room. If I feel a buzz in my pocket, I find a discreet nook behind a row of slot machines and say hello.

While I am waiting for instructions, one of the early games, Maryland vs. Valparaiso, starts rocketing up, from 18 to 19½ to 20½. I ask the Pencil when this game is going to hit 21, and he says, "Never!" He rapidly writes the figure about six times. Then he says, "Of course, I could change my mind."

I'm just making small talk, yet, after two years of immersion in this racket, I've developed a keen sense for when a game we weren't the slightest bit interested in all week suddenly becomes, well, interesting. I suspect this might be one of them.

Sure as a flush beats a straight, Brother Herbie buzzes me five minutes later. "Call your guys over the water and bet 'em up to thirty thousand on Valpo plus twenty-one."

I do. (By the time I get through to Victor Chandler, in Gibraltar, the line has ticked to 21½.) But Caesars stands firm at the lower number, and I'm forced to pass.

The only bet I can give Stevie the Pencil all morning is UCLA −1 against Detroit, the same bet I've given my offshore shops. Given the nature of Stevie's sharp linemaking, I have to hope that the hordes of casual gamblers thronging his counter will push the point spreads around enough to warrant a bet. In the meantime, I'm free to enjoy the electric fun of being at the Palace during March Madness—with several hundred thousand dollars to play with.

The giddy sense of pleasure diminishes rapidly when your 21½-point underdog loses at the buzzer by 22 points. Especially when every other sports fan in the joint is screaming his brains out in support of the over-valued favorite. Regarding Valparaiso's heart-wrenching loss I console myself with a maxim torn from the Book of Rick: It's all one big long game, with hundreds of little results adding up to one big victory.

Day Two. I'm worried.

I fire $110,000 worth of bets at Caesars. The first $66,000 of them are losers. Heartbreaking losers. By 12:00 noon I have only $44,000 of my original $200,000 to bet with. I need at least two of my three outstanding bets to come home winners.

Happily, all of them do, netting another $100,000. Now I have plenty to play with, as well as a nice profit. When my biggest college basketball bet to date—Purdue, getting 2½ points from Texas—wins, I add another $90,000 to the coffers.

It's a good day to be a sports bettor. And I'm learning to appreciate the fleeting triumphs, because depressing days of equal magnitude will surely follow. Up, down, profit, loss—it's all about grinding out an edge. As long as I'm in action, the short-term thrills and chills shouldn't really matter—but if you're human, they do.

I'm mystified how Big Daddy has managed all these years to avoid a gastric ulcer the size of a grapefruit. Money stolen, plays hijacked, reputation impugned—he weathers the constant indignities of trying to win at sports betting with something like noble equanimity. Like a monk.

The former theologian in our organization, however, doesn't subscribe to the concept of "turn the other cheek." Brother Herbie believes somebody is picking off my bets at Caesars and siphoning the information to another betting syndicate. He's been noticing that almost every time I bet, the number starts jumping almost immediately all over the world. And he's livid.

Hissing, he queries me, "I already know the answer, but I gotta ask you this, 44. Are you telling these plays to anyone?"

"No," I say flatly, slightly hurt that after all this time he could suspect me.

"Not a soul?"

"Not a soul," I reply. And it's true.

"All right," Herbie says, sounding relieved. Then he tells me the culprit might be the Pencil at Caesars, or a couple of runners for another betting crew, or maybe even the management at WWTS. Or—and this is likely, too—it may all be a troubling coincidence. He tells me to keep an eye out at the Caesars counter for two guys in particular, a couple of large, unkempt fellows who have a reputation for pirating wiseguy plays. In the meantime, he's concocted a cunning plan, which involves my betting an opposite side in Vegas and then betting the other real team offshore.

It works. The followers drive the price up on St. John's, the wrong team; we bet a bunch on Indiana, the right team. Only problem: The wrong team crushes the right one, and the followers get rich.

"I'm gonna look into this," Herbie promises.

Despite the suspected information leaks, we continue to triumph. We can't seem to lose. Here and there, yes. Over the course of the entire tournament, no.

The remainder of college basketball passes without incident—unless you count winning at nearly a 70 percent clip an "incident." But since most of my bets are on the cold side, playing against the line moves, the bookies are all thrilled to have my business. When almost all the underdogs come in winners, the books and I make a pile of money. It's a perfect scenario to play with impunity, without complaining, whining, or interrogation from the people holding our money. If only football season were so effortless. Knowing this will be my last weekend in Las Vegas as an RFB guest for many months, I enjoy a celebratory dinner with Vivian at Palace Court, where we toast a $1.1 million season. "Here's to Caesars Palace! Here's to sports betting! And," I say, hoisting a glass of first-growth claret, "here's to the greatest gambler of all time, Rick 'Big Daddy' Matthews!"

• • •

Spring 1999 is blissfully devoid of sports. I return to being a full-time writer with no interest in televised athletics. After four months of fun and fruitful travel, much of it with Vivian, who probably enjoys the gambling off-season even more than her boyfriend, I meet Big Daddy at his estate in Santa Barbara for our annual strategy session. After a splendid round of golf—splendid because I play out of my mind and manage to lose only one proposition bet to the notoriously heartless golf hustler—we retire to his home to plan our football campaign. Over iced tea and corn chowder, Big Daddy predicts that in the coming football campaign I should plan on earning some serious money: My piece of the Brain Trust will officially be increased to 15 percent.

He smiles at me broadly, showing his dimples. "Good ol' 44's gotta little bark on his trees these days, huh? You seem to have gotten the hang of this whole gambling deal. It ain't that complicated, is it? You just find some good numbers and bet as much as you can. I think you're turning into a real sharpie. And I want you to have a bigger stake in our mutual success."

"I don't know if I should be flattered or offended," I admit. "You sure you aren't just taking pity on another golf victim?"

"I love you like a son, 44. But hell, I ain't gonna give away the store out of charity. You know me better than that."

"Yes, I do, Rick."

"My friend, I couldn't be happier with your performance." Rick glances around the veranda of his mansion, which overlooks the Pacific, twinkling in the distance like an animated painting. "You deserve everything you've earned, and I'm happy—really, 44, it pleases me—that you've learned so much. One day you might take over the whole operation. See, Herbie's a great guy, and I love him like a brother. But I don't know if he could run an organization that's this demanding."

I shrug. "I don't know if I could either."

"See, it ain't just enough to pick some winners. Anyone can do that if he's got good enough information and he understands how the lines are made, which, obviously, you do. You also got to manage the money, the individual accounts, the personnel. I don't know if you know this," Big

Daddy says, raising an eyebrow, "but the Brain Trust has about a dozen people making bets for us simultaneously when we go out on an open order."

"You mean when I'm betting at Caesars Palace there are eleven other guys betting simultaneously at other casinos?"

"No, see, I wouldn't heat you up like that, 44. That's what I mean about keeping you cool. The games you play, we gotta bet strategically, take a bite here and another taste there. A little at a time. I'm talking about the games where we just want to get down all at once, just chew up all the good numbers in a minute. The open orders."

"So this is how the steam happens," I say, nodding.

"Right. We got a call center in Ireland. It's staffed by a temp agency. No shit. We pay them by the hour. They come in each night—you know, cuz the time is all screwed up—and when we're ready to move on a game, they all call their accounts at the same time. This way we get the good numbers before someone can steal our play."

I say, "It sounds like currency trading, or the stock market."

"Exactly. Now, 44, maybe it would be beneficial for all of us if you opened up a call center of your own. Get a bunch of people to bet for you—since, hell, ol' Mikey K ain't much good anymore. Your name ain't exactly popular with our friends the bookmakers, is it?"

"Come on, now. Mr. Konik is known as the bookmaker's best friend," I quip.

Rick replies seriously, "You know, pards, once you get a reputation for being able to win, they treat you like a terrorist. All these names and addresses you came up with this year, that was smart. But it ain't gonna last forever. You and me both know that. You better start getting some people to bet for you."

"My own group of 44s."

"A whole bunch of them. A whole bunch of twenty-twos and thirty-threes."

I guffaw outwardly, but inside I feel the kind of queasy excitement one associates with first kisses. As a teenager, I had flashes of adolescent insecurity: *Does she really like me? Does this pretty girl really want me to touch her?* And now, a grown man, I'm light-headed with anticipation and glee: *Does Rick Matthews really want me to be his right-hand man?*

SEASON THREE

Summer 1999–Spring 2000

Thirteen

A LITTLE KNOWLEDGE IS DANGEROUS

Throughout the summer of 1999, I dedicate myself to opening additional offshore accounts that will accept large wagers. This last bit—the *large* part—is far easier dreamed of than accomplished. By now, every time someone from Southern California, no matter his name, tries to pass himself off as a big player, an action fiend with no regard for money, the world's bookies instantly assume the newbie is an agent of the Brain Trust.

My task is made exponentially more difficult by an essay published by the Doc on The Sports Cure. He fingers me as a beard for Big Daddy Rick Matthews. Though his tirade is filled with factual errors (not to mention spelling errors), the circumstantial connection to the Man "in print" harms my relationships with several bookmaking shops. This is the second time I've been outed; the law of averages says that eventually the wrong people will stumble across the damning information. The people at World Sports Exchange, for example, deeply troubled by this revelation, tell me they no longer wish to book my action. They later relent, albeit at ridiculously low limits meant to purchase my opinion at wholesale prices. I do my best to institute damage control, but the longer I'm in this business, the more volatile my name becomes.

For this reason, Rick and I agree that from now on *all* of my betting will be under fictitious names, the aka identities that the banker Lucy Davino helped arrange. This way, when I set up a new account with a suspicious bookie, my real name will never be uttered. The man formerly known as Michael Konik is officially retired from sports betting.

Using this strategy, I manage to open eight fresh accounts for the upcoming football season, generating nearly $150,000 per game of potential outs.

I also recruit a stable of friends and business acquaintances to make wagers on my behalf. The chief criterion for becoming part of the 44 syndicate is trustworthiness, a rare quality that severely limits the pool of applicants. How many people do you know whom you would feel comfortable letting hold $100,000 or more of your money—at a bookmaking shop? The comrades I end up using are fellows who've previously expressed zero interest in gambling, guys who couldn't tell you the difference between making your point on the dice table and taking the points on a football game. In fact, some of them actually have to be coached on how to make a bet. During preseason training, when I tell one dear boy hypothetically to take Texas Tech at +8 or better, he confesses that he's not sure what's better than +8.

"Plus eight and a half, or nine," I explain.

He's still not sure. "What about ten?"

Poker buddies; golf buddies; music buddies; theater buddies; former classmates—they all get pitched. "Hey, pards, howya'd like to make some money this football season," I propose, just as I was once seduced. Only one fellow declines, and solely because his father, a reformed gambling addict, is mortally certain that there's got to be a catch, an unexplained circumstance that will somehow rob the son of a financially secure future. The truth is, there isn't any catch: My players are on a free-roll. Lose and it doesn't cost them a penny. Win and they get 5 percent of the profits.

Although I've got people working with me out of several states, we call ourselves the Hollywood Boys, primarily because a few of us actually live in Hollywood, and subordinately because it sounds better than the Suburban Atlanta Boys. Each member of my crew earns 5 percent of the net profits on the games he bets. I keep 10 percent and the rest goes to the

Brains. Each member understands that he's to wager as instructed, that he's being included for his dependability and competence, not his handicapping ability. Each fellow understands that when the point spreads are flying off the board I don't have time to explain why we're betting on certain teams at certain prices. We just are. To the young men waiting by their phones, hoping I'll send action in their direction, I'm a regular Big Daddy.

The truth is, I'm more like a Medium Daddy. I'm forbidden to bet on the same games Rick bets on, to add a little something on top of what I'm already betting for the Brain Trust. But that doesn't mean I'm prohibited from betting on games that Rick and Company have disregarded. If I have a strong opinion, I'm more than welcome to express it monetarily in the language of 11–10. The problem is, as Rick Matthews has warned repeatedly, strong opinions are what get people in trouble betting sports—or almost any gambling venture. The draconian laws of mathematics don't care what your local newspaper columnist said about the Raiders. Billions of computer simulations don't pay attention to what your Uncle Jed, the lifelong Giants fan, says about the rival Cowboys. And the linemakers, the ones who are paid to convey in numerals the power disparity between two football teams, certainly don't care about the vivid dream you had about the Patriots and Ravens the other night—the one in which you could see the scoreboard down at the end of the stadium, with the final tally up in lights.

By now it's ingrained in me: To beat sports, you need access to better numbers than everyone else. If I've learned anything from Rick Matthews—and, in fact, I've learned *everything* from him—the only way to get a better number than the bookmakers is to use a computer, a thinking machine that can have the vivid dreams for you.

When I went to high school, two of my classmates were so smart (and so socially maladjusted) that almost no one would talk to them. I liked them both. Though you couldn't call us friends—we never *did* anything together, except feel vaguely disliked by our school's various cliques—I would sometimes join one or both guys in the school cafeteria for lunch, sitting at their otherwise unoccupied table while the cool kids huddled at a superior spot near the vending machines. One of the geniuses, Ben, ended up working for the space program and, according to apocryphal rumors, was a lead engineer on the Challenger shuttle. The other, Andy, attended Caltech on a full scholarship, where he happily immersed himself in calculus and discussions of Fermat with other preternaturally gifted young men (and women), who found in numbers the kind of excitement and comfort most people discover in wet kisses and fried foods.

I never spoke to Ben after high school. Andy, however, called me once or twice a year for more than a decade. These were awkward conversations, filled with lengthy longueurs. We were never close to begin with; during high school I was just trying to be a kind person to a classmate who was accustomed to unrelenting cruelty. Andy had a speech impediment, as well as unstylish, 1970s porno star hair that refused to obey the comb. When I'd pick up the phone and hear his voice on the other end, I'd panic. What could I tell him? What common ground did we share? After several years of "Hi, how are you? Fine. And you?" calls, Andy finally admitted that he had a crush on me, and that he used to attend my wrestling matches for reasons other than a finely cultivated appreciation of single-leg takedowns.

After that revelation, which I handled as well as I could—which is to say rather clumsily—Andy seemed liberated to talk about what was really happening in his life, including the groundbreaking work he was doing on something called parallel processing—a concept I wouldn't grasp until many years later. He was building artificial brains.

Sometime later, Andy fell in love with a nice young man and accepted a professorship at MIT, where he continued to tinker with the infinite possibilities that the digits 1 and 0 presented. In the summer of 1999, kismet brought Andy and my Hollywood Boys together. Mick, a musician pal and former bandmate, forsook the rewards of the underground indie rock scene in Los Angeles and matriculated at MIT, where he intended to pursue his doctorate in robotics. Andy—my high school "friend" Andy—was one of his professors.

"Very cool guy," Mick the musician reported. "Very into Bach."

I asked for Andy's direct phone number and told my pal Mick to warn Algorithm Andy that Mr. Konik, his old classmate from Nicolet High, would be calling.

When I dial the professor's number, I'm not sure what I'm going to tell him. I just know we need to talk. Andy answers after one ring. After the standard pleasantries, I ask, "Hey, Andy, do you know anything about football?"

"Um, other than a bunch of large men run around in tight pants and fall on each other? Not really," he says.

I tell him what I do, how I bet on sports. And I tell Algorithm Andy that he's the smartest person I've ever met, and if he could help me figure out how to derive a slightly better line than the oddsmakers, he's going to be a very rich man.

Andy says, "That doesn't sound very difficult."

"It doesn't?" I say cautiously.

"No. It's all rules-based. If we tell the program the rules, and keep adding rules, and throwing out the ones that don't apply, and continue adding data, and refining the rules—you know, testing them in simulations—and we can compare them with a historical record (I assume you have all that) and then test your hypotheses (and, again, I assume you have plenty of assumptions, since you've been doing this for many, many years, right?) it's rather easy to get a couple of computers working against each other to assign values to every aspect of the data we feed them. In other words, if you can tell me what to tell the machine, I can tell you what it thinks about what you know. Does that make sense?"

"Sure," I reply.

"Really?"

"Well, not really. Well, not at all, actually. But that doesn't mean it wouldn't work. It just means I'm too stupid to understand why."

Andy continues, "It's actually very low-level stuff. A high school kid could program this. Sorry, I don't mean to insult you. It's just not a very complicated problem."

"So why haven't more people done this?" I wonder.

"I'm sure many people have," Andy remarks. "But the trick is what we say the rules are. I guess that would be where you come in. You can help decide where to start, what seems like rule number one. You know, like: 'The team wearing yellow shirts always wins.' "

"I get it." I say, not completely getting it, but abuzz with possibilities.

We agree in principle to make a partnership. I'll put up the money and the gambling expertise. Andy will put up the algorithm and the computing power. Neither of us will breathe a word of this project that dare not speak its name.

The next morning, I e-mail Algorithm Andy ten years of NFL point spreads results, culled from an Internet database. Then I send him three years of Brain Trust results based on those same point spreads. Two hours later I get a reply.

He tells me, "It's a start."

Throughout September, while I wait for Algo Andy to crack the code, I let the faint possibility of handicapping mastery independent of the Brains go to my addled head. Because I can single-handedly move the line around the world, I start to fancy myself a sports-gambling luminary. This can be dangerous, I know. Nonetheless, directing my mini-syndicate of Hollywood Boys with the same crisp, formal tone Rick Matthews uses with me, I bet about $25,000 worth of games for my own account. Some of my selections are based on handicapping, which I already know is nearly impossible without a computer. Others are based on my finely developed sense of what the Brains (and the competing syndicates) are likely to do later in the week. Spookily, about two-thirds of my games do turn out to be Brain Trust or Ferdinand & Blair specials. Thus, I (and my Boys) get the absolute best number from the bookies, which makes it seem to them, I'm sure, that the new players flooding their shops are *really* well connected.

All of a sudden I convince myself I'm a sharpie. I bet way too many games and end up on the wrong side on a few of them. But since I've made my buys at a good number, I can always come back and purchase the other side at an attractive price, giving myself an opportunity to middle some games. For example, I play Wisconsin −19 vs. Minnesota, knowing this is the kind of number the syndicates will likely jump all over. And when they in fact make Wisconsin a buy later in the week, the point spread goes to −23. I then purchase Minnesota +23, enjoying a 3-point middle chance as well as two additional free-roll points (19 and 23) for a total of five key numbers. If a middle such as this comes in once out of nineteen times, it's profitable.

More than anything else, though, riding the coattails of the master is what gets the cash. If, while waiting for Andy's toils in Boston, I can avoid gambling too much on my own wits and, instead, merely maximize my investments on Big Daddy stock, I should do just fine. The urge to be someone, however, is hard to ignore. Earning money from sports betting is nice. Earning money from your own ingeniousness is nirvana; it brings a sense of accomplishment that just getting paid doesn't. After only two years of working with the Brain Trust, merely stacking up the cash bores me. I have the dangerous impulse to do something grander and more satisfying. I have the impulse to be the smart money.

After one full week of aggressive freelancing, I—and my syndicate of 5 percent colleagues—go 19–12 and win $29,000. These highly unscientific results lead me to believe that I'm on to something. My suspicions are further confirmed when the next week I win another $10,000.

Eventually, though, my so-called handicapping crumbles in the face of multiple trials and I lose $17,000, including several thousand on games in which I've selected the wrong side of a Brain Trust game. I've learned my lesson—sort of. No matter how wise a guy I fancy myself, Big Rick is right: it's folly for me to play on my own opinion. Better to maximize my investment when I have solid information from the Brain Trust.

Or Algo Andy.

After several weeks of six-hour late-night phone calls, dismal false starts, and the kind of comical misunderstandings that usually occur in door-slamming British bedroom farces (he thinks, for instance, that a safety is when a team refuses a penalty), we finally have a program to predict the final score of NFL football games. It's full of bugs and prone to mistakes—I mean, there's no way Cleveland, the worst team in the league, is a 24-point underdog to any squad, even the Super Bowl champion Rams—but it seems to sort of kind of possibly work. Andy cautions that the program has a low "efficiency ratio," or something like that, and that he can't make any performance promises other than "It will get better the more it learns."

"Is it safe to bet on?" I ask Andy, hoping he'll allay my doubts with one blithe pronouncement.

"You're the gambling expert, my dear," he reminds me. "If it were me, I wouldn't put too much faith in our little baby until she matures a little."

"Like a fine wine," I propose.

"Or a teenage boy," Andy retorts.

"So just tell me this: If it were your money at risk, would you bet on football games based on our new program?"

"Hmmm." I hear Algo Andy click-clacking on a computer keyboard. I imagine him scrolling through long strings of numbers, integers flying across his screen, until he sees what he needs to see—whatever that may be. "If you compare the historical point-spread numbers with the ones our baby spits up, they're pretty close. I mean, if you were to bet on every game you might get—let's see—oh, like, call it a fifty-two percent success rate against the point spread, which I've been led to believe isn't enough of an advantage."

"Right. But we're not going to bet every game."

Andy titters. "Oh, right. Well then," he says, flamboyantly, "let the fun begin!"

I fairly beg him to keep feeding information to our fledgling program—which we informally call "Baby"—and to e-mail me the predicted final scores of the upcoming week's NFL games. We've consciously avoided the college matchups, since, Algo Andy claims, the amount of data to be processed would overtax his personal system, and he doesn't feel comfortable using MIT equipment for betting on intercollegiate athletics. "And, Andy," I caution him, "please, not a word about this to anyone. We could be sitting on a gold mine. Granted, there might not be anything but granite at the bottom of the shaft, but there's a chance, however slim, that we'll hit the jackpot."

"Don't get your hopes up too high, Michael. This isn't a very large sample. Let's not get seduced by the fallacy of small numbers."

Feeling momentarily very much like Rick Matthews, I say, "Andy, my friend, it's the big numbers I'm interested in."

In my third season of football betting, for the first time in my sports-gambling career, I experience anxiety. Not nervousness. Not excitement. *Anxiety.* It's the night before Baby's late-September debut, and I can't sleep.

My pulse is racing as if I'm cranked up on amphetamines. My mind won't shut off: it's filled with thoughts of betting lines and point spreads.

My dog looks at me like I'm insane. She can tell something's wrong.

While Vivian sleeps soundly, her mind uncluttered with sports-gambling concerns, I envision touchdowns and field goals, fumbles and interceptions. At 3:00 a.m., I do something I never do: I get out of bed, lace up my shoes, and go for a three-mile run in the almost deserted streets around my Hollywood home. The hound goes with me, per-plexed but happy. After a post-run shower and check of the betting lines on my computer—nothing's changed at 4:00 in the morning—I sleep for three hours and awake less than refreshed, with a twelve-hour workday ahead of me.

Were I a superstitious lad, I might look upon my anxiety attack in the wee small hours as some sort of harbinger, a Shakespearean foreshadow-ing of impending doom.

The day will live in infamy.

The Brain Trust goes 2–8, losing more than $250,000. At our low point, before a couple of late winners come in to soften the blow, we're down close to $400,000. And since I've boldly chosen to follow Baby's in-fantile gurglings, I lose an additional $20,000 of my own syndicate's bankroll. I fleetingly attribute this bloodbath to karmic retribution, my cosmic punishment for disobeying Big Daddy's warnings, for mistakenly believing that I could do something I haven't been anointed to do.

But then I come to my senses. These fluctuations happen. They're cruel and bizarre and extraordinarily painful, but anyone who gambles for a living knows that sooner or later one of these vicious streaks will hit you like a three-hundred-pound lineman going for a quarterback's knees. If you have the bankroll and the fortitude to ride it out you sur-vive. If you don't you quit gambling.

Algo Andy suggests I give him a week or two to do some "tweaking," as he puts it. "Obviously, these things aren't perfect predictors," he notes. "But I'm sure we can make Baby more effective. I've got some ideas, which I could explain to you, but you'd have to be pretty well versed in some advanced concepts to get where I'm going on this. Are you up for it?"

"No, I'm really not, Andy," I admit. "Just do your thing and let me know when it's safe to use Baby again. In the meantime, I'm going to try to disinfect and bandage the gaping wounds in my bankroll."

I have a brief talk with Big Daddy during the carnage. He sounds tired and worn, and genuinely rueful. "I've never worked so hard in my life," he tells me. "If someone would have suggested to me I'd have to work this hard to lay a man eleven to ten . . ." He chuckles bitterly. "I'll tell you what, pardsy-wardsy . . ." For a moment I think he's going to tell me he's through with all the nonsense, the elaborately choreographed charade he must dance every week, all to lose $1 million or more.

Instead, he says, "I love it. It's my favorite thing in the world, 44. The cat-and-mouse. It's all a big game. And I truly enjoy it."

He can't possibly enjoy blowing second-home-on-the-water money on football games. It's the winning, I'm sure, that inspires him to keep going, the knowledge that he and his partners can beat a game that no one is supposed to be able to beat. Big Daddy can handle the fluctuations. Brother Herbie can handle them. I think even I can handle them. None of us are happy—indeed, a nice group crying session would be rather cathartic at the moment. But we'll survive. And besides, it's great advertising. Any bookie who doesn't want my action now is either crazy or a genius. This kind of catastrophic loss should buy me many weeks of life.

Still, it's hard to think cheerily when you've just hemorrhaged $57,000 of your own money on sports gambling. So I drown my sorrows in a glass (or two) of Scotch whiskey and hope the night will pass quickly.

I have a very bad week. And it has nothing to do with bookmakers.

On Thursday, shortly before a college football game on which I lose another $60,000, Vivian walks into my office and announces that she's moving out and moving on. "We're through," she says robotically, as though all her emotions have been extinguished. I knew we were having problems, but I never expected this.

"Hold on," I say, turning away from the odds screen on my computer. "Let's talk about this."

"There's nothing to talk about anymore. The well has already been poisoned," she says, cryptically. "We can't grow together. I'm sorry." She kisses me on my forehead and walks away.

The phone rings. I don't answer it. It rings again, several times in succession. I pick it up to make it stop. It's Brother Herbie. "Where you been, Doc? I got an updated order for you."

I tell him I can't work just now. "Sorry," I say, and hang up.

Ten minutes later, just before the game kicks, a taxi pulls up in front of our house. Vivian gets in it and says, "Good-bye, Michael."

For the next two lost days I'm despondent. I have no interest in gambling—or much else, for that matter. I feel frighteningly bleak. By Saturday, I can execute my betting responsibilities, although my heart (and every other corporeal part of me) isn't in it. The Brain Trust launches into an 8–0 tear before finally booking a loser. Is this, as my father claimed for many years, the phenomenon of "lucky in cards, unlucky in love"?

After a late, prolonged run of bad picks, the Brains finish the day 9–6. But most of our winners are smaller positions and most of our losers are bigger ones. Most improbably, one of our favorites, Baylor, about to plunge into the end zone to cover the spread with seconds left on the clock, fumbles at the one-yard line and allows the underdog, UNLV, to scamper ninety-nine yards the other way for a game-winning (and spread-beating) touchdown. What looked to be a get even from last week returns a modest $17,500 profit.

Despite the gloom, I have faith that one day I'll be reborn. Somewhere in Boston, one of the smartest men in America is ably tinkering with a computer program that could turn Mr. 44 and his Hollywood Boys into a betting syndicate worthy of Big Daddy's respect.

The bookies have long believed that the NFL lines are more or less unassailable. All the information about the teams is public knowledge. Bettors, the bookies assume, can't have more knowledge about the celebrated mercenaries than the blabbering TV commentators, or statistic services, or newspaper columnists. So the well-capitalized shops have little fear in extending $30,000 to $50,000 limits per game.

On the basis of our results over the past couple of weekends they have nothing to worry about. We get slaughtered. Nearly every pick is a loser, a big loser. I forfeit another $245,000.

So much for the theory about cards and love.

Early Monday morning, Big Daddy calls to check on some figures with me. For a moment the fierce leader of the world's biggest sports-betting syndicate sounds like a sweet old man.

"Tough weekend," I offer.

"These things happen," Rick remarks. "You just gotta have faith that they'll get better eventually."

I recall Big Daddy's words several nights later, when I'm staring at the ceiling, wondering where my former lover is, replaying all that has gone wrong. I feel hopeless. This I'm sure would alarm Rick, who, if he knew my dismal state of affairs, might see me as a threat to the security of the many hundreds of thousands of dollars under my stewardship. Indeed, knowing that I'm partnerless in the world, he might want me to close my accounts and send him back what's left. Because were I to die tomorrow, how would he get his money?

I soldier on, pretending to care about how many points the Utah Utes are giving New Mexico State. But I don't pretend very well. My malaise is obvious as hair plugs. Both Brother Herbie and Big Daddy can tell something is wrong with me.

"Are you all right, 44?" Big Daddy asks.

I tell him the truth: No, not really.

He offers a few words of comfort to me—talking this way, I can tell, is difficult for him—and makes me promise him I'm really okay. And then we get back to business, monitoring the point spreads, allocating our funds. We wager hardly anything for the rest of the day. But it may be one of the most memorable Saturdays of my Brain Trust career.

During a quiet moment, while the afternoon games are well under way, Big Daddy calls me. "I'm just checking on you, pards. I want you to know I care about you and that you're my friend. I'm here for you."

I tell Rick Matthews I'm genuinely touched. We chat idly for a few minutes. Big Daddy shares with me some of his homespun wisdom. And then, signing off, he says, "I love you, pards."

I'm dumbstruck. And, for the briefest moment, a tiny bit happy.

. . .

One of my newest accounts, a place called Betmaker.com, shuts down my action after exactly four bets—four bets that result in a net loss of $4,500. When I call to make a wager, the boss, a man who claims his name is Ralph, gets on the line and says, no offense intended, that I'm not the kind of player he wants in his shop. "You're too smart," he says. "I don't want to take bets from the smart money." He makes no mention of Big Daddy or syndicates or moving funds for unseen nefarious forces. I'm just not a desirable customer. End of discussion. Money on the wire tomorrow morning. Thanks for your interest.

Big Daddy, who has the persistence of a badger, refuses to quit or slow down, or even stand in place. He orders me to check out another Costa Rican joint he's heard about, called SBG Global, that takes very large wagers. "See what they're all about, pards, and maybe we'll be able to give 'em some business."

So I go through my usual due diligence, employing a phony name and voice, asking for references and credit history so that I might "get comfortable" with sending $100,000 or more to some heretofore anonymous enterprise somewhere in Central America. At SBG Global, the boss man gives me the name and number of his sales rep from Sprint so that I might see what a big (and sturdy) operation he runs. He offers me every assurance he can think of short of telling me his real name and providing the direct number to his bank manager. I've come to understand that there's really no way to gain complete confidence in these matters. You have to make a gut call, send the dough, and hope it isn't stolen.

This is what I tell Big Daddy. And I tell him my gut call is that the money will be okay. But I can't 100 percent guarantee it.

"All right, then, 44, we'll just have to start them out small, I don't know, send them what? A couple hundred thousand?" he asks.

"Let's try one hundred for now," I suggest. "And if and when we get more comfortable we'll pump it up."

"Fine. Let's see what ol' Mister Global is all about."

Even with new outs the results are old. We have yet another miserable, losing weekend. We blow only another $60,000 or so—which is equivalent to maybe two bets—but the losses are mounting to a point where I'm troubled, and I say so to Brother Herbie.

"This ain't nothin' to worry about. I'll tell you when you should start worrying. And we're not even close to that time!" He assures me that the hole we're in will be easy to dig out of: we just have to persevere.

I can't help recalling that at this point last season, rolling through October, I was up nearly $500,000, about the exact amount I'm *down* this year. And what makes matters even less palatable is that every weekend starts out looking so very promising, with enormous, early profits. Then we seem to give all those profits back, plus more. I don't bother watching the games; it's too disturbing. Instead, I try unsuccessfully to read and write. My concentration's shot.

At the end of the day I check the final results and do my accounting. Not only do the losses always seem to add up to more than the wins, our handicapping percentage is below 50 percent, worse than what a monkey could accomplish flipping a coin. This is not the form of the world's greatest sports bettor. Even I, who admittedly know next to nothing, am managing slightly better than 50 percent in my personal accounts, where, without Baby's artificial intelligence to guide me, I frequently pursue investments on the basis of that most dangerous of motivations: my own unassisted opinion.

Algo Andy tells me Baby still isn't ready to return to work. "Don't worry, Michael, I'll figure this one out. I said this isn't rocket science—but it sort of is in a way." He laughs uncontrollably and wishes me good night.

I'm driving in a rental car from the Napa Valley Country Club, where I've spent the day doing research for an upcoming golf article, to the Oakland airport, where I hope to arrive in time to place a slew of wagers before the Thursday night college football games. The bookies at SBG Global have given me a lovely welcome gift that's even better than the 15 percent sign-up bonus added to my account: They're willing to let me bet $50,000 on a college side and an astounding $25,000 on a college total.

Before I can negotiate the late-afternoon traffic tangle around San Francisco, my cell phone rings. It's Big Daddy. He's got the hungry, predatory sound in his voice he gets when someone offers him big limits, as though he were a salivating wolf and the prospect of a five-dime bet on a football game were an injured lamb. Thus I'm experiencing something I never envisioned doing: driving a Pontiac Grand Am in bumper-to-bumper northern California traffic while placing more than $100,000 worth of bets on the Syracuse Orangemen (–10 points).

This should do wonders for my image with the fellows at SBG Global. Only a hopelessly addicted maniac tosses off six figures worth of football bets a few hours before game time, *from his car.*

When I arrive at the airport, the craziness continues. With my cell phone in one hand and two pay phones juggled in the other. I place a rope of disparate bets for Big Daddy with almost every one of my accounts. A casual onlooker might mistake me for a harried business traveler attempting to keep up with the new sales projections back at the home office. But I'm merely a hard-core sports gambler, trying to keep up with the insatiable betting appetites of my friend and colleague, Rick Matthews.

My tenure with the allegedly high-limit gambling shop of SBG Global lasts exactly five bets. Management there decides to shut me down after noticing that on three out of three bets placed on college football Saturday I managed to get a good number. Since the line didn't move against me—as it did on the Thursday night Syracuse game, when I took a bad number—I must therefore be part of a well-connected and powerful betting syndicate.

Which is true, of course. Never mind that during my brief relationship with the Global folks I haven't won a penny. In fact, I've lost $7,500. But they see in my consistent refusal to take a poor point spread the potential to earn a profit over the long run, and that just won't do.

I'm glad that at least *someone* foresees me winning.

. . .

Throughout the dark days of my breakup with Viv, Big Daddy has proved a perceptive and kind friend. He'll interrupt our bet making to ask, "Are you okay, pal? Are you really all right?" Over the past few weeks, during which we've lost more than half a million dollars, I've grown eager to hear which homespun term of endearment he'll use next. I'm alternately "slap-daddy," "pardsy-wardsy," "young friend," and my favorite, "daddy rabbit." Big Rick frequently solicits my advice about the particulars of getting our money down; more heartening, he frequently follows it. Even as we lose our shirts, Big Daddy confides in me more and more.

Still, he's no Brother Herbie, who tends to speak frankly and (I would suppose in Big Daddy's eyes) loosely about what's going on in the world of sports betting: which syndicate is betting on what; how much is getting wagered on which teams; insider gossip. So it's with some regret that I listen to him tell me that my old pal Little Mikey Brown from Caesars Palace is getting a reputation in sophisticated sports-betting circles as a shady character.

A few months ago, during baseball season, the onetime boxer left the Palace to assume a managerial position at the MGM Grand. I always assumed that Mikey Brown moved to MGM because he didn't want to work for the suffocating Hilton administration, which bought Caesars earlier in the year. Now Brother Herbie tells me that Mikey's move may have been because the suits at Caesars had gotten wind of the former fighter's antics.

According to Herbie, Little Mikey is doing at MGM Grand what he did at Caesars: letting a group of professional gamblers bet into badly off lines on Sunday night. "Let's say the line is three everywhere else," Herbie explains. "Mikey Brown will put up the number as one and a half and let his boys lay it. Later in the week they'll take three and a half from somewhere else."

I don't know if it's true. And I almost don't want to know. I'm just sorry to realize that everyone in this dirty business—including me, I suppose—is constantly looking for an angle to beat the game, even if that angle isn't completely honest. In a perfect world, the bookies would put up a line, the bettors would bet into it, the good handicappers would win and the bad ones would lose, and everyone would go home feeling as though he got a fair deal.

But that would be too easy.

When I brief Brother Herbie on some of my upcoming travel plans, including weekly visits for couples counseling with a completely uninterested Vivian *and* individual counseling to deal with my dismally ineffectual couples counseling, he offers me his unsolicited advice.

"I've never done the therapy thing," Herbie says in his gentle backwoods drawl. "But I've always found that a really expensive gift seems to do wonders for a relationship."

Just when I'm convinced that the only thing that matters is the absent affection in my life, in one splendid day of college football wagering we erase $330,000 of our $470,000 seasonal deficit. I can see faintly what I've been seeking for the past six weeks: many very big wins. All our important games, the ones where the Brain Trust has $75,000 or more on the line, come home on the happy side, and though money isn't everything, when it's all you have, it's something.

Returning from a story assignment in the Channel Islands, minutes after touching down at LAX after a twelve-hour flight from London, I call Brother Herbie to see if we're doing any business. (I spent the interminable hours at 37,000 feet poring over statistical charts and early-in-the-week line moves. My point-spread divining rod managed to find nine games that were "off.") He tells me it can wait until tomorrow morning, Saturday, and that I should get a good night's rest.

On the taxicab ride home, I call my Hollywood Boys and, in true sicko fashion, bet a string of games. Am I becoming an action junkie, or do I really know something?

Rick Matthews indubitably is on to something. For the second Saturday in a row we win more than $300,000, eliminating the season's deficit and settling nicely into a six-figure profit. Meanwhile, my personal accounts continue to produce dividends. Indeed, my handicapping percentage, I note with some pride, is measurably better than Big Daddy's at this point in the campaign. Of course, some of his positions are opposites, phony signals meant to throw meddling bookmakers off the scent of a hot play. Still, I'm up more than $40,000 on my own.

But there's that little problem with winning: When I call to get the

Sunday morning NFL lines, two of my most reliable outs, WWTS and William Hill, the august London outfit, inform me my account has been terminated. They give the usual reasons—smart money plays, etc. But the truth is this: While I sent them cash every week for five weeks to cover my mounting losses, they didn't care what games I bet on. Now that I've put together two winning weeks in a row, they care.

The closure of WWTS hurts especially. This was my largest out, taking $30,000 on a college side. I don't know how I'll replace WWTS—except to send in a "different" player, with a fresh name, address, bank account, and voice. When I report the bad news to Big Daddy, he takes it calmly. "You're just too tough, I guess," he says, chuckling darkly.

I'm a sports-betting hero only when cloaked in the super-powerful cape of the Brain Trust. When I return to my desk at *The Daily Gambler*, bespectacled and anonymous, I'm a pretend hero. What's worse, I'm channeling my emotional problems into odds analysis. I'm so lonely and heartsick, I find myself turning to gambling to fill the hole in my life. I can see how a gambling addict, despairing about things other than money, can easily narcotize himself with the adrenaline infusion of an uncertain bet.

But freshly earned money doesn't help me sleep any better. I still miss my girlfriend terribly. Cold hundred-dollar bills can't press warm breasts against you or kiss your lips.

Herbie gives me two conflicting orders: one at one shop for over on the Thursday night college game and one at another shop for under. When I question this strategy, he advises me to make like Eli Whitney with his cotton gin. "Sit chilly and don't ask too many questions, and everything will be all right."

"I don't get the Eli Whitney reference," I confess.

I'm mystified. But I'm also inspired. Surely I can do better than this. Surely opportunities exist that don't require the permission (and expertise) of the Brain Trust. Instead of brooding over my solitude, waiting for Rick Matthews or Brother Herbie to lead me into action, I ought to discover my own secrets, my own closely guarded keys to the sports-betting vault.

Algo Andy assures me that everything is progressing nicely and that he's noticing some interesting trends. But unless I want to gamble for the sake of gambling, he wouldn't recommend following Baby's advice just yet. "She's having growing pains," he says.

It's almost the weekend and Big Daddy has yet to instruct me on a single bet. (Apparently he's waiting to make his move early Saturday morning.) I look at my ledger book and note that I've already got $35,000 in action on the weekend, all based on my own handicapping, without a computer to show me the way to salvation. Have I gone insane? Has lovesickness rendered me an utter buffoon? Or—and this is my devout hope—am I starting to get the hang of this whole racket?

Based on my dismal results on this college football Saturday, I don't know a damn thing about sports betting. I go 3–7 and bleed away nearly $15,000. Furthermore, Big Daddy has me execute exactly five bets: one an opposite; two on totals; and the other two on Ivy League games, where the limit is $2,000. Are the lines too tough? Have the outs become too unreliable? Has Big Daddy gotten wind of my freelancing? I'm not sure I want to know the answer, but I *am* sure I don't want to have to hang around my house all day, every day, if there's no reason to be here. I'd much rather be hiking with Ella in the Hollywood Hills, chatting up starlets, and pretending I haven't a care in the world. It's a boring and unprofitable Sunday, and I become more disconsolate when I talk to Viv, who's supposed to be meeting me later in the evening to attend a mutual friend's wedding. She sounds, as always these days, cold and distant, speaking to me as if I'm a foreign clerk booking her sports bets.

We barely talk at the nuptials. Vivian is icy—if a woman so ridiculously hot, radiating lasciviousness through her dark green dress, can be called that. Feeling like a stranger with the closest person in my life sends me reeling back to Mistress Gambling.

The next week I blow close to $30,000 on college football. Some of the games are Brain Trust specials—which continue to lose. Most of them, though, are my homegrown stinkers.

Something weird has happened to me. I'm no longer scared of money. I spend it freely and, when everything is working correctly, I earn it easily. Maybe it's only the recklessness born of heartbreak, but I'm convinced that Big Daddy has had a powerful influence on me. No longer do I have "piss running through my veins," as do many of the bookies Big Daddy derides. Now, I've discovered, I've got heart. I'm not sure that's a good thing.

If I were to lose another $30,000 on NFL games this November Sunday, maybe I'd smarten up and quit my solo enterprises. Maybe I'd learn an expensive lesson. Regrettably, the only enlightenment I glean is that I'm pretty damn good at selecting professional football sides. I win back more than $15,000 of Saturday's losses—and my confidence, if not my entire bankroll, returns. This, I realize, may not be the best result for long-term financial wellness. But I'm not complaining about going 4–1 and taking down the dough.

I'm only sorry I didn't bet more.

Fourteen

BRINGING HOME BABY

"Let's not get carried away until I can run some more simulations. But, Michael, I'm starting to see indications that we might be on to something here."

It's nearly midnight on the Pacific coast, in the middle of the night back east, and during a freezing November storm gripping the Atlantic coast the insomniac genius Algo Andy is delivering the news I've been longing to hear.

"Andy, tell me, is 'cautiously optimistic' a fair way to put it?" I ask, hoping my programmer will tell me to hurl restraint aside and start betting on Baby's opinions with both fists.

"Ummmmm . . ." Andy inhales leisurely, keeping me in suspense. "Weeeelllllll . . ."

"Andy, come on, man, you're killing me."

He titters. "Let's put it this way. *I* would bet on football games now—and I don't even know what 'positive yards after catch' signifies, although it obviously means something important to Baby."

I scream. "Oh, man! I could kiss you!"

"That's an intriguing proposition," he says.

"So, wow—I'm just. *Wow.* So Baby is really working? I mean, you're seeing—what are you seeing, Andy?"

He mentions "improved efficiency" and "probably accurate to a tenth of a point" and "two standard deviations" and a bunch of other things I can't quite comprehend. But I understand the essential message: the Brain Trust is no longer the only betting group with a computer that's smarter than the linemakers. Indeed, Andy is so confident in the improved Baby that he wants to put some of his capital into the pool and make bets himself.

"Have you ever talked with a bookie?" I ask the academic.

"Oh, dear God, no," he replies. "But how hard can it be?"

"Well, when you're betting a couple hundred dollars per game, it's easy. No one pays any attention. But if you try betting the kind of sums that will make this whole venture worthwhile, you're going to be under a microscope. I'd have to train you."

Andy says, "I'm a quick learner."

I tell Algo Andy that it's probably best to leave the betting to me and my Hollywood Boys. But if he's determined to be a player (and not just a computer savant) I can give him a script, a rubric to follow.

He says it sounds like fun.

"That's not the word I would use, pards," I warn him, slipping into the Vernacular of Rick. "But, sure, you want to gamble with these fellas, we'll give 'em some business."

"Was that a southern accent?"

The next morning, I send Algo Andy a draft of how a conversation might go between him and a big offshore bookie, the kind of shop that would be willing to take $25,000 per game—which is slightly larger than we can afford to bet on our own, but comfortably within our means if I borrow funds from my Brain Trust bankroll. The Antiguan store, WWTS, seems like the best candidate for Andy. The bookmakers there don't steal, they're accustomed to big bettors, and the owner, Buckeye Bill Scott, has probably heard every smooth-talking wiseguy in the business—including several versions of me—make his pitch. The best technique for dealing with legitimate bookmakers, I've found, is to tell them something very close to the truth. Tell them you're smart. Tell them you've got a system. Tell them you've got a computer.

Don't waste your time with someone in marketing. Talk directly with the boss. Go right to the top. He's the one who will have to approve you anyway. Just say:

Hello, may I speak with Bill Scott, the owner? I'm hoping to have him approve some large betting limits on pro and college football.

When he comes on, say: Hello, Mr. Scott. My name is Andy Algo. I'm calling you from Boston, where I'm a professor in the computer science program at Harvard.

Don't be offended. He'll definitely have heard of Harvard. MIT might not mean anything to a guy who used to operate out of Toledo, Ohio.

I'm thirty-six years old and I'm not really a gambler, but I do probably know more about artificial intelligence than 99.99 percent of the people in America. A group of us had some extra time on our hands, and we came up with an algorithm for a computer program to predict the outcome of football games, and it turned out to be extremely powerful. We were hitting 56 percent on college and 58.5 percent on pro, but we were betting only very small amounts of money—just a few thousand a game—to test out the program. We managed to put one of the local campus bookies here in Cambridge out of business. I think we've really got something special here—which I'm sure you hear all the time from people who think they can handicap football games! I know there's supposedly been some other computer betting programs that supposedly work very well—I've heard about the Brain Trust group, which everyone says is very successful, but I'm sure its code isn't nearly as sophisticated as ours. But anyway, I don't mean to boast, I'm just excited about what I've come up with.

This year we've rounded up a pool of investors, including some of my colleagues at Harvard, and we're ready to put our money where our mouth is, so to speak. I'm calling you because everyone I talk to about bookmakers says you're the oldest, most trustworthy place to bet in the world, that our money would be safe with you. And also because you take the biggest bets. The people at Right Away Odds speak very highly of you, and so does every watchdog site on the Internet. I've researched WWTS, and unless it's all a scam, you seem like the top legal bookmaker in the industry. Plus, Antigua seems to have a fairly reputable gaming commission, in case there's a problem.

Our group is looking to bet between $25,000 and $50,000 a game. I'd like to pick the best three or four games each day and bet them with you exclusively. Now, I'm telling you in advance, I think we're going to win. But my understanding is that you handle lots of action from big Las Vegas syndicates and so forth. I'm sure that sometimes my picks will be very different from what the Las Vegas people bet. And sometimes maybe they won't. But in any case, that's an awful lot of juice you'll be pocketing.

He'll probably suggest letting you bet more like $10,000 to $20,000 (if we're lucky!). If he offers smaller limits than that—and I don't think he will—ask him for other places he would personally recommend, and ask if he'll make an introduction.

Then say: What are the mechanics of this? Do I need to send you all the money in advance, or do we settle up at the end of the week?

He'll tell you need to post up all the money with his bank.

Propose this: If I put up, say, $300,000 in cash, can I bet up to, say $600,000 in action? I'm not going to lose all my games. In fact, I'm probably going to win most of them!

In essence, you're asking for partial credit. If you show good faith in shipping so much money offshore, you want him to show good faith by letting you bet on collateral.

Ask him: Is everything recorded? How does the actual betting work? I've never dealt with an offshore bookmaker before.

In fact, everything is recorded. When WWTS opens your account, you'll be given an account number, something like AA24601; and they'll ask for a password, which I think you should make something like "BoyGenius" or "MathWizard."

The key here is to sound like you really know what you're talking about when it comes to computer handicapping but that you don't know shit about betting, which is true, I guess.

"Oh, this is going to be too fun!" Andy exclaims.

"You have no idea, partner," I say, trying mightily to abstain from an invective-laced monologue in the style of Rick Matthews, Aggrieved Bettor. "No idea."

Within twenty-four hours, Algo Andy has an account up and running at WWTS—as do two other members of the Hollywood Boys. Within forty-eight hours, I have the scores—or at least what Baby says they ought to be if the NFL contests were played several million times. How strange to see the difference between teams expressed in hundredths of a point. Indianapolis, Baby says, is a 5.29 point favorite over Miami. The Bears shouldn't be getting 7 points from the Packers; they should be getting 7.14. This is because, according to Baby's simulations. Green Bay is supposed to score an average of 23.74 points and Chicago is supposed to score an average of 16.60. I notice that almost all the matchups are closer than one might reckon initially, that the (long-term) difference between NFL teams isn't as large as most people assume. Which means there's inherent value in the underdogs.

I analyze the numbers for two hours, drawing a neat rectangle around the games that have the largest disparity between the current point spread and our predicted point spread. The fact that *most* of the "theirs" and "ours" are within a point of each other gives me faith that Baby is largely producing the same power ratings as the linemakers. In the four sides (and six totals) where the discrepancy is a point and a half or more—especially around the key football scoring numbers of 1, 3, 4, 6, 7, and 10—Baby apparently noticed something the oddsmakers didn't. This could be because she weighted some batch of data—scoring average on artificial turf, for instance—differently from the guys who make the line. Or because the people who set the official betting spreads have to consider public perception and media hype, factors from which a computer is blissfully immune.

I'd like to know how Baby's figures stack up against the Brain Trust's. I'd like to have incontrovertible evidence that I'm not seeing just what I want to see. But I have to keep my love child's existence a secret. Because I know that to remain even a little bit useful to the Brains, I must mine new (and substantial) outs. For them, not me.

I don't yet have any proof whatsoever that Baby's extrapolations are worth anything more than a two-dollar lottery ticket. Keeping a bridle on my ambitions might not only avert financial ruin, it will also help me retain membership in the most elite betting club in America. Despite Algo Andy's confidence in the accuracy of our intelligence, I use the first Sunday with Baby II to conduct some modest real-money tests. I realize that there isn't really any reliable way to gauge the value of our program, on the basis of such a tiny sample of trials. We could win (or lose) everything and I wouldn't know more (or less) about Baby's power. Only Andy can really say—and he says, "Yes! Yes!"

I know that if I had the heart of a Rick Matthews, I'd have the courage to back my knowledge with as much money as I could get my hands on. Maybe I'm not even a Medium Daddy. I'm a guy who wants to be that kind of man without facing the calamitous consequences that plague such bold characters.

I direct my Boys to play New England and New Orleans, Atlanta and Carolina, for a measly $10,000 per team. As I'm giving the orders, I feel simultaneously relieved and sickened. Am I throwing away money on fantasies or am I throwing away money because I'm too meek to take the financial plunge?

Several of the point spreads offered by the bookmakers match almost exactly what Baby says they ought to be. Normally, this would mean abstaining from wagering. But one opportunity piques my interest. Baby says the Jacksonville Jaguars should be a 7-point favorite (actually, 6.96) over the Baltimore Ravens. But at one of my shops, in Australia, I find Jacksonville –6.5 over Baltimore. At another, in Costa Rica, I find Jacksonville a –7.5 favorite. So I lay the low number on the Jaguars and take the high number on Baltimore, betting $22,000 on each side, effectively risking $2,000 to win $40,000.

With two minutes to go in the game, Jacksonville, driving furiously, trails Baltimore by 1 point. This scenario gives me a faint chance that the final point spread will fall exactly on the magic 7. If Jacksonville can score a touchdown, it will be leading by 5. Correct game strategy dictates going for a 2-point conversion, making the margin 7 instead of 6. Just as Baby hath decreed.

Serendipity, thy name is Jacksonville. Rather than settle for a field goal from inside the Baltimore 20, the Jaguars continue to drive. And on third and goal, with seconds remaining, they dive into the end zone for a touchdown. Without hesitation, the Jags line up for the strategically compulsory 2-point conversion. And succeed.

Final score: Jacksonville 30, Baltimore 23.

And 44, Algo Andy, and our very smart Baby: plus $40,000.

For the weekend, the Hollywood Boys win nearly $70,000, only $110,000 less than the Brain Trust.

Every morning between 8:30 and 9:30, Brother Herbie and I bet on college basketball games. And like the year before and the year before that, we win. Some days are bigger and better than others, but, lordy, our success at college hoops can't be explained by mere luck. We're on the right side with way too much consistency.

College basketball, I've learned after only a few weeks of action with the Brain Trust, garners only a fraction of the betting interest that football does. A $50,000 bet on an NFL game disappears into the giant ocean of money that's wagered every week on the helmeted gladiators. That same $50,000 bet on a Pac-10 basketball game can easily turn the line inside out. So when the opening numbers come out of the Caribbean and I place a whole bunch of money on the Oregon Ducks, laying 1 point against my hometown UCLA Bruins, the point spread changes all around the world. By the time I'm done with the few bookies that take early-week action, the line has crawled up to 2.5.

Two days later I see the brilliantly funny sportswriter T. J. Simers's column on page two of the *Los Angeles Times* sports section:

> Oregon is not ranked in the AP Top 25, but in the past few days the public has wagered so much on the Ducks, Las Vegas oddsmakers have moved sixth-ranked UCLA from a one-point underdog to a 2½-point underdog to encourage more bettors to go with the Bruins. I know from experience the public doesn't know what it's talking about.

I grin when I read this over my morning bagel. What T. J. doesn't understand is this: The public doesn't move the line on anything. Brother Herbie and I do.

The Brains go ten days straight without losing. Sure, there are a few defeats sprinkled among our victories, like truffle shavings on a bed of pasta. But each day, when I tally the results—at this point I don't bother watching any of the games—I always find more winners than losers. It's like a license to print money.

Brother Herbie says our picks are about as hot as he's ever seen. "And don't you worry, 44, it'll get cold on us eventually. So you better enjoy it while it lasts."

I take particular glee in watching the money pour into my bank account via wire transfer, pumping up my net worth by substantial percentages every week. This must be what it feels like to be a Wall Street bond trader, or a sitcom star, when every day brings another $10,000 or $15,000 profit, sometimes more.

I only wish I had someone special with whom to share my fortune, someone to climb into a limo with and take off for the best restaurant in town. Someone to surprise with tickets for the Concorde and a suite at the Ritz. Someone to laugh with. Vivian left couples therapy after two sessions. "What's the point?" she complained. "Nothing's ever going to change."

The basketball games don't interest me. The point spreads don't interest me. The players and their illiterate locker room interviews don't interest me. I want only to extract as much money as possible from the grasp of the bookmakers and eventually find something wonderful to do with it. Maybe Viv was right.

I get a brusque good-bye from my oldest offshore out. World Sports Exchange, one of the first offshore bookmaking shops I discovered, throws me out. Its bookmakers are sick and tired of my picking 70 percent winners in the college hoops; they're sick of every game moving 2 points in my favor after I bet them; and, most to the point, they're sick of sending me tens of thousands of dollars every other week. Sherm, the co-owner, says, "You tell Rick Matthews that if you or anyone else connected with the Brain Trust tries to sneak back in here under another name, I'm just going to keep the money!"

"Isn't that against the law?" I ask. "Wouldn't the gaming commission take away your license for that?"

"Try me!" he yells. "Go ahead, try me!" I do, two days later, posing as an Asian gentleman from San Francisco.

The fact that the formerly polite proprietors of WSEX have become surly, larcenous, and exceedingly rude about my exit—"You're not smart enough to pick all these winners yourself, sir"—doesn't bother me as it might have two years ago. I've grown accustomed to bookies throwing me out for winning, and, like Brother Herbie and Big Daddy, all I can do about it at this point is laugh smugly. And find someplace else to lay 11–10.

My life is seriously out of balance. And the funny things is, I don't really mind it that way.

Each week my results—my personal results—involve wins and losses of $30,000 to $90,000. Each week I watch my net worth rise and fall significantly on the outcome of some football game in which I don't even know the names of the quarterbacks, let alone the team nicknames. Each week I'm alternately richer and poorer, and I feel hardly anything either way. Indeed, I hardly even care what happens to my bets for Big Daddy and the Brains; I have so much riding on my Baby-guided freelance action that I hardly pay attention to the real plays.

To my amazement, I realize I'm now routinely betting $25,000 a game on professional football. Three years ago I would have been frightened to bet $1,000. Now? What the hell. It's only money.

Up and down my bankroll goes. Since all I truly care about is how miserable I am without my woman, I notice the swings clinically, not emotionally. It helps, of course, that despite the wicked fluctuations, the general direction of my swings is upward. Truth is, I almost never get a bad number, and I almost never end up on the wrong side. Truth is, I beat the game.

Still, when I take a moment to look at my gambling career objectively. I'm slightly stunned. Am I really this heavy a bettor? Am I really throwing around money like so many blades of freshly mown grass? Am I really this sharp? Based on the paranoia displayed by every bookie I play with, I suppose the answer is yes.

• • •

If there's some way to pop a bookie, Big Daddy will figure it out. He's like some demented antihero from one of the Great Books, constantly on a solitary mission of revenge and redemption. Now he wants me to sign up for executive consultations with the Jim Snow Sports Service, a bunch of know-nothing touts who sell worthless "information" to sucker gamblers too stupid or lazy to make their own picks. For prices as high as $3,750 a month, the Snow people will supposedly supply me with a steady stream of hot picks, the same selections on which Jimmy himself is allegedly betting "hundreds of thousands." The marketing literature is so slimy I want to take a shower.

Nevertheless, I subject myself to this boiler-room operation because, according to Big Daddy, they'll steer me into a huge offshore bookmaking shop: our old buddies at Nautica—run by Larry Houston and half owned, coincidentally, by Jim Snow. Once firmly established as a total idiot—and who else but a total idiot would pay thousands of bucks for "20-star Platinum Picks"—I'll get big limits and a long shelf life. Later, a former Snow employee would admit to me that these super-duper VIP selections consisted of one side of a contest for half the clients and the other side for the other half.

I congratulate Rick on his clever idea. But what happens when I start betting the *real* hot stuff, instead of the phony random picks put out by Snow? Then what?

Big Daddy's got an answer for everything. "You tell 'em you've got more than one service, that you're part of a betting club, that you pick some games on your own. Shit, 44, if you get put into Nautica through Snow, paying 'em all that money for nothing, they *know* you're a sucker."

So I begin a phone relationship with a young salesman who identifies himself as Ken and immediately begins asking me prying questions about how much I bet per game, how many games I bet on a weekend, and what kind of teams I like to bet on. I can almost hear his saliva glands kicking into overdrive, drooling over me as though I were a prime cut of tenderloin. Ken claims to bet $5,000 per game on Jim's Super Selections, which, he guarantees, will go 13–2—or better!—for the first fifteen games, or I'll get the next month free!

Now, I'm no math genius, but I figure if Ken is indeed doing what he claims, he must be clearing around $50,000 a week from his sure-thing winners. Which makes me wonder just a little why he's wasting his time on the phone with chumps like me when he could be tooling around Vegas in a Ferrari convertible, with a Bally's showgirl in the passenger seat.

I sort of admire Ken's slick web of nonsense. He says all the right things to entice anyone who doesn't really know how sports betting works, and with my stupid questions and suggestive hints I encourage him to lay it on thick. Stifling the urge to laugh, I tell him I'll be back in touch very soon—after I consult with Big Daddy, who, I know, will enjoy a chuckle when I recount my conversation with these con artists. "Ken," I assure the fellow on the other end of the phone, "I want to become a big winner just like you."

Like any good salesman ever eager to close the deal, Ken doesn't want to let me off the line until I commit to some sort of package. He even promises me a free winner for the weekend, a "super big play" Jim Snow is giving out only to his very best customers. Unfortunately, I hear my "wife" calling for me from the other room and hastily hang up.

I shudder with revulsion and instinctively head to the sink to wash my hands.

On Christmas Eve, I sit in my underwear in my office until 2:00 a.m. getting my accounts in order for the all-important college bowl game season.

Basketball has been a tremendous success. Pro football, with the assistance of Baby, has been solidly profitable for both the Brain Trust and my Hollywood Boys. College football, however, has been only modestly profitable. But Brother Herbie says he has a real good feeling about our prospects for the bowls. And I believe him. I've got to believe him: I've got nothing else to believe in. My life has been reduced to meeting strange women on the Internet, as I pine for my lost companion. Meanwhile, I bet incessantly on athletic events for which I couldn't otherwise muster the slightest interest.

Brother Herbie is a dice man, a hard-core craps player, so I tend to discount his premonitions, his good feelings about what lies ahead in our wagering fortunes. But this time, this year, he's utterly, indisputably *right*. Thanks to an almost uninterrupted streak of games going under (the side the Brains bet on almost every televised contest, it seems), our record in the college bowl games is an astounding-bordering-on-miraculous 18–4. (And two of the four losses come on wickedly improbable last-second disasters.) Otherwise, in Herbie's charming parlance, we mutilate the bookies.

In ten days my season goes from mildly profitable to wildly profitable. Steadily, surely, my personal win for the season breaks the magic $100,000 mark, and then $125,000. And then $150,000. And as the money piles up, something strange happens: I forget what it's like to lose. I believe every bet I make will come a winner. I'm certain.

This, I know, is a dangerous outlook. But the results have me bamboozled. I make $5,000 and $10,000 bets with hardly a second thought. I total up my wins and losses at the end of a fervent day and I'm not at all surprised to see I've pocketed another $20,000. At the end of the holiday week. I watch the bottom-line figure on my computer accounting software eclipse $175,000, and my heartbeat barely accelerates.

It's all too easy.

Fifteen

GOOD-BYE AND HELLO

For a man who allegedly knows nothing about professional football, Las Vegas point spreads, or betting odds, Algo Andy sure knows a lot about professional football, Las Vegas point spreads, and betting odds.

His tenure as a big gambler lasted four weeks. Three successive bookmakers, all of whom advertised themselves as "where the pros play" and "home of the world's best gamblers" and other nice-sounding (but empty) words of encouragement, unceremoniously requested that Andy take his money, his hot picks, and his regular account withdrawals and stay far away from their operations. By the end of 1999 he was no longer welcome to bet more than $5,000 a game anywhere. "They called me names," Andy told me, "like I had done something wrong."

"You did, brother," I reminded him. "You didn't turn your pockets inside out and leave all your money on the floor."

"Pretty funny," he said.

"The first hundred times it's faintly amusing."

With his interest in sports gambling piqued and nowhere to play, Algo Andy turned his attention to further refining Baby's oracular capabilities. And he started to notice something. In the past six years of action, the NFL results, he observed, had begun "regressing toward the mean."

"Ah, yes," I remarked learnedly. "I hate when that happens."

"Well, you shouldn't necessarily, Michael," Andy replied. "Maybe we could exploit this somehow."

"Sure we could—if I knew what you were talking about."

Andy explained to me that if Baby's analysis was accurate—and he was pretty sure that was the case—each year the final scores of the NFL games were landing perceptibly closer than the previous year to the predicted point-spread number. Exactly why, he wasn't certain. "Could be that the linemakers are getting better. Could be that Baby's getting better. Could be rule changes. Could be a conspiracy created by the television networks to keep couch potatoes watching longer."

"Could be that the fraternity of NFL coaches have an unspoken agreement to play nice, you know, so that they don't make the other guy look bad. And they're scared of the media. It's like they play not to lose instead of to win. Or something."

"I really can't say," Andy says. "But the data don't lie. Every year the correlation between the predicted number and the actual number is relatively closer. Not dramatic, but measurable. Just thought you'd like to know that."

It's Super Bowl Sunday, January of 2000, the beginning of the next thousand years, and for the second year in a row the Brain Trust has no play. Big Daddy believes the line—St. Louis giving up 7—is solid. (Baby says the line should be 6.72 points; close enough.) Brother Herbie, however, likes the underdog, Tennessee. "Man, I think Tennessee plus seven and a half or eight would be the nuts," Herbie says.

It would indeed. Through some highly unlikely circumstances, including a last-second pass play that leaves the Titans five feet from paydirt, the game falls directly on 7, resulting in a point-spread push.

Watching the Rams douse each other with champagne, I recall Andy's evaluation, which, at this moment, seems akin to biblical prophecy. Maybe there's something to his theory. Maybe we're witnessing a demonstrable trend. In fact, Big Daddy Rick decided that *none* of the NFL playoff games were worth betting on this post-season. Baby spotted only one glaring opportunity. But for the most part, she agreed with the Brains that the NFL numbers were too tough to fool with. I realize suddenly that it's almost February and I haven't made a single

Brain Trust football bet since New Year's Eve—and that was on a college game.

If the golden well is running dry, perhaps it's time for me and my crew to bid farewell and tramp off in search of more fertile pastures. If Andy and Big Daddy and Baby are right, there's just not enough variance, enough volatility, to bet the NFL games. How can you show a long-term profit if the final scores cleave so closely to the point spread?

I turn off the television, pour myself a glass of Scotch, place a live recording of Ella Fitzgerald in the CD player, and commence to sulk. As I'm musing on the spiritual differences between gambling on football and making immortal music—the latter seems, oh, just a wee bit more fulfilling—Ella launches into the old Fats Waller tune "Just Squeeze Me."

Treat me sweet and gentle . . .

Just squeeze me, don't tease me.

Whenever I'm really enjoying the music in my living room, I have the habit of serenading my dog. (She hardly ever complains.) I'm lying on the couch, melting into the cushions, petting my Ella behind her ears. *"Please don't tease me!"* I warble.

I get a sloppy kiss on the nose. Then she scurries away to her bolster bed beneath the piano.

"Why are you teasing me?" I cry out in mock dismay. "You hairy teaser."

She stares at me impassively. And I say, "Hey."

If my life was a novel, I might exclaim "Eureka!" or "By George, I think I've got it!" But I'm just a guy who bets on sports in the twenty-first century. So I say, "Hey."

Then I go to my office and get in touch with my partner the genius. "Andy," I say, trying vainly to remain calm, "I need you to run some numbers for me."

Algo Andy has become a football fan. "Did you see the end of the Super Bowl? Oh my God, what a finish. Right on the point spread!"

"Andy, listen to me," I say calmly. "I need you to run some numbers for me as soon as possible. Do you know what a teaser is?"

"A good-looking straight man who likes opera and ballet? Is this a trick question?"

"A teaser bet. Do you know how a teaser bet works?"

"No idea."

I explain. It's one of the all-time classic sucker propositions, a wagering innovation that has made many a bookmaker fabulously rich. The bettor gets to move the bookie's line 6 or 7 or even 10 points, so instead of getting, say, 9 points, your team now gets *15* points. (The original 9 plus the additional 6.) You can even turn a favorite into an underdog. If you play a 4-point favorite in a 6-point teaser proposition, that team now *gets* 2 points. The only catch is that when you make these bets, you have to wager on two, three, or more teams—and they *all* have to win, or else your bet goes down in flames. "That's why they call them 'teasers,' my friend. They look so good on paper, but they usually end up breaking your heart."

"I don't think anyone likes getting teased. Do you remember what they used to call me back in high school?"

"Look, Andy, we can deal with your pain in a few minutes. I'm trying to tell you that maybe, I don't know exactly, but maybe there's an opportunity here. With the NFL, I mean. Do you get where I'm going with this?"

Andy giggles. Numbers make him giddy. "If you have a set of trials where everything regresses toward the mean, and there's not a lot of variance—"

"Which is what we've been seeing—"

"Which is what we've been seeing lately in the football games. Well, then I suppose it would make sense to create your own variance—"

"By moving the point spread yourself. Exactly!" I shout.

"Exactly. Hmmm. Fascinating. If there's a lot of volatility you get killed. But if things stay within an acceptable range, like . . . oh, maybe one standard deviation—but don't hold me to that. Off the top of my head . . . I mean, well, for instance, if you had a season like the last two, I imagine you could do pretty well."

I fairly plead with Algo Andy to drop everything and start running some numbers. "Show me what happens when you start moving the point spread. Show me how much it comes into play, how much you win when you move it six points, or seven or, whatever—fourteen. We've got to figure out if you can win enough to overcome the juice."

"I get it," Andy says confidently. "I'll see what I can tease out." He laughs hysterically.

"Very clever."

"Good night, my dear. May the tease be with you."

I switch off my computer, trudge upstairs, and sing myself to sleep.

Throughout January and into February, the Brain Trust suffers a prolonged losing streak in the college hoops, the cold spell Brother Herbie predicted would eventually come. I've become so sour on the whole stinking enterprise of sports betting, the indignities of trying to get paid when you're lucky enough to pick more winners than losers, that I barely notice the intermittent victories. A month ago I felt invincible; now, I've become resigned to the inevitable losses. This is not a good attitude for gambling, or anything else in life for that matter. A prolonged winning streak normally has a way of cleansing the bad memories from a bettor's brain. The trouble is, I can't remember what those kinds of streaks are like, how they feel. I've come down with gambler's amnesia. The bad kind.

Two days after I've opened yet another new account under yet another new identity with yet another inscrutable accent, the chief line manager at the industry giant WWTS dies of a heart attack. I had talked to this fellow, Roger, several times on the phone, usually about things like getting my limits raised, and he always struck me as a decent and likable man—which is rare in a sordid industry filled with punks and worse. In the last conversation I had with him, about forty-eight hours before he collapsed at his office, he urged me—"me" being a French-Canadian chap named Jacques—"Go pick some winners, fer crissakes!"

At the risk of repeating an obvious cliché, I learn again that none of this gambling bullshit matters. Not at all. As Roger gasped on an ambulance stretcher, heading for the hospital he would never see, I know he didn't worry about the point spread on the Laker game, or if a certain new player from Beverly Hills was too sharp, or if his store was winning or losing money that week.

None of that stuff matters. None of it. It's the living that counts.

Which is why, after the football season fizzled to a conclusion in January, I announced to my colleagues that I was taking a few weeks off. I told them I wanted some time to evaluate the state of the universe and, parenthetically, my little place in it. The truth, I confided to my father confessor, Brother Herbert Curtis, was that I had actually started to think about something I hadn't thought about for three months: the financial implications. For the professional gambler this kind of ruminating can be dangerous, a slippery slope that leads toward self-doubt and intermittent anguish. When you're able to divorce yourself from the money, treating it merely as the primary tool you use in your profession, the comings and goings don't bother you. But when you start to realize, "Fuck! I've lost a new car in the last three days," then the money begins to mean something other than the commodity you trade with bookmakers.

Lately I've had the impulse to pull down all my remaining funds, call it a season, and enjoy the profits. Perhaps after a hiatus I'll feel refreshed; I'll be eager again to bet, bet, bet, and win, lose, win. Maybe. Or perhaps I'll discover I've had enough of the stress and irritation and euphoria chased with despair. Perhaps I'll be ready to quit, to walk away from this netherworld and its forbidden charms.

But then I start thinking: What would Big Daddy do? Would he display the "heart of a mouse, with piss-water in his veins," or would he come out firing on all cylinders, determined to blast through the miasma of doubt with sheer willpower?

I'm conflicted, which isn't a salutary state when you're dealing with a business that's all about black and white, right and wrong. "Herbie, I just need some time. Time to think. I'm sort of confused at the moment."

"Listen, 44, if you're spooked 'cause I told you we're getting murdered in the buckets, you can put it out of your mind. You know how these things work. Everything in life goes in cycles, 44," he says, paraphrasing verses from Ecclesiastes. "For every season there's a reason. I think our winter might just be turning to spring right about now. I really do. I got me a good feeling about this."

Considering this hunch is coming from an unrepentant dice player, a man who routinely blows five figures at the craps tables of Las Vegas, I'm not exactly rushing out to put a reverse mortgage on my house. But then I hear from Big Rick.

"Hey, pardsy-wardsy, how's life treating you?"

I tell him the truth. I don't know how much longer I'm going to be a part of the Brain Trust.

Big Daddy can't understand how anyone, even someone with aspirations beyond winning money in a casino, would excuse himself from such an exalted relationship. "I know we haven't had the greatest year. But, man, you're on a free-roll. It don't get better than that."

I hem and haw and try unsuccessfully not to sound like a self-absorbed neurotic.

"You know what I told you at the start, 44. It still stands. Anytime you want out, you're free to go. I just think, well, obviously, it benefits all of us to have you as part of the team. You know I count on you, pardsy."

Rick Matthews is a hard man to say no to. I tell him, "I'm just taking a short break, Big Daddy. I guess I'll see you and all the boys in March. For the Madness."

"All right, then, sweet face. March it is." Rick promises, "We gonna have us some fun."

Big Daddy has trained me well. I'm no longer a reflective pragmatist. I'm no longer entirely in control of my destiny. (Are any of us?) I'm a gambler. And soon it'll be time once more to sublimate my fears and gamble.

For the third year in a row I'm in Las Vegas for the NCAA Men's Basketball Tournament, the most heavily bet sporting event in America other than the Super Bowl. Little Mikey Brown, former sportsbook night manager at Caesars Palace, now the vice president of race and sports at the MGM Grand, has personally invited me to be his casino's guest for the week. Over the telephone he's agreed to let me wager $10,000 a game. He says, "I'd *love* to let you bet more, but we've got a much more recreational player base. We just don't write that kind of business here."

He's not kidding. Whereas Caesars always had a $5,000 minimum window, the top counter slot at MGM is $1,000 minimum—and I seem to be the only one using it. What's happened to all the monster sports bettors in Las Vegas? They're all playing offshore, where the bookies will take a decent wager.

Given the state of the Brain Trust's handicapping skills maybe I ought to be thankful that I'm limited to $10,000-a-game bets. Herbie's admitted to me that while I've been off playing golf and musing about my future, the syndicate has been treading water for the past two weeks, barely breaking even. In my darkest moments I can't wait for the season to be over. No more phone calls; no more line moves; no more wire transfers; no more crabby supervisors; no more cat-and-mouse; no more last-second bad beats; no more fluctuations in my net worth; no more.

The first day of March Madness we go 4–1, and all of a sudden I like this gambling business a tiny bit better. Plus, it's fun to be back in Vegas, flush with $100,000 in cash and chips, armed with the privilege of signing for all my meals and beverages, knowing the tariff will never show up on my final bill.

But I'm lonely—lonely enough to call Algo Andy in Boston every evening. We're like a couple of old matrons trading gossip. He tells me the latest Baby developments. ("*Very* interesting opportunities for football next year. *Very* interesting.") I tell him the latest Madness moves, with the understanding that he's not to bet any of the Brain Trust games. Given his newfound penchant for point spreads and power ratings, I know it's an oath that's hard to keep. He talks about football. I talk about basketball. He talks about offshore bookmakers. I talk about Las Vegas casinos. He tells me he wishes he could be at the sportsbook, in the eye of the gambling storm. I tell him I wish I could be anywhere but here.

Strolling through the cavernous hallways of the MGM, the world's largest hotel-casino, I miss Vivian terribly. How many happy times we had together in Las Vegas, the high-rolling RFB gambler and his moll, swimming in money and sex and good wine, living out the kind of fantasy life most visitors to Vegas dream of but seldom taste. It's been nearly six months since she moved out, and I still think of her daily. Being in Las Vegas again, gambling on sports, deciding between one glorious gourmet restaurant and another, makes me long for her vivacious presence, so full of lust and hunger and excitement. I'm alone. And I miss her. No amount of winning basketball picks, it seems, can change that.

As the season grinds to a finish over the next few days, we need the Michigan State Spartans to defeat the Florida Gators in the championship game of the NCAA Men's Basketball Tournament. Now back home in Los Angeles, I'm holding a $10,000 future ticket, at 3½–1 odds, that will be worth $35,000 if Michigan State wins. The Spartans are something like a 4-point favorite, but the point spread is immaterial. If they win—by one or a dozen—we finish our campaign on a successful note. The extra $5,250 I'll earn on this game suddenly seems sort of meaningful. This has been the least profitable season of the three I've had with Big Daddy and the Brains. For the year I've won only a bit more than $700,000—*only!* The two previous seasons have yielded $1 million gains. If not for the $100,000+ I've managed to accumulate on my own accord (with the help of Baby and my Hollywood Boys), I'd have to consider the 1999 results disappointing, a lot of work and time commitment for a relatively modest return. (And no weekly subsidized high-roller jaunts to Vegas, replete with $300 bottles of Bordeaux and trips to the spa.) I'm like the ardent golfer who shoots a lousy score but manages a birdie on the eighteenth: Going out with a memorable winner will not only assuage my financial avarice but also leave a lingering taste of sweet redemption, a hunger to come back and play another round.

Michigan State never trails, never looks anything but dominant, and rolls to the national championship.

A couple of weeks later I return to Las Vegas to convert the winning ticket into legal tender. While there, I meet Big Daddy and Brother Herbie for a round of golf at a swanky private club; a gourmet meal at Prime, the steakhouse in Bellagio; and an evening of blithe conversation over a stack of 350 hundred-dollar bills. At dinner, Rick talks about his growing collection of restaurants and his new electronic massage chair and the European trip he's planning to take with his wife. Everything but sports.

Herbie talks about dice.

I love these men, my friends and colleagues, the accomplished safe-crackers who've taught me how to break into impenetrable vaults. I respect them. I admire them. I try halfheartedly and with limited success to emulate them. But when I look across the table, I wonder if this is the last time I'll share a meal with them. The dancing water show begins on the man-made lake in front of Bellagio. I hear Sarah Brightman and Andrea Bocelli singing, and I, too, wonder if it's time to say good-bye.

Rick Matthews and Brother Herbie aren't much into speeches. They measure a man by what he does, not what he says. I propose a toast anyway. "Here's to another successful season for the Brain Trust," I say, lifting my glass of Opus One. "Here's to Brother Herbie. Here's to Big Daddy Rick. And here's to all of us working with each other in a happy partnership."

"Well," Big Daddy says modestly, "we did the best we could." He looks around the table and nods. "And we'll get 'em again next year."

Ah, next year. For six months, I can look forward to a life that has nothing to do with bookmakers and point spreads and wire transfers and early morning phone calls and late night account reviews and close calls that go against us and lucky breaks that do—and everything else.

And I suspect I won't miss it at all.

SEASON FOUR

Summer 2000–Winter 2001

Sixteen

SUPERSTARS

The high desert of Nevada, in July, scorching and persistent, reduces energetic strivers to partially melted zombies incapable of clear thought or decisive action. Algorithm Andy, however, isn't one of those people. He seems immune to the searing sun and the Mojave-borne siroccos that make the great outdoors feel like an industrial hair dryer. It's his first trip to Sin City, and he's like a child at an amusement park, animated and awestruck, bursting with more energy than an adult man should be allowed to have.

"Are you on crystal meth?" I ask him.

"High on life," he says, laughing way too loudly.

I've agreed to meet him for a Vegas weekend of harmless blackjack and baseball betting, which is my computer programmer's newest recreation, an "intellectual challenge" that apparently stimulates him in ways that teaching MIT's undergraduate Einsteins can't match. "Baseball is all numbers, Michael," he announces with a cocked eyebrow. "A cornucopia of statistics. Very beatable."

"I'm sure it is. I mean, I know it is. The Poker Players kill baseball every summer."

"So why not the Brain Trust? Or if they're not interested, why not the Hollywood Boys?" Andy asks.

We're at the MGM Grand, at the Wolfgang Puck Café, near the sports-book. I put down my smoked-salmon and cream-cheese pizza and lean forward emphatically. "Because, Andy, a guy's gotta have a life. There's so much more to living than making money. I mean, even a man like Big Daddy Rick Matthews—even he needs a vacation from all this," I say, gesturing broadly at the casino around us.

"I understand, Michael. On the other hand, if you were an academic and not a fabulously wealthy type, and there was a bunch of money lying in the street, and all you had to do was bend down to scoop it up, wouldn't you?" He smiles crookedly and starts to laugh, a wheezy coughing sound, like someone hyperventilating. I haven't seen Andy in person for almost twenty years; he looks just as I remember him from high school, albeit slightly better dressed and with a significantly smaller Jewish afro. I have great affection for the man, even if I'm incapable of comprehending the mathematical mysteries that swirl inside his brilliant mind. I don't want to hurt him. But I can't help him.

"Look, Andy, you're more than welcome to take a crack at baseball on your own. I'll lend you some money if you need a bankroll to get started. I'll even advise you on how to get your money down safely. But I can't be a sports bettor all year round. I'd slash my wrists. Seriously, I'm thinking of retiring this season. Not just taking a break. Quitting."

"You're kidding!" Andy says. "What's wrong?"

"Nothing. I'm just tired of . . . I don't know. I just feel like I should be doing something more constructive with my life."

"Like what? Writing the great American novel?" he says sarcastically.

"Even the mediocre one," I joke. "Anything where I'm actually making something, doing something productive, not just piling up the money. Sports betting, gambling—I might as well be trading soybean futures."

Andy nods thoughtfully. "I get it."

We momentarily sit in silence. I feel like I've ruined Andy's vacation. "You're more than welcome to continue on your own, of course."

He shrugs. "Knowing the right teams to bet on doesn't do any good if you can't actually make the bets. You know, Michael? Dealing with the bookmakers and the money transfers. All that."

"I could always introduce you to people who know how to do that kind of stuff. And I'm sure they'd be delighted to know a guy as smart as you," I say, grinning.

"You're really retiring?" Andy asks. "I'm skeptical."

"I haven't decided. Maybe I just need to recharge my batteries, get some distance. Stay the hell out of casinos!"

We both chuckle. "Well, I guess this is sort of anticlimactic, then," Algo Andy says, pulling a neatly folded piece of paper from his shirt pocket. "But I thought you'd like to look at it, anyway, even if you're not interested whatsoever in sports gambling." He starts his unbridled laughing again.

I unfold the quarto. Across the top, in block type, it says:

POSITIVE EXPECTATION TEASER BETS

Beneath the title, in uniform columns, I see rows of numbers and percentages, with all the minus figures in a regular font and all the plus figures in bold. I scan the calculations. The vast majority of the bets are negative expectation, returning less than 100 percent for every dollar wagered. A few of them, though, are positive. Double-digit positive.

I stifle the urge to scream and wonder if it's too late: maybe someone has already seen what I've just seen. I stuff the paper into my pants. "Andy," I whisper, "don't say another word until we're out of the casino."

He smiles broadly. "I knew you wouldn't be interested. It's only the greatest discovery in the history of sports betting."

"I'm serious! Shut the fuck up. Especially," I whisper, "when we're around . . ." I tilt my head toward the sportsbook.

"You mean people would be interested in this information? You don't say!"

"So how's Terry? Everything good with the family?" I say, motioning to the waitress for the check.

Safely barricaded behind a dead-bolted door in my twenty-eighth-floor suite, after an elevator ride that I feared would involve grievous bodily harm at the hands of a large man demanding that I hand over the paper, I sit across from Andy in the living room. He giggles. "Are you hyperventilating?"

I catch my breath. "No," I say with forced nonchalance. "I'm just, you know, sort of—oh my God! Tell me everything!" I yell.

Algo Andy nods emphatically. "Of course. But just promise me that my discovery won't go to waste. I've got to have something to show for this."

I look him in the eye. "Andy, listen to me. If this works, you're going to be rich. Whether it's me or Rick Matthews or someone else, you're going to be taken care of. You have my word."

"Promise?"

"I promise."

"All right, then," he says, reaching for a notepad and pen beside the telephone on the coffee table. "Let me explain how I came up with these numbers."

Listening to Andy go through the mathematics of positive expectation teaser bets—of which I comprehend maybe half the concepts, even with his laboriously dumbed-down explanations—I realize I'm having a life-changing moment. There are precious few times in life when any of us can say with certainty, *"It was then that I saw my destiny unfold before me,"* since so much of our existence is built on the gradual accretion of circumstances and relationships, not dramatic epiphanies and tragic (or glorious) occasions that suddenly shatter the constancy of our daily routine. I'm hearing Andy explain how and why certain highly particular teaser bets involving certain highly particular numbers can be beaten. But what I'm thinking has nothing to do with point spreads and underdogs being transformed into favorites. I'm thinking that if what he's saying is true, I'm not going to be leaving the sports-betting world this football season. I'll only be leaving the Brain Trust.

Contrary to the myths the media aims at viewers who aren't here, when you live in L.A. you don't see movie stars in the grocery store. You do see them in the park, walking their dogs. You don't see them picking up their dry cleaning. You do see them in restaurants, attempting to enjoy a meal—if that's possible to do while being stared at. You don't see them at the video store. You do see them at movie screenings, opera performances, and live sporting events.

Especially live sporting events.

Especially live sporting events that people like to bet on.

One of the comforting clichés that get repeated by people who know celebrities to people who don't know celebrities is "They're just like any other normal person." Common examples: They have families that they worry about. They're insecure and anxious. Never mind that famous people are trailed by packs of photographers, and that their most uninteresting perambulations are reported upon with more thoroughness and gravity than Middle East peace negotiations. Deep down, *they're just like you and me.* Only richer and more beautiful.

And some famous people like to gamble; they just play for higher stakes. I've personally witnessed both the World's Greatest Basketball Player and the World's Greatest Golfer playing blackjack, in public, on the main casino floor, for stakes that would stagger anyone for whom $5,000 doesn't represent what the world's top athletes earn *per minute* in endorsement deals.

The tabloids do a remarkably assiduous job of detailing the wagering proclivities of our culture's court jesters and dancing girls, and I don't intend to further invade the privacy of famous people who like to bet. Except to say that the hordes of celebrities who show up in Las Vegas for ringside seats at boxing matches, gala concerts, and culturally significant events like, say, the Super Bowl, March Madness, the World Series (of baseball and poker), the Stanley Cup, and the NBA Playoffs are not there to enjoy the ninety-nine-cent shrimp cocktails.

Many of these celebrities have large lines of credit established at various casinos along Las Vegas Boulevard. And many others, I discover in the summer of 2000, have large lines of credit established at casinos in Costa Rica, Jamaica, Curaçao, and everywhere else offshore bookmakers ply their trade.

The week after I return from my revelatory weekend with Algo Andy, my pal the Heartthrob invites me to be his guest at a Dodgers game. The studio that produces his hit television show and his hit movies has a private skybox available on Wednesday night, and he's welcome to use it, along with a dozen or so of his closest friends. Apparently I'm one of them. We met two years ago at the Hollywood dog park, where the Heartthrob noted with some regret that his boy, Diddles, a rambunctious pit bull, did not behave as nicely as my mutt. He had taken the naughty pup to a school some of his celebrity friends had recommended, but higher education, it seems, didn't appeal to his hound Diddles, who had gotten into a fracas with Renée Zellweger's sheltie. He wanted to know what the secret was. "How do you make them just *chill out?*"

The Heartthrob and I ended up talking about dogs and walking home together—which was a strange and funny experience, since, even though he had a baseball cap pulled low over his much-photographed brow, members of the female sex, particularly those under the age of sixteen, seemed to recognize him with uncommon ease (and hysteria). Turned out he and I lived around the corner from each other, close enough that I could see the roof of his estate from my upstairs bathroom. Dog walks and moderately successful training sessions became a weekly custom, and soon I was the friend of someone whose face I'd often see on billboards, at bus stops, and almost every time I turned on the television.

At the Dodgers game, where I suspect I'm the only one in our group of spectators who hasn't appeared in *People* magazine, the Heartthrob introduces me to a pretty young woman who smokes like a decrepit motor and swears like an Appalachian prison guard. She's actually quite charming. I innocently ask her if, like all the other people in the skybox, she's in the entertainment business.

She takes a drag, nods, and phlegmatically says, "Fuckin' A."

"Oh," I say politely, avoiding the cloud of fumes traveling toward my face. "Theater? Film?"

"I'm on a show on NBC," she says, nodding.

"Oh, wow. Cool," I say suavely. "Which one?"

She tells me the name of a hit prime-time program, which I've never watched. "Can't say I've seen it," I admit. "I don't watch television very much. But I've heard of it. Very popular show. Do you have, like, a recurring role?"

She smiles, not sure if I'm putting her on. "I play the title character."

Before the phrase "You look so different without makeup, when you're not on the cover of *Maxim*" can escape my lips, the Heartthrob pulls me aside and says, "Dodgers win by at least three. Mark it down, Mikey. Dodgers by three."

"You think so?" I ask innocently, knowing that the visitors, the Cardinals, are in fact a small favorite according to the linemakers.

"Money in the bank, my friend," the Heartthrob insists, flashing his multimillion-dollar smile. "You wanna bet?"

"Sure," I say, "although I don't pretend to know anything about baseball. I'm more of a football man."

"Football? Football? Don't even get me started on football!" the Heartthrob says, turning on the charisma. "I'm only like America's number-one fan," he says. "I mean, I *live* football. You know, if I didn't end up going into acting, I probably would have played in the NFL."

The Heartthrob has the kind of physique that begs to be draped in couture suits, not shoulder pads. But that's not what's important. What's important is that he loves football.

"So tell me," I ask him, "do you ever bet on the games?"

He laughs. "I'm only like the best handicapper in America. I probably picked, like, seventy-five percent winners last season. I'm serious! I *love* football, man. I'm a football freak!"

"You picked three out of four against the spread?"

"Oh, yeah! I'm telling you, Mikey, if you ever want the hot plays . . ." He nods suggestively.

I lead him to a corner of the skybox unoccupied by movie industry pulchritude. Murmuring softly, I ask him, "Do you have a bookie? Offshore?"

He grins. "Three of them."

Big Daddy calls a summit meeting in Santa Barbara. Brother Herbie and I are invited to be his guests for thirty-six holes of golf, gambling, and, oh yeah, some discussion on our strategy for the 2000–2001 Brain Trust sports campaign. If we're the Rat Pack, Big Daddy is Frank, Herbie is Dino, and I'm Sammy, the integral part of the team who nonetheless always feels like an outsider. I tell Big Rick that of course I'll be there and that I'm looking forward to seeing him and the gambling monk. But the truth is I'm dreading being there, knowing that I'll be forced to finally make up my mind. Once I overcome my Hamlet-like vacillations, I'll be compelled to essentially tell my mentor, *"Thank you for teaching me enough about sports betting that I no longer need you. Now I'm able to defect from your organization and lead my own crew."*

Driving up the 101, with the Pacific Ocean sparkling over my left shoulder, I lose and regain my nerve about forty-seven times. When I pull into the driveway at Santa Barbara Country Club, I'm still not sure what I'm going to say. Or if I'm going to say anything at all.

I meet the boys on the practice range, where the turf is finer than the belly fur on a Labrador puppy. "Gentlemen!" I call out. "Your pigeon has arrived."

"Mr. 44, pleasure to see you," Big Daddy exclaims warmly, patting me on the shoulder. Brother Herbie shakes my hand and commences to haggle. "You know, 44, Rick here tells me you're playing pretty good lately. I'm not sure I should be gambling with a young buck like you, but, then again, I don't want to be unsociable or nothing."

Already, before I can lace up my spikes, the negotiations have started. When one plays golf in this crowd, it's not for $2. Brother Herbie wants to play a $500 Nassau, with two-down automatic presses and a $500 bonus for birdies and $1,000 for eagles. It's a big game—one of the biggest I've played—but I think I'm a little better than ol' Herb. And if Big Daddy has taught me anything, it's to bet big when you have an edge and retreat when you don't. "What the hell," I say, shrugging, "I'll give you a game. If I lose, I guess I'll just have to go and pick some more hockey winners."

Big Daddy had infamously lost his shirt on hockey the year before I joined the Brains. It's the only topic I can tease him and Brother Herbie about.

"We're officially out of the hockey business. I convinced this stubborn old donkey. 'Course, blowing two hundred thousand a day doesn't make a man need much convincin'. Then again, knowing him," Herbie says, pointing his thumb at Rick, "this may not be a final decision. Let's just say the hockey is on probation."

"We'll see about the hockey, fellas," Big Daddy says mischievously. "Come on, now. Let's go play some golf. I wanna watch this match between the young lion and the sly old fox." He winks at me conspiratorially, and, sotto voce, says, "You should destroy this guy, 44. I'd love a piece of your action."

I want to win the Brother Herbie golf bet. But even more I want to show Big Daddy Rick I've got heart and courage and all those other intangible qualities that supposedly make a great gambler. I want to show him I'm not merely a responsible and trustworthy associate; I want him to see I'm a *player*.

After eighteen holes of countless laughs and smiles (and many superb golf shots), Big Daddy Rick proclaims wistfully, "We really should do this more often."

I probably couldn't afford to. On the eighteenth hole, I dunk my approach shot in the water and end up losing about $2,000 to the former man of the cloth, who can barely contain his smirk.

We instantly make plans to play again tomorrow.

After golf, we meet the wives at an oceanfront restaurant in Montecito. I'm traveling solo. Big Daddy drives his cherry red Mercedes roadster. Brother Herbie's got a shiny new Cadillac. The girls' caravan is a luxury SUV. The food is delicious. The wine is superb. The view is spectacular. The crowd is rich and beautiful. All this, I suppose, amounts to the spoils of war. The Good Life. It's very seductive. Except that it all comes at a cost that extends beyond money. Another season is upon us, which, should I choose to continue with the Brains, means I must endure my least favorite part of being a sports bettor: setting up accounts, creating business relationships, lying. The dance is the same every year. These operations are like Hydra: each one that gets chopped off by sharp wiseguys grows back as two fresh bookmakers, eager to make his fortune off the mediocrity of the average sports gambler.

The wives excuse themselves to freshen up, leaving me with Rick and Herb. "How you doin', pardsy-wardsy?" Big Daddy asks. "You ready for another great year?"

"Well, Big Daddy, it's a tough business," I say, not veiling my disenchantment.

"Well, 44, I'm hoping to make it easier," he says. Then Rick Matthews shares a radical strategy he's devised for camouflaging the Brain Trust's supersharp play from the bookmakers, a plan he hopes to implement in the upcoming football season. "We're done with the pros. No more NFL sides for us. They're just too tough to beat. We'll bet our usual college football, and college hoops, and maybe some NBA, too. Maybe a little dash of hockey here and there. And here's the unique part. We're going to make these bets in all sorts of combinations that only suckers do. Parlays and such."

"Parlays?" I ask, skeptical. The vig on these wagers, in which the player has to win two or three or more games to score a giant payoff, is much higher than the typical one-result bet. "That's giving up an awful lot of advantage," I complain.

"Not as much as you think," he corrects me. "We're going to be concentrating on halftime bets, parlaying the first half of a game with the overall game. There's a formula—and I'll show it to you if you want—where we can make all these parlays and get the best of it. No more straight NFL sides for us, pardsy. Our future is in parlays."

Rick thinks we have a big enough edge on our pure handicapping skills that we can overcome the inherently poor odds. And if we bombard them with sucker bets, the bookies, according to Big Daddy's theory, won't be able to tell the smart money from the square.

Anything that makes it easier to get a bet down I'm all for. But a world-class gambler like Big Daddy surely knows the huge expenses involved in betting exotics. Parlays can be twice as bad (in pure math terms) as straight wagers. A two-team parlay, for example, usually pays 13–5. The true price is 15–5. This means bettors are giving up 10 percent of every dollar they bet to the bookie. A classic straight wager—one team against another—should pay 10–10; but the bookies charge a standard 11 to win 10, which translates into a hefty 4.54 percent edge. That's a lot of disadvantage to overcome, but not nearly as much as the double-digit imposts thrown up by exotics. Apparently, though, Rick's got it all figured. If there's an angle to be exploited, Big Daddy will be on it like a terrier on a rabbit hole. But I also know a strategy like this creates a vertiginous amount of fluctuation, the kind of up- and downswings that can give you ulcers.

"I guess it'll work," I say halfheartedly. My essential misgiving about Big Daddy's new order is this: No matter how stupid you make yourself look, betting hockey and round-robins and three-team parlays, if you end up being a big winner in the long term, most bookmakers are going to chase you out of their shop anyway. I've already been booted from more than three dozen offshore casinos.

"Oh, it'll work, 44," Big Daddy says confidently. "Shit, you call up a bookmaker, I don't care how suspicious he is, when the first words out of your mouth are 'Hello, I wanna bet me a three-team teaser,' I guarantee he's gonna love you."

My heart stops. "Teaser."

"Yeah. Imagine that," Big Daddy jeers.

"We're going to betting teasers?"

"No, of course not, 44. I'm just giving an example. So long as I'm alive the Brain Trust ain't gonna be betting no teasers," Big Daddy says, rolling his eyes. "Every year some hotshot kid comes along thinking he's got a system for beating teasers, and every year he goes broke before he figures out that they can't be beat."

"Not under any circumstances?"

He shakes his head. "No. Not in a million years. Which is why it'll sound like sweet music to these bookmakers when we call up and say we want to bet parlays and teasers and all these sucker bets."

"I get it," I say. "But—and of course you know more about this than I do—but I've heard that if you catch the right numbers at the right price—"

"Listen, 44," Big Daddy interrupts me. "The Brains ain't betting teasers. The only people that do are too smart for their own good, college boys with math degrees. I'm sure there's some kid at some prestigious university trying to work it out right now. And if he decides to put his money where his theories are he's gonna get busted like everyone else."

I feel short of breath and queasy. "Excuse me, gentlemen. I'm going to the restroom."

Instead, I walk directly out the restaurant's front door, onto the sidewalk, under a star-filled sky. And I call Algo Andy in Boston. When he answers, I demand, "Tell me the truth. Did you contact Rick Matthews about our teaser discovery?"

"What are you talking about?"

I tell him Rick's grand plan for the upcoming season. "He said specifically that he knew someone was looking into NFL teasers," I report, infuriated.

"It wasn't me, my dear," Andy assures me. "Scout's honor."

"So it's just a weird and awful coincidence?"

"I've never talked to Rick Matthews in my life, Michael. But you promised to introduce me one day. Is he there? Say hello for me!"

"Andy, this is serious," I remind him. "I'm not sure what's the right thing to do. Should I just tell him about you? Should I just quit and *not* tell him about you? I don't know."

"Hmmmmm." I can hear what sounds like Andy scratching his scalp, or possibly his beard. "It's not like anyone owns the numbers, Michael. They're born free, free as the wind blows."

"Stop it."

"My point is . . . hmmm. Well, my point is that it's like in science. Everyone is chasing the same solutions, the same breakthroughs. You can patent drugs and chip designs and fungible things like that, but nobody owns the right to bet on football games, you know, at whatever point spread seems attractive. Right?"

"Andy, I can't handle anything philosophical right now."

"I'm just saying, Michael, it's not a yes or no proposition."

"Well, you don't know Big Daddy. *Everything* is yes or no with him. Are you with him or against him?"

"How about a little of both? A 'yo.' Get it?" Andy, amused with himself, breaks into convulsive laughter. I tell him I'll call back later and hang up.

When I return to the dining table, the ladies have rejoined their gents. Everyone seems to be in high spirits, smiling and drinking and howling at one of Herb's stories. To the other patrons in this sublime restaurant, our group of revelers probably looks like a trio of successful real estate brokers, respectable businessmen and their pampered wives out for an evening of bonhomie. The other diners would never guess that the tropical-weight cashmere sweaters and silk scarves and glittering diamonds, the $200 bottles of wine, the freshly caught halibut, and the fantastic *bounty* that radiates from this table are the result of knowing that the Eagles should be giving 6½ points to the Bengals, not 9.

I feel tears welling, my breath quickening. "Excuse me, everyone," I say, forcing a smile. "I have something I have to tell you."

"He's super cool," the Heartthrob assures me. "Totally sweet guy. Very down-to-earth. Very easy to talk with. You'll love him."

We're in the Heartthrob's Porsche convertible, winding through the hills of Bel Air, on our way to meet one of the biggest movie stars in the world, someone I've seen in numerous films, someone, therefore, whom I feel I already know, if only through repeated exposure to his unmistakable face. The Heartthrob, though, really *does* know Captain Beefcake. They're friends.

Seems Captain Beefcake, like my pal the Heartthrob, is a football fan. A *big* football fan. A bets-up-to-$250,000-a-game football fan.

When the Heartthrob revealed to me at Dodger Stadium that he had a trio of bookmaking shops he played with regularly, I was thrilled at the possibilities. Here was a young man with more money than common sense, a maniacal sports fan who gambled on every televised football game, no matter what the point spread was. I assumed the bookmakers had to be accustomed to his firing huge wagers, and, despite the Heartthrob's claim of handicapping supremacy, none of the bet-takers could be scared of a genuine Hollywood dude whose only association with wiseguys was sharing a business manager with the star of *The Sopranos.* Here was the perfect beard: a monster bettor with a proven pedigree.

Then I found out the Heartthrob's usual wager was a thousand dollars a game.

"I thought you make, like, five million per movie," I said, perplexed. "And the TV show—I was under the impression you had more money than you could ever spend."

"Right. But I'm not *stupid*, Mikey," he replied. "I don't have a gambling problem, like some people I know."

I explained to the Heartthrob that, strange as it sounded, I was more interested in his friends with gambling problems than the clever ones like him who knew how to manage their money. "Let's say, theoretically, we're playing with a ten percent advantage over the bookies. Betting a grand a game is going to net us a hundred-dollar profit. We couldn't bet enough games to make it worth our while. Now, if we're betting fifty, a hundred thousand a pop—well, that starts to add up."

The Heartthrob told me he knew three Hollywood stars who bet big, *really* big. One of them, Mr. Sick, whose gambling exploits, according to the gossip sheets, were allegedly compromising his financial future, wasn't exactly a friend. "But we have the same publicist. I could have her set up a meeting, no problem." The other two were intimate acquaintances. Boy Wonder, whose youthful beauty belies his artistic maturity, is a frequent visitor at the Heartthrob's pool parties, pickup basketball games, and Sunday football extravaganzas, where a collection of movie industry heavyweights (and their lingerie-model girlfriends) congregate on the Heartthrob's U-shaped couch and scream at the ninety-seven-inch TV screen together.

And then there was Captain Beefcake.

"Great guy, Mikey," the Heartthrob remarked. "But totally out of control. He's probably lost, like, I don't know, ten million in the last two years betting on football."

"You've got to have a complete disregard for money to blow that much with bookies. Then again, at a quarter-mill a throw, it doesn't take much to get bruised," I commented. "It almost sounds like Beefcake doesn't care if he wins or loses. He just wants the action."

"You know what, Mikey? I don't care how much money you've got, *nobody* likes to lose. You know what I mean? Even if it's not about the money, nobody likes to be known as a loser, especially someone who's used to having his ass kissed. You know what I'm saying?"

"Do you think Beefcake would mind having someone tell him which teams to bet on? Or is there too much ego involved?"

The Heartthrob smiled. "Fuck the ego. I don't care if you're making twenty million a picture. You don't like sending those fucking bookies money every month. You want to beat them."

The Heartthrob warned me, though: Everyone is always trying to get a piece of Beefcake. His time, his money, his influence—everyone in

Hollywood wants to bask in his glow, if not outright rob him. He has finely developed scammer radar. "I don't care if you promise him your left nut," my pal the movie star joked, "he's still going to be, you know, a little skeptical."

I recall the Heartthrob's prediction when we arrive at Beefcake's estate, a ridiculously magnificent slice of English countryside transplanted to the arboreal moraines above Sunset Boulevard. The man himself, dressed in white pajamas and a black silk robe (it's 2:00 p.m.), answers the door. "Hey, brother," he says, giving the Heartthrob one of those intimate handshakes that morph into a back-patting man hug.

"This is my friend, Michael."

"Hey," Beefcake says, extending his hand. "Pleasure. Come in, come in."

We walk down a long marble corridor that leads to a living room that looks out on what normal people would call a backyard. Beefcake's version has an Olympic swimming pool, multiple tennis courts, and a well-bunkered putting green. "Sit down, make yourself comfortable," he urges, motioning to a leather sofa. "Smoke?" he offers.

I decline. The Heartthrob joins Beefcake in defiling their heavily insured lungs. They talk about family and travels and movie industry developments while I try to look around Beefcake's home without appearing to gawk. He has a vibrantly green and yellow Matisse hanging above the fireplace, and in the corner, near the bar, a concert grand piano of the type one typically sees on the stage of Carnegie Hall.

"So, Mike," Beefcake says, flashing the smile I've seen countless times on celluloid, "they tell me you're the football genius."

"I don't know about that," I say nervously. "But this much I can tell you: I have a hard time getting any bookmaker to take my bets."

"You're kidding," Beefcake says, snorting. "That's outrageous."

I start to explain to him how a group like the Brain Trust works. Before I can make my pitch, Beefcake interrupts me. "You're part of the Brains? No shit?"

"You've heard of the Brains?"

He shoots me a look that conveys *What do you take me for, an idiot?* "Of course. Rick, Ricky. You know, what's his name? Sure. So you're tied up with that group?"

"Confidentially, yes. I mean, I was. I was and I sort of still am. But I run my own group, the, um—well, actually, we're known as the Hollywood Boys."

Captain Beefcake smirks. "Cute."

"And here's our problem." I explain to Captain Beefcake that we don't have any trouble picking winners, it's finding bookmakers to take our bets that's the challenge. I propose to the movie star that he can go on betting just as always, but I'd like him to make bets on my behalf, too. If I lose, I'll pay immediately. If I win—and I'm going to—I collect. "I'm not asking for a loan. I'm not asking for an investor, none of the bullshit I'm sure you're used to dealing with. I'm just hoping to capitalize on your . . ." I search for the right word.

"Relationship?" Beefcake proposes.

I was thinking "reputation." But "relationship" is better. "Yes. That's right," I agree. "Your *relationship.* Your bookmakers, I assume they're very comfortable with you."

"They should be," Beefcake cracks. "I've donated a shitload of money over the years."

"Like, what? A million?" I ask innocently.

He takes a long drag on his cigarette. "I wish. More like twelve."

I catch the Heartthrob's eye. He nods.

I address Captain Beefcake directly. "Well, I'm not saying you're going to get it all back at once. But if you follow my advice—and, I'll be honest, you're not always going to want to—you'll finish the season a winner."

Beefcake smirks, and in a hoarse whisper, says, "So what's the catch?"

I shrug. "I can't think of one."

The Heartthrob jumps in. "I'm doing it." He adds that Boy Wonder is, too. "I mean, if you're already losing, it's not like Mike is going to make you lose more than you already are. And if he's as good as he says he is, you're going win like you never did before."

"Right. And, again, I'm not asking you to advance me any money. I'm only asking you to make my bets at the numbers I'm looking for, and when I win, you make sure I get paid." I hold Beefcake's gaze, letting him assess me.

He squeezes his nose and scratches his ear. Then he stifles a yawn. "All right."

"Do you mind telling me who you're playing with?" I ask.

"They call themselves Nautica," Captain Beefcake says.

I howl. "Oh! Larry Houston? In Costa Rica? That Nautica?"

"That's them," he says. "You know them?"

I tell the movie star I've been booted out of the joint three times.

Beefcake can't believe it. "They seem like the nicest guys in the world. I can't imagine."

"Let's see if they're still so nice after you kick their asses. See what they're like when *they* have to send the money."

Beefcake smiles. The Heartthrob smiles. I smile. "That would be a change," Beefcake says. "What the hell, chief. Let's have some fun."

Seventeen

THE SMART MONEY

I spend the month of August 2000 coping with the crushing logistics involved in running a betting syndicate, dealing with the hundreds of niggling details that Big Daddy and Brother Herb, I now fully realize, contend with on an exponentially larger scale. Everyone has his agenda.

Algo Andy wants half the action—without putting up any of the capital. We settle on 25 percent.

The Heartthrob, unconvinced of my financial solvency, wants me to let him hold the money in his business manager's account so that if we lose he can be certain the debt will be retired promptly and that his reputation will remain pristine. We settle on a joint account at my bank with both our names on it, with all wire transfers requiring authorization from both parties. When he comes to Lucy Davino's office to sign the paperwork, an estrogen riot nearly erupts.

Captain Beefcake doesn't want me calling him at home. He prefers all football orders to come through the Heartthrob. We settle on a special cell phone, turned on twenty-four hours a day, that serves as my dedicated hotline to his much-photographed ear.

Boy Wonder, who was briefed in advance by the Heartthrob and talked directly with me for less than five minutes before declaring the arrangement "sweet," wants to make bets only after 9:30 a.m. on Sunday mornings so he can get his beauty rest. We settle on 9:00 a.m.

My other Hollywood Boys—the ones in San Francisco, Las Vegas, Atlanta, and Tulsa—want to get the plays *before* Sunday morning, for reasons that are never made clear to me. (Perhaps they intend to make renegade bets on their own.) We settle on the plays' being released when I feel the number is as good as it's going to get. I give the most worrisome Boys an extra 5 percent of the free-roll, hoping this will assuage their greed.

After everyone is taken care of, my piece of the betting action comes out to approximately $25,000 per game if we're betting $75,000 a pop, which includes the few thousand I'm able to bet on my own under an alias and an unintelligible accent.

We're ready to rock. We're not playing for Big Daddy anymore; we're playing for ourselves. Now would be an excellent time for Baby to find a bushel of juicy numbers, for the game results to fall within a statistically predictable range, for us to *win*.

I'm so nervous I start to get a bald spot on the side of my head.

Gamblers in the grip of fear, racked with doubt and regretful that they didn't do something reasonable with their money, like invest in municipal bonds, are apt to see signs in the most insignificant places. The bird that didn't (or did) squawk at his feeder; the television announcer who didn't (or did) pick his team to win; the lightbulb that didn't (or did) blow out when the field-goal kicker lined up for the extra-point try— everything is freighted with meaning, with the kind of dense semiotics French academics write unreadable books about. I'm starting to believe some supernatural force is attempting to send me a darkly ominous message, and he's using the Cleveland Browns as his medium.

Per Algorithm Andy's advice, the Hollywood Boys have forsaken teaser bets this first NFL Sunday. Our programmer wants at least one week of current data to feed Baby before we start experimenting with our precious bankroll. Instead, we make a few straight bets on the sides that are most undervalued, including the pathetic Browns. To say our season begins inauspiciously would be more diplomatic than the Greek ambassador to Turkey. Our first morning of the 2000 campaign is a disaster. Every game loses—all three, including a heartbreaking travesty in the Cleveland tilt, during which our sure-thing under bet gets obliterated, thanks to 14 unwelcome points that are scored in the last dozen seconds.

Within moments of the game clock expiring, I get apoplectic phone calls from three international movie stars, cursing, whining, and theorizing. "Game was fixed," Captain Beefcake declares. Although I want to theorize and whine and curse in sympathy with my soldiers, I'm supposed to be the stoic general who's immune to the obscene jokes football teams play on their faithful investors. Trying my best to emulate Big Daddy, I say as calmly as my racing heart and churning intestines will let me, "That's gambling. These things happen sometimes. Next time the breaks will go our way." Then I hang up and stifle the urge to kick my TV.

To compound the indignity of having our lock winner transformed into a painful loser, the (losing) bet attracts tremendous heat at two shops, since the line moved two points after we bet it. The Brain Trust, I suspect, liked the same position as us. SBG Global, which prominently advertises its willingness to accept the world's biggest bets, temporarily deactivates my man Timid Joe's account while conducting an "investigation." (The ads neglect to mention that you're invited to bet at SBG only if you certify in advance that you'll donate your mortgage money to the shop.) Another Costa Rican shop, Diamond, accuses Algo Andy of being a wiseguy and demands to know where gets his picks. Both Boys tell Diamond and SBG the usual fiction of insider tout services straight out of Las Vegas, but neither place is buying the story. After two bets (for which the results are one loss and one tie), Andy's limit at Diamond goes from $20,000 per game to $2,000, and he closes his account.

"We're in a serious hole, Mike," the Heartthrob complains. "Not making a very good first impression."

Boy Wonder wants to know what exactly made the Patriots such a compelling bet at –4. "Artificial turf instead of natural grass?" he hypothesizes.

And Captain Beefcake wants me to know, just for the record, and not because he's upset or anything, that he would *never* have bet on Chicago, no matter how many points you gave him.

We're not halfway through the first day of a sixteen-week season and already the crew is threatening mutiny.

Miraculously—or, in Andy's impassively calculating view, *predictably*—not only do we recover most of our morning losses in the afternoon, we actually turn a $31,000 profit.

All our games win.

All of a sudden I'm a genius again, worthy of telling absurdly handsome men which football teams to bet on.

I celebrate with my new girlfriend, Blanca, over pizza and beer, hoping the late St. Louis vs. Denver game falls exactly on 7, our perfect middle number. The Rams miss a 2-point conversion try with less than two minutes to go and win by 5. Blanca, an intense Argentine who understands NFL football better than most American men, goes berserk, yelling at the television in Spanish. I'm not complaining. I know this kind of thing will happen a hundred times before the season ends, and whether the bounces are for or against me I ought to accept the outcome with placid stoicism.

Of course, that kind of spiritual equanimity is easier to manifest when you're winning.

The following week, in the best Big Daddy tradition, I rescue Timid Joe from the larcenous intimidators at SBG, the allegedly big-time bookmakers who really want to deal only to squares. After "an internal investigation," the bookmakers there have concluded that the Welshman Joe isn't connected with the Brain Trust, or Ferdinand & Blair, or any other syndicate they fear. His account has been reactivated, accompanied by an earful of thinly veiled threats and warnings. He's under microscopic scrutiny.

So I instruct him to bet eight games that the smart money has already moved on, including a couple where I suspect the Brain Trust is responsible for skewing the point spread. On each of these hot games, Joe's betting SBG on the wrong side.

The beauty of this tactic is that though we're investing thousands of dollars on the disfavored team, we're betting at the absolute best number possible. The money moves have warped the lines so much on these games that the bookies are desperate to have counterbalancing action on the other side, even at the risk of a disastrous middle. After Timid Joe makes his bets, including a stone-cold play on the Monday night game (for which SBG offers him a bonus half point, on the mistaken assumption that he was going to bet the smart side), the clerk says the manager wants to talk with him.

"Sure," Joe says, knowing what kind of threatening lecture he's about to get, acutely aware that he shouldn't encourage a heated confrontation—not when they're holding more than $100,000 of our money.

The boss, Bobby Dixon, gets on. He explains why Joe was put on hold for so long. Seems his shop has had a whole bunch of wiseguys opening accounts and betting them big amounts, and, well, they want to keep a close eye on any large activity. "What I'm saying is, if you're betting steam, or moving for someone like Rick Matthews, you won't have the luxury of playing in my shop. And I *will* confiscate your funds."

Joe, as trained, feigns ignorance.

The boss uses words like "wiseguys" and "syndicate."

Joe, laying on his most charming Welsh accent, tells him the only syndicate he's aware of is one neither he nor the bookies want anything to do with. Heh-heh-heh.

The bookmaker mentions games moving after Joe bets them.

As rehearsed, Joe tells him, sure, he hopes so, since the services he's using promised him they'd get all the latest smart money moves straight out of Vegas, all the sharp plays.

Bobby Dixon takes a moment to clarify things for Timid Joe, to educate his slightly naïve customer. "There's a bunch of guys out of North Carolina and Arkansas," he says. "The Matthews group."

"Who are these guys in Arkansas?" Joe asks, genuinely curious. "I'd like their phone number!"

"Well, we're not giving that away," Bobby says, laughing.

"Oh, I'll pay you for it," Joe says.

Bobby thanks Joe for his patronage, urges him to enjoy the games, and wishes his newly restored friend the best of luck. The bookie, I imagine, hangs up the phone with a smile, pleased to have snared another sucker.

"You handled that perfectly, my man," I tell Joe. " 'Sure I'm playing the smart money teams. That's what my services promised me!' Well done."

But the next week, even though we've bet SBG Global on sides that are cold as a well-digger's ass, we win. When Joe tries to wager $10,000 on NFL Sunday, the clerk informs him that a $1,000 limit has been put on all his bets, per management's direction. Joe asks to speak to the management. The clerk tells Timid Joe that the man in charge isn't in yet. (It's two hours before the first kickoff.) Then he asks if Joe still wants to make the bets for $1,000. Joe declines and, per my instruction, closes his account.

If it were Big Daddy's operative who got the bait-and-switch treatment, I know how he would respond. Once Rick gets a hard-on for someplace that done him wrong, he doesn't rest until he's made their life miserable. At least triply as miserable as they've made him. He's like the count of Monte Cristo with a big bankroll. Me? I'm content to know the truth about some of these worms and move on to truer playing fields. Sure, I'd like the world to know what kind of charlatans these bookmakers are. I'd love to expose a fraud like Joe Schlockman at The Sports Cure, who's nothing more than a paid shill. The Doctor makes money off the credulity of unthinking acolytes. But none of the suckers really want to listen, anyway. They're all chasing any tiny morsel of reassurance, like most addicts. His faithful readers deserve the Doctor, just as adherents of the prosperity gospel deserve their creepy televangelists.

With my Hollywood stars comfortably installed as longtime customers, the bookmakers they play with aren't frightened of their NFL action. It's common knowledge that nobody can beat the Vegas NFL lines, including the Brains. There's just too much information available with only fifteen games played a week, each one covered by every imaginable form of media. How can anyone know anything that someone else doesn't? I'm not sure. Baby just somehow does—although Algo Andy remains unconvinced that we'd be gaining much betting teasers this early in the season, despite the priceless public-relations value. He says, "Let's just stick with the straight bets for another week or two, Michael. Those numbers are solid. I'm confident of that. I'm certain."

All I'm certain of is that for the first two weeks of the season our little group of recreational gamblers has been able to identify a handful of five-star specials and, whaddya know, there have been more winners than losers. Thanks to the New York Giants and Minnesota Vikings and Buffalo Bills, we end the second week up a whopping $12,000.

It feels like a monumental victory. Even if the total profit is less than Captain Beefcake tips his gardening staff, *it's not a loss.* And in the early going I'm desperately eager to prove to him and the others who've chosen to trust me that their confidence isn't misplaced. I've made a big deal out of how the Hearthrob and his friends mustn't breathe a word about their relationship with me, how the information I'm passing on must be kept as secret as which of their sexy costars they're banging on the side. To begin the season losing would make a mockery of all my solemn talk, even if I explained that downward swings are an expected precursor to upward ones.

A win, even a small one, somehow validates all the fuss.

I've personally closed two more accounts (with bookmakers who realized that they really *didn't* want to let people bet $20,000 on football games) and opened two new ones. I have high hopes for one of these places, Royal Sports, since the head man there, Victor, talks a very savvy game and seems utterly willing to book sharp business. Such willingness is usually a sign that the bookie is eager to get good information on $10,000 bets and then turn around and bet $50,000 himself on the identical games, knowing they're hot. So we'll have to be careful with Mr. Royal. Still, it's nice to know I won't be treated like a criminal for making a house-limit bet. The other place, Horizon, is slightly more wary of wiseguys. The line manager there, Nick, tells me he doesn't chase out sharpies—but he does cut their limits from $20,000 on an NFL game to $2,000. He tells me (the "me" that has a pronounced Long Island accent and shares the name of my nephew) that I'm welcome to bet the max limits at first, but that he's going to be watching me carefully.

Late in the day, when I'm trying to reclaim a $2,000 bonus that a shop called International Island has stolen when I closed down my account, I get put through to the main man, the owner, I recognize his voice instantly: It's Ron Blutstein, Rio Ron, the crook from Rio International who took six months to pay off his $287,000 debt to me two years ago.

I disguise my voice, using a thick Chicago accent, and explain my situation. After gambling through my post-up money twice, his deputies confiscated my $2,000 bonus when I closed down my account.

He doesn't recognize me. Not even slightly. In fact, Rio Ron senses in me a customer he should desperately want to keep. After listening to my tale of woe, he wants to know why I left International Island in such a hurry.

I explain that the limits I was promised were soon dishonored, so I figured my business was better off elsewhere.

He explains the usual reasoning for the limits—I'm sharp; no one was buying back the other side; etc.—and makes me a juicy offer. "If you'll sign up with my major sportsbook, Rio, I'll honor the high limits you were promised *and* I'll let you bet at a reduced juice of eight cents."

"I'm intrigued," I say, intrigued. "But tell me a little about this 'Rio' joint."

Ron informs me that his store has "the best reputation in the business." That gamblers around the world "feel completely safe" keeping their funds under his watchful eye. That they've "never had a problem" in five years.

"You've been around five years?" I ask, knowing this is impossible.

"Well, let's see. Umm. Four. Four years. Never a problem."

"You always pay your winners promptly?" I query.

"Immediately!" he assures me.

"And you won't kick me out for winning?"

Ron claims, "We love winners!"

"Well, then, you gotta deal," I tell him, basking in a pool of delicious irony. The one guy he never wanted in his shop, the one he tried to cheat, the one he wished had never come into his life—that one guy, little old me, he's courting like a debutante with big tits.

Now *I'm* the count of Monte Cristo. And the revenge I've dreamed about for months is only a few vulnerable point spreads away.

The first weekend of October brings the official commencement of our Great NFL Teaser Experiment. Algo Andy has reviewed the numbers with me exhaustively, like an insurance salesman converting a skeptical buyer to the merits of a term-life policy. Still, I'm nervous. "Bottom line, Michael," he reiterates, "each leg of the six-point teaser has to win around seventy percent of the time to show a profit. The key numbers I've shown you win more than seventy-five percent. Do the math."

"That's what I pay *you* for," I joke.

Andy is all business. "Well, the math doesn't have an opinion. It's clear. If we bet the Baby picks at the key point spreads, we're going to win."

"Guarantee it?" I say, whimsically.

"Didn't someone tell me there aren't any guarantees in gambling?" Andy replies, breaking into a coughing-laughing fit.

Even with the facts—or Andy's version of the facts—displayed before me in unblinking black letters, I have to fight years of conditioning that have prejudiced me against making any bet that seems to give the bookies an ungodly advantage. As I look over the list of teams that fit into our teaser formula, I think, *If the bookmakers don't love this action, they don't love money. Lord help me: I'm about to bet a teaser.* When the clerk asks, "How may I help you this morning," I almost can't get the words "I want to bet a three-team teaser" out of my mouth.

Yet there I am Sunday afternoon, marveling that I've got three teams who would have lost against the normal point spread but who are winning with the additional bonus points I'm getting from the tease. By the end of the day I've won as many of these foolish bets as I've lost, breaking exactly even on the deal, and earning who knows how much goodwill from the bookies. Plus, a whole parcel of my teasers ($86,000 worth) survive two of the three prongs on Sunday and carry over to Monday, when the Kansas City Chiefs play Seattle on national television. If the Chiefs can win—or, thanks to the teaser, lose by five or less—I'll be dancing a victory jig once more.

Now, given the inflated points we're getting on the Chiefs, I strongly consider hedging a little on the underdog, Seattle, at +4½. With this strategy, not only do we lock in profits, we also have a huge middle working for us. As long as the game stays reasonably close (a field goal either way) we'll win *both* bets.

Algo Andy's against the move. "Look, Kansas City is supposed to be . . ." I hear him fumbling with papers. "Okay, Baby says they're, well, let's call it six—they're supposed to be almost a six-point favorite and we're effectively *getting* five. I think we've got so much the best of the proposition, and the bet size is well within our bankroll parameters, so, hmmm. . . . No, I would advise against it. But," he says lasciviously, "you're the boss, Daddy Michael."

Though the foolish, hunch-playing, just-feel-it-in-my-gut handicapper in me says Seattle is the play, I'm rational enough not to argue with a computer that's immeasurably smarter than I am.

On Monday, as the game clock winds down, I call Andy and sarcastically remonstrate, "How many times do I have to tell you? Don't hedge when you've got the best of it!" Kansas City mounts a furious comeback in the fourth quarter and wins by 7 points.

We cash $86,000 in teaser tickets.

Life is grand.

A week later, I'm through with gambling. I hate gambling. Gambling is a terrible vice that should be avoided by all decent people.

These are the times that try a sports bettor's soul. Hot on the heels of last week's phenomenal triumph, the next week we lose more than $200,000, most of it on NFL underdogs that, according to Baby, were getting more points than they ought to. The whole thing nauseates me, and I would be inconsolable if I didn't know that ups and downs—and arounds and overs and unders—were all part of this ugly (but profitable) business.

Alas. There's always another week, another game, another bet.

The movie stars are so accustomed to having everything in life thrown at their feet that their sense of entitlement extends to professional football scores. "What the fuck?" the Heartthrob complains. "What the fuck is going on?"

I explain as calmly as humanly possible—which, in my agitated state, probably isn't as calmly as I imagine—that what we're experiencing is known as "fluctuation," the unpalatable yet statically predictable variance in results that most people call "bad luck." Even though I catch myself sounding like a pathetic loser, the kind of guy who blows his child's college fund at the Vegas dice tables, I vow, "I'll get it back. I'll definitely get it back."

I *will* get it back. I will.

But sometimes I wonder.

We get slaughtered again the next week, losing another $95,000 of the Hollywood Boys' bankroll.

I lose. I lose. I lose. (I win). I lose.

All the syndicates, Brother Herbie confides, have had a rough couple of weeks. "The Poker Players are close to quitting. Same with Ferdy and them guys. College, pros, it's all pretty much stunk to high heaven. Hell, we done blown about a million last week," he reports.

I don't tell him about my relatively inconsequential travails. Neither he nor Big Daddy knows that I'm not completely retired. Neither of them knows about Algo Andy and Baby, or about my celebrity partners. As far as the Brains are concerned, I'm enjoying a quiet dotage far removed from the pulse-pounding point-spread action. I surmise, "I guess the bookies are pretty happy."

"Delirious," he says bitterly.

"Well, I'm sure we'll get it back." Catching myself, I say. "I mean, I'm sure *you'll* get it back. Just give it time. Everything will turn out."

Brother Herbie laughs. "Don't you worry about that, 44. We'll get out of this trap, I promise you. It's like blackjack, when you're doubling down on eleven against a stiff and losing every time. But eventually if you keep on doing the right thing you'll get what's comin' to you. It always does."

Indeed it does. One Sunday later, we put the train back on its rails, winning more than $90,000, thanks to a dizzying array of NFL teaser-bet combinations. But after seven weeks, even with Sunday's sizable haul, I'm still down, deep in the red. This is the unpleasant circumstance most casual gamblers find themselves stuck in after two or three weeks. Tasting it now, halfway through the season, I'm slightly panicked, as though the prospect that I might actually lose my hard-earned money had never occurred to me. (It had, but it really hadn't.) Now, I foresee blowing $200,000 or more of my cautiously constructed bankroll, and I get nauseous.

Big Daddy often says of certain bookmakers, "He's got a heart the size of a pea," meaning true gamblers like Daddy himself can persevere and show courage when the chips are down.

I'm discovering my heart may not be pea-sized, but it's probably no bigger than a lima bean.

Ironically, even amid the ongoing carnage, one joint, Olympic, cuts my limits from $20,000 to $3,000. (Olympic accuses me, falsely, of following the Brain Trust picks.) Another, GameDay, cancels one of my bets after I've made it (but before the game starts) because I've played both sides of the game, both at good numbers. GameDay's explanation: Middling is not allowed at this shop. One would think that after three years of putting up with all the nonsense one confronts in the gambling business I wouldn't take it personally when some neophyte bookie kicks me out because he doesn't like my style of play. Yet, when Victor Chandler, one of my English shops, boots me for "chasing the steam"—not understanding that I *am* the steam—I feel the sting of a terrible injustice.

I shouldn't, but I do. I should simply let it go and move on to another, more willing bet broker. The hypocrisy of a clone bookie, who doesn't make up his own betting lines in the first place, accusing a player of betting someone else's plays makes me want to scream. Instead, I bite my tongue, and politely apologize, because the bookies are holding my money (what's left of it) hostage and can basically do as they wish—including unthinkable antics that would never happen in Las Vegas. They want to cancel a bet? Here's what I can do about it: nothing.

I hate this ugly business, populated by clumsy extortionists and liars. We could probably bear it if we were winning, but when we're hemorrhaging money, it's intolerable. In the midst of our losing streak, one of my least favorite bookies, a guy named Benny from a ragged little Belize-based shop called Loose Lines, accuses me of taking cheap shots at his pitiful operation by trying to bet after games have kicked off. It's a practice called past-posting, made famous by horse players and roulette cheaters. And it's something I've never done.

"I don't have to cheat to beat your lines," I fume. Then I explain to him that there have been several times I've been forced to bet him late because he has a habit of waiting until seconds before the kickoff to hang an attractive number. I don't appreciate his insinuation that I'm trying to shoot an angle. I'm just betting his offered point spread when he makes it available.

Benny calls me a "fuckin' lowlife" and tells me he's going to close my account and confiscate my bonus.

Then I let him have it. I yell. I curse. And I make this guy the convenient target for a season's worth of pent-up hatred and aggression against all the unscrupulous bookmakers who treat winning players as though we were transmitting a contagious disease. After my eruption, after my fury is spent, he tells me he's going to check his records and see if maybe he hasn't been wrong about my pattern of play. And if he has been, he says, "I owe you an apology."

"I'll look forward to hearing that," I say furiously and hang up on him.

I'm sick of this whole dirty business. I want to get my money back and quit and interact with nice people again, people who don't care about moving the line and buying a half point. But when you're chasing your debits, quitting only guarantees a loss. You can win only if you keep playing. The problem for most amateur gamblers is that they're facing an inherent disadvantage, the kind of insurmountable edge produced by slot machines and roulette wheels. For professional sports bettors—or anyone who can consistently find weakness in the point spreads—each bet has an inherent *advantage*. As painful as our prolonged losing streak is, I'd have to be crazy to stop.

We have fifteen teaser bets working this October Sunday, all of them keyed on Pittsburgh −2.5 points. At game time, the teaser line is up to −7 points, since Pitt's opponent, the Browns, lost the services of their starting quarterback (about three hours after I've had my Boys make all our bets). The Heartthrob remarks excitedly, "On paper, we're in good shape on this one, Mikey."

Sometimes, one finds, the paper version of events closely mirrors the real-life one. Pittsburgh is *supposed* to win this game. And does.

And Indianapolis, and Minnesota, and Oakland win theirs.

And, therefore, so we win ours.

I cash fifteen out of fifteen teaser tickets, dinging the bookmakers for $203,000 in one magical day. This is how it's all meant to be. "Yeah, baby," Mr. Heartthrob croons. "Now we're playing the game!" He's personally earned less money today then he probably receives in one residual check. But he's no longer a loser. And that makes all the difference.

Even with this monumental sweep, though, the Hollywood Boys have barely broken even for the season, netting a little more than $900 for our trouble.

"Look at it this way," Algo Andy points out, "you've done better than minimum wage!" He almost falls out of his chair laughing.

Captain Beefcake, unable to control his compulsions, bets every game on the schedule and, therefore, continues to struggle, even with my guidance. He's a nice man, and I hate to see him donate a prodigious chunk of his movie fortune to the bookmakers. But, on the other hand, he's inadvertently laying so much cover for the smart-money plays I give him that Nautica won't begrudge its most prized sucker getting the best of the number once every four or five times. I know Nautica will *never* bar him. No matter how much he wins on my behalf.

Boy Wonder shows up at my door one afternoon unannounced (and unshaven, and carrying a backpack). Seems he wants to see the computer that the Heartthrob has told him about. "I just want to see how you do it," he admits. "Is that cool?"

The less everyone understands about our handicapping, the better. I don't want Boy Wonder to know about Algorithm Andy. I don't want him to know how we come up with our magic numbers. I just want him to bet, no questions asked. I see now why Big Daddy is always so furtive: the fewer people who are privy to your secrets, the more likely they'll stay secrets. Boy Wonder has his girlfriend with him, a young actress whose face I recognize but whose name escapes me. I glance her way and flash him a pained look. "Oh, this is Mel," he says. "She's totally cool."

"My lips are sealed," she says, zipping her mouth shut with a manicured finger.

"No, it's fine, I just, umm, sure," I mumble. "Come on in. My teenage cousins would never forgive me if they knew you wanted to visit and I said I was too busy."

Boy Wonder laughs graciously and offers to send them an auto-graphed picture. "I mean, if they'd like that," he adds.

We three go to my office, where my computer screen displays the Right Away Odds page. "Here it is," I say, presenting the monitor with a Vanna White flourish. "All the bookies around the world and their lines." I know this isn't exactly what Boy Wonder has come to see, but I'm hoping it will sate his curiosity for the time being.

"That's cool," he says, nodding. He explains to Mel the point-spread number and the total number, and then he asks me, "What does it mean when one of the numbers gets highlighted in black?"

"That means it's recently changed," I answer. "When a big syndicate like the Brain Trust moves on a game, the whole screen turns black. When you're betting on a Sunday, we try to avoid turning the screen black. The more it stays blue, the happier your bookies are."

He smiles knowingly. Mel bends over my desk to get a closer look, and Boy Wonder absentmindedly pats her pronounced butt, round as a ripe peach, as he peers over her shoulder. "So, like, where it says Mirage, or, like, Stardust, that's the point spread at the Mirage in Vegas?"

"Yep. Up to the second."

"It's like currency trading," he comments, running his fingers through fashionably unwashed hair that sticks out in every direction.

"Very similar," I agree.

He points to a list of names along the top of the screen. "And these—Del Mar, Grande, CRIS—what are those? Smaller casinos?"

"Those are actually some of the biggest offshore casinos. The places in the Caribbean. They probably write more sports betting business than all the Vegas casinos combined."

"There's mine," he tells Mel, pointing to one of the major Costa Rican shops. Boy Wonder scans the names, chuckling at some of the fanciful names—First Deposit Guarantee Corp, Guardian Trust—meant to make the bookmaking shops sound like august financial institutions. Then he says, "I'm looking for this one place. Have you ever heard of a place called Betsports?"

"You mean, Betonsports?"

Boy Wonder nods. "Maybe that's it. They say they're like the biggest one offshore. Guy calls himself Greg Champion."

I snort derisively. "Oh, I know him. He stole a bunch of money from the Brain Trust. He's a crook."

"Huh. Good to know," Boy Wonder says, frowning. "Guess we shouldn't mess around with him then."

"What do you mean?"

"I guess he's opening some casino down there—what is it, San Jose?—and they were trying to get some celebrities to attend. Charter a jet, the whole deal. They give you free casino chips to play with. It's like a paid vacation."

Mel turns her head from the monitor and says, "We went to another one last year in the Bahamas. Super fun. I was saying maybe we could all go." She brushes her blond hair behind her ear. "Right? In the car on the way here, I was just saying we should take Mike with us. The gambling guru."

"I appreciate you thinking of me," I reply, "but I don't think Mr. Champion would be too glad to see me. He's not a fan of winning players. In fact, it's been pretty well documented that he refused to pay off a nine-team parlay ticket some dope was lucky enough to hit. And that's just the tip of the iceberg. On the other hand . . ." As I peruse the point spreads on my computer screen, an idea hits me. "On the other hand, he'd probably be thrilled to have you bet on football at his casino. He'd probably go out of his way to make things smooth for you."

Boy Wonder nods in agreement. "It's funny you say that, 'cause I was just going to mention that when they were putting together this grand opening party his people said they had a full-service sportsbook and I could play there on credit."

"Meaning you wouldn't have to post up any money?"

Boy Wonder grins. "Right."

"So you could bet as many games as you wanted and you don't have to pay in advance? Like the arrangement Captain Beefcake has with his bookie?"

"That's the impression I got," Boy Wonder confirms.

"And did Mr. Champion mention how much you could bet? Surely he wouldn't expect a person in your position to bet a thousand a game. He's got to know that wouldn't get your heart beating. He knows how much you like to bet, right?"

Unzipping his backpack, Boy Wonder says, "I've got his direct number right here. I'll just call him and ask. Mind if I use your phone?"

I shake my head. "Better not. The caller ID is blocked, but you never know with the bookies. They've got all the latest technology."

"No problem." Boy Wonder retrieves a cell phone from his pack and commences to dial. I can faintly hear a female voice through the speaker asking, "May I tell him who's calling?" When Boy Wonder says his name, there's stunned silence. Then, "One moment, please."

"Hey, how's it going?" Boy Wonder says, turning on the charm. I can't make out what's happening on the other end, but both parties seem to find each other hilariously entertaining, as though they were trading rabbi-walks-into-a-bar jokes, not arranging hundreds of thousands of dollars in gambling credit. Boy Wonder says, "Uh-huh, uh-huh, okay" often, which I take as a good sign. "Cool. Very cool," he says. "I'll take a look at the lines and call back with some winners. Yeah. Thanks. You, too. Ciao."

I look at him expectantly.

Boy Wonder nods. "He said I can bet my normal fifty grand a game, up to half a million total. We settle up every Monday."

We bump fists. "You da man!" I say.

"No," Boy Wonder corrects me, "*you* da man. Now you better prove it."

I notice an old Buick parked across the street from my house.

My neighborhood requires a parking permit, so you get used to seeing the same cars sitting beside the curb. Unfamiliar vehicles stand out. On an otherwise quiet Wednesday morning, when I walk out my front door and down to the gate at the sidewalk to retrieve some takeout menus left there, the Buick peels away quickly—a little too quickly, I'm thinking, given the preponderance of dogs, cats, and children in the neighborhood. Three years ago, I would have been mildly upset if someone in the neighborhood drove recklessly, endangering helpless pets and youngsters. Today I'm additionally concerned about myself. Maybe whoever is in the Buick is after me, even if I can't say exactly how or what he's hunting. My picks? A clear view of my face? My innocent dog?

I chuckle to myself. It's amazing what kind of dark plots an overactive imagination can conjure. I've got to stop being so dramatic.

But before I can laugh away the incident and retreat to the safety of my office, I realize that more people than I can count probably want a good look at what goes on inside this little house: bookies, betting colleagues, even, I suppose, Big Daddy himself.

No. That's ridiculous, I tell myself. He wouldn't be interested in my small-potatoes operation, and he certainly wouldn't do anything to harm me. No. It's an absurd notion.

So why am I even entertaining the possibility? Am I losing my mind?

I can feel my chest tightening and my back beginning to ache. I feel dizzy.

After closing the front gate securely, I sit on my front porch steps, with my head in my hands, attempting to breathe deeply and slowly so that the synaptic chaos in my brain might recede and let me think clearly. I tell myself that no one is trying to hurt me—or spy on me, or anything out of the ordinary. It's just one of those weird circumstantial quirks that make you think something is connected to something else, like a roulette wheel that comes up red seven times in a row and puts dangerous thoughts into a superstitious gambler's head, even though he knows each spin is an independent event. It was just a random car parked across the street; that's all. Nothing bad happened. The driver just pulled away a little too rapidly. Forget about it. Sometimes things happen too slowly—like when you've got the favorite and they're trying to run out the clock—and sometimes things happen too fast.

And some things happen at just the right time. Momentarily refreshed and with ominous delusions temporarily banished from my mind, I trudge back inside and check the balance sheets. My movie star's new relationship with the self-ordained king of the Costa Rican bookmakers couldn't have come quickly enough.

During week eight of the NFL season, when Baby has orchards of fresh data to pick through, the ultimate sucker bet blazes a path to righteous gambling salvation. As I monitor the scores on my computer throughout Sunday afternoon, a feeling of omniscience fills me. I remember what it's like to expect you'll win everything you bet on. When the games go final, I tally the results. At one shop, the Heartthrob bet fifteen different combinations. They all win. At another, Captain Beefcake bet eight combinations. They all win. And Boy Wonder introduced himself to Greg Champion's bookmaking operation with seven crazy teaser plays. They all win. "Boys," I announce to my ecstatic crew, allowing a hint of southern accent to creep into my voice, "that's what's known in this business as a 'clean sheet.' Not a blemish on it." By the end of the day—and it's a long one, from 6 a.m. to 8 p.m.—we've pocketed close to $350,000 in profits from our friends the bookmakers.

Recalling my former Vegas excursions, I take Blanca out for a fine dinner, with jazz singing, champagne, and numerous in absentia toasts to Algo Andy, his brilliant Baby, and the cooperative mercenaries of the NFL. When you're in the chips, I've learned from Brother Herbie, you've got to live it up, because those chips have a way of slipping through your fingers when you least expect it. Conversely, you can't celebrate too vigorously, because even if you're not superstitious, the lessons gleaned from a childhood reading Sophoclean tragedies haunt your memory. You know that hubris requires punishment, a righting of karmic equilibrium. And so you enjoy the triumph, but all the while you temper yourself, too. Because the next week's results, you understand, can't possibly be as sweet.

Blanca doesn't believe that a countervailing dose of bitterness must inevitably follow a big win. "The force is coming on your side," she says in her unique version of English. "When the good is yours, you have to let it live in you, yes?" She has a sunny outlook on life, an optimism that I find tremendously appealing, if slightly irrational. I'm attracted to her ability to be happy when the circumstances warrant it, rather than looking glumly toward a less scintillating future.

I wonder who or what supervises the fickle nature of gambling. Is there a god of football betting? A divine teaser spirit? Or is everything in this glorious, maddening, inexplicable world merely, as Algo Andy claims, explainable by math? "Sometimes circumstances make it seem like they're not telling the truth," I recall him saying during one of our rambling late-night colloquies. "But unlike human beings, numbers don't lie."

The next weekend, our big underdog Chicago, which Baby says should be a small underdog, upsets Peyton Manning and Indianapolis. The Broncos, a small underdog that Baby says should be a tiny favorite, win straight up against the Jets. The Redskins, the numbers say, aren't as good as the public thinks. The Dolphins are slightly better. And Tampa Bay isn't getting nearly the amount of respect it deserves.

That's what the numbers say.

And though they may tell a wee fib every now and then, a naughty prevarication that tests your faith, numbers don't lie.

We win $608,000.

It's the best week of my career as a professional gambler.

Algo Andy is suddenly rich. Timid Joe doubles his net worth overnight. And along with a cute story to tell at the lodge in Sun Valley or on the beach at Cannes, the movie stars have another small parcel of lucre to stack onto their giant heap.

The next week we win $502,000 more.

If every week were like these two—filled with victories, lacking vicious threats and impending doom—I might continue betting sports indefinitely, or until I could afford to retire to a country cottage, where I might spend my days singing songs, making love, and writing unpublishable poetry. In a fortnight, we've amassed a small fortune, more money than I thought a nonfamous writer could ever see.

But. Yet. However.

I don't want to do this anymore.

I feel like I'm about to crack.

It's true: There's no such thing as easy money. Betting on sports is making me clinically depressed. The rampant incivility. The spirit-crushing realization that the only thing in life allegedly worth caring about is winning and losing, profiting and despairing. The liars and cheats and con men, the vulgarians who make their millions off the miseries of their customers. And I fear I'm becoming eerily like them, that my soul is slowly being replaced by dollar lust. Every day of the week, for more hours than I want to admit to my friends and family, I'm devoting my too-brief life to making hundreds of miniature deals with bookmakers. Not historians and songwriters, scientists and sculptors. Bookies.

When I examine what makes me glad to be alive, thankful to be a human being, I know it's not money; and in gambling, that's all there is to care about.

Is this my destiny? Betting on football games? All the time and psychic energy I devote to wagering on sports surely could be better spent on something else. Anything else.

One can be forgiven, I think, for having pretensions of leaving the world a slightly better place than one found it. Of making something worth keeping, something lasting. Though I write several thousand words a week, I'm by many measures a full-time gambler, talking with bookmakers almost hourly. And it's making me ill. The color is draining from my face.

The walk I take at the end of the day with my dog, the trip to the gym, the meal out and away from my office, the possibility of blooming love—these are the things to which I look forward, not the ersatz glamour of gambling more on sporting events every day than most people earn in a year, or maybe a lifetime.

My participation with the Brain Trust (and now my Hollywood Boys) has sometimes felt like paying off a mortgage. I always believed I'd eventually have all I need, whatever that was. And then I could say good-bye to the thrilling squalor. But it's hard to stop. The money is a drug. Even when the high has worn off, you want more; you feel you *need* more, if only to recapture for a moment what it was like that first time your heart raced and your head spun.

I've had my fix.

Besides, practically speaking, how many millions of dollars can I win before the industry collectively says "No more!"? How many aliases can I play under? How many silly accents can I affect? How many voice changers and bank accounts and mailing addresses can I find? Eventually, I know, this must all come crashing down. At this stage, even the most benighted bookmakers know about (or strongly suspect) my former relationship with Big Daddy Rick and my present one with the stars of the big screen. These people talk. They hang out in the same bars, scoff at the same bad officiating, chase the same Costa Rican whores. When one of them mentions a group of monster bettors from Hollywood comprising certified losers who now wager like the smart money, bells ring and lights flash. Connections are made.

For the past two weeks, during which Captain Beefcake has taxed his paymasters in Costa Rica for more than $1 million, the conspicuous Buick has been intermittently parked on my street. When I spotted the car while walking the dog, I thought it might be a coincidence. Now, while looking for exotic birds that might be migrating through the area, I see the car again. I can vaguely make out the driver, a balding man in a leather jacket, peering in my direction through what look alarmingly like miniature binoculars, similar to the kind people rent at the opera. When I start down the steps to investigate more closely, the man speeds away.

I'm alarmed. But I tell myself that I couldn't possibly be under surveillance: a professional spook wouldn't be so obvious. (Not unless he was a character out of a Coen Brothers comedy.) It's just one of those weird and unexplainable incidents. Still, my first impulse is to call someone for comfort and reassurance—someone like Big Daddy Rick. Except I'm worried that maybe—possibly, because you never know, and nothing's certain in this world—maybe he's behind the stakeout, masterfully pulling the strings as he always has done, controlling the lines, controlling who gets smart, who gets rich.

The instant the thought crosses my mind, I dismiss it. I want to slap myself and say, "Get hold of yourself, man! You're losing it! Stop already with this whole descent-into-madness foolishness. This isn't Dostoyevsky. It's just sports betting." And after a forced laugh, I feel a little better.

Later that morning, though, Boy Wonder's back at my door, this time without his girlfriend. He looks shaken. "Dude, we gotta talk," he says breathlessly.

"What's wrong?" I ask, assuming one of his bookmakers has refused to pay off his winnings.

"We're finished with Greg Champion. And he's *pissed*. No joke, he is *pissed*," Boy Wonder repeats, the agitation playing across his gorgeous cheekbones.

"Sure. You beat him out of more than six hundred thousand. He doesn't appreciate that," I say, trying to defuse the situation.

"No, I mean, he calls me and he's like, 'I know you're getting your plays from somewhere and if I find out it's Matty, or Matt'—do you know who he's talking about?" Boy Wonder asks.

"I think he means Matthews," I say, suddenly frightened that our spectacular triumph has turned into a colossal theft. "He said he's not going to pay you?"

"No, no," Boy Wonder clarifies. "He said *if* he could prove that I was betting money for Matthew he wouldn't pay me. But Champion said that even though he strongly suspected I was connected with this Matt guy, he couldn't prove it, so he was going to pay me off. But also he doesn't want me as a customer at his sportsbook anymore."

Only one piece of news matters to me. "He said he's going to pay you?"

"Actually," Boy Wonder reports, "he already did. It was wired to my bank. All of it."

I nearly collapse in his arms. "Oh, man, you scared me!" I confess.

Smiling gamely, Boy Wonder says, "Sorry, dude. No, that's cool. I'm just, like, a little freaked out. Champion said some nasty things. You know, very threatening. I don't need any hassle, Mike, you know? It's so not worth it to me."

"I understand," I say understandingly. "I've been there. Just tell me, did he mention my name specifically?"

Boy Wonder shakes his handsome head. "No, just this Matt guy. I told him the truth, I never heard of the man."

We agree that Boy Wonder should stop betting on sports, at least on my behalf. "You don't have anything to worry about," I assure him, "but I guess you're seeing for yourself: these aren't very nice people we're dealing with."

Boy Wonder grimaces. "Worse than the movie business."

Shortly after one celebrity departs from my home, another calls. The Heartthrob is screaming. "Unfuckingbelievable! Those motherfuckers. They shut down my betting account! I win two fucking weeks in a row and they kick me out. What kind of bullshit is that?"

I just want to hear that we haven't been ripped off (again).

"Of course they're sending my money. I told them I would personally go down there and kick their motherfucking asses if they didn't. I told them don't even *think* of playing games with me," he snaps. Either the Heartthrob is a far better thespian than I ever credited him with being, or he's genuinely furious.

"So they didn't like you winning," I say calmly.

"Get this," the Heartthrob says. "They said they didn't mind me winning, but they did a little investigation, they said, and they figured out somehow that you and me are neighbors. So they figured I was getting my plays from you. You must really be serious shit, Mike. I mean, come on! I'm neighbors with you, so I can't bet on football games?"

I'm shaken, but I don't tell my colleague. I don't want him to know I'm scared.

He's still venting. "Unfuckingbelievable. My house isn't even in my name. My business manager owns it in a trust. They must have hired a private detective."

I start to tell the Heartthrob about the Buick, about the rank stakeout of my house. But instead I just say, "Well, it was fun while it lasted. Unfortunately, I guess we're finished."

"Hell, no," he retorts. "I'll just find someplace else to bet. There's gotta be a thousand places that would want me as a customer. I'm not running away just because some pussy wants to take his ball and go home."

I explain to him that once his cover has been blown, his career as a sports bettor (playing on credit and the strength of his celebrity reputation) is effectively finished—unless he plans on getting a new name, domicile, and face, all of which are going to be a tiny bit problematic, considering he's one of the most famous people in America.

"Such bullshit, man," he says disconsolately. "Well, at least I got a nice piece of their loot," he says, calming himself. "Tomorrow morning I'm going to go pay cash for a new Escalade, courtesy of the bookies."

I spend the rest of the day explaining to my other colleagues, including Captain Beefcake, that because of extenuating circumstances that may (or may not) involve my facing physical threats, all of which I'm purposefully vague about, we're going to have to go on a betting hiatus until further notice. Everyone should close all his accounts and ship the money back home. "The present environment has become too dangerous—potentially dangerous—to continue," I say.

Which might be true. There could be people trying to hurt me and my friends, or at the very least make our lives fraught with constant trepidation and misery. There could be people who would like to damage me, even people I thought I could trust. Or perhaps it's all in my increasingly addled head, and I'm making much ado about nothing, like a bookmaker moving the line because some second-string tackle goes on the injured list. I don't know the truth. I don't want to know the truth. I just want to be free. Of this I'm certain: I want to be free.

I want to be normal again.

I've extracted as much money from the bookies as my effete constitution can handle. Blessed with the sudden emergence of face-saving circumstances, I know it's time to walk away, to leave the game while I'm ahead. Just as Rick Matthews has always taught me: Find your edge, make good decisions, and get paid in full.

Be a winner.

I check to make sure all the doors are locked, and that nobody is lurking around the front yard. Then I go to my computer for one last look at the weekend football lines, just for nostalgia, one final fling before settling back into a life of blissful ordinariness. As I sit, the cushions of my desk chair seem to exhale in sympathy with my audible sigh. Through the office window I look at the few remaining birds in the backyard, a family of motley finches and sparrows huddled together in the dying light, a ragged group of bench-warmers put into the contest when the margin of victory matters only to gamblers. For a mad moment I wonder how many points the Cardinals are getting from the Seahawks, and if there's any value in the Eagles at home.

Then I turn the machine off and wipe away a little teardrop, unsure if I'm already suffering the melancholy of withdrawal from a fantastic dream or if I'm the luckiest guy on the planet.

EPILOGUE

The season after I left the Brain Trust, in 2000, Rick Matthews moved his operations to another nation, where sports gambling is an established industry (and heavily taxed). Given the contentious and increasingly uncertain legal climate in the United States, Big Daddy Rick reluctantly retired from sports betting after the 2003 football season. "It stopped being fun, 44," he told me. "And I'm too old not to be having fun." Bookmakers around the world breathed a collective sigh of relief, happy to know that the most fearsomely successful gambler of all time would be sating his wagering appetite on the golf course.

Brother Herbie inherited the Brain Trust's key asset, the computer. He continues to bet on sports from a beautiful island estate he purchased in the Caribbean. Whenever you see the point spreads move, it's probably Mr. Herb picking off the good numbers.

He has competition, though. Algo Andy now heads his own syndicate of bettors, known throughout the industry as the Nerds, many of whom were once his students. He no longer teaches at MIT, though rumors of a triumphant return to academia persist, particularly whenever the concept of game theory is mentioned. Our original Baby is now BabyIV, and according to Andy, "She's dramatically more efficient than anything else out there. Honestly, I don't know how the Brains ever made a profit.

Their program just isn't very visionary." Andy claims that the Nerds win at every sport (and I believe him), but baseball, the statistician's smorgasbord, is his favorite.

I haven't made a sports bet in several years. Occasionally, a friend or former colleague will ask me my opinion on a game or a point spread, and I'll usually offer my meager advice with a serious caveat. Sure, I know a little something about the betting lines, and, yes, every week presents a few profitable betting opportunities that I can recognize. But these days I'm just a casual sports fan, like everyone else.

I'm no longer the smart money.

ACKNOWLEDGMENTS

Thanks to:

The S&S team: David Rosenthal, Victoria Meyer, Nancy Inglis, Tara Parsons, and especially Marysue Rucci, an editor with the kind of eye and ear that puts the wise in *wiseguy.*

Jeremy Warren, for looking after me.

And my advocate and friend, Jennifer "Big Mama" Joel, who's as sharp as the best sports handicapper.